THE
TELESCOPE
HANDBOOK
AND
STAR ATLAS

THE TELESCOPE HANDBOOK AND STAR ATLAS

UPDATED EDITION

by Neale E. Howard

Thomas Y. Crowell, Publishers
Established 1834
New York

DESIGNED BY Slavomir Dratewka

Manufactured in the United States of America

Library of Congress Cataloging in Publication Data

Howard, Neale E
The telescope handbook and star atlas.

Bibliography: p.
Includes index.
1. Astronomy—Observers' manuals. I. Title.
QB63.H68 1975   523′.002′02   75-6601
ISBN 0-690-00686-1

3   4   5   6   7   8   9   10

TO MY WIFE,
Barbara S. Howard

Foreword to the
Updated Edition

This book is the outcome of some thirty years of work with secondary school students in the field of astronomy. The sequence was typical of most programs in amateur astronomy: building various telescopes, then learning how to use them to best advantage. The first phase resulted in the *Standard Handbook for Telescope Making*, while THE TELESCOPE HANDBOOK AND STAR ATLAS is the product of the second.

Ideas, information, and techniques change very rapidly in astronomy, perhaps faster than in any other area of science. This is due largely to advances in the means of observing the heavens. Optical and radio telescopes have increased in size, number, and scope, as have long-range radar and spectroscopic instruments. Since publication of the HANDBOOK in 1967, data collected by these earthbound instruments and by numerous space probes have revolutionized some of our concepts of the solar system and have given us a better understanding of our galaxy. Much of this recent information, and some striking new photographs, have been incorporated into the updated edition.

The procedures, discussions, and techniques presented here have all been tested and evaluated by students. The star maps and charts, the lists of celestial objects, and most of the other tabular material are the result of student discussion and help. I wish space were available to list all the students who have contributed to the book in greater or smaller part; as it is, I can only express my very profound gratitude to them as a group. The original idea for this book came from Gorton Carruth, then editor of reference books at Crowell. Mr. Carruth was most helpful with the early stages, and his encouragement and good judgment were invaluable. Thanks are due to Ned Barnard for his editing of the early chapters. I also owe deepest thanks to Barbara Clark for her skillful editing and excellent suggestions for changes and revisions in the text, and to Patrick Barrett for his invaluable help in the updated edition of this book.

The book has been written with two purposes in mind: To help the telescope owner understand what he may reasonably expect in the way of performance, and to list a number of heavenly objects he may reasonably expect to find and observe. Many beginning astronomers are puzzled by what seems to be a lack of performance by their telescopes. The objects which appear so sharply defined and beautifully detailed when photographed by the big telescopes of the world somehow don't look that way in the eyepiece of the amateur's telescope. So it is important to understand the factors which have a bearing on how much can be seen through *any* telescope. For this reason much space in the first two chapters has been devoted to a discussion of the capabilities and limitations of various instruments in terms of the factors which influence them. Readers who are already aware of these factors may wish to bypass the early chapters in favor of those which present the second objective—a list of heavenly objects which are within easy grasp of most amateur telescopes.

Millbrook School for Boys   N. E. HOWARD
Millbrook, New York

Contents

CHAPTER I   Telescopes in General | 1
CHAPTER II   Telescopes in Particular | 17
CHAPTER III   The Sky | 33
CHAPTER IV   Celestial Geography, Time, and Telescope Mountings | 47
CHAPTER V   The Sun and Moon | 55
CHAPTER VI   Occultations, Appulses, and Eclipses | 71
CHAPTER VII   The Planets | 78
CHAPTER VIII   The Stars—Single, Double, Variable | 104
CHAPTER IX   Celestial Showpieces | 111
CHAPTER X   Wanderers of the Heavens | 122
CHAPTER XI   Sky Glows | 132
CHAPTER XII   Celestial Photography | 136

STAR ATLAS | 147

Star Maps | 149
Gazetteer | 165
The Messier Catalog | 190
Appendixes | 203
Glossary | 209
Reference Material | 213
Index | 215

THE
TELESCOPE
HANDBOOK
AND
STAR ATLAS

CHAPTER I

Telescopes in General

What can you expect from a telescope—not *your* instrument in particular but *any* telescope? What part does telescope diameter play in what you can see? How important is focal length? What effect does the optical system have upon telescope performance? What role does light itself have? How important are the deficiencies or qualities of the human eye? The answers to these and many other questions will help you predict the ultimate performance of any instrument you may now own or wish to acquire. Before we can talk about any particular type of telescope, we must discuss telescopes in general.

The Principle of the Telescope

Every telescope, whether it be a homemade instrument or one of the giants of the western observatories, operates in essentially the same manner. It gathers a part of the light produced by, or reflected from, an object or objects, concentrates this light in a single area—the focal plane—and then, by means of an eyepiece, magnifies the image formed there. That part of the telescope which gathers the light is called the objective. In the reflecting telescope, the objective is a curved, aluminized mirror of some sort. The rays of light from the object to be viewed are reflected from the mirror surface directly to the eyepiece (as in the off-axis reflector), or are picked up by the eyepiece after being reflected from a flat secondary mirror (as in the Newtonian reflector). In the simple refracting telescope, or refractor, the light rays are bent toward the focal plane as they pass through a curved lens. This lens serves the same purpose as the mirror of the reflector, although it is usually referred to as an object glass instead of an objective. The compound telescope is a combination of lenses and mirrors; each plays a part in bending the train of light toward the focal plane. No matter what the type of telescope, the basic principle is always the same. The cone of light from an object is reduced in diameter and is concentrated at the focal plane, where it can be examined by means of either a photographic plate or an eyepiece. The result is always a magnified image of the original object.

What Is a Good Telescope?

A good telescope must perform five main functions:

1. It must gather sufficient light from an object to produce a brightly illuminated image. The amount of illumination depends on the diameter of the mirror or the aperture of the object glass.

2. It must have sufficient resolving power to separate close-together objects that appear as one to the naked eye. This ability to reproduce detailed images of good resolution depends on the aperture.

3. It must be able to produce images with good definition; that is, sharp images of uniformly excellent quality. Here the quality of the optical elements is all-important.

1

4. It must magnify the image. Both the objective and the eyepiece take part in this function, and the magnification produced depends on their focal lengths.

5. It must have a range, or field of view, wide enough for a number of objects to be seen in relation to each other. Here again focal length is the main factor.

Some Telescope Terminology

It will be worth our while to go into these aspects of the telescope's function a little more deeply, but it will first be necessary to define a few of the terms used in describing telescopes.

The useful diameter of the objective, *D,* or aperture, is the diameter of that portion which transmits light to the eyepiece. It may be varied, as in a camera, by using a diaphragm to cover part of the surface. Don't judge the aperture of your telescope by the size of the tube (as many people do.) The term refers to the *effective* diameter of the mirror or object glass.

The *focal length, F,* is the distance from the objective to the focal plane (the area where the rays of light cross each other to produce an image).

The focal ratio (usually called the f-number) is the focal length divided by the aperture, or *F/D*. This often misunderstood term applies only to the objective, never to a combination of focal lengths of objective and eyepiece. The focal ratio is ordinarily indicated by a single number. For example, a refractor of 60-inch focal length and 4-inch aperture is referred to as an f/15 refractor. But if a circular stop is applied to the lens so that the diameter is cut in half, the instrument becomes an f/30 refractor.

The exit pupil consists of the light which emerges from the eyepiece. A cross section of this light at its narrowest point is known as the Ramsden disk.

Magnification is the increase of the apparent size of the image, as compared with the apparent size of the object. It is measured in terms of the relative diameter, never in terms of the area.

These are only a few of the fundamental terms we must know and understand to talk about the telescope. We will introduce and define others as the occasion demands.

Image Brightness

Why is it that in the late afternoon, stars which are invisible to the naked eye can readily be seen through a telescope? Part of the answer to the question is that the light from the sky causes the pupil of the eye to contract and thus reduces its ability to register faint objects. The telescope, however, is not trained on the full sky, only a very small part of it. Thus, the total light is reduced, the contrast between starlight and sky light is increased, and the star becomes visible. But the important factor is the light-gathering power of the telescope compared with that of the eye alone. The telescope amplifies the light of both star and sky and the brighter object becomes still brighter by contrast.

The theoretical ability of your telescope to gather light depends primarily on its aperture and, to a lesser degree, upon the magnification used. This theoretical value can be found from the formula

$$\text{light-grasp} = \text{transmission factor} \times \frac{D^2}{d_e^2 \times M^2}$$

where D is the aperture of the objective, M is the magnification, and d_e is the diameter of the pupil of the eye. The pupil when fully open for nighttime vision is about three tenths of an inch in diameter. (The size of the pupil varies, of course, from one individual to another, but three tenths of an inch is a good average.)

Telescopes waste some of the light they take in. Much of it is lost by partial reflection and absorption at the objective lens (or by poor reflectivity of the primary and secondary mirrors in reflectors) and by absorption in the eyepiece. In reflectors the loss is about 38 percent; in refractors it is slightly less—about 36 percent. If we take 37 percent as an average value for any instrument, only 63 percent of the light gets through the telescope. This percentage loss appears as the transmission factor (t.f.) in the formula above. This formula is for use with telescopes up to 7 inches in diameter. Above this size, because of the increasing thickness of the objective lens of the refractor, the reflector becomes superior in light-grasp.

In spite of the fact that telescopes actually waste light, they are still infinitely superior to the human eye as light-gathering instruments. We can see that this is true by applying the formula given above, ignoring magnification for the moment:

$$\text{light-grasp} = .63 \times \frac{D^2}{.3^2} = 7D^2$$

As a rule of thumb, then, for telescopes up to 7 inches of aperture used at the same magnification, the light-grasp equals the square of the aperture multiplied by 7. As an example, let us take two telescopes of 3-inch and 6-inch aperture, respectively. The light-grasp of the 3-inch is 63 times as great as that of the human eye and the light-grasp of the 6-inch is 252 times as great! The point of this discussion is that if you are interested in the very faint objects of the heavens, the aperture of your telescope is very important. Stars and other objects

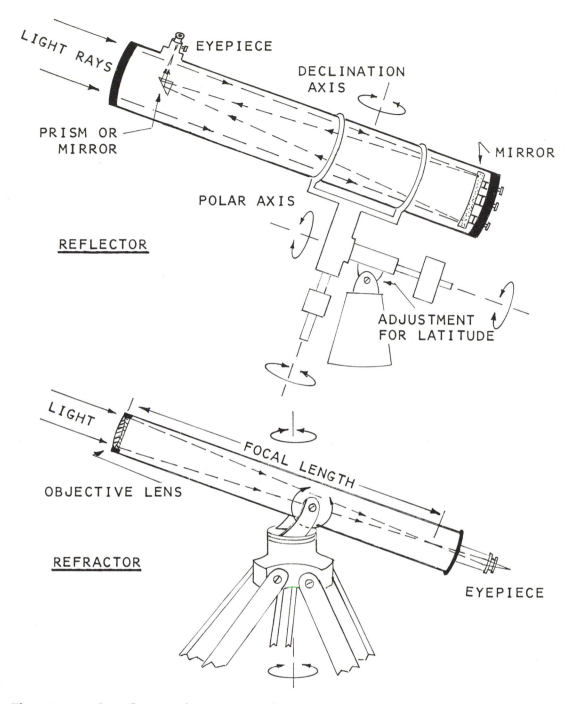

LIGHT RAYS

EYEPIECE

DECLINATION
AXIS

PRISM OR
MIRROR

MIRROR

POLAR AXIS

REFLECTOR

ADJUSTMENT
FOR LATITUDE

LIGHT

FOCAL LENGTH

OBJECTIVE LENS

REFRACTOR

EYEPIECE

The mirror in the reflecting telescope serves the same function as the objective lens in the refractor: Both bring light rays to a focus, where the image they produce can be examined by an eyepiece. Two types of mounting are shown—The reflector is mounted with one axis parallel to the axis of the earth, while the refractor's main axis is perpendicular to the plane of the observer. However, either type of telescope may have either type of mount.

that cannot even be seen with small telescopes immediately become visible with large ones.

STELLAR MAGNITUDES

How do we measure the brightness of a star? Apparent star brightness, or *apparent magnitude,* is based on a system in which a first magnitude star

is 100 times as bright as its sixth magnitude cousin. The limit of human vision, on this scale, is about magnitude 6.5,* and that of telescopic vision is mag-

* A commonly accepted value although, like all values based upon human attributes, it is only an average. Many people have difficulty seeing stars of sixth magnitude, but there are some who can see stars below seventh magnitude on clear, dark nights. A chosen few can, on occasion, pick up stars as dim as magnitude 8.5.

nitude 23 (the 200-inch giant at Mount Palomar in California). As the magnitude decreases in numerical value each star is 2.512 times as bright as those in the preceding group. This relationship gives us a way of comparing brightness. For example, how much brighter than a star of fifth magnitude is one of the second? The difference is three magnitudes, each representing a 2.512 increase in brightness. Then $2.512^3 = 15.85$, or the second magnitude star is approximately sixteen times brighter.

But there are stars brighter than first magnitude. What numbers are assigned to these? The scale is continued into negative numbers, so that magnitude 0 is 2.512 times brighter than magnitude 1, magnitude -1 is 2.512 times brighter than magnitude 0, and so on. On this scale Venus at her brightest shines with magnitude -4.4, the full moon is about -12, and the sun is represented by the figure -27.

Actually, there is no star which is *exactly* first magnitude, even though there are about twenty-one which come close. These stars range from 1.48 for Adara to -1.42 for the glittering Sirius.

TELESCOPES AND STAR MAGNITUDES

Now let's apply these facts to your own telescope. What are the faintest stars you can expect to see with it? A rule of thumb is that a 1-inch objective will reveal stars of the ninth magnitude, and the rest can be scaled accordingly. More exact, and much more applicable to our problem, is the formula

$$m = 8.8 + 5 \log D$$

where m is the magnitude and D the aperture of your telescope in inches. Using this formula and a table of logarithms, we can make a table for various apertures.

Limiting Magnitudes

D (inches)	Limiting magnitude	D (inches)	Limiting magnitude
1	8.8	9	13.6
2	10.3	10	13.8
3	11.2	12	14.2
4	11.8	13	14.4
5	12.3	16	14.8
6	12.7	18	15.1
7	13.0	20	15.3
8	13.3	200	23.0 (*approx.*)

The magnitudes in this table can be converted to relative brightness as they appear to the human eye. Earlier it was pointed out that a 6-inch telescope can pick up stars 252 times fainter than those visible to the unaided human eye. What magnitude would such a star have? By trial and error, or by using some simple algebra,* we find that 252 is the sixth power of 2.512. Therefore the star is six magnitudes dimmer than those seen with the naked eye. But we started with magnitude 6.5, the usual limit of the human eye, and six magnitudes less than this gives a value of 12.5, which compares roughly with the 12.7 listed in the table. This table is only an approximation—it shows the theoretical limits of magnitude for a telescope of given aperture. When seeing conditions are excellent, you may be able to find stars one and a half magnitudes dimmer than those listed. When conditions are poor, you may fail to see stars that are several magnitudes brighter. There are a number of reasons for this variation:

1. Your own vision. How good are your eyes and how well do you employ them? When you are looking for faint objects it is best to use averted vision; that is, look out of the corner of your eye. Test the truth of this by looking at some point in the heavens where there is a reasonable concentration of stars—the Little Dipper, for example. You will be able to see some very faint stars at either side of the point on which your eyes are focused. But if you shift your gaze directly toward these stars they will disappear, only to reappear as soon as you look slightly away from them. This happens because your most acute vision is at a point off to one side of the center of the retina.

The quality of your eyesight is, of course, very important in the performance of your telescope. The telescope can do its part within the limit of its capabilities, but no two pairs of human eyes interpret what the telescope presents to them in quite the same way. Perhaps you would like to test your eyes against a time-honored standard. If you can see all the stars in the Little Dipper, you need not worry about oculists. The Pleiades (Seven Sisters) also provides a good trial ground. Five of them seen in bright moonlight is a good score; on a dark night, six is normal, ten is very good, thirteen is exceptional.

2. The telescope itself. Defects in objective and eyepiece, dirt on the optical surfaces, a poor reflective coating on the mirror, improper adjustment (collimation) of the optical elements—all are factors that reduce the efficiency of the instrument. You can precisely check your telescope's performance by checking it against the stars of the North Polar sequence. This list of ninety-six stars located near the polar region provides tests for magnitudes between the fourth and the twenty-first.† The excellent charts issued by the American Association

$$2.512^x = 252$$
$$x \log 2.512 = \log 252$$
$$x = 6$$

† E. C. Pickering, *Adopted Photographic Magnitudes of 96 Polar Stars*, Harvard Circ. 170.

of Variable Star Observers (AAVSO) list star magnitudes down to the fifteenth.

3. Poor seeing conditions. There are many causes of poor seeing conditions, the chief of which is turbulence of the atmosphere. Turbulence may occur at any level from the ground up and, curiously enough, may at times be completely unsuspected as a source of poor telescope performance. Lens-shaped masses of air high in the atmosphere are usually invisible until their rapid passage distorts the image of a star. At ground level, the atmosphere may appear to be completely calm and transparent.

A rapidly falling or rising temperature during the observing period will create changes in the "figure" on your mirror or object glass. The only remedy for the resulting distortion is to wait for the mirror temperature to reach the same level as that of the surrounding air. If your telescope is portable, don't attempt to use it immediately after taking it from a warm house to the cold outdoors. Wait at least half an hour for it to cool off. Air currents within the tube of the telescope—these are caused by differences in temperature inside and outside the tube—also have disastrous effects upon good seeing; again, the only recourse is to wait for the temperature to level. You can recognize temperature effects easily because the stars appear to jump and twinkle.

4. Background light. The lights of a nearby town, the presence of the moon, and even the light from a bright star in the field can cut visibility by an amazing amount—sometimes by as much as 50 percent.

5. Excessive magnification. Ordinary magnification has little or no effect on the visibility of point sources such as the stars. When the optics of the telescope are pushed to their magnifying limit, however, the attenuation of light from dim objects such as nebulae, faint clusters, and distant galaxies may become so great as to make them invisible to the viewer.

SOME CONCLUSIONS

The light-gathering power of your telescope is one of its most important qualities. It is the factor that determines the visibility of objects far up in the scale of magnitude—the dim comparison stars used in variable star work, faint nebulae, the distant planets, and the feeble light of many galaxies. Some authorities think that a 6-inch reflector or a 4-inch refractor is the smallest useful telescope for planetary work, and they recommend larger instruments. Yet even if your telescope is small there are many objects you can find and observe with it. Even a 2-inch refractor will pick up objects as faint as the tenth or eleventh magnitude under good seeing conditions!

Resolution

Because light travels in waves rather than in a straight, undeviating line, the light produced by a star can never be focused to a sharp point. These light waves, wiggling up, down, sideways, and at all possible angles to their line of travel, produce in a telescope a bright blob called a *spurious disk* or, in honor of its discoverer, *Airy disk*.* At definite

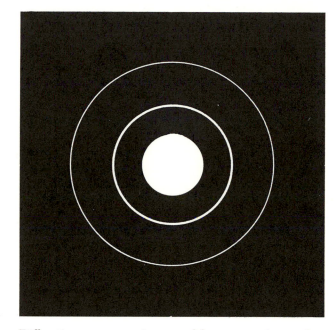

Diffraction pattern: An out-of-focus star image has interference rings where light is diffracted.

distances from this disk the light waves interfere with each other and cancel each other out. At such distances a dark ring is formed around the spurious disk. At other points, however, the waves reinforce each other and produce bright rings. The resulting image, a bright central disk surrounded by alternating bright and dark rings, is known as a diffraction pattern. About 86 percent of the light from the star is concentrated in the central disk; the remainder is distributed through the illuminated rings. Because of this concentration, the rings of many stars, especially the fainter ones, may not be apparent.

The fact that stars observed through a telescope do not register as points of light, but as disks, is very important, for the size and distribution of these disks determine how much detail will be evident. For example, if two stars are so close together that their disks overlap, they will appear as one. So, to determine what double stars you can expect to separate you must know something about the rela-

* Named for Sir George Airy, Astronomer Royal at the Greenwich Observatory from 1835 to 1892.

tionship between the size of spurious disks and the aperture of the telescope.

There are two formulas that can be used to measure spurious disks; one gives the disk's *linear* size, the other its *angular* size:

$$1. \text{ linear radius of disk} = \frac{1.22 \, \lambda \, F}{D}$$

where $\lambda =$ the wavelength of green-yellow light, .000022 inch
$F =$ the focal length of the telescope in inches
$D =$ the aperture of the telescope in inches

This first formula shows that the linear size of the disk is very small indeed. As an example, the typical instrument built by many amateurs (56-inch focal length, 8-inch diameter) produces a disk only two ten-thousandths of an inch in radius.

$$2. \text{ angular radius of disk} = \frac{1.22 \, \lambda}{D} \times 206,265$$

For our purposes, this second formula is the more important of the two, because it is the *angle* between two objects that determines whether or not we can distinguish one from the other. But each formula shows that the radius of the disk is inversely proportional to the diameter of the objective producing it. In other words, a larger aperture produces a smaller disk. Why is this important? Well, as we learned earlier, if the disks of two stars overlap, the two stars appear as one.

DAWES' LIMIT

If the spurious disks of two stars overlap only enough so that the center of one lies in the first dark ring of the other, each can be seen. The distance between them must be equal to the radius of one of the disks. You can find the resolving, or separating, power of your telescope from the above formula.

$$R = \frac{1.22 \, \lambda}{D} \times 206,265^* = \frac{5.45 \text{ seconds of arc}}{D}$$

In practice, however, this limit is even lower. As the result of a series of tests made with various apertures, the great English astronomer W. R. Dawes established a practical value of

$$R = \frac{4.56 \text{ seconds of arc}}{D}$$

which is still used as a standard for testing the resolving power of telescopes. Suppose, for example, that you have a 3-inch refractor. Its resolving power,

---

* In this expression λ is expressed in radians. (1 radian = 57.3°.) Since there are 206,265 seconds of arc in a radian, the final result is given in seconds of arc.

using Dawes' criterion, should be 1.52 seconds of arc and your telescope should show clear separation between two equally bright stars separated only by this amount in the heavens. A list of double stars is given in the star atlas. Try your telescope out on pairs above and below this theoretical value, but remember that in such a test there are several additional factors you must take into consideration:

1. As in tests for light-gathering power, the test for resolution is very much influenced by the sharpness of your own vision. How does the resolution of unaided vision compare with that of a telescope? Experiments have shown that the smallest separation of stars that can be observed with the naked eye is in the vicinity of 2 *minutes* of arc, while in a 3-inch telescope the smallest separation is about 2 *seconds* of arc. In other words, the resolving power of a telescope of this size is about sixty times that of the eye alone. You can test your eyes for this kind of vision on a few familiar objects, if you wish. Alcor, the companion of Mizar (which lies at the crook of the handle of the Big Dipper—map 4), is separated from its bright neighbor by about 12 minutes of arc. Good eyes can "split" these two easily on a dark night. Much more difficult is the separation of the two stars that make Epsilon Lyrae (map 5). They lie only 3.5 minutes of arc from one another.

2. If the test stars are too bright, or of unequal brightness, the eye becomes dazzled and the lower limit of vision increases. Mizar, for instance, has a tendency to "flood out" its dimmer companion. In fact, if the two components of a double star differ by more than three magnitudes, Dawes' limit must be quadrupled, and if the difference is six magnitudes Dawes' limit increases over seven times. Curiously enough, stars that are of equal brightness but that are dim—say, of the eighth or ninth magnitude—also increase the Dawes criterion. To be safe, find a pair in which each star is around the sixth magnitude.

3. As in testing for light-grasp, watch out for atmospheric turbulence, because seeing conditions must be excellent when testing for double-star separation. If the light from the stars varies or if the stars jump around in the field of view, wait for another night. The best time to test for resolution is when stars seem to glow rather than twinkle.

4. Finally, refractors are slightly inferior to reflectors in resolving power, assuming the quality of the optical system to be the same. Even though this difference is small—only about 5 percent—it must be taken into consideration.

Now let's sum up. The resolving power of your telescope is its ability to present detail, and this depends chiefly upon its aperture. Obviously, then, a big telescope is superior to a smaller one in this respect. But before you rush out to exchange your

3-inch for a bigger model, remember that an increase in aperture also increases the effect of atmospheric disturbances, and that you can take advantage of your new telescope's greater resolving power only when the seeing conditions are good. So if you live in a locality where the skies are troubled —a big city or an industrial area—you may actually be happier with your smaller telescope.

Definition

Definition is a term applied to the extended image of an object, such as the moon or a planet. It refers mainly to the fidelity of the reproduction of the object in all parts of the image, and this, of course, includes sharpness of the image and the amount of detail in it. Although definition depends to some extent on the resolving power of the telescope, and therefore is also a function of the aperture, it depends chiefly on the quality of the optical system.

The image of any extended surface, such as the moon, is composed of diffraction patterns formed by light coming from a multitude of tiny areas. If these light patterns were of equal value, they would form an overlapping pattern to the extent that *no* resolution would be possible and therefore no detail could be seen. Fortunately, different light values produce spurious disks of varying intensity, and this is what creates the image. Each part of the surface of the objective is instrumental in building up the final image, so absolute uniformity in the delicate curvature of the optical surfaces is of paramount importance. This is why definition depends to such a large extent upon the quality of the optical system.

Dawes' limit, which is so important in the separation of double stars, does not apply to extended images. You can distinguish objects much closer together than the Dawes criterion calls for, sometimes separated by as little as one fifteenth of the amount theoretically possible. As an illustration, the Cassini Division (the fine dark line between two of the rings of the planet Saturn) is only .5 second of arc in width. But it was discovered with a 2½-inch telescope!* Applying Dawes' formula, such a telescope should have been capable of separating objects no more than 1.8 seconds of arc apart. Thus the instrument was performing three and one half times better than Dawes' limit predicts.

We shall in many instances refer to telescopes in terms of definition. No matter what other qualities your telescope may have, its ability to produce sharply defined images is the final measure of its performance.

Magnification

Magnification is what is usually referred to as a telescope's "power." It is, of course, only one of the "powers" which the telescope possesses, for the final image depends on the capability of the telescope to collect light (light-grasp), to produce detail (resolving power), to present a clear image (defining power), as well as to enlarge the image. But it is clearly one of the most important functions of the telescope, without which most of the other "powers" would be meaningless. The total magnification of a telescope depends on objective and eyepiece acting in unison; each plays a part in the process.

MAGNIFICATION BY THE OBJECTIVE

The size of the image produced by the objective at its focus (called the *prime focus* of the telescope) depends only on focal length. This is given by the formula

$$\text{image size (inches)} = \frac{\theta F}{57.3}$$

where θ is the angular diameter of the object as seen from the center of the objective, F is the focal length of the telescope in inches, and 57.3 is the approximate number of degrees in a radian.

Let's suppose you have a telescope of focal length 48 inches, and want to make a practical application of this formula. Train the telescope on a 1-foot rule placed 100 feet away, remove the eyepiece, and bring a piece of ground glass (semitransparent paper will do) up to the focal plane. When the image of the rule is in sharpest focus, measure it with a pair of dividers. You will find it to be about ½ inch long.

The angular height of a 1-foot rule at a distance of 100 feet is 36 minutes of arc. Substituting into the equation, we get

$$\text{image size (inches)} = \frac{36 \times 48}{57.3 \times 60} \text{ or .51 inch}$$

Having verified our formula by experiment, we can use it to find the size of the image formed at the focal plane if we know the angular size of the object at which we are looking. This is very important in astronomical photography, where we wish to know the actual dimensions of the image as it is formed on the photographic plate. Take, for example, the moon, whose angular diameter is 31 minutes of arc. If we plan to take its picture at the prime focus of a telescope whose focal length is

---

* Cassini's discovery is all the more remarkable because his telescope was over twenty feet long, and its mounting was none too secure. Guiding this elongated pencil of a telescope must have been a task in itself, to say nothing of seeing anything with it.

forty-eight inches, we should expect to get an image size of just over four tenths of an inch.

THE NATURE OF MAGNIFICATION

How can we consider the result of the experiment with the foot rule as magnification? All we seem to have done is to reduce an object twelve inches long to an image that is only one half inch in length. The key to the riddle is the distance of the *eye* from what is seen. After all, the rule was one hundred feet away from the eye and its twelve inches of length seems much shorter than the half-inch image which is close to the eye.

dary magnification is large and the magnification of the telescope is also large. The total magnification is in inverse proportion to the focal length of the eyepiece. But there is a limit to the minimum focal length of an eyepiece, as we shall see later on, so the focal length of the objective is of prime importance in magnification.

To sum up, we may say that magnification in a telescope is in inverse proportion to the focal length of the eyepiece and in direct proportion to that of the objective. We can write this relationship as

$$M = \frac{F_o}{F_e}$$

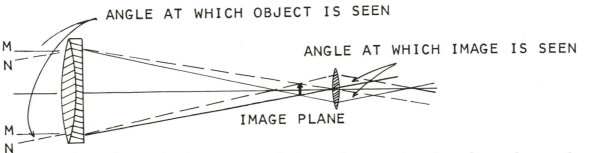

The nature of magnification: An object appears to be larger when seen through a telescope because the viewing angle is larger.

To make this point more real, try this practical demonstration. Support a fifty-cent piece in an upright position on a shelf about three feet away. Now hold a dime between the fingers and bring it slowly toward the eye, looking at both coins simultaneously. The coin closer to the eye appears larger than the other, and as it approaches the eye, the difference between the two becomes increasingly great. This illusion is caused by the difference in the angular diameter of the coins. Because the fifty-cent piece is seen at a greater distance, the angle it makes with the eye is smaller, and it therefore appears smaller than the dime.

THE FUNCTION OF THE EYEPIECE

In the coin demonstration, the one closer to the eye is blurred and out of focus. But if you hold a magnifying glass between your eye and the closer coin, you can see both coins simultaneously in sharp focus. The shorter the focal length of the magnifying glass, the closer the coin can be held to the eye, and the greater the apparent difference in size between the two.

A telescope operates under the same principle, except that the image is magnified both by the objective and by the eyepiece. In other words, the objective produces a magnified image of the object; then the eyepiece magnifies this image still more. If the focal length of the eyepiece is short, the secon-

This simple formula is very important because it gives us an easy way to find magnification: Divide the focal length of the objective by the focal length of the eyepiece. Thus, if your telescope has a focal length of 50 inches, an eyepiece with a 1-inch focal length will give a total magnification of 50, while one of ¼-inch focal length produces a magnification

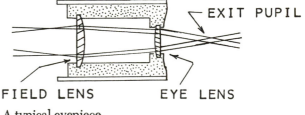

A typical eyepiece.

of 200. To yield a complete range of magnification, therefore, a telescope must have several eyepieces. An alternative is a single eyepiece of variable focal length, a development in telescopes that has grown out of the "zoom" lenses in cameras.

Limits of Magnification

You probably know that there is an upper limit to magnification—too much magnification destroys the original clarity of the image just as blowing up a photographic print reduces its sharpness. But you may not know that there is a lower limit of magnification as well. In order to discuss this we must bring in exit pupil size, which depends upon the magnification as well as the aperture of the objective. The three factors are related by the formula

$$d = \frac{D}{M}$$

where d = exit pupil diameter
D = aperture of the objective
M = magnification

You can see that if the magnification is decreased, the diameter of the exit pupil must increase. If the exit pupil diameter becomes larger than the diameter of the pupil of the eye (about .3 inches for the night-adapted eye), much of the light will be wasted, for it will be blocked off by the iris. So it is important to use magnifications in which this limit is not exceeded, and the smallest that can be employed without wasting light is therefore

$$M = \frac{D}{.3} \text{, or about } 3D$$

Even this figure, three magnifications per inch of aperture, is high unless the pupil of the eye is opened to its fullest extent. Under bright sky conditions, in which the pupil diameter shrinks, the lower limit of magnification is increased even more. On a bright day, for instance, if you are using your telescope to look around the countryside, the lowest magnification you can use profitably is 8D. If you have a 3-inch telescope you are probably wasting light if you use it at less than 24-power.

Theory and practice do not always agree about the limit of high magnification; theory sets a much lower limit than practice allows. The minimum diameter to which the pupil of the average person's eye can contract is about .025 inch. If we admit a light beam whose diameter is smaller than this we are wasting eye potential rather than light. Using the formula to find out what the limit might be, we have

$$M = \frac{D}{.025} = 40M$$

or 40 magnifications per inch of aperture. Yet many amateurs who own telescopes with well-figured mirrors or object glasses know that on a good night this limit can be pushed up to 60D, or even higher. We often find it advantageous to crowd the limit in this way when we wish to separate close double stars. Usually, however, an extended image magnified beyond theoretical limits suffers a serious loss, or dilution, of detail. High magnification also tends to exaggerate atmospheric disturbances, decrease image brightness, and diminish the field of view. Loss of light is the most serious drawback to high magnification. The amount of light gathered by a telescope is inversely proportional to the *square* of

the magnification. Thus, when you double the magnification of your telescope you reduce the illumination of any given area of an expanded image to one quarter of its original value. To a lesser degree, this is also true of stars. You can actually magnify the image of a faint star into invisibility!

Yet, within the limits mentioned above, high magnification is something greatly to be desired. On a clear night, look at Mars under low power. Then increase the magnification by using eyepieces of shorter and shorter focal length until you pass the limit of useful magnification. (You can raise this limit a little by using an amber filter to improve contrast.) You will find an optimum value somewhere along the line—one that probably exceeds the theoretical one.

There are many tables that show upper and lower limits of magnification. Most of them are based on theoretical values. The one given below is intended for the average observer using an average telescope under good seeing conditions. It will be useful to you only insofar as the performance of your own telescope approaches that of such an average instrument.

Magnification Limits

Aperture (inches)	Highest Based on theory	Highest Based on 60M per inch	Highest For average telescope	Lowest
2	60	120	130	6
3	90	180	170	9
4	120	240	210	12
5	150	300	250	15
6	180	360	290	18
7	210	420	330	21
8	240	480	370	24
9	270	540	410	27
10	300	600	450	30
12	360	720	530	36
16	480	960	690	48
20	600	1200	850	60

Telescope Field

Telescope eyepieces are designed to cover an area of the focal plane called the apparent field. The angular diameter of this area is usually limited to about 40° by a circular fixed diaphragm, called a stop, placed in the eyepiece itself. The apparent field is limited in this way because the eye itself can take in only about 45° without moving, and because images usually deteriorate in quality as they near the edge of the field.

The true field of the telescope is the angular diameter of the sky whose image is included in the apparent field of the eyepiece or, put more simply, it is the area of the sky you can see through your telescope with any given eyepiece.

You have probably noticed that when you increase the magnification of your telescope the true field becomes smaller and dimmer. The relationship between true field size and magnification can be expressed by the formula

$$\text{true field} = \frac{\text{apparent field}}{\text{magnification}}$$

Suppose you have an eyepiece whose apparent field is 40° and whose focal length is one inch. If your telescope objective has a focal length of, say, fifty inches, this eyepiece gives a magnification of 50. How much of the sky does this combination cover? We can easily find out:

$$\text{true field} = \frac{40}{50} = .8°$$

But if the eyepiece has a focal length of one half inch, the magnification is now 100, and the diameter of the true field shrinks to .4°.

Although eyepieces usually have an apparent field of about 40°, special wide-angle eyepieces may spread as much as 90°. If we use one of these, again assuming a focal length of one inch, then

$$\text{true field} = \frac{90}{50} = 1.8°$$

FINDING APPARENT FIELD

But suppose you know neither the apparent field of an eyepiece nor the true field of the telescope when you use it. You can then let your telescope find the true field for you by rearranging the formula:

$$\text{apparent field} = \text{true field} \times \text{magnification}$$

From this you can compute the apparent field. The process is a little complicated, but here is how it's done:

Set the telescope on a star, let the star trail across a diameter of the field, and time its passage accurately. Now look up the declination of the star and the cosine of the declination in the star atlas. Then apply the formula

$$\text{true field} = 15 \times \text{time} \times \text{cosine of declination}^{*}$$

Here is an example: You observe the star Pollux (declination 31°59′) under a magnification of 50. You find that when the telescope is held motionless

* This formula will transform minutes and seconds of *time* into minutes and seconds of *arc*.

the star takes 4 minutes and 20 seconds to go across the field. Thus

$$\text{true field} = 15 \times 4 \text{ mins } 20 \text{ secs} \times .8479$$
$$\text{true field} = 55\tfrac{1}{4} \text{ mins of arc}$$

This is the true field—in this case less than one degree—and is what you really want to know when you use the eyepiece in your telescope. The apparent field of the eyepiece is

$$55\tfrac{1}{4} \times 50 = 2{,}763 \text{ mins} = 49°13'$$

But you need not use these formulas to find true field unless you have an eyepiece of odd apparent field size. The following table will help you estimate the true field size of almost any combination of apparent field and magnification:

Table of True Field Sizes

| Magnification | If the apparent field diameter is | | | | | |
	20°	30°	40°	50°	60°	70°
	the true field diameter will be					
50	24′	36′	48′	60′	1°12	1°24
100	12	18	24	30	36′	42′
150	8	12	16	20	24	28
200	6	9	12	15	18	21
300	4	6	8	10	12	14
400	3	4.5	6	7.5	9	10.5
500	2.4	3.6	4.8	6	7.2	8.4

FIELD ILLUMINATION

There is little point in trying to use the complete field that can be taken in by the objective of the telescope. Light rays which come from an object far from the optical axis (the straight line passing through eyepiece, objective, and out into the sky) are bent to such an angle that some of them do not fall into the area of the focal plane taken in by the eyepiece. Such an object will not appear as bright (or as fully illuminated) as those nearer the axis. This is another reason for limiting the apparent field of the eyepiece, and in practice the eyepiece stop is of a size and position to provide equal brightness over all parts of the true field.

IMPORTANCE OF FIELD SIZE

There are many occasions when a wide field can increase your observing enjoyment. Open star clusters or the bright diffuse nebulae observed under high power and narrow fields are often disappointing, for only sections of these beautiful objects are visible. But under low power and in wide fields, these objects can be seen in their entirety and be really appreciated. Wait for the crisp nights when the sky is transparent,* then train your telescope on the great star clouds in Sagittarius, the brilliant Cygnus area, or the glittering stars of the Perseus double cluster. Views of these objects, as well as of the moon in eclipse, the rare thrill of seeing a comet, and the awe-inspiring spectacle of the Andromeda galaxy, call for low power and a wide field. But on nights of good seeing, when the planets "hang" and the close double stars separate themselves, shift to high power and look for detail.

THE EXIT PUPIL AND FIELD SIZE

The exit pupil is also a very important factor in utilizing full field size. Unless the pupil of the eye and the exit pupil coincide both horizontally and longitudinally, loss in field size results. Field illumination is also greatest at this point. We speak of longitudinal displacement of the eye because there is only one area of the exit pupil, a cross section called the *Ramsden disk*,† where the rays cross

EYEPIECE BARREL
EYE LENS
AREA OF BEST IMAGE
LIGHT

The Ramsden disk: The cross-hatched area is actually an image of the objective of the telescope.

each other. This point is where the eye must be placed. Many eyepieces have a cap back of the lens so that the eye can easily be placed at the point of fullest illumination and widest field. Test the importance of locating your eye at precisely the proper place by moving your head away from the lens. Notice how the width of field narrows. There is a relationship between field size and three other factors: diameter of the eye pupil, diameter of the exit pupil, and distance of the eye from the Ramsden disk. If the difference between eye pupil and exit pupil is .01 inch and the eye is placed .01 inch back

of the Ramsden disk, the diameter of the field will be about 52°. If the eye is moved only .01 inch farther back, the field shrinks to 28°!

It is astonishing how many observers sacrifice width of field by failing to "crowd" the eyepiece a little. Of course, the wearer of glasses faces a special problem with short-focal-length eyepieces because the lens keeps his eye away from the Ramsden disk. The only way to avoid this difficulty is to remove the glasses and refocus.

Optical Deficiencies

The quality of the glass surfaces which produce the image is a very important telescope factor—the *sine qua non* of telescope performance. Your telescope is only as good as its glassware. There are, of course, many other important considerations—trim design, a solid mounting, moving parts that are vibrationless and that work easily in all temperatures, and accessories such as setting circles, slow-motion devices, finders, filters, and the like. But most of these features are added for your comfort or convenience and have little to do directly with how much and how well you can see with the instrument itself.

It is important to remember that when we speak of optical deficiencies we are not necessarily referring to sloppy workmanship or poor quality. The nature of light itself is such that certain image defects can be eliminated only at the expense of adding others; it is impossible to eliminate all of them simultaneously.

What telescope shortcomings can be attributed to the optical system and what specific aberrations cause them? Unfortunately, the list is rather long, consisting of defects which affect either the quality of the image, its position, or both. Among them are spherical aberration, coma, astigmatism and field curvature, distortion, and chromatic aberration. Space does not permit a full treatment of these defects, so we must be content to point out only the nature of each one, its source, and some ways to recognize it.

---

* The word *transparent* applies to the atmosphere when it is clear, rather than steady. At such times the stars glitter against the background in their brightest glory. But on nights when the stars appear clearest and brightest they are apt to jump around in the eyepiece because of turbulence.

† It is easy to find the exact location of the Ramsden disk for any eyepiece. Point the telescope at the sky in daylight and look at the eyepiece from a distance of a foot or so. The round spot of light which apparently floats in mid-air just outside the eye lens is the Ramsden disk. You can measure its diameter if you move a piece of ground glass toward the eyepiece until the circle of light is in sharpest focus. The distance of the glass from the eyepiece is where your eye should be when observing.

SPHERICAL ABERRATION

The term spherical aberration refers to the fact that spherical reflecting surfaces do not bring rays from different parts of the mirror to a focus in the same focal plane. But the defect is not limited to mirrors; it is also a shortcoming of lenses. The effect of spherical aberration is a series of poorly defined images spaced along the axis of the objective (a line passing through its center and at right angles to its plane). The point at which the best image is obtained is called, appropriately enough, the *least circle of confusion*. To produce a sharp, well-defined image, a mirror must be curved in the shape of a paraboloid (the three-dimensional curve whose cross sections are all parabolas), and lenses must have a combination of curves for the same result.

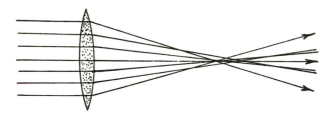

Spherical aberration is a defect of both mirror and lenses. The focal plane is not sharp because the rays focus at different points.

If the rays from both the center and edges of the objective fall within an area of very small limiting size, the objective is said to be fully corrected. This area is cone-shaped, and is known as a caustic surface. The cross section of the caustic at its narrowest point is the least circle of confusion mentioned above. Its minimum size is determined by the Rayleigh limit (to be discussed in the next section). If rays from the periphery of the objective focus at a point closer to the objective than those from the central section, the curves are undercorrected. If the opposite is true, they are overcorrected.

A variant of spherical aberration (where the fault lies in the general curve of the surface) is termed zonal aberration. Here the objective has definite zones or areas, each of which has its own focal length. This is an intolerable defect in a professionally made telescope, as it indicates carelessness in workmanship and insufficient testing of the finished product. It is, needless to say, a characteristic of cheap, mass-produced instruments.

Unless of gross proportions, spherical aberration has little effect on resolving power; hence it does not greatly diminish the telescope's capacity for separating double stars. But it reduces contrast in such objects as the planets; thus an improperly corrected objective is a very serious defect.

The Rayleigh Limit

When light is reflected from a mirror or passes through a lens it travels toward the focal plane in a spherical wave front, much as the upper surface of a soap bubble emerges from the bubble pipe. If the objective is perfect, all parts of the wave front are contained in the same spherical surface. If imperfect, the surface has "dents" or "bumps." If these defects are small enough to be contained between two concentric spheres whose distance apart is one quarter of the wavelength of yellow-green light (or the unbelievably tiny distance of 55 ten-millionths of an inch), the objective from which they come can be considered perfect for all practical purposes. This distance is called *Rayleigh's limit*.

To produce a near-perfect wave front, a mirror can have no imperfection larger than ⅛ wave, or for a lens, ½ wave. This is why good telescopes cost so much. No machine can create curves within these tolerances, and the final work must be done by hand. The Hale telescope on Mount Palomar in California, for example, was polished to the point where no bump or dent larger than two millionths of an inch appears anywhere on the entire 31,400 square inches of its gleaming, curved surface. Even closer to perfection, the 60-inch astrometric (star-measuring) telescope at Flagstaff, Arizona, has no defect larger than ⅟₃₀ wave.

In lenses, the tolerances are less exacting because the light is refracted instead of reflected, and the effect of imperfections is less marked. To reduce spherical aberration, a lens can be ground so that the curvature of one convex surface is about six times that of the other. Since telescope object glasses are made up of two lenses, one converging (convex) and one diverging (concave), the four surfaces are ground to share the total refraction as equally as possible. The spherical undercorrection of one lens is thus compensated for by the undercorrection of the other. However lenses can never be completely corrected except for a single wavelength; the one chosen for visual work is the yellow-green part of white light, as we shall see later.

Testing for Spherical Aberration

You can check your telescope for spherical aberration by watching the appearance of a star as you move the eyepiece inside and outside of its position of sharpest focus. Perform this test on a night of good seeing, and wait at least a half hour after you set up the telescope to be sure the optical parts have reached a constant temperature.

Choose a moderately bright star as near the zenith as possible. Focus the telescope; then move the eyepiece inside focus (toward the objective) until you can see diffraction rings around the star. Now move the eyepiece the same distance outside

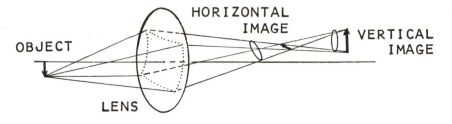

Astigmatism: The image assumes different shapes and positions for different places on the optical axis.

focus. If the diffraction rings appear the same at both sides of focus, the telescope is well corrected. If your telescope is a refractor, you may be bothered by the appearance of color—a red fringe on the rings when inside focus that changes to green outside. But this phenomenon is normal and indicates no fault in the spherical correction of the objective.

If the objective is overcorrected, you will notice that the image inside of focus is almost the same as at focus; *i.e.*, the central disk remains about the same size and brightness. The only difference in the appearance of the rings is that they diminish markedly in brightness the farther they are from the central disk. The outside focus image has a weak central disk, and the outside rings are much brighter than those near the center. An undercorrected objective exactly reverses the above: The central disk is bright when outside focus and weak when inside. The appearance of the rings is also reversed.

Zonal aberrations in an objective show up in this test as a lack of uniformity in the brightness of the rings, most apparent inside focus in an undercorrected mirror and outside focus in an overcorrected mirror. A word of warning: Don't condemn your telescope for zonal errors on the basis of a single test. Nonuniform changes in the brightness of the rings are difficult to estimate at best, and the trouble may lie in seeing conditions or in the eye rather than the telescope—or even in your mood at the time of the test.

ASTIGMATISM AND FIELD CURVATURE

Astigmatism and field curvature must be considered at the same time, since they arise from the same source. Astigmatism affects the images of points of light that are not on the axis of the lens; in other words, it affects images other than those in the center of the field. Field curvature is, as the name implies, a condition in which the image lies on a curved surface rather than on a plane.

Astigmatism results either when the incident light from a point source does not strike the objective perpendicular to the plane of the objective surface, or when the mirror or object glass is not uniform in its curvature for all diameters; *i.e.*, when the curve across one diameter differs from that across any other. The result of either condition is a series of images, none of which looks very much like the

object it represents, strung along a line parallel to the optical axis. You can check your telescope for astigmatism by observing the same star both inside and outside of focus. Any change in shape of the stellar image as you change the focus is an indication of astigmatism, especially if the pattern rotates 90° on opposite sides of the focus.

Textbooks on optics define the image seen inside focus as the *primary* image and the one outside focus as the *secondary* image. The best image lies in between, in the least circle of confusion. All three images are curved. Telescope makers can eliminate astigmatism by grinding the lens curves so that primary and secondary images coincide, but this adjustment increases the field curvature in the resulting surface of best focus. If, on the other hand, the primary and secondary images are given equal and opposite curvature, the result is a flat field, but astigmatism is back again! Field curvature being the lesser of the two evils, since it can be corrected to a great extent by the eyepiece, objective lenses are corrected for astigmatism.

An astigmatic objective is fatal to good definition; clear, well-defined images are an impossibility no matter how carefully the eyepiece is focused. Increased magnification does make the defect less noticeable. Furthermore, astigmatism is rarely so pronounced, except in very cheap instruments, that visual observation is ruined. But it is a very serious defect in photographic work, especially when wide fields are used. The photographic plate registers details invisible to the eye, and although the eye compensates to some extent for visual defects, the camera is less kind.

In testing for astigmatism be sure that the defect lies in the objective and not in the eyepiece. You can check the eyepiece by rotating it in its adapter tube. If the aberration rotates along with the eyepiece, try another. If you can spot the same defect with several eyepieces, the trouble must lie in the objective.

COMA

Coma is an aberration that creates an umbrella-like (or pear-shaped) distortion of images away from the center of the field. Unlike astigmatism, the change in the image takes place in the focal plane, not on either side of it. But like it, the fault lies in images lying on either side of the optical axis

This schematic sketch represents the distortion of an object due to coma. It is characteristic of short-focus lenses and mirrors.

of the objective. As a matter of fact, it is sometimes difficult to distinguish between the two defects because they usually occur together.

Coma is a characteristic of telescopes with large apertures and short focal lengths; it is therefore more likely to occur in reflectors than in refractors. Often it is caused not by faults in the optical system itself, but by incorrect alignment or "squaring on" of the optical elements. If the coma is caused by too small a focal ratio, however, there is little that can be done except stopping down the aperture. While coma interferes with visual enjoyment of the heavens, it is not necessarily fatal to telescope performance.* It is disastrous only in photographic work, for the image is not only malformed but is actually shifted from its true position.

DISTORTION

Distortion is the condition by which a square object is transformed to a shape whose sides bulge outward. This is called negative (barrel) distortion; when the sides curve toward the center of the

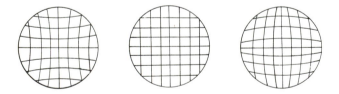

Distortion: left, "pincushion" distortion; right, "barrel" distortion. The center lens shows no distortion—grid lines are straight and perpendicular to one another.

square, the defect is known as positive (pincushion) distortion. Each condition arises from unequal magnification for parts of the image lying at varying distances from the center of the field. An objective that permits equal magnification over all parts of the

* One of the principal objections to the so-called "richest-field telescope" (RFT) is the presence of coma. But these telescopes are not intended for photographic work; they are designed primarily for panoramic visual enjoyment of the heavens and a certain lack of precision at the edge of the field is the price of their other qualities.

field is said to be *orthoscopic*, but this is a condition that is rarely fulfilled. Coma and distortion are interdependent; if the objective is completely corrected for coma, distortion is likely to be present.

DIFFRACTION

Diffraction is a modification of light into patterns caused by the supporting elements of an optical system, not by the optical system itself. A common defect of reflectors, especially Newtonians, it occurs because an object placed in a train of light sets up interference patterns in the light waves. These patterns arise from the same causes and for the same reasons as the Airy disk, but their effect is different. A sharp-edged object placed in a beam of light causes alternate dark and bright lines to form on its shadow, with the brightest lines at the edge of the shadow itself. The "spider" support that holds the secondary mirror or prism in place in a Newtonian reflector is just such an obstacle, and its shadow falls on the primary mirror. But the mirror is also illuminated by light from other sources, so what is reflected to the image plane is not the shadow of the support but the intensification of light at the shadow edges. This light can be seen radiating from the edges of bright stars as tiny projections, or spikes, and it is what gives bright stars their "star-shaped" appearance in photographs.

CHROMATIC ABERRATION

The bane of refracting telescopes, chromatic aberration is inherent in lenses, never in mirrors. It occurs because so-called "white" light is actually a composite of all colors, from red to violet. When white light passes through a piece of glass at any angle other than the perpendicular, it is bent, or *refracted*. The smaller the angle at which the light meets the glass, the more it is bent; as a consequence, fat convex lenses have short focal lengths. Some of the colored rays are bent more than others and the light is spread out, or dispersed, into a band of colors, or spectrum. The amount of bending is inversely proportional to the wavelength of the color concerned. Thus violet light, with its short wavelength, is bent away from its path more than the

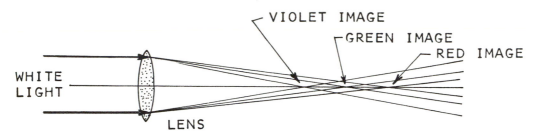

Chromatic aberration: Because the colored rays into which white light is separated by an uncorrected lens come to a focus at different points on the optical axis, an image formed at any point always has colored fringe areas.

longer wavelength red rays, and it comes to a focus closer to the lens than does red, with the other colors strung out in between. This displacement has two unhappy consequences: first, the images produced by each color do not coincide in a common focal plane; second, they are not equally magnified. The first is called *longitudinal chromatic aberration,* the second, *lateral chromatic aberration.* Their combination in a telescope with a single lens as an objective produces a fuzzy, colored image, much worse in short-focus lenses than in long ones. Because of this fact, the early astronomers made lenses of tremendous focal length. In the late seventeenth and early eighteenth centuries, few refracting telescopes had focal lengths of less than twenty feet and some were as long as two hundred feet.

The wavelengths of visible light range from about 4,000 to 7,000 angstrom units.* These wavelengths can be measured by a spectroscope, each color occupying a fixed position on the spread-out spectrum. In an absorption spectrum, numerous dark lines cross the colored bands, and the position of these lines has been very carefully measured. A line in the red regions at 6,563 Å is called a *C* line, one in the blue at 4,681 Å is the *F* line, and the *D* line appears at 5,890 Å in the yellow region. Color correction in lenses is usually referred to in terms of these lines; the typical correction is for the *C* (red) and *F* (blue) regions.

How is this correction accomplished? The lens-maker takes advantage of the fact that different types of glass may have similar refracting powers but wide differences in dispersion. Combinations of lenses made of different glasses will therefore bring two colors to the same focus. Such a combination occurs when crown glass and flint glass are used as the elements in a two-lens objective. The flint glass corrects the dispersion of the crown glass, although each refracts light by approximately the same amount. When a compound lens is made in this way, with a double-convex (biconvex) crown glass

lens placed in front of a plano-concave flint glass lens, the result is an *achromatic doublet.* If the two lenses are separated, the combination is called an *air-spaced* doublet; if the two lenses are glued together with a transparent adhesive (usually Canada balsam) of the same refractive power, we have a *cemented* doublet. Unfortunately it is possible to correct only *two* colors this way. The remaining color is called *secondary spectrum* and it appears to a greater or lesser degree in all refractors. Usually the greater the aperture, the more noticeable the secondary spectrum.

The human eye is most sensitive to yellow-green light (wavelength about 5,500 Å). Since the *C* and *F* lines fall on either side of this wavelength, telescope makers choose glasses of dispersive powers such that the *C* and *F* lines are each shifted toward a common meeting ground, the *D* line.

What is the effect of chromatic aberration and why is it so objectionable? If you were to look through a telescope with an uncorrected objective, you might get the impression that you were looking at a poorly adjusted color television set in a fringe area. Images inside focus would have a red central area with blue fringes on the edges. At focus the colors would fade but the image would not be sharp; outside focus you would see an expanded image, blue on the inside, fringed with red. Even with a telescope corrected for color, the residual color is bothersome. Yet it is only about one twentieth as strong as that of the uncorrected lens.

Secondary spectrum has unfortunate side effects. One is a reduction in light grasp, not serious but still to be taken into account on the over-all performance of the telescope. The other is loss of contrast on extended images, such as the moon and planets. Delicate shadings are obscured or lost in the remaining blue and violet light, although this loss can be minimized by use of a red filter.

Secondary spectrum is not really objectionable, however, unless the aperture of the telescope is greater than 8 inches. But even in telescopes smaller than this, the focal length must increase with aperture. A useful formula for this relationship is that

* 1 angstrom unit (Å) = one hundred-millionth of a centimeter.

the focal length of any refractor must be at least three times the square of the aperture. For example, an aperture of 2 inches must have a focal length of at least 12 inches (f/6), one of 3 inches a focal length of at least 27 inches (f/9), and so on. Most small refractors go well beyond these limits, with f/15 almost standard.

Objectives corrected for color are subject to the other lens aberrations, chiefly coma and astigmatism. Each is present to a considerable degree in the various forms of cemented doublets, although much less so than in air-spaced objectives. The long focal lengths associated with refractors tend to minimize lens aberrations unless they are of gross proportions.

More serious, though, is the fact that the eye and the photographic plate do not react alike to color. The refractor used for photography must be corrected differently from one used for visual purposes only. In the visual telescope, the C and F lines are shifted to fall close to the D line, but for photographic purposes they are changed to fall on either side of the D line, with the F line in front. A visual refractor can be used photographically only if filters are used to blot up the unwanted colors.

CHAPTER II

Telescopes
in Particular

Both the variety of telescopes and the wide divergence in their prices can be confusing to the prospective buyer. A 6-inch Newtonian reflector costs about $300; a Cassegrainian of the same size, $600; a Maksutov, $1,800; and a refractor, as much as $5,000. Furthermore, the prices of different-sized models of the same type vary widely. The 12-inch Newtonian, instead of costing twice as much as its 6-inch counterpart, is usually at least six times as expensive.

Why should there be this great variation in cost? Let's look at the Newtonian again, considering only basic requirements and forgoing fancy fittings. Doubling the diameter of a mirror increases its area only four times, but it increases the difficulty of producing the same smooth curve by a factor of 16. In addition, the tube must be longer (if we want the same f-ratio) as well as wider, the mounting must be heavier and more solid, the drive system more rugged, and everything else disproportionately larger, and therefore more costly.

The cause of the great disparity in price between one type of telescope and another lies in their optical systems. The Newtonian requires a precise curve over only one surface of glass, the Cassegrainian over two, the Maksutov over three, and the refractor must have four delicately curved and polished surfaces. Moreover, when more than one curve is required in an optical system, each must match the others with the same precision possessed by each individual curve. To complicate the problem even further, instruments that refract light must have glass of infinitely higher quality than those that only

reflect it. No wonder a good refractor costs so much more than a reflector of corresponding size and quality!

Now the question arises whether one type of telescope possesses enough better qualities than another to justify a large price difference. We have pointed out some of the variations in telescopic performance, but to answer the question fully, we will here consider the advantages and drawbacks of each of the main types of telescope.

The Refractor

The most appealing attribute of the refractor is its permanence. Once the optical system is aligned, it need never again be adjusted in normal use. Of course no telescope can stand rough handling, but a well-made refractor is more resistant to misuse than any other type of telescope. Properly cared for, it lasts practically forever. The inside glass surfaces are sealed from the atmosphere and rarely need cleaning. In the unlikely event that some interior housekeeping is required—probably as the result of allowing the eyepiece end of the tube to remain open—it is easy to remove the cell that holds the objective. In almost all refractor objectives, the crown glass element is on the outside. Because it is harder and tougher than flint glass it can be cleaned many times without deterioration, provided only that reasonable care is exercised in the cleaning process.

There are two main types of refractors: the Gali-

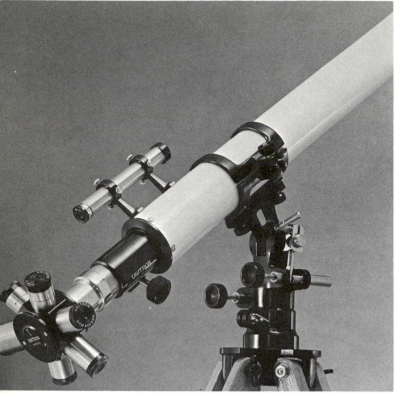

Unitron Instrument Company

A refracting telescope on an altazimuth mounting. Note that six different eyepieces with varying degrees of magnification can be turned into place with a minimum of fuss.

lean and the astronomical. The Galilean—the "spyglass" type of refractor—gives an erect image, seldom has a magnifying power greater than 5 and usually has an aperture of less than 2 inches. Its great deficiencies as an astronomical instrument are its low resolving power, its small field, and its lack of image brightness.

The astronomical refractor gives an inverted image and requires an erecting eyepiece or prism system if you wish to use it for looking around the countryside. It may have one of several types of objective lens. For small apertures—up to 2 inches —the objective is a cemented doublet, used because of its efficient light transmission and good contrast. These advantages are paid for, however, by coma and astigmatism, which limit the usable field. Larger refractors have objectives of either the Fraunhofer or air-spaced type. The Fraunhofer is a contact doublet: the two lenses touch each other but are not cemented together. It is free from coma and has a wide field of excellent definition with very little astigmatism. The lenses of the air-spaced objective are usually separated by a distance equal to about 1.5 percent of the focal length. This distance is very important because it influences the color correction, and should never be disturbed once it

has been set by the manufacturer. The air-spaced doublet is well corrected for color, has only a moderate amount of coma—it is midway between the cemented objective and the Fraunhofer type in this respect—and yields a flat, well-defined image. There is a very small difference in chromatic magnification, but the discrepancy in the size of the images formed at the red and violet foci is only about .2 percent.

Another advantage of the refractor is its portability. In sizes up to 4 or 5 inches it is easy to carry around and set up for use. This is an important feature—not only for the city dweller who must observe away from home, but also for the man who can stargaze in his back yard. And, besides being portable, the refractor is easy to use: the eyepiece is conveniently located for viewing heavenly objects with altitudes of less than 45°, and a star diagonal can quickly be attached for viewing objects with altitudes of more than 45°. Most observers like the convenience of merely sighting along the tube to find the approximate location of a planet or star and then moving their eye just an inch or so to the eyepiece.

But the refractor's greatest appeal lies in its optical qualities. It is little affected by changing temperatures; the closed tube eliminates the bothersome air currents that are the bane of many reflectors, especially those constructed by amateurs. It is an "all-weather" instrument. Under bad seeing conditions its images are steadier than a reflector's and it will stand higher magnification with less loss of definition, especially at the edge of the field. It is also free from diffraction patterns, since there is no secondary mirror or prism to set up interference effects. Star images are sharp, double stars are well resolved, and extended images show good contrast since almost no extraneous light can reach the eyepiece.

The large focal ratio of the refractor gives it several advantages over shorter-focus, reflecting instruments of the same size:

1. The refractor produces a higher magnification with the same eyepiece. *Example:* A 1-inch eyepiece used with a 6-inch f/8 reflector magnifies 48 times. The same eyepiece used with a 6-inch f/15 refractor magnifies 90 times. Conversely, the refractor can produce the *same* magnification as a reflector with an eyepiece of longer focal length, a characteristic that is a boon to the average observer, since long-focus eyepieces are easy to use.

2. The refractor does not require expensive, highly corrected eyepieces.

3. The "average" refractor is likely to perform better than the "average" reflector because the longer the focal length of a telescope, the less apparent its optical defects.

The many advantages of the refractor are quite

impressive. Yet there are observers who feel that the one disadvantage of secondary spectrum outweighs all of them. It is true that in larger refractors secondary spectrum can be obtrusive and at times very annoying. But in smaller instruments, of 2- to 6-inch range, it is hardly noticeable. Certainly for those who want only to get acquainted with the heavens and for those who need a small, portable, rugged telescope, the refractor cannot be surpassed. In any size its merits outweigh its deficiencies by a wide margin.

Simple Reflectors

The simplest type of reflector is the Newtonian. In the 6- and 8-inch sizes, it has been constructed by thousands of amateurs, and is the choice of the great observatories of the world. It can be constructed in almost endless variations, from the short-focus telescopes designed for wide-field observing, to the long-focus giants used in studying remote galaxies. If any one telescope can be designated as a universal instrument, the Newtonian must be the choice.

The most appealing aspect of the Newtonian to the majority of amateurs is its relative inexpensiveness. A 12½-inch model costs about as much as a 4-inch refractor, and a 6-inch can be built at home for as little as $50. Inch for inch of aperture, it is the cheapest telescope one can buy.

But it has many other advantages as well. In the first place, the Newtonian, regardless of its aperture, is the perfect achromatic telescope. Whether its images are viewed directly through an eyepiece or are recorded on film, they are flat and color free. In apertures of over 7 inches, reflectors are superior in light-gathering power to refractors of equal size. With good seeing conditions, the reflector equals and often surpasses the refractor for observations of nebulae, the planets, and the moon. In some respects, it is easier to use than a refractor. Its short focal length permits a more compact instrument that is simple to mount and often more stable than the equivalent-sized refractor with its longer tube. But when it is mounted equatorially, the Newtonian can be a very awkward instrument indeed, for the eyepiece sometimes presents itself at difficult angles. Many an amateur has ended an evening's observing with a stiff neck and aching muscles. Fortunately, this is now almost a condition of the past, for the manufacturers of today's Newtonians provide for rotation of either the tube or the eyepiece so the latter can be turned to a comfortable position for observing.

Perhaps the most serious limitation of the Newtonian, especially a portable instrument, is its tendency to get out of alignment. The optical train

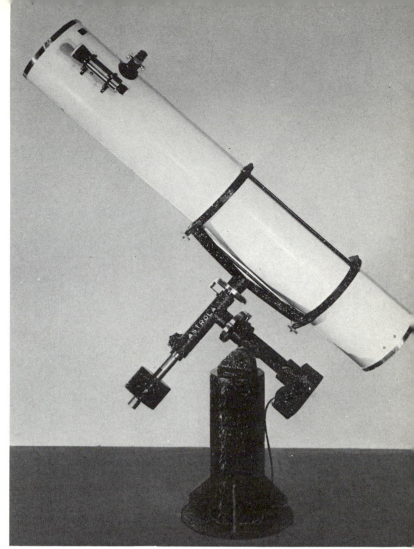

A 10-inch Newtonian reflector. The rugged construction of the equatorial mounting reduces vibration to a minimum.

involves a right angle at the diagonal, and a very small shift in the position of either the primary mirror or the diagonal has drastic effects on the image. Then, too, the diagonal causes diffraction effects because it must be mounted in the path of incoming light. The final objection to this reflector is that its short focal length emphasizes any imperfections in the optical elements. A poor-quality Newtonian, therefore, is almost useless for serious observing.

It is difficult to make rigorous comparisons between refractors and reflectors. Both are, in a sense, special-purpose instruments. The small refractor is probably to be preferred to the small reflector, especially when portability is required. But there is one notable exception to this general statement. If you are looking for expanded views of the heavens—the open star clusters, the gaseous and galactic nebulae, the star clouds of the Milky Way—there is no finer instrument than a short-focus Newtonian. These are called RFT's (richest-field telescopes), and they are so compact they can be carried under the arm. Although they can be made in any size,

Millbrook School Observatory

From left to right: an 8-inch reflector, a commercial Maksutov-type with camera, a 6-inch reflector, and a 6-inch RFT.

the two most widely used models are the 4-inch f/5 and the 6-inch f/4. The 6-inch size gives a magnification of about 20 and has a tube a little over 2 feet long. The field is nearly 2½°—about five full moons —enough to take in most of the big objects of the sky, such as the Andromeda Galaxy (dimensions: 160′ × 40′). Like all short-focus instruments, the RFT produces poor images at the edge of its field, but this distortion is a minor inconvenience when you consider the beautiful views that such a wide and brilliant field affords.

Permanently mounted, the large reflector of 12 inches or more is superior to the refractor of equal size in nearly every respect. Indeed, the long-focus reflector in the f/10 to f/15 range is probably the best instrument available for viewing the moon and planets.

Compound Telescopes

Although the term *compound* may be applied to any telescope with more than one reflecting surface, we shall apply it only to instruments with more than one curved optical element, excluding eyepieces.

Compound telescopes can be subdivided into two main groups: Cassegrainian and catadioptric. The essential difference between the two is in their method of correcting for aberrations. The catadioptrics use large lenses, or plates; the Cassegrainians, special curves in the primary and secondary mirrors.

CASSEGRAIN TELESCOPES

There are many variations of the Cassegrainian, all characterized by short tubes but long equivalent

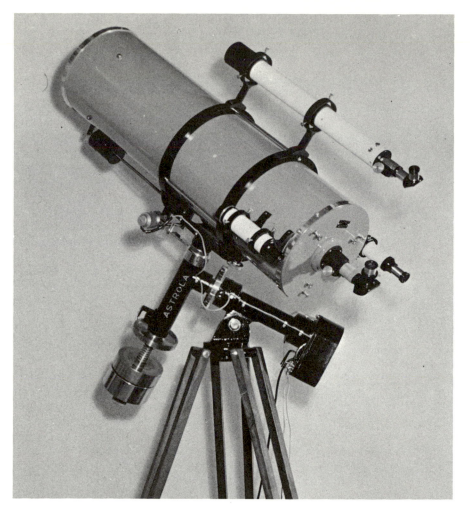

Above: A 10-inch Cassegrainian telescope. Below: Two possibilities in the Cassegrainian design for telescopes.

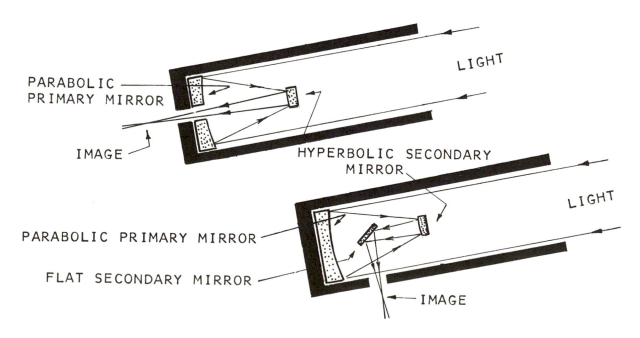

focal lengths, which allow high magnifications with greatly reduced coma (as compared to short-focus Newtonians) and almost no spherical or chromatic aberration. This combination would seem to produce the "perfect" telescope. The fact is, however, that although the Cassegrainians are excellent telescopes they have a few shortcomings, such as astigmatism, field curvature, a limited field of view, and reduced contrast. Manufacturers of Cassegrainians compensate for this latter defect either by placing field stops near the Ramsden disk or by placing one baffle tube at the exit hole in the primary mirror and another behind the secondary mirror.

How can the Cassegrainian simultaneously have a short tube and a long focal length? The secondary mirror, acting as a sort of amplifier, narrows the angle of the cone of light produced by the primary until the equivalent focal length becomes very long. The amplification factor is the distance of the secondary mirror from the final focal plane (P_1) divided by the distance of the secondary inside the focus of the primary (P_2). This result multiplied by the focal length of the primary mirror gives the equivalent focal length. Let's suppose we have a 6-inch Cassegrainian in which $P_1 = 21$ inches, $P_2 = 3.5$ inches, and the focal length of the primary is 15 inches. Then,

$$\text{equivalent focal length} = \frac{P_1}{P_2} F = \frac{21}{3.5} \times 15 = 90 \text{ inches}$$

and the telescope is therefore a 6-inch f/15 Cassegrainian.

The short tubes, long focal lengths, and large focal ratios (a 10-inch is usually f/16, for example) give Cassegrainians most of the advantages of both reflectors and refractors, plus the added convenience of simplicity in mounting, excellent portability, and steady performance, since the shortness of the tube almost eliminates the air currents that plague the Newtonian.

Three variations of the Cassegrainian are in wide use.

The true Cassegrainian exemplifies most of the characteristics noted above. It is free from spherical aberration and has only about the same coma as an ordinary reflector of equal focal length—which is not much. The primary mirror is a paraboloid,* the secondary a convex hyperboloid. The primary (paraboloidal) mirror brings parallel rays to a perfect focus, but they are intercepted before they reach this focus by the secondary (hyperboloidal) mirror, which reflects them to another focus, usually

through a hole in the primary mirror. Some forms have a nonperforated primary and the rays are reflected to the side of the tube by a diagonal. This form has some advantage over the ordinary Cassegrainian, for it does not allow extraneous light to fog the image and it has a more conveniently placed eyepiece. But it also produces a reversed image—bothersome to lunar and planetary observers—and it has a smaller field of full illumination.

Since the curves of the true Cassegrainian are difficult to produce and test, this type is relatively expensive. Another type of Cassegrainian, the Dall-Kirkham, employs simpler curves, an ellipsoid primary mirror, and a spherical secondary. In performance this telescope parallels the true Cassegrainian except for increased coma and a consequent narrowing of the usable field. But Dall-Kirkhams are simpler to make than true Cassegrainians and so are more favored by amateur telescope-makers. More important to the observer who buys a telescope, professionally made Dall-Kirkhams are less expensive than their more complex cousins. In common with all Cassegrainians, they are excellent instruments.

A third Cassegrainian type, the Ritchey-Chretien, has more complex curves than either of its companion instruments and hence is much more difficult to make. The curves employed, hyperboloidal sur-

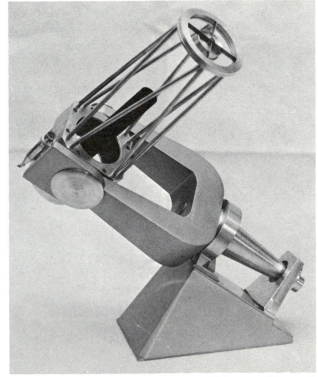

A model of the 61-inch telescope at the U.S. Naval Observatory, Flagstaff, Arizona. This exemplifies beauty as well as rugged design in a telescope.

---

* The terms paraboloid, hyperboloid, etc., represent 3-dimensional curves derived from their 2-dimensional counterparts in plane geometry. The sphere is a curve of uniform radius of curvature, the paraboloid is deeper in the center than at the edges, the hyperboloid is still deeper than the paraboloid and flattens more at the edges, and the ellipsoid is the curve generated by rotating an ellipse around its long axis.

faces on both primary and secondary mirrors, yield a completely coma-free image, and the only remaining defects are astigmatism and curvature of field. Because it is difficult to manufacture, it is usually made only in large apertures for observatory use. An example of this type is the beautiful 61-inch telescope at the Naval Observatory at Flagstaff, Arizona. Many experts regard the Ritchey-Chretien as the Cassegrainian telescope at its best.

CATADIOPTRIC TELESCOPES

The mouth-filling adjective catadioptric refers to a pair of optical elements that oppose one another. One element is a lens that causes negative spherical aberration; the other is a mirror that causes positive spherical aberration. The result is cancellation, and a system that has no spherical aberration at all. As we shall see, the catadioptrics have many other merits.

Like their close cousins, the Cassegrainians, the catadioptrics come in several variations. They range from telescopes designed for photography only—the Schmidts—to the photovisual instruments called Maksutovs. Unlike the Cassegrainians, these telescopes represent brand-new ideas in optics, relatively speaking. Bernard Schmidt developed his telescopic camera in 1930; A. Bouwers patented his

chromatic aberrations, astigmatism, and curvature of field are reduced to negligible proportions.

We shall not be much concerned with the Schmidt telescope itself, since it is primarily a photographic instrument. But it is interesting as a prototype—the first telescope to use a correcting plate or lens in front of the center of curvature of the primary mirror. As Schmidt used it, the correcting plate was a thin, almost flat piece of glass, plane on the outside but curved on the inside facing the mirror. This curve is convex at its center and is surrounded by a concave ring that extends to the edge of the plate. The primary mirror is spherical, focusing at a curved focal plane that acts as the plate-holder. The combination produces a very fast telescopic camera, free from coma, astigmatism, distortion, and chromatic aberration. Its most remarkable feature (as if those already mentioned are not unusual enough in themselves) is its tremendous field of excellent definition. An f/1 Schmidt yields beautifully sharp images over a 20° field; the field of good definition of other telescopes is measured in *minutes* of arc rather than in degrees.

There are several visual adaptations of the Schmidt principle, but these have been superseded in large part by the Maksutov-type telescopes. A notable exception is the Schmidt-Cassegrain, which has all the Maksutov characteristics as well as a

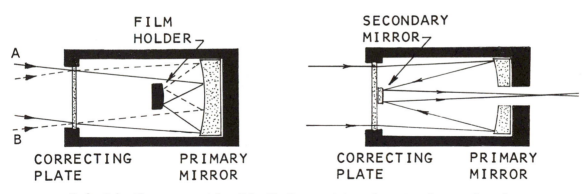

Left; Schmidt camera; right, Schmidt-Cassegrainian adaptation for visual work.

idea for a photovisual catadioptric telescope in February of 1941, and eight months later D. Maksutov was granted a patent on exactly the same principle. Bouwers worked in Amsterdam, Maksutov in Moscow. Neither, apparently, knew what the other was doing, yet each came up with an idea that was to change the whole concept of small telescope design. In contrast to these recent designs, the principle of the Cassegrain has been well known since the seventeenth century.

The claims made for catadioptric telescopes are perhaps somewhat exaggerated, yet it is true that these instruments are nearly aberration-free: Spherical aberration is eliminated, as noted earlier; coma,

larger clear aperture than a comparable Maksutov. The optics are complex: a Schmidt-type correcting plate, a spherical primary mirror, and an elliptical secondary. Hence it is difficult to construct and expensive to buy. But it is a particularly fine instrument, providing well-defined images whose quality is limited only by small diffraction effects from the secondary.

The outstanding feature of the Maksutov is a meniscus lens—a lens that looks very much like a large, deep watch crystal—placed inside the radius of curvature of the primary mirror. In the original design, a secondary mirror, located immediately behind the correcting lens, reflected rays back

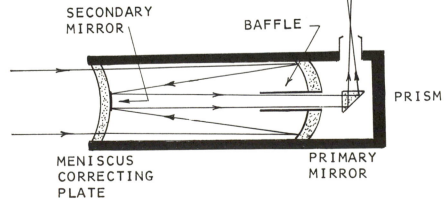

SECONDARY MIRROR

BAFFLE

PRISM

MENISCUS CORRECTING PLATE

PRIMARY MIRROR

Left: one arrangement for the elements of the Maksutov design, as developed by Lawrence Braymer. The light train is bent by a totally reflecting prism to reach the eyepiece. Above: a cutaway view of a particularly fine and compact telescope, showing the elements arranged as in the diagram. In the base of the telescope can be seen part of the gear system for the right ascension drive mechanism, which operates on 110-volt, 60-cycle current.

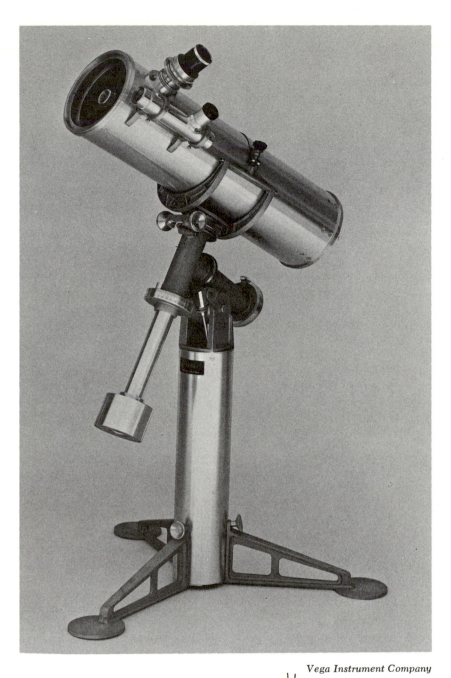

Vega Instrument Company

Above: an exceptionally fine and sturdy design in a Maksutov telescope. The optical system for this telescope is shown at right.

MENISCUS
CORRECTING
PLATE

DIAGONAL
MIRROR OR
PRISM

PRIMARY
MIRROR

through a hole in the primary to the eyepiece. With the formation of the now-famous Maksutov Club (founded by Allan Mackintosh in Glen Cove, Long Island), the Maksutov telescope caught on like wildfire with amateur telescope-makers. As could be expected, there are several variations in design and construction. The most widely used was designed by John Gregory; it employs spherical surfaces for both the correcting plate and the primary mirror. The secondary has been eliminated and replaced by an aluminized spot on the back of the corrector. The Gregory-Maksutov, as it is now known, is designed in two focal ratios, an f/15 and an f/23. The f/15 is intended as an all-round instrument with a wide field at low powers and excellent definition at high powers. The f/23 is primarily a planet-observing instrument, but it too is amazingly versatile. Another variation, the Newtonian-Maksutov, replaces the Cassegrain-type secondary with a Newtonian diagonal. This arrangement turns the Maksutov into a low-focal-ratio (f/4) RFT, but with none of the coma of the short-focus Newtonian. The addition of a Barlow lens increases the focal ratio to f/12, making possible high powers with good definition.

The Maksutovs are extremely sensitive to any maladjustment of the optical train, but once the optical elements are fixed in position they are practically immovable. The tube is short; as a result, it can be ruggedly constructed without becoming too heavy. For the observer's comfort, a diagonal is usually added behind the secondary mirror so that the eyepiece can be placed at right angles to the tube. Like the refractor, the Maksutov is a sealed instrument. Hence, the tube is free from air currents that might distort the image, and the optical surfaces are protected. The correcting lens is usually a tough borosilicate glass, which, properly cared for, will last almost forever. They are light, portable, easy to set up and use.

The Maksutov, again like the refractor, is limited in size of aperture because of the difficulty of producing optically clear glass in large diameters. Since light passes *through* it, the correcting plate obviously must be flawless. Maksutovs are thus pretty much restricted to amateur use, where great light-gathering power is not required, and for amateurs they are ideal. Consider the qualities of a commercial model, similar to the Gregory-Maksutov, which the author has used for six years for teaching purposes. It has been handled by hundreds of teen-age boys, and consequently has had some very rough usage, but it still performs as well as when it was first unpacked from its shipping case. Its aperture is 3.5 inches, focal length 44.5 inches, f/14.4. It has no observable spherical aberration, coma, astigmatism, or chromatic aberration. Resolving power exceeds Dawes' limit and definition is excellent over the entire field.

The Maksutov, aperture for aperture, is superior to any other telescope, provided its optics are of high quality. Tolerances are very small; slight imperfections in the mirrors or lens or in the optical alignment become glaring defects. Workmanship must be painstaking, tedious, and near-perfect. Consequently, the Maksutov is an expensive instrument, but in the long run well worth its price.

Many observers start with a small telescope, then graduate to ever larger ones as they find their pursuit of the multitudinous heavenly objects ever more fascinating. A good telescope is a lifetime investment; starting with the best is the most sensible approach. But not everyone is fortunate enough to be able to do this, and even a poor telescope is better than none. After all, the great astronomical discoveries were made with "poor" telescopes. Galileo would have been delighted to have the telescope now gathering dust in your attic because you think you have exhausted its possibilities.

Thus far we have discussed only the main telescope types and have ignored many others. The Gregorian reflector, the off-axis telescopes (Herschelian, neobrachytes, and many others), the Schwartzchild, the Couder reflector, the Sampson telescope—all these have been omitted, not because they are unimportant, but chiefly because they are variations of the main types of telescopes. Before we proceed to our primary objective—a discussion of how to use telescopes—we have one other important topic to consider: eyepieces.

Eyepieces

Much of the blame for the inferior performance of a telescope should be put squarely where it belongs: on the eyepiece. The eyepiece itself may not actually be inferior, but perhaps a poor choice. Few people realize that eyepieces should match the optics with which they are used. You can demonstrate this for yourself by trying an eyepiece that works perfectly well with a refractor in an f/5 Newtonian, or by trying a Ramsden eyepiece (designed for short-focus Newtonians) in a refractor. The result is likely to be unsatisfactory in both cases. And for this reason many of the war-surplus eyepiece "bargains" are not bargains at all; usually they are designed for instruments with entirely different characteristics than those of astronomical telescopes.

What are the characteristics of a good eyepiece? Here are a few of the most obvious:

1. Since eyepieces exhibit the same aberrations as objectives, ideal performance would be characterized by freedom from spherical aberration, astigmatism, coma, curvature of field, distortion, and chromatic aberration. Curiously enough, an eyepiece which has one or more of these aberrations may

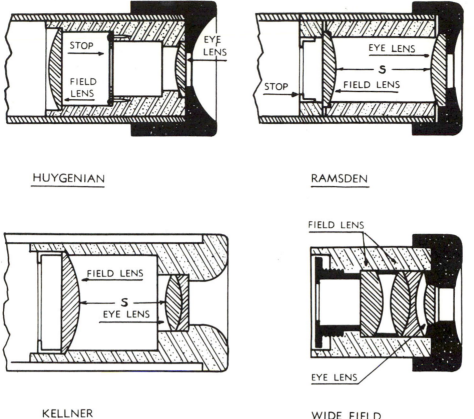

HUYGENIAN

RAMSDEN

KELLNER

WIDE FIELD

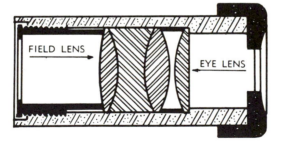

ORTHOSCOPIC

Types of eyepieces.

still be useful, provided the objective with which it is used exhibits a defect that is identical but opposite in degree. In such cases, the aberration is canceled to a large extent. For example, if the residual spherical aberration of an eyepiece is positive (undercorrected), it will work very well with an overcorrected objective.

In general, eyepiece aberrations become more noticeable as relative apertures increase; short-focal-length telescopes demand a greater degree of perfection than those of long focal length. This also applies to the eyepiece itself; deficiencies appear more pronounced with an increase in eyepiece focal length. Since longer focal length decreases magnification, it follows that defects in a low-power eyepiece are more noticeable than the same defects in one of high power.

2. The field of an eyepiece should be dark, flat, and wide. Dark fields help increase contrast; a flat field brings more parts of the image into focus at one time. And of course the wider the field, the better, provided definition is good over all of it.

3. Images must be bright, with no annoying "ghosts" from internal reflections.

4. Eye-relief should be as large as possible. A large-eye-relief eyepiece is not only a boon to the wearer of glasses, but also a great help to the beginning observer. Many people looking through a telescope for the first time can see no image at all simply because they find it difficult to get close enough to short-eye-relief eyepieces.

5. Finally, eyepieces used with relatively large aperture objectives should be achromatic, because chromatic aberration becomes more objectionable as apertures increase. This applies to reflectors as well as refractors. When you see color in a Newtonian image, blame the eyepiece rather than the mirror.

As a general rule, long-focus telescopes do not require exceptionally high-quality eyepieces unless they are used at low magnifications. Nevertheless, *all* telescopes deserve the best eyepieces obtainable, no matter what magnification is used. A cheap eyepiece may perform reasonably well at high powers, but getting full potentialities out of an excellent objective demands equal excellence in the remainder of the telescope optics.

There are literally hundreds of different kinds of eyepieces, ranging from simple single-element units to those employing half a dozen elements or more. Fortunately, they can all be divided into three broad groups, each including wide variations in performance and quality. The first group includes eyepieces consisting of only one lens; the second, eyepieces consisting of two lenses separated from each other; the third, eyepieces consisting of more than two separated lenses. This is an arbitrary grouping, for some of the single-lens eyepieces are actually made up of several pieces of glass cemented together. But because they act as a unit, we consider them single lenses.

SINGLE-ELEMENT EYEPIECES

This group includes three types of eyepieces: the thin-lens, the thick-lens (made from a single piece of glass), and the thick-lens cemented.

Thin-lens eyepieces, the simplest type, are chiefly of historical interest, although some cheap telescopes still employ them. The Kepler, a plano-convex lens, is used with the plane side toward the eye. Even though it produces bright images and has good eye-relief, it is practically useless because of its chromatic aberration, small field, and distortion. The Galilean is a double-concave lens; its greatest advantage is an erect image, good for terrestrial use but of doubtful value in astronomy.

Solid, or thick-lens, eyepieces are cut from crown glass rods and are usually ground spherical at each end. One form, the Tolles, has a groove cut around it two thirds of its length from the eye. When blackened, the groove acts as a lens stop. Eyepieces of this type suffer from chromatism and poor eye-relief, but they have wide, dark fields without internal reflections (ghost images) and produce bright images.

Cemented eyepieces represent an attempt—usually successful—to combine the virtues of the single lens with those of the two-element eyepiece. The cemented doublets (Steinheil, Hastings, Chevalier), give good eye-relief and produce bright images without ghosts and flat fields of good definition. They suffer from slight distortion, but not enough to impair their usefulness.

Cemented triplets, such as the monocentric Steinheil and Zeiss eyepieces (so called because the curves in the three elements are sections of concentric spheres, or very close to it), are excellent in all respects. Some observers, indeed, think these are the best eyepieces now available, chiefly because they work well in any telescope no matter what the focal length of the primary. They have wide fields of good definition; excellent light transmission that produces a bright image; no ghost images or scattered light, so that the bright image is seen against a dark field; almost perfect achromatism; and good eye-relief.

TWO-LENS EYEPIECES

The *Huygenian* eyepiece is made up of two Kepler lenses of different curvature, both of which have their plane surfaces facing the eye. It is called a "negative" eyepiece because the image is formed between the two lenses; for this reason it cannot be used as a magnifying glass.

The Huygenian is a standard eyepiece for the refractor and it works very well with objectives of long focal ratios—f/15 and over—especially at low and medium powers. When it is used with short-focus Newtonians, however, strong color appears, accompanied by spherical aberration and distortion at the field edges. But properly employed, it produces a field of good definition and illumination and it has less obvious ghost images than any other two-lens eyepiece. One of its deficiencies is poor eye-relief; also, because the image is formed between the lenses, it is difficult to use a reticle successfully.

In the Ramsden the lenses are turned so that their convex surfaces face one another. In all two-lens eyepieces, the lens nearest the objective is called the *field lens;* the one nearest the eye, the *eye lens.* The function of the eye lens is to magnify the image formed by the field lens, which acts more as a light collector than as a magnifier. The two lenses are placed just far enough from one another so that the image is formed on the eye-side of the eye lens. One difficulty with this arrangement is that if the image plane is far enough from the lens to allow comfortable eye-relief, serious color is introduced. Consequently most Ramsdens are somewhat hard to use. Nevertheless, they have enough advantages—wide field, less spherical aberration and less field curvature than the Huygenian, low cost—to be very widely used, especially with short-focus reflecting systems.

The chromatic aberration of the Ramsden can be greatly reduced by adding another element to the eye lens, making it a cemented doublet. In this form the eyepiece is called an achromatic Ramsden, or Kellner. Some observers refer to this combination as a "haunted ocular," since it is more subject to ghost images than any other type. Because it has wide (up to 45°), flat fields of excellent definition and almost no chromatism, it is very useful in short-focus telescopes.

There are many other variations of two-lens systems—too many, indeed, to include here. But there are at least three which must be mentioned: the Euryscopic, the Ploessel, and the orthoscopic. The Euryscopic is similar to the Kellner, but its field lens is double-convex; as an even further departure, the Ploessel's field lens is a cemented doublet exactly like the eye lens except reversed in direction. Because of this similarity of eye and field lenses, the Ploessel is called a *symmetrical* eyepiece. Both the Euryscopic and the Ploessel give excellent definition over a wide, flat field and are particularly adapted to short-focus systems. In the *orthoscopic* eyepiece the field lens becomes a cemented triplet while the eye lens reverts to a single, plano-convex piece of glass. The principle operating here is simple: The field lens produces color aberrations exactly opposite to those of the eye lens; color neutralization is the outcome. In addition, the usual eyepiece aberrations, especially spherical aberration and distortion, are reduced almost to the point of disappearance. The field is wide and flat, ghost images are negligible, scattered light is practically eliminated, and the result is an excellently defined image against a dark background. Add good eye-relief and the end product is a very fine eyepiece that can be used in telescopes of almost any focal ratio.

COMPOUND EYEPIECES

The addition of a third element between eye and field lenses transforms the two-lens eyepiece into a compound eyepiece. The extra element may be a simple lens or a cemented combination. It further reduces residual aberrations, but at the cost of a slight loss of light. Its advantages make up for this loss, however. A compound lens is completely achromatic and has only traces of distortion, coma, astigmatism, field curvature, and spherical aberration. Definition is exceptional over most of its tremendous dark field—up to 80° in some lenses. Examples are the Erfle, the fine component of so many Moonwatch telescopes; the Koenig, supplied as standard equipment on at least one fine commercially made instrument; and the Bertele and Goerz, used on many military instruments.

An important adjunct to many eyepieces, especially those with short eye-relief, is the Barlow lens. This is an additional lens, mounted in its own bushing, which is slipped into the eyepiece tube in front of the eyepiece itself. It is usually either a single negative lens, or an achromatic, cemented negative doublet. Its function is to act as a magnifier by lengthening the cone of light which enters the field lens of the eyepiece. The simple Barlow is usually made to magnify from 1½ × to 2 ×, the achromatic up to 4 ×. These figures are multipliers. If an eyepiece yields a total telescope magnification of 100 ×, the addition of a 3 × Barlow lens increases the total magnification to 300 × and at the same time increases the eye-relief to a comfortable margin.

The recently developed "zoom" eyepiece is a combination of lenses with one movable component. By simply twisting a knurled ring on the barrel, the observer may vary the effective focal length. The zoom eyepiece retains the excellent characteristics of the orthoscopic lens throughout its range of magnification and is a boon to the observer who doesn't like switching oculars. When he is using a zoom eyepiece with an f/8 Newtonian, for example, the observer may shift from a magnification of 55 × to 250 ×, or to any magnification between, in a

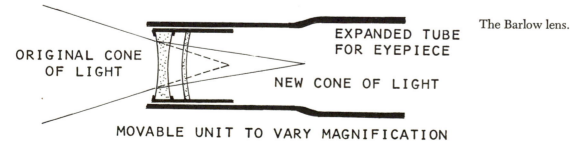

ORIGINAL CONE
OF LIGHT

EXPANDED TUBE
FOR EYEPIECE

NEW CONE OF LIGHT

MOVABLE UNIT TO VARY MAGNIFICATION

The Barlow lens.

matter of seconds. Zoom eyepieces are, of course, more expensive than most of the highly corrected oculars, but since they encompass the range of several individual units they are well worth the extra cost.

USING EYEPIECES

It is a great temptation to blame inferior telescope performance on the eyepiece; sometimes, but rarely, this is justified. If you possess a high-quality, commercially made telescope, the manufacturer has carefully matched the eyepieces he supplies with the characteristics of his particular telescope. On the other hand, if your telescope is homemade, you must make your own eyepiece selection. A cardinal rule is that large-aperture telescopes demand good-quality eyepieces; a corollary is that long-focal-length eyepieces should be coupled with good quality. The characteristics we have listed for eyepiece types speak pretty much for themselves; beyond this only a few generalizations need be made. Huygenians, Kellners, and symmetrical eyepieces work well with refractors; Ramsdens and monocentrics with reflectors. Orthoscopics and compound eyepieces can be used with any telescope.

If you plan to buy a new eyepiece for your telescope, try it out first, if possible. Check all parts of the field by looking at as many different objects as you can under a variety of seeing conditions. Remember that almost any eyepiece will give good images at the center of the field; you are looking for "fringe" benefits. Finally, there is no substitute for quality; in eyepieces, as in anything else, you get what you pay for. Fine telescope objectives must be matched by fine eyepieces if their full capabilities are to be realized.

Eyepieces are supplied in focal lengths from 4 mm (.16 inch) to 102 mm (4 inches). The outside diameter of the bushings is usually 1¼ inches, a standard width for the adapter tubes of focusing mounts. The simpler eyepieces (Ramsdens, Kellners, Ploessels, Huygenians) cost from $3 to $8, depending on their source. The more highly corrected types (orthoscopics, triplets, compound eyepieces) cost from $10 to $20. Add a dollar or two if the lenses are coated.* They should be carefully chosen to give the correct range of magnification for your telescope: 3 diameters per inch of aperture for lower limits, 60 per inch for upper limits. Thus, if you own a 6-inch f/8 Newtonian, a full range of eyepieces might run from 6-mm (¼-inch) to 75-mm (3-inch) focal length. You will probably find that the intermediate focal lengths will get the most use.

Telescope Accessories

What extra equipment do you need for your telescope? The answer to this depends on the answer to another question: What is the principal use to which you are going to put the instrument? If you are interested in solar observation, you will need high-density filters, a Herschel wedge, or some other device to cut down on light and heat. If you are primarily interested in planetary or lunar work you will want an array of filters to bring out contrast. If you wish to hunt for Messier† objects or faint nebulae, you will find that a good finder telescope is a great help. For pinpointing objects beyond the reach of a finder, setting circles become a necessity. If you are interested in photography, your telescope must be fitted with a drive and slow-motion devices, both of which require an equatorial mounting. If you own a refractor, you must have a star diagonal for your eyepieces in order to view objects near the zenith. Any accessory that increases your comfort is usually worth what you spend for it.

We shall talk about the various types of telescope mountings, drives, and setting circles in the next chapter. For the moment, let's confine our attention to some of the other accessories.

FINDER TELESCOPES

A finder is a wide-field, low-power telescope with an optical axis parallel to that of the main telescope. Although not needed on RFT telescopes—where the field of the telescope is so wide that objects can be easily located—a good finder is an essential addition to all others, even if setting circles are also provided. There are few requirements for finders, but those that apply are important:

1. The field must be oriented in the same direction as that of the main telescope. Many amateur telescope-makers use elbow telescopes for finders because of the convenient position of their eyepieces. An elbow telescope, however, is little better than no finder at all because the fields of finder and telescope are exactly reversed—a star appearing to the right in one will be on the left in the other, and the observer must constantly make allowance for the difference. For the same reason, when a star diagonal is used with the main eyepiece a diagonal should also be added to the finder eyepiece.

2. The finder must be located near the eyepiece of the main telescope and must be mounted high enough that the tube of the main telescope does not interfere with viewing. If the telescope is a Newto-

* Coated lenses have a thin application of magnesium fluoride, which reduces reflections and therefore increases light transmission.

† The list of 103 star clusters and nebulae compiled in 1781 by Charles Messier, the great comet hunter.

nian, there should be *two* finders. When a telescope is mounted equatorially the finder may sometimes be in an awkward position. The observer may find himself crouching under the telescope, twisting his neck in a tiring attempt to bring his "seeing" eye to the eyepiece—most of us are left- or right-eyed, just as we are left- or right-handed. The addition of a second finder obviates this difficulty, since one will always be in a convenient position.

3. A reticle or cross hairs should be placed on the field lens of the eyepiece. The wide field (3° to 6°) makes centering an object difficult unless there are some guide lines to help. Triple cross hairs that form a small triangle at the center of the field or a glass reticle with a small circle in its center are particularly helpful. The supports of the finder must be strong, and the adjusting screws must be kept tight. A finder that gets out of adjustment is more of a nuisance than a help.

Ordinarily, a finder has a much shorter focal length and a wider field than its companion telescope. But if the finder is to be used as a guide telescope for photography, its focal length must approach that of the main instrument. If there is a great disparity in the two focal lengths, a change in position of the telescope may produce only a small shift in the finder, and at the same time move an object out of the field of the telescope eyepiece or the photographic plate.

FILTERS

Filters have two main purposes: to reduce the glare of bright objects at low power—e.g., the moon, Venus, Jupiter—and to improve definition by providing more contrast in extended images.

Neutral density filters are used to reduce glare. These filters have no color and are usually made of partially silvered glass or of colloidal carbon deposited on a glass surface. You can make your own by exposing black-and-white photographic film for different periods of time and then developing it to maximum density.

The density of a filter can be determined by this formula:

$$D = \log \frac{\text{incident light}}{\text{transmitted light}}$$

The range in density is from 0 to 5, the former transmitting 100 percent of the light that strikes it and the latter, none. Some typical values follow:

Density	Percentage of transmitted light
0	100
.3	50
.5	32
.8	16
1	10
1.3	5
1.6	2.5
2	1
3	0.1

Neutral density filters are useful in bringing out details often obscured by the brightness of the object being viewed: irregularities on the terminator of Venus, double stars (when one is much brighter than the other, as in the case of Pollux and its companion), details on maria of the moon, and so forth.

There are a great many colored filters to choose from. The Wratten series (Eastman Kodak), for example, offers more than one hundred. Filters are invaluable in bringing out lunar and planetary detail. Amber, yellow, or orange are excellent for improving the contrast of Martian details. Jupiter's belts show up well with green filters, and the white markings on the belts are enhanced by blue filters. Green, blue, and yellow filters used when viewing the moon may change your ideas about some of the lunar configurations, especially the inside areas of the wide craters, such as Plato.

Never use a filter at the eyepiece to view the sun unless the light and heat in the optical train are

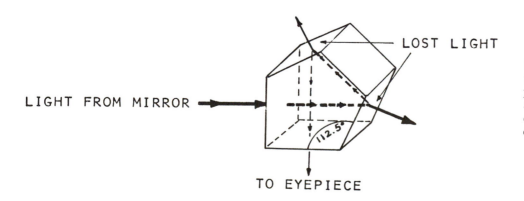

LOST LIGHT

LIGHT FROM MIRROR →

112.5°

TO EYEPIECE

Some of the light that enters the unsilvered pentaprism is reflected internally and eventually reaches the eyepiece, but most of it escapes and is lost.

being reduced by some other means as well. The danger involved is equivalent to placing your eye at the focus of a burning glass. The heat at the focus of a telescope objective is intense enough to crack glass filters and allow the full power of the sun to strike the observer's unprotected eye. But this light can be cut down by a Herschel wedge or an un-silvered penta-prism, for when light strikes an un-silvered glass surface at any angle other than the critical angle (where it is completely reflected), some of it is reflected and some transmitted through the glass. The transmitted light is again only par-tially reflected by the inner surfaces of a prism, some of it passing through. In the Herschel wedge, only a small percentage of the original light and heat is reflected to the eyepiece; the remainder is safely reflected or transmitted in other directions. The penta-prism acts in the same way. Each of these devices is placed in the train of light in front of the eyepiece, and each should be supplemented by a medium neutral density filter. With these prisms, the telescope may now be used safely for direct solar viewing. In the absence of such safety devices, you can view the sun by projecting its image onto a piece of white cardboard or screen. Don't use ce-mented eyepieces for this purpose, however, because the heat may melt the Canada balsam that holds the lens elements together. A Herschelian or Ramsden eyepiece is best for projection purposes.

Some telescope manufacturers avoid the use of Herschel wedges or other devices by filtering light *before* it enters the telescope. This is done in two steps: First, the aperture of the telescope is reduced by placing a mask with a small hole cut in it over the front of the telescope. The amount of light entering the telescope is thus diminished by a factor proportional to the squares of the diameters of hole and mirror. Then this hole is covered by heavily silvered, optically flat (to $\frac{1}{10}$ wavelength of light) glass. The result is to cut down light transmission to about one part in 50,000, or by 99.998 percent! The eyepiece needs no further protection and filters are not necessary with this arrangement.

STAR DIAGONALS

Unless you lie flat on your back, it is almost im-possible to use a plain refractor to observe heavenly objects at the zenith. The addition of a right-angle prism or mirror diagonal to the adapter tube in front of the eyepiece makes it possible to observe zenith objects in comfort. You cannot use just *any* prism or *any* diagonal, however, for their optical qualities must be in keeping with other telescope elements, or flat to within $\frac{1}{4}$ wavelength of light. And remember that a diagonal will change the orientation of the field under observation in one plane (right and left, or up and down, depending on the way the diagonal is turned with respect to the rest of the telescope).

CHAPTER III

The Sky

Our Observation Platform

If we were to make a catalog of the worst possible places from which to observe the myriad objects of the heavens, the earth would probably head the list. In the first place, we are surrounded by an atmosphere some three hundred miles deep, parts of which are filled with dust particles, water vapor, and other obscuring material. This in itself wouldn't be so bad, but in addition we must contend with constantly shifting layers of air of different densities, which bend light back and forth until images jump like Mexican beans in our telescope eyepieces. Beyond the atmosphere things are not much better, for "empty" space seems to be filled with vast dust clouds and great areas of illuminated gases that completely block our view of some of the things we would like to see most. We can't even see the center of our own galaxy as earth is far out, near its rim.

When you observe the sky for several hours, you notice that the stars appear to move slowly across the sky from east to west. And you know that the stars you see in the summer are not the same ones that you see in winter. The sky is ever-changing— an observer who went out at the same time every night for a year would see a slightly different picture each night.

The apparent drift of the stars is, of course, caused by the rotation of the earth. And the movement of the stars from season to season is caused by the earth's revolution around the sun. But revolution and rotation do not explain certain other changes which can be observed—minute changes admittedly, but nonetheless important to the telescope user over a period of years. Each year the sky seems to shift ever so slightly to the west. This change too can be ascribed to a motion of the earth —a 26,000-year wobble of the earth's axis which we call precession. Similar to the wobble of a gyroscope, it is caused by the gravitational pull of the moon. There are other, even more minute, changes that are important only over tens of centuries.

And getting a good look at the heavenly object is another matter. Our only means of interpreting the nature of the things we see in the heavens is from their emitted or reflected light. Light, unfortunately, does not have instantaneous speed; it pokes along at about 186,000 miles a second. This rate sounds pretty fast, but when we consider stellar distances it really is incredibly slow, as we shall see in a moment. Astronomers work always with the past; because light takes time to move from one place to another, they see things as they *were*, not as they *are*.

Consider just a few examples. We see the moon as it *was* about a second ago, the sun as it *was* eight minutes ago. If an explosion were to blast Jupiter out of the sky right now, we would not know of it for thirty-five minutes. The bright blaze of the great star Sirius might have been extinguished four years before you read this, yet you would go on admiring it for another four and a half years without realizing that anything was wrong. The vast panoply of the Andromeda Galaxy appears in a telescope eyepiece as it looked nearly 2 million

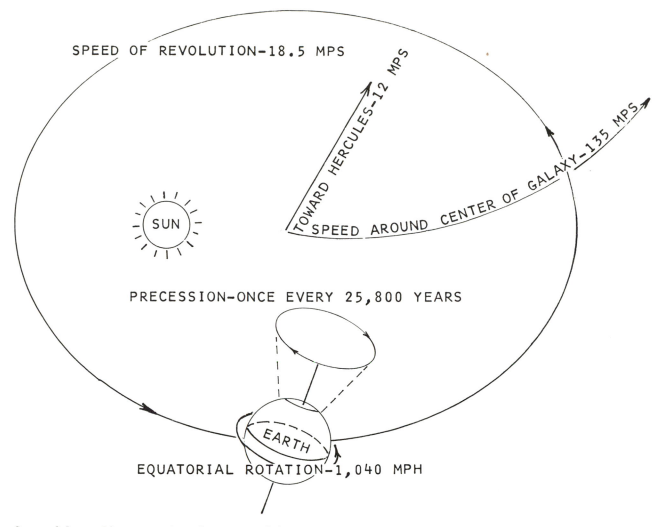

SPEED OF REVOLUTION-18.5 MPS

TOWARD HERCULES-12 MPS

SPEED AROUND CENTER OF GALAXY-135 MPS

SUN

PRECESSION-ONCE EVERY 25,800 YEARS

EARTH

EQUATORIAL ROTATION-1,040 MPH

Some of the earth's motions (not drawn to scale).

years ago, not as it is today. At this moment, photons of light emitted from far-distant galaxies bombard the photographic plates of the great Palomar telescope after having traveled through space for *9 billion* years! Light is indeed a slow messenger and hardly keeps us up to date on what is going on in the heavens.

Taking all these factors into consideration—atmosphere, obscuring matter, motions, distance—the earth seems to qualify rather poorly as an observation post. But since it is our only one, for a few more years at least, we must try to make up for its deficiencies by the excellence of the instruments we use.

Getting Acquainted with the Heavens

It is easy to train a telescope on the moon or a bright planet. But suppose we want to look at the Ring Nebula in Lyra. A look at map 5 will show that the famous "doughnut" lies just off a line connecting the stars Gamma Lyrae (Sulaphat) and Beta Lyrae (Sheliak), which are separated from one another by about a degree. But how do we locate Lyra in the heavens, and how long a distance in the sky is a degree?

MEASURING THE SKY

To start with, both the moon and the sun extend across about half a degree of the sky. This sets a scale, but since we can't move the moon and sun around for measurement purposes, we must find a substitute that is easy and simple to use. Any round object held at a distance of 110 times its diameter will just cover the full moon. A dime, for example, has a diameter just over $^{11}/_{16}$ inch and this figure times 110 is 76 inches. So if you place a dime 76 inches from your eye it will cover ½° of the sky. Unfortunately, few of us have arms 76 inches long, or even half that length, but we can use a proportion based on a comfortable position of the arm holding a coin. For the average person this is about 19 inches. The proportion is:

$$\frac{110 \times \text{width of coin}}{\text{distance from eye}} \times \frac{1}{2}°$$

Therefore:

$$\frac{110 \times \frac{11}{16}}{19} \times \frac{1}{2}° = 2°$$

People with long arms will probably find it more convenient to use a quarter which is 1 inch across. A comfortable distance in this case is 28 inches. Thus,

$$\frac{110 \times 1}{28} \times \frac{1}{2}° = 2°$$

Either coin, then, can provide you with a 2° unit to measure angular distances between close stars. For stars that are more widely separated, or for angular distances between constellations, use the width of the knuckles of your closed fist from little finger to forefinger. Let's say this is 3 inches and that you measure 28 inches from eye to outstretched knuckles. In this case,

$$\frac{110 \times 3}{28} \times \frac{1}{2}° = 6°$$

For even more, try the outspread fingers from thumb to little finger. If the distance is, say, 8 inches, then

$$\frac{110 \times 8}{28} \times \frac{1}{2}° = 16°$$

Work out your own measurements and try them on a few test objects. Here are some familiar trial horses:

Across the top of the bowl of the Big Dipper	10°
Between the "pointers"	5°
From top pointer to the North Star	29°
From the end of the Dipper's handle to Arcturus	32°
Across the W of Cassiopeia	13°

Locating Celestial Objects

Before we start looking for star patterns, let's get an idea of the stars' positions relative to each other in the sky and learn how these positions are measured on star maps. A simple way is to imagine that the stars lie on a huge spherical shell surrounding the earth, all at the same distance from it. The equator of this shell is simply an extension of the equator of the earth.

Star distances are measured in degrees from this celestial equator, the two celestial poles lying 90°

from it. To avoid confusion, southward measurements are indicated by a minus sign or by a line drawn under the figure used. Thus, a star 38° south of the celestial equator has its position indicated by either −38 or 38. To differentiate these measurements from those of the earth, we use the term *declination* instead of latitude. For east-west distances, we start with a spot in the constellation Pisces (called the First Point of Aries) and locate all stars by their eastward distance from it. We express these distances in hours, minutes, and seconds of arc to avoid mixing them up with time measurements. Here an hour equals 15°, a minute ¼°, and a second 1/240°. This east-west measurement is called the *right ascension* of the star. When both measurements are put together, right ascension is written first (four digits) followed by declination to the nearest degree (two digits). *Example:* 163208 indicates that a star has right ascension 16h 32m and is located 8° north of the celestial equator.

LOCATING CONSTELLATIONS BY BRIGHT STARS

There are few constellations that are recognizable as the mythological figures for which they are named. In the long run, it is easier to learn them from the geometrical arrangement of their stars— triangles, trapezoids, parallelograms, and so on. But how do you locate them in the first place? A simple method is to get acquainted with some key bright stars, many of which are associated with a single constellation. A familiarity with these easily found constellation beacons will soon lead to a recognition of the figure as a whole. Of course, you cannot expect to learn all eighty-nine constellations by this means, for many of them have no outstanding stars. Nevertheless, the method will introduce a sufficient number so the rest can be learned more easily later.

Some Spring Constellations

Because any given star rises approximately four minutes earlier each night, the constellations gradually shift to the west. This shift is barely noticeable from night to night, but over a three-month period a whole new set of constellations come into view. Just what constellations will be overhead on any given night depends on the position of the observer north or south of the equator and the time of night he does his stargazing. The seasonal constellation charts show the constellations as seen from 40° North latitude at about 8:30 P.M. Each chart shows a set of constellations for one of the four seasons.

To use one of these maps outside at night, illuminate it with a dim red flashlight, just bright enough so you can see the figures. (Cover the lens with sev-

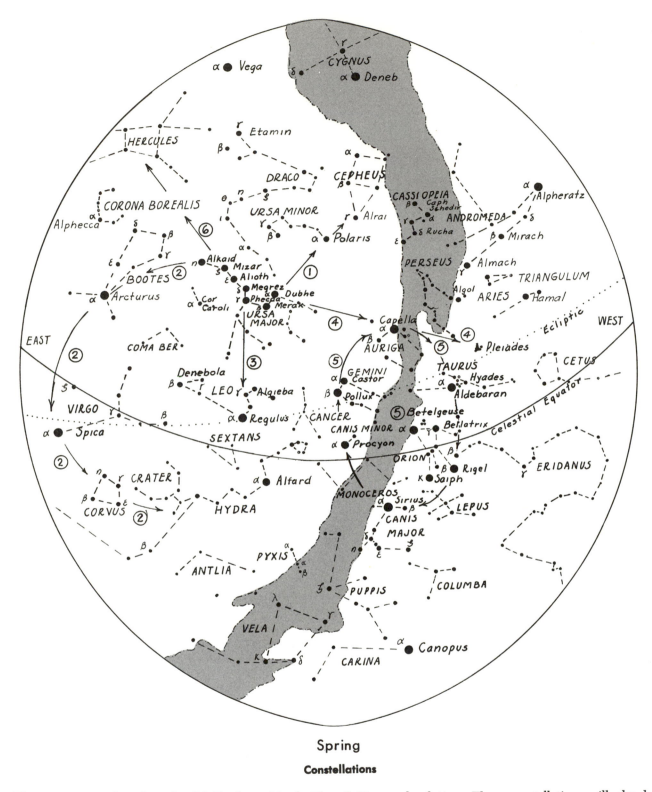

Spring

Constellations

The stars as seen from latitude 40° North on March 15 at 8:30 P.M. local time. These constellations will also be found on maps 2, 3, 6, 7, 10 and 11.

eral thicknesses of red cellophane, kept in place with an elastic band.) Hold the map overhead with its north point facing north. See how many of the constellations you can pick out, starting with the bright "key" stars. Then put the map down and identify these stars without its help. You will be surprised how quickly you will become familiar with both individual stars and constellations.

Let's take such a set and find some of the constellations by means of the bright star patterns. We pick the spring stars to start because the Big Dipper (part of *Ursa Major*), which we shall use as a guide, is high in the sky. We can see it from any latitude north of 38°.* The accompanying chart shows the stars as they look about 8:30 P.M. local time on March 15 from a latitude of about 40° North. The heavy black dots represent "bright" stars of magnitude 2.5 or brighter.

The two stars on the right-hand side of the bowl of the Big Dipper are called the *pointers* because an imaginary line drawn through them also passes through Polaris, the North Star. Actually, the Dipper contains several more pointers, as shown on the map.

The first pointer (1) leads from the stars Merak and Dubhe† and passes through Polaris, about 29° away. If the night is dark and clear, you can see that Polaris lies at the end of the handle of the Little Dipper, *Ursa Minor,* and you can follow the curve of the handle around to the bowl. Otherwise you will probably see only the two outside stars of the bowl, Beta and Gamma Ursae Minoris, called the "Guardians of the Pole."

A continuation of the first pointer past the pole for about 12° ends near Alrai, a third-magnitude star in the constellation *Cepheus.* This star, Gamma Cephei, lies at the apex of a triangle whose base is the top of a parallelogram. The five stars form a figure that looks like a dunce cap, with Alrai at the peak.

A secondary line drawn from Mizar (at the crook of the handle in Ursa Major) through Polaris leads

* Here are two convenient rules about what stars are visible, to be reversed if used for the southern hemisphere: (1) Subtract your latitude from 90°. Any star whose declination is greater than the resulting figure is always above the horizon; it never sets. (2) Any star in the southern hemisphere whose declination is greater than this figure is always below the horizon; it never rises.

† The stars are usually named for the constellations in which they appear; relatively few have names of their own. The constellation names are all Latin—*Ursa Major,* the Great Bear, for example. Individual stars are identified by a Greek letter followed by the genitive form of the Latin name of the constellation in which they appear; thus, Dubhe is Alpha Ursae Majoris. Ordinarily, the alpha star of a constellation is the brightest of the group, the others following in decreasing brightness according to the order of the letters of the Greek alphabet. Ursa Major is one of the exceptions: here the letters are in the sequence of their position in the constellation, from right to left.

to Rucha, the delta star in the W-shaped constellation *Cassiopeia,* the Lady in the Chair. Rucha is 28° from the Pole.

The Big Dipper's handle is also a pointer (2). Follow the curve of the handle for about 32° across the sky and you will find the red-orange star Arcturus, fourth brightest in the heavens. Arcturus lies at the foot of the kite-shaped constellation *Boötes,* the Herdsman. By continuing the same curve for another 32° you will locate Spica, brightest star in *Virgo,* the Virgin, a constellation which sprawls east and west across the sky for some 45°. And, if you continue 15° more, the long curve will pass near the trapezoid of stars that make up *Corvus,* the Crow, and finally end with the constellation *Crater,* whose dim stars (fourth magnitude or less) form a figure that looks very much like a wineglass. The brightest star in Corvus is Gamma—strangely enough, the only one in the trapezoid without a name.

The third pointer (3) leads from the *inside* stars of the Dipper's bowl, but in the opposite direction from the line that picks out Polaris. When followed for about 45°, it ends near Regulus in *Leo,* the Lion. This first-magnitude star lies at the butt of the handle of the Sickle on one side of the constellation. The other side of Leo is a triangle of stars marked by bright Denebola, Beta Leonis.

Now if you can follow an imaginary line from Denebola passing through Algieba, the first bright star in the blade of the Sickle, you will come to a dim constellation called *Cancer,* the Crab. None of Cancer's stars is brighter than fourth magnitude, the relatively dim group looking like an inverted Y. We mention it here because it contains the beautiful, naked-eye (on a dark night) open cluster called *Praesepe,* or the Beehive.

The fourth pointer (4) starts with the two stars at the top of the Dipper's bowl, goes as far as Capella in Auriga, and then continues to the lovely *Pleiades,* or the Seven Sisters. Capella, the Goat, is a brilliant red-orange star of magnitude .2, and is the key to a pentagon of stars forming *Auriga,* the Charioteer. Menkalinan (Beta Aurigae), a neighbor of Capella in the five-sided figure, is the starting point of a line that passes through Capella and ends at Algol, the "Demon Star." Algol, which got its name from the Arabs, decreases in brightness from 2.3 to 3.5 in a period of a little less than 69 hours, and then increases to its original brightness in the same interval. But we are interested in Algol chiefly because it is a means of finding the constellation *Perseus,* the Champion, a string of stars stretching between the Pleiades and Cassiopeia.

Capella is also the key to the great loop of bright stars (5) that surrounds the brilliant constellation *Orion,* the Hunter. The main body of Orion's stars is a clockwise parallelogram starting with the red giant Betelgeuse, with Bellatrix, Rigel, and Saiph following, in that order. Cutting diagonally across the parallelogram is a chain of three stars (Orion's Belt), pointing downward to Sirius, the heavens' brightest star, and pointing roughly upward in the opposite direction to orange Aldebaran. Orion's Belt is of further interest because the celestial equator passes through it. Once you spot it and then turn to look at Polaris, the apparent dimensions of the great sphere of stars that make up the celestial globe becomes strikingly clear.

Because of its brilliance, Sirius makes a good starting place to follow the loop around Orion. Sirius is the key star in the constellation *Canis Major*, the Big Dog. Above this group, about 28° away, is *Canis Minor*, the Little Dog, marked by the bright star Procyon. Still farther along, the twin stars Castor and Pollux lie at the top of the constellation *Gemini*, the Twins. Next in order is Capella, almost directly above Orion. On the downward sweep of the loop lies Aldebaran, key star of *Taurus*, the Bull. Taurus is an interesting constellation because it includes another open star cluster called the *Hyades*, not as spectacular as the Pleiades, perhaps, but still a fine sight through field glasses or a small telescope. The loop continues until it passes through Rigel, a beautiful blue-white star in the base of the parallelogram, then goes on until it ends at its beginning point, Sirius.

The sixth and final pointer (6) follows a line set up by the two stars in the middle of the Big Dipper's handle and directs us to the constellation *Hercules*. Here again there are few bright stars, but you can recognize the group because it looks similar to Orion but has only two stars in the belt as compared with Orion's three. Lying about halfway between Hercules and Boötes is *Corona Borealis*, the Northern Crown, one of the few constellations that looks like what it purports to be. You will probably be able to pick out the chief star of this semicircular group, called Alphecca.

Some Summer Constellations

By the time June 15 comes around we have almost a whole new team of stars at the 8:30 P.M. observing time. Some of the "regulars" are still with us—the circumpolar constellations, for example—but the great loop around Orion has disappeared to the west, taking its associated constellations with it. But their replacements have risen in the east and will be with us until fall.

The Big Dipper in Ursa Major has swung around the pole until the curved pointer (2) generated by its handle is almost on the zenith and moving toward the west. Corona Borealis and Hercules are approaching an overhead position. The pointers of

the spring map are still useful in finding old friends—Regulus in Leo (3), the Keystone in Hercules, Polaris (1), and others. Now we can introduce a few new ones.

Protected by the curve of the Dipper's handle and lying in the area bounded by Boötes, Virgo, and Leo are two small constellations which often escape notice. They are *Coma Berenices*, Berenice's Hair, and *Canes Venatici*, the Hunting Dogs. The latter is distinguished by Cor Caroli, lead star of the "Diamond of Virgo." The other three in the diamond are Denebola, Arcturus, and Spica. This is perhaps the largest "jewel" ever seen—it stretches 50° from Cor Caroli to Spica. Coma Berenices, lying just below the Hunting Dogs, is easily distinguished on a dark night as a sparkling handful of little stars.

The two inside stars of the Dipper's bowl, Phecda and Megrez, were useful in finding Leo's sickle when we looked at them in the spring skies. Now if we follow this pointer in the opposite direction—(7) on the map—for about 65° across the sky, we arrive at Deneb, principal star of *Cygnus*, the Swan. Cygnus is more easily recognized as the *Northern Cross*, with Deneb at the top of the upright shaft and the beautiful double star Albireo at the bottom. Unlike its counterpart in southern skies, the Northern Cross really suggests its name.

About halfway between the Big Dipper and Deneb pointer (7) crosses pointer (8), which starts with the outside stars of the bowl of the Little Dipper, Pherkad and Kochab, and heads 45° across the sky to brilliant Vega in *Lyra*, the Lyre. On its way, pointer (8) passes Etamin, the bright star in the head of *Draco*, the Dragon. On a dark, clear night you can see Draco winding between the two Dippers, his tail almost dipping into the open bowl of Ursa Major.

Vega, fifth brightest star in the heavens, is placed at the right angle of a huge right triangle of stars, a familiar landmark of the summer skies. The other two stars are Deneb, 30° away, and Altair, just rising in the east at a distance of about 40°. Altair is the key star of *Aquila*, the Eagle, a constellation which looks more like a kite than a bird. Enclosed in the great right triangle are two small groups, *Sagitta*, the Arrow, about 15° from Altair, and *Vulpecula*, the Fox. Vulpecula lies between Sagitta and the foot of the Northern Cross.

Vega and Altair also form one side of a tremendous equilateral triangle whose third vertex is the star Ras Alhague in the sprawling and otherwise undistinguished constellation *Ophiuchus*, the Serpent Bearer. Ras Alhague lies on one side of the line connecting Vega and Altair, Deneb on the other. As might be expected, the Serpent Bearer is connected with (or seems to stand upon) *Serpens*, the Serpent. The Serpent's head (*Serpens Caput*) lies halfway between Ras Alhague and Arcturus,

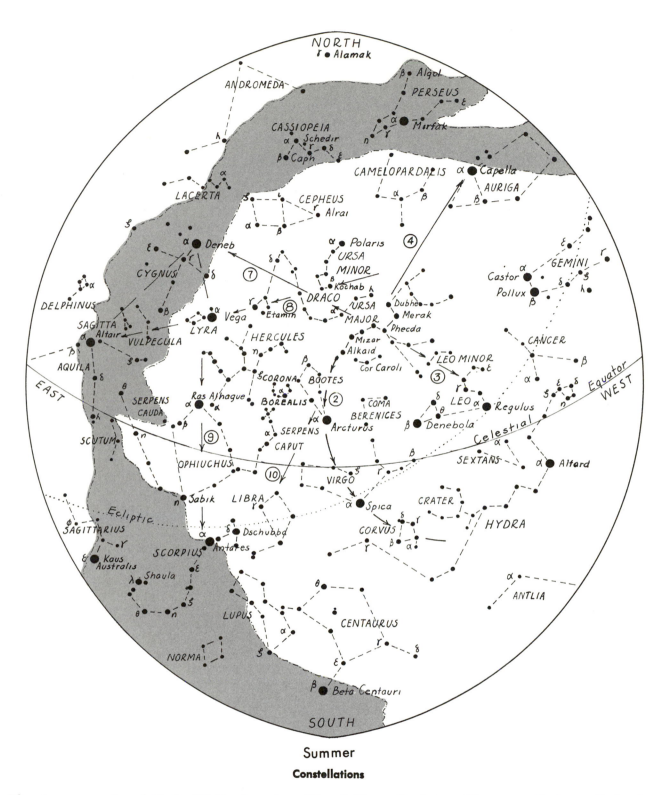

Summer

Constellations

The stars as seen from latitude 40° North on June 15 at 8:30 P.M. local time. These constellations will also be found on maps 3, 4, 7, 8, 11 and 12.

while his tail (*Serpens Cauda*) twists upward from the base of Ophiuchus toward Altair.

In the southern sky, almost on a line (9) passing through Vega and Ras Alhague, appears Antares, the great red giant of *Scorpius*, the Scorpion. At this time of year the tail of Scorpius dips toward the horizon, but the stinger reappears farther to the east as Lambda Scorpii, the star Shaula. *Libra,* the Scales, is another trapezoid of stars (larger than Corvus), which appears halfway between Antares and Spica, in Virgo. Libra can also be found by following a pointer (10) formed by the final two stars of the handle of the Dipper, Mizar and Alkaid.

Finally, strung all the way across the southern sky from Libra to a point just below Cancer is the tenuous constellation *Hydra*, the Sea Serpent. It has only a single bright star in its entire length, called Alfard, the "Solitary One." Alfard forms a right triangle with Spica and Regulus.

Some Fall Constellations

Many of the summer constellations have fallen below the horizon because of the swing of the heavens to the west. The Little Dipper is now dumping its contents into the bowl of the Big Dipper instead of the reverse, as in the spring. The edges of a few of the winter constellations are just beginning to poke above the horizon to the east. Overhead, the bright stars of the fall constellations can be seen in their full glory.

Again we can use the Big Dipper as a pointer to start exploring the groups of the autumn skies. The North Star pointer (1), if followed through the peak of Cepheus, leads to Alpheratz, chief star of the constellation *Andromeda*, the Queen. Alpheratz is about 60° from Polaris and forms one of the corners of the great square of *Pegasus*, the Winged Horse. The other stars in the square, reading clockwise, are Scheat (Beta), Markab (Alpha), and Algenib (Gamma).

Pegasus serves as a good signpost for the other constellations of the eastern sky. Pointer 11 drawn from Markab through Alpheratz to the north passes almost directly through the stars Mirach and Almach in Andromeda and thence to Algol in Perseus. To the east of the line, looking exactly like its name, is *Triangulum,* the Triangle. A little farther east still, on a line through Cassiopeia and Triangulum, is the small group *Aries,* the Ram. Hamal is the chief star in Aries, which at one time held the Vernal Equinox, the point at which the ecliptic (the path followed by sun, moon, and planets) crosses the celestial equator.

Pointer 11 followed to the south for about 22° passes through the *Water Jar,* four close stars lo-cated in the central part of *Aquarius,* the Water Carrier. Aquarius spreads east and west in the southern sky for some 45°. Continuing south from the Water Jar we come to Deneb Algiedi, delta star of *Capricornus,* the Sea Goat. Capricornus is a bat-shaped group, with Deneb Algiedi on one wing and Dabih and Giedi (Beta and Alpha Capricorni) on the other. We can locate Dabih by drawing a line (12) from Vega through Altair.

Lying below Aquarius is the bright star Fomalhaut, all alone in this part of the heavens and therefore easy to find. Fomalhaut is the lead star of *Piscis Austrinus,* the Southern Fish. In the southwest, close to the horizon, you may be able to see a small trapezoid of stars, about 3° high, which lies in the constellation *Sagittarius,* the Archer. The brightest star in the trapezoid is Nunki, and at the opposite corner is Ascella. Some observers have thought this little group looks like the bowl of a dipper with a third-magnitude star, Kaus Borealis, serving as the handle. Because the Milky Way is particularly dense in this region (the center of our galaxy is located here) the group is usually called the *Milk Dipper.* About 10° below its bowl you can find the circlet of stars *Corona Australis,* the Southern Crown.

Piscis Austrinus is only one of the "fish" constellations. Another is *Pisces,* the Fishes, lying to the east of Pegasus. The head of one of the fishes is the *Circlet,* just below Pegasus; the head of the other is near Mirach in Andromeda. The two fishes join at the star Alrisha, Alpha Piscium.

If we draw another pointer (13) from Alpheratz to Algenib in Pegasus, its extension will pass Deneb Kaitos near the tail of *Cetus,* the Whale. Another line (14), from Markab through Algenib, locates Cetus's head. We are interested in Deneb Kaitos because it is the eastern terminus of a great sweep of bright stars stretching all the way across the southern horizon. These stars (from west to east) are Antares in Scorpius, Kaus Australis (lying below the Milk Dipper) in Sagittarius, Fomalhaut in Piscis Austrinus, and finally Deneb Kaitos in Cetus.

Overhead, the great triangle of Vega, Deneb, and Altair appears with its associated constellations. From it we can pick up one or two small groups we have neglected before. Part way between the triangle and the Water Jar in Aquarius lies another dipperlike constellation called *Delphinus,* the Dolphin. All of the five stars in this group are of the fourth magnitude, but two of them are interesting because of their names. These are Sualocin and Rotanev—Nicolaus Venator spelled backward. Venator, a seventeenth-century astronomer, was honored in this way by the astronomer Piazzi, whom he assisted. Between Delphinus and the Water Jar, *Equuleus,* the Little Horse, appears.

Finally, lying at the foot of Aquila (whose chief

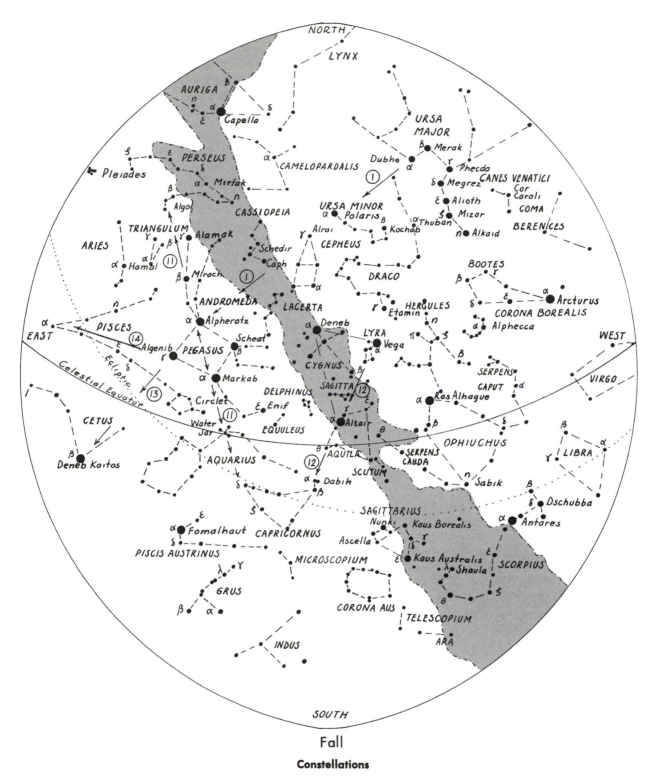

Fall

Constellations

The stars as seen from latitude 40° North on September 15 at 8:30 P.M. local time. These constellations will also be found on maps 4, 5, 8, 9, 12 and 13.

star is Altair) an undistinguished little constellation called *Scutum,* the Shield, can be found if you look hard enough. Visually, Scutum is dull; telescopically it actually is anything but that, as we shall discover later.

Some Winter Constellations

By December 15, the date of our winter map, the Big Dipper's handle has swung all the way down to the northern horizon. The Dragon, as it arches its way across the sky, really looks like one. The line (4) from Megrez to Dubhe points across the sky to brilliant Capella. The great loop (5) of first-magnitude stars around Orion is prominent in the eastern skies, while to the west the square of Pegasus dominates the heavens.

About 10° south of the line connecting Saiph and Rigel at the base of Orion, you can pick out the double trapezoid of *Lepus,* the Hare. Above Rigel, Beta Eridani appears, lead star of *Eridanus,* the River. The tenuous length of this great constellation winds southward all the way to its alpha star, Achernar, 130° away. From our position in the north, Eridanus disappears as we catch a glimpse of Acamar, about three fourths of the way along the "river's" path. At a point just east of the sprawling Cetus, Eridanus swings into a great horseshoe bend before continuing on southward.

This is a good part of the sky to use for orienting yourself in declination. The star Delta Ceti lies 50° across the sky from the belt of Orion; a line drawn from the belt to this star roughly parallels the celestial equator. Continued, it passes just under the Circlet of Pisces on its way through the Water Jar of Aquarius.

In the northwest, the Northern Cross is approaching the horizon. A line drawn from Deneb through Schedir, in Cassiopeia, helps to locate the indistinct group *Lacerta,* the Lizard, lying on the edge of the Milky Way just south of the mid-point of the line. Vega is almost on the horizon, while Altair, the third member of the great right triangle, has disappeared.

Almost overhead, the Pleiades and Hyades glow against the cold winter sky, even though they are often overlooked at this time of year because of the competition of the great, brilliant suns of Orion and the loop of constellations around him.

Along the southern horizon, we catch glimpses of some of the southern constellations. Starting with Fomalhaut in Piscis Austrinus in the southwest and moving around to the east we pass *Sculptor,* whose only distinction is that it lies near the south pole of our galaxy; *Phoenix,* whose second-magnitude alpha star helps to locate it; *Fornax,* the Furnace, distinguished only by its name; *Caelum,* the Chisel; and *Columba,* the Dove. This eastward swing finally takes us to Sirius. If we look a little farther to the north we see Procyon and pass over *Monoceros,* the Unicorn, a constellation of dim stars. Most of the constellations just named lie in the haze close to the horizon and we rarely see them, but because they are a fringe group of the southern constellations, they are mentioned briefly in the next section.

THE SOUTHERN CONSTELLATIONS (see maps 10–14)

Up to this point, we have identified fifty of the eighty-nine constellations, all of them lying north of declination −45°. Thirty-five more groups lie to the south of this line. They can be roughly divided into two main groups, those known to the ancients and named in the days when the earth's precession made them visible from points north of the equator, and those named by the astronomer Lacaille in the 1750's. Those in this latter group are all supposed to represent parts of the ship *Argus—Octans,* the Octant; *Horologium,* the Clock; *Mensa,* the Table; *Reticulum,* the Net; *Puppis,* the Deck; *Norma,* the Level; *Pyxis,* the Compass; *Antlia,* the Pump; *Circinus,* the Drawing Compasses; *Telescopium,* the Telescope; and *Microscopium,* the Microscope. We lump these together in a group, even though they spread far and wide across the southern skies, because of their indistinct forms and because they possess few objects of any importance.

There is no southern polestar. The nearest star of the brightness of Polaris lies 20° away, and so we find no pointers in this region as we did in the north. But there are several objects we can use as starting points, among them the two great subgalaxies called the *Magellanic Clouds.* Two other groups useful for this purpose are *Crux,* the Southern Cross, and *Triangulum Australe,* the Southern Triangle. Now, if we draw a line from the center of the Small Magellanic Cloud (*Nebecula Minor*) to Beta Crucis, and another from the center of the Large Magellanic Cloud (*Nebecula Major*) to Alpha Trianguli Australis, the intersection of these lines comes close to locating the South Pole of the heavens (within 3°; Polaris is 1° away from the *true* North Pole). Fortunately, both Crux and Triangulum Australe are easy to find; the former consists of four close-together bright stars, the latter of two third-magnitude and one second-magnitude stars.

Another line drawn from Alpha Trianguli Australis through the mid-point of the triangle's base locates Toliman, chief star of *Centaurus,* the Centaur. Most of the remainder of this constellation swings around the Southern Cross. Toliman is particularly interesting to us because of its nearness to earth—only 4.3 light-years away.

Not far from the Southern Cross—about 25°—

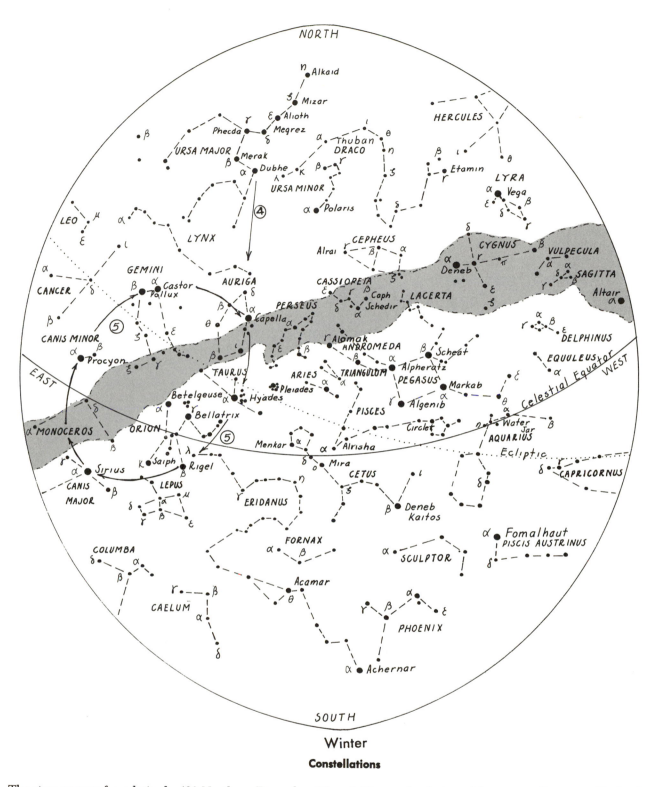

Winter

Constellations

The stars as seen from latitude 40° North on December 15 at 8:30 P.M. local time. These constellations will also be found on maps 2, 5, 6, 9, 10 and 13.

is the *False Cross,* made up of stars from the constellations *Carina,* the Keel, and *Vela,* the Sails (two more Lacaille constellations). This is actually a better cruciform shape than the true Southern Cross, although neither is as representative as the Northern Cross. Miaplacidus, at one end of Carina, Canopus at the other end, and the Large Magellanic Cloud form a triangle. Canopus is to southern skies what Sirius is to those of the north.

The Small Magellanic Cloud lies on one side of a triangular constellation called *Hydrus,* the Water Serpent, interesting to us chiefly because the apex of the triangle points to Achernar, alpha star of Eridanus. Surrounding the Large Magellanic Cloud are four constellations: *Dorado,* the Goldfish (northwest); *Reticulum* (west); *Mensa* (south); and *Volans,* the Flying Fish (east). The directions given are their positions in the summer skies of the southern hemisphere. Like the northern circumpolar constellations, they rotate about the South Pole and consequently change their positions relative to each other as the seasons progress.

The Constellations Month by Month

Earlier we suggested a model for the heavens in which all the stars were pictured as lining the inside of a great sphere surrounding the earth. This sphere is divided north and south into parallels of declination, and east and west into meridians of right ascension. The meridians are called *hour circles;* they are spaced 15° apart, so there are twenty-four of them lining our imaginary sphere. The earth spins slowly inside the sphere, and the stars appear to move across the sky from east to west because of the rotation. If the sun were to be blacked out, we should see all the stars visible from our particular latitude each twenty-four-hour period; *i.e.,* an observer could sweep the whole heavens each day. Because we are also swinging around the sun, the particular meridian that is directly overhead at a given time each night varies from month to month at a rate of two meridians a month. We call the hour circle that is directly overhead the *local meridian.*

Constellations Visible from 40° N

Circumpolar (visible all year)

Ursa Major
Ursa Minor
Draco
Cepheus
Cassiopeia
Camelopardalis

Constellations listed below will be on or near the meridian at 8:30 P.M., local time, on the fifteenth of each month:

January (4 hours)	February (6 hours)	March (8 hours)	April (10 hours)	May (12 hours)	June (14 hours)
Auriga	Taurus	Lynx	Leo Minor	Canes Venatici	Boötes
Perseus	Orion	Gemini	Leo	Coma Berenices	Centaurus
Caelum	Lepus	Cancer	Sextans	Virgo	
Eridanus	Columba	Canis Minor	Hydra	Crater	
	Canis Major	Monoceros	Antlia	Corvus	
		Puppis	Vela		
		Pyxis			

July (16 hours)	August (18 hours)	September (20 hours)	October (22 hours)	November (0 hours)	December (2 hours)
Corona Borealis	Lyra	Cygnus	Lacerta	Andromeda	Triangulum
Hercules	Ophiuchus	Vulpecula	Pegasus	Pisces	Aries
Serpens Caput	Serpens Cauda	Sagitta	Aquarius	Sculptor	Cetus
Libra	Scutum	Delphinus	Piscis Austrinus	Phoenix	Fornax
Scorpius	Sagittarius	Aquila	Grus		
Lupus	Corona Australis	Capricornus	Equuleus		
Norma	Telescopium	Microscopium			

THE SKY | 45

On November 15, the zero hour circle is directly overhead at about 8:30 P.M., local time. A month later the western movement of the heavens has brought the constellations located along the 2-hour meridian to the overhead position, and so on throughout the year. As you look to the north you can see the circumpolar constellations (those with declinations greater than 60°) on *any* night, provided you live north of the thirtieth parallel of latitude.

Star Designations

There are many systems for naming the stars and other heavenly bodies. Most of the stellar names come from antiquity—from the Persians, Arabs, Greeks, Romans. These usually apply to the brighter stars or to those possessing unusual characteristics of color or position. Some of the stars have several names. The pole star, for example, is variously called Polaris, Cynosura, Alruccaba. The star at the end of the Dipper's handle is listed as Benetnash on some charts, Alkaid on others. Some have names of recent origin, usually associated with their discoverers, as Ross 128, Kruger 60, van Maanen's star, Barnard's star, and many others.

Obviously, nobody could remember names for all the stars visible to the naked eye, so astronomers started working out systematic methods for identifying them. One of the first systems, still in effect today, was the one devised by Bayer in 1603 and later adopted by Lacaille (1757) for the southern constellations. Here the stars in each constellation are listed by Greek letters. Sometimes the letter has a subscript which indicates a positional sequence in a constellation; the stars in Orion's arm are an example. We use this system in the charts in this book.

Because there aren't enough letters in the Greek alphabet to name all the stars in a big constellation,* the English astronomer John Flamsteed (1646–1719)† adopted numbers for the members of a constellation, thus making it possible for the dimmer stars to have designations. Flamsteed numbered the stars in a given constellation in order of increasing right ascension. Thus, in the constellation Cygnus, the star 61 Cygni is found at approximately sixteenth-hour right ascension while 26 Cygni is at fifteenth hour.

Further study of the stars and their positions gave rise to new and varied charts, some of them for lo-

calized areas, such as the circumpolar constellations, until the list of star catalogs became very long. New designations appeared, most of them based upon increasing right ascension without regard to the constellations. Today, a casual glance at a star chart may make it appear that there are almost as many different ways for naming stars as there are stars themselves. Although the charts in this book list only Bayer letters and Flamsteed numbers, we include a list of some of the other systems as a matter of interest.

I xxxx   From the Index Catalog, an extension of the New General Catalog.

M xx   Messier's list of 103 nebulous objects, compiled in 1784.

GC xx   Boss's General Catalog of stars.

Mel xx   Melbourne Observatory Designation.

Using Star Charts

Star charts can be confusing until you get used to them because their orientation is just the opposite of terrestrial maps and charts. This is because our point of orientation is different. Perhaps we can explain the difficulty by using two views of the earth as examples.

Let's assume our globe is transparent. You are standing at its center, your head toward the North Pole, facing the continent of North America. Points on the East Coast appear on your left; San Francisco and the West are on your right. Now transpose yourself back to the surface and again face north. East and west have changed positions, for San Francisco is now on your left. The analogy may help to show why star charts appear to be reversed —it is because you are at the apparent center of the great sphere of stars, looking at them from the inside out. If you hold the chart over your head with its north point toward the North Pole, the directions come right again and west is once more where it should be. Many observers forget this fundamental of star chart use; thus they have difficulty connecting what they see on the chart with what actually appears in the heavens.

Another difficulty is the difference in scale between the chart and the heavens. On most charts the stars are large and distinct and, even in the big constellations, appear close together. But in the heavens they shrink to widely scattered points of light, brilliant and multitudinous on some nights, indistinct and sparse on others. The dotted lines that outline constellations so clearly on star charts,

---

* Since Bayer's time, his system has been expanded to include Roman as well as Greek letters. There are 24 letters in the Greek alphabet, 26 lower case Roman letters, and 17 Roman capitals (those beyond Q are used for another system)—67 in all.

† *Historia Coelestis Britannica* (1712).

as well as the scales of declination and right ascension, are missing in the skies.

Most of us have a tendency to hurry when using charts. We look at the chart inside a building, then rush outside to match up our recollections with the skies. Or, equally bad, we use bright flashlights to read the charts. The human eye sometimes takes as much as thirty minutes to become adapted from light to dark, which is why both of these methods are self-defeating. Instead, use a dim red flashlight to illuminate your chart. Wait for at least ten minutes before even attempting to make any identifications. You can spend this time picking out the bright stars and arranging them mentally into squares, triangles, or other geometric figures. During this time you will be aware that the number of stars increases as your dark-adapting eye increases the diameter of its pupil. Now, using the flashlight as sparingly as possible, take quick looks at the chart. Use the "pointer" system in going from one constellation to another. For dim constellations, such as Cancer and Scutum, try averted vision: Don't look directly at the group; turn away from it a little and attempt to see it out of the "corner of your eye."

Before you cope with the wealth of detail on the large charts, you may want to try using planispheres or model celestial globes. Planispheres consist of two parts, a map of the heavens covered with a rotating mask. The mask has a large opening to expose the part of the heavens visible for a particular date and time, and smaller openings to expose the scales used for month, day, and hour. You "dial" a setting for a particular time, then hold the planisphere overhead.

A variation of this is the "see-through" chart. Here the constellations are indicated on a transparent plastic sheet by means of luminous paint. The scale is such that when the chart is held the proper distance from the eye the spots of paint match up with the main features of a constellation. As you might expect, these charts are relatively expensive, but a good one is worth the price. The model celestial globe employs the same principle —luminous paint on a transparent background. If you look *through* the globe, the stars are oriented as they are in the sky; when you look *at* it, they are reversed as when you look down on a chart.

CHAPTER IV

Celestial Geography, Time, and Telescope Mountings

Imagine a huge disk passing through the center of the sun and extending countless miles into space. Then picture the earth as a marble rolling in a tremendous ellipse around the sun, always staying on the surface of the disk. The paths of the rest of the planets as they circle the sun are very close to the plane of the disk, most of them never rising above or dropping below the disk by more than 2¼°. The exceptions are Mercury, which varies by 7° from the path traced by the remainder of the

planets; Venus, by 3¼°; and erratic Pluto, by 17°. This great flat path, and the space 9° above and below it, is called the *ecliptic*.

As viewed from a spinning earth, the planets follow a well-defined path through the skies. But the path seems to vary in altitude from season to season because the earth spins at an angle of 23½° from the plane of the disk mentioned above. Each day an observer at the earth's equator spends half his time below the disk and the remainder above it.

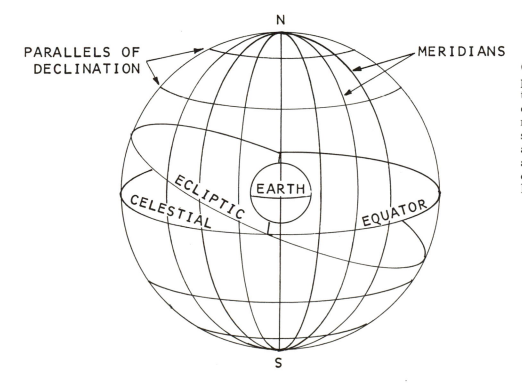

Celestial coordinates: The plane of the celestial equator intersects earth at the equator. Parallels of declination on the celestial sphere correspond to parallels of latitude on earth, and the meridians are equivalent to meridians of longitude.

The inclination of the earth's axis to the great planetary disk never changes. Thus, on June 22 the North Pole of the earth leans 23½° toward the sun; on December 22, the same amount away from it. This not only explains the seasons—in northern latitudes the sun's rays are more nearly perpendicular during summer, and therefore hotter—but also explains why the apparent path of the planets appears to rise and fall relative to an observer on the earth.

Now let's visualize another disk, this one simply an extension of the plane of the earth's equator, one which also extends into space. The intersection of this second disk with the apparent great globe of stars surrounding us is called the *celestial equator*. Now we have two base lines in the sky, the ecliptic and the celestial equator, each passing through the center of the earth but tipped at an angle of 23½° to one another. Each line is useful, the first for locating planets, the second for star measurements.

The Ecliptic and the Zodiac

The ecliptic is the path followed by planets, moon, sun, and most of the asteroids. It passes through twelve constellations, called by the ancients the Signs of the Zodiac. Each constellation, as used in modern astronomy, covers a section of the sky 30° long by 18°. The boundaries of the zodiacal

Precession of the Equinoxes

As we have mentioned earlier, the earth not only spins on its axis, but wobbles slightly as it spins. This axial revolution, much like the wavering of a spinning gyroscope, is clockwise for an observer looking down on the North Pole. The consequence is that the celestial equator slides along the ecliptic to the west. This causes the intersection of the two circles to move west as well. Since the earth's axis completes a full wobble in 26,000 years, in that time the vernal equinox will have moved all the way around the ecliptic. Such a rate of motion involves only about one minute of arc each year. The rate, slow as it is, explains why a point that was once in the constellation Aries has moved westward until it is now located in Pisces.

The precession is of course not noticeable to a day-to-day observer, but it is a great source of annoyance to makers of sky charts, who must use this shifting point as zero point for their measurement of the heavens.

The chartmaker draws a circle through the vernal equinox and the poles of the heavens and uses it as his base line, or zero meridian. Because he is really measuring time—the time needed for the earth to rotate once inside the great sphere of stars—he calls this line 0 hours (0h) instead of 0 degrees. Then, at one-hour intervals, he draws circles to the east until he has once more reached his starting point. For all practical purposes, it is as easy

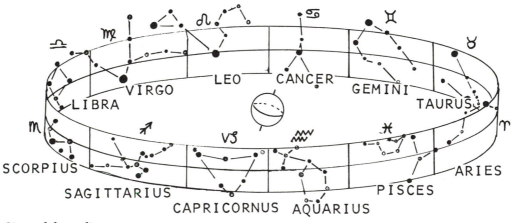

Signs of the zodiac.

constellations are not quite the same as the original signs, but the names are still the same. Here is a rhyme to help you remember them:

> The Ram, the Bull, the heavenly Twins,
> And next the Crab, the Lion shines.
> The Virgin and the Scales,
> The Scorpion, Archer, and the Goat.
> The Man who pours the water out,
> And Fish with glittering tails.

to think of the stars swinging around the earth from east to west as it is to imagine the earth turning from west to east inside the great sphere of stars. The hour circles, spaced 15° apart along the celestial equator, swing across the sky carrying their stars with them. The particular hour circle on which a star is located is called its *right ascension* (RA), usually designated by the Greek letter alpha. Thus, one with RA 10h is ten hour circles to the east of the vernal equinox. Conversely, a star with RA 18h

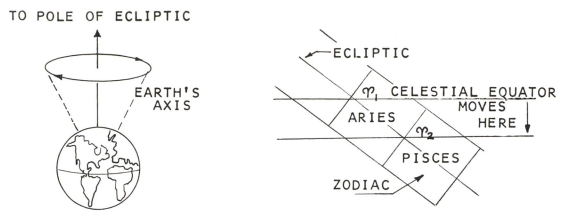

The wobble of earth's axis causes the celestial equator to move across the sky, thus producing a westward shift of the vernal equinox. Over the last 2,000 years the vernal equinox has shifted from Aries to Pisces, γ_1 to γ_2.

is eighteen hours east of the vernal equinox, or six hours *west* of it.

At any instant of time, one of these hour circles is passing overhead and at this instant is called the meridian of the observer. The position of any star in the sky may be measured from this meridian. Based thus, the star's position is known as its *local hour angle* (LHA). We shall find this form useful later on.

To complete the system of celestial coordinates, the chart maker draws parallel circles of declination every ten degrees from the celestial equator to the north, which he labels N or +, and to the south, labeled S or −.

Sidereal Time

The system of time based on everyday needs is the interval required for the sun to appear in the same place in the sky (usually from noon to noon) on two successive days. This interval is divided into twenty-four hours. Now, because the earth travels around the sun at an average rate of 18.5 miles a second, it must complete a *little more* than one rotation for the sun to appear in the same place on two successive days. On the other hand, the earth is so far from the stars that its motion among them is negligible, and the same star will appear in the same place for every single rotation of the earth. The difference in time is about 4 minutes, so that a complete rotation actually takes only 23 hours 56 minutes. The length of the day, based on the stars, is a sidereal (star) day and is measured in *sidereal time*. Sidereal clocks are therefore adjusted to run a little faster than ordinary clocks.

TIMING THE STARS

All this sounds complicated in theory, but in practice it is very simple. Let's imagine ourselves at a fixed location on an immovable earth watching the stars chase each other across the sky. Overhead, bisecting the heavens from north to south, is our local meridian. The stars move across this meridian from east to west. Now suppose we notice a star crossing the meridian. We identify it and look up its position (right ascension and declination) in a chart or star atlas. Let's say its right ascension is eight hours. On the same star chart we see another star whose right ascension is, say, nine hours. Since the two stars are an hour apart, and since the higher-numbered hour circles are to the east, it is apparent that if we wait an hour (as indicated on our sidereal clock), the second star will also pass over our meridian. Conversely, we could swing the telescope 15° to the east and view the star without waiting for its appearance on the meridian. (We explain below how to use setting circles on a telescope to do this.)

Earth Time

Each area of the earth must have its own local time based on an appropriate noon hour when the sun is directly overhead. This is impossible in practice because, if rigorously adhered to, the watches of the inhabitants of two neighboring towns would always be a few minutes apart. So it has been found convenient to divide the earth into *time zones*, each 15° of longitude in width. The time in two neighboring zones differs by one hour. Thus a traveler moving west must set his watch back; if he moves eastward, he must set it ahead. By convention earth's time zones are numbered westward from Greenwich, England. The time zones in North America are Zone 4 (Atlantic Coastal), Zone 5 (Eastern), Zone 6 (Central), Zone 7 (Mountain), and Zone 8 (Pacific). When it is noon in Philadelphia, for example, it is 1 P.M. in Halifax and 9 A.M. in San Francisco. Since the day gets younger as we move westward, it would seem that by making a complete trip westward around the globe we would lose a whole day, or that, conversely, by making a trip eastward around the globe we would gain a day.

This gain and loss has been avoided by the establishment of the International Date Line, a long, jagged line running from pole to pole through the central Pacific Ocean. Crossing the line from east to west increases the date by one day; crossing from west to east decreases the date by one day. From the foregoing, it should be apparent that we can tell what time it is anywhere on the globe by applying the proper time-zone number. Earlier, we mentioned that time zones increase westward from the prime meridian at Greenwich. But they also increase eastward, except that here the numbers are negative. The rule is simple: Add the zone number to your local time to obtain the time at Greenwich. *Examples:* When it is 7 P.M. in New York (Zone 5) it is midnight in London. When it is 7 P.M. in Durban (Zone −3) it is 4 P.M. in London.

Universal Time

In order to avoid mix-ups in the timing of a particular event—*e.g.*, the passage of a meteor or the occultation of a star by the moon—astronomers record any instant of time as it would appear on a clock in Greenwich. Here the hours of the day are numbered from 0 to 24, using a four-digit number. Thus, 1315 is the same as 1:15 P.M. and 0015 is equivalent to 12:15 A.M. Any local time may be changed to the time at Greenwich by adding the time zone, as in the example above. This system of reducing time in all parts of the world to the corresponding instant at Greenwich is called *Universal Time* (UT).

Ephemeris Time

The time systems we have been talking about so far are all based on an unvarying rotation of the earth. Unfortunately, the rotation of the earth is not unvarying, and for very exacting predictions for the positions of heavenly bodies another time system must be used. This is known as *Ephemeris Time* (ET), so called because it was first used by the *American Ephemeris* in 1960. It is based on the orbital motions of the moon and planets, rather than on the rotation of the earth. The length of the Ephemeris day is defined as equal to a day measured in Greenwich time during the year 1900. According to this concept, the earth is slowing down, for the accumulated time-difference between Ephemeris Time and Universal Time is about 36 seconds. (We mention Ephemeris Time here because some readers may wish to use the *American Ephemeris* as a source of reference.)

Time Relationships

How can we establish a relationship among the various kinds of time? Fortunately, it is not often necessary to make transformations from one kind of time to another, and when we must we can do so by referring to tables or by using our telescopes.

A. Using charts to determine sidereal time. If you know your longitude (you can find this from a Coast and Geodetic Survey Map) you can use tables to find the sidereal time of your locality. Tables for this purpose are given in the appendix. Appendix I shows the exact relationship between sidereal time and mean solar (ordinary) time; Appendix II gives the sidereal time at Greenwich for the beginning of each day of the year. Using these two you can convert your local civil time into Greenwich sidereal time. We can best demonstrate the method by giving an example:

Suppose your longitude is 80° west, and your local time is 9 P.M., June 5; 80° west is in time zone 5, so your Universal Time must be 2100 (9 P.M.) plus 5 hours, or 0200, June 6. Appendix II shows you that at 0 hours, June 6, the sidereal time at Greenwich is 16h 58m. But a two-hour interval must be added, and since this time-interval was measured in solar time, it must be converted into a sidereal time-interval. Here's where appendix I enters the picture. It shows that the sidereal time-interval must be 20 seconds greater, so the correct sidereal time is 16h 58m plus 2h 20s, or 18h 58m 20s. Now the only remaining step is to change the Greenwich sidereal time into your local sidereal time. You do this by applying the longitude difference between Greenwich and your own locality. You are 80° to the west of Greenwich, which really means that you are 80° away in time. If you convert this angular difference to a time difference, using appendix III to make things easier, you find that 80° equals 5h 20m. Subtracting this time from the Greenwich sidereal time (you subtract because you are west of Greenwich and therefore behind in time; if you were east of Greenwich you would add the difference), you obtain 13h 38m 20s, your sidereal time.

This method is for the purist who wants to know the *exact* sidereal time; in practice (as we shall see) it is an unnecessary refinement. Actually, once you have transformed your longitude into a time factor, you can determine your sidereal time in a matter of only a few minutes by using appendix I.

B. Using your telescope to determine sidereal time. Buy an inexpensive alarm clock. Set up your telescope until it is pointing directly south, wait until a known star in the vicinity of the celestial equator is in the center of the field of your eyepiece, look up the star's right ascension in the star atlas, set your clock to this time and you are in business. The alarm clock now reads sidereal time. The fact that it is not a sidereal clock makes very little difference, for during the average observing period—say, four hours or so—the difference between a sidereal time-interval and the one shown on your clock is so slight as to be negligible. In four hours the clock will lose only 40 *seconds* of sidereal time. Over a period of several days, of course, the difference becomes significant and you can no longer rely on your alarm clock.

The principle involved in the explanation given above is based on the fact that your sidereal day starts the instant the vernal equinox crosses your local meridian. The right ascension of any star is its time-distance from the vernal equinox. Consequently, if a star of RA 8h 28m is on your meridian, the vernal equinox must have passed overhead 8 hours 28 minutes before, and these figures therefore represent your sidereal time.

C. The importance of understanding time relationships. Why all this discussion of time? What purpose does it serve the amateur? There are several good reasons for including it here:

1. Knowing what the sidereal time is (even approximately) tells you what star charts to use for any night of the year. If you know, for example, that your sidereal time is 15h, you turn to the charts which include this meridian—maps 4, 8, and 12. These show all stars visible within three hours (45°) on either side of the meridian. Stars farther east or west will be found on the neighboring maps.

2. If your telescope is equipped with setting circles, you must understand sidereal time in order to use them properly.

3. Astronomical magazines, observer's guides, almanacs, and so on, usually give data in terms of Universal Time (UT) or Ephemeris Time (ET). You must be able to transpose these figures into local time to be able to use them properly.

4. A knowledge of the time and space relationships of the stars and planets deepens your understanding of the heavens as a whole. Knowing which stars are visible on any given night is important to any observer, but understanding *why* they are visible leads to a real comprehension of the heavens and its mechanics.

Telescope Mountings

The mounting of a telescope not only must provide a firm support for its optical system but also should serve as a means of finding and following the stars. The latter feature is a great convenience for any observer and is essential for the serious amateur.

The simplest possible mounting is a ball-and-socket connecting the telescope tube to the tripod or other support. But while this is probably the most satisfactory arrangement for a low-power instrument used for looking around the countryside, its deficiencies for astronomical work are manifold. Its sole advantage is its ease of operation. The telescope with a ball-and-socket mounting can be quickly moved into position to locate a star, and as long as the observer guides it manually the star remains somewhere in the field of view. We say "somewhere" because although the telescope may be moved in any direction, it is very difficult to adjust its motion to correspond exactly with the movement of a star—consequently sometimes the star's image is in the center of the field, sometimes on the edge. At no time is it possible to hold the image in one place long enough to get a good look at it, and it is practically impossible to use such a mounting for photographic purposes.

The altazimuth mounting is better than the ball-and-socket type, but still there are disadvantages. With this mounting the telescope is movable in two axes at right angles to one another: a vertical axis (altitude) and a horizontal axis (azimuth). The base of an altazimuth mounting is perpendicular to the earth's radius to whatever point the observer happens to be. This means that two telescopes with altazimuth mountings located at different points on the surface of the earth must be moved differently in order to follow the same heavenly body. Again direct observation of stars is difficult, because the telescope must be moved in two directions simultaneously; photography is next to impossible. Finder telescopes and slow-motion devices help a great deal when one is using altazimuth mountings. The great advantage of this kind of a mounting is that it is very steady if the axes are heavy enough. It is also very easy to set up and use, and one doesn't have to bother with orienting the telescope in any particular direction, a great convenience for those who use their instruments only for casual observing.

Another type of mounting, the equatorial, makes use of two axes set at right angles to each other, but there is one vital difference. The axis on which the telescope turns in right ascension is not horizontal, but rather is parallel to the axis of the earth. The effect is the same as if the telescope were mounted on the earth's axis itself. As the earth turns toward the east, the observer pushes the telescope around the axis to the west. Because the declination axis is at right angles to the axis of the earth, the declination of the telescope remains constant. Only the movement of the instrument in right ascension is

required to keep an object constantly in view. Now if the observer connects a drive to the polar axis to turn the telescope at the same rate that the stars appear to move—*i.e.*, a complete circle in 23 hours 56 minutes—he need not touch the telescope again, for it is now following the object automatically. All equatorially mounted telescopes, therefore, turn on polar axes mounted parallel to each other and to the axis of the earth, and all can use the same scales for finding and following stars.

The equatorial mounting will not work perfectly for objects in the solar system. The sun, moon, and planets move in the plane of the ecliptic and constantly change in declination. Although the telescope will still follow these objects in right ascension, the observer must operate it manually in declination. This one drawback of the equatorial mounting is minor, however, compared to the many drawbacks of the altazimuth.

Although all equatorial mountings operate on the same principle, there are several different variations, each with its own merits.

1. The *German mounting* is a T-shaped arrangement in which the telescope itself is mounted on the declination axis (the crossbar), which in turn is mounted on the polar axis (the shaft of the T). The telescope is at one end of the declination axis and must be counterbalanced by a weight placed at the other end. This counterweight must be very carefully adjusted if true balance is to be achieved.

German mounting constructed by Charles Fallier.

The polar axis must be strong enough both to support the telescope and counterweight and to prevent vibration.

If the German mounting is used, there are two possible positions for the telescope to assume. An object can always be seen from one position or the other, but not from both. When an object is east of the meridian, the telescope is swung to the west of the mounting. But when it passes to the west of the meridian, the telescope must be swung to the east of the mounting and turned 180° in declination. This maneuver, inconvenient for visual observing, is disastrous for photographic work, since the plate has been turned over as the telescope is moved in declination. Consequently, when an object being photographed nears the meridian, the remaining exposure time must be postponed until the following night. In spite of these disadvantages, some of the great telescopes of the world are mounted this way, as well as the majority of commercially-made small refractors and reflectors.

2. The *English mounting* employs a yoke or elliptical ring supported at each end for a polar axis, with the telescope mounted in supports on either side of the yoke. The telescope is free to move in its supports; and its motion back and forth inside the yoke acts as a declination axis. Here neither telescope nor yoke requires counterbalancing and the action is smooth and convenient. The great drawback of the system is that the polar region of the sky is screened from view by the north end of the yoke. In a modified version, the yoke is replaced by a single beam with the telescope mounted on an axis at right angles to the beam. This provides clearance so the northern sky can be viewed, but it also requires counterweighting on the side of the beam opposite the telescope tube. Both versions of the English mounting are much favored by amateur telescope-makers because of their ease of construction.

3. The *fork mounting* is the simplest and easiest to use with short-focus or compound telescopes. The ends of a two-pronged fork serve as the polar axis, and the telescope is balanced in declination between the prongs of the fork. Most of the Dall-Kirkhams, Cassegrainians, Maksutovs, and other professionally made telescopes are mounted in this way.

There are many variations on these three types, too many to mention here. Your telescope probably uses one of them. All possess the great advantage of being easy to fit with slow-motion devices, setting circles, and mechanical-drive systems.

Setting Circles and How to Use Them

Many of the more obscure nebulae, dim star clusters, faint variables, and double stars that appear on a good star map are difficult to locate with finders. Setting circles enable you to transfer the coordinates—right ascension and declination—from the star map to your telescope. Once the telescope is moved to the proper settings on the circles, only very small adjustments need be made to pick up an otherwise elusive object in the eyepiece.

Each axis of the telescope has its own setting circle. The polar axis circle positions the telescope to the proper hour circle, the declination circle to the correct declination. The declination circle is the easier to use: when it indicates 0, the telescope points toward the celestial equator; when +90, the telescope points to the North Pole. From 0 to −90°, it sweeps the southern skies.

Fork or English mountings require only half a circle to find all possible objects in declination. The German mounting, on the other hand, must have a full circle with identical halves, one for use on each side of the mounting. The number and spacing of declination scale divisions depend on the size of the circle. On most small telescopes the scales read only to the nearest degree, which seems like a rather large spread. However, when you consider that your low-power eyepiece probably has a field of a degree or more, this spread is well within the limits of easy and convenient use. If an object does not appear in the field when the setting circles indicate that it should, you can usually pick it up very easily by moving the telescope only slightly.

Declination circles are easy to use. Look up the declination of the sought-for object on a star chart; then move the telescope in declination until the reading is under the pointer.

The right ascension circle on the polar axis is a bit more complicated to use, but a little practice will soon make you proficient. On fork-type and English yoke mountings the circles are usually numbered from 0 to 23 hours, with subsidiary divisions down to five minutes or less. As with the declination circle, the number and spacing of the divisions varies with the diameter. On German mountings, the circle may be divided into four units of six hours each—0, 6, 0, 6, again divided into five-minute intervals.

There are several ways you can use the right ascension circle, all of which depend on sidereal time. Here is possibly the simplest, an easy combination of theory and practice: Pick a bright star near the celestial equator and look up its declination and right ascension. Set the declination circle to the proper figure; then move the telescope in hour angle until the star is in the field of view. After it is centered, move the right ascension circle on its shaft until its reading is the same as that of the star; then clamp it in position. We must consider the type of circle you have. If it is divided into twenty-four numbered hours, you need only set the pointer

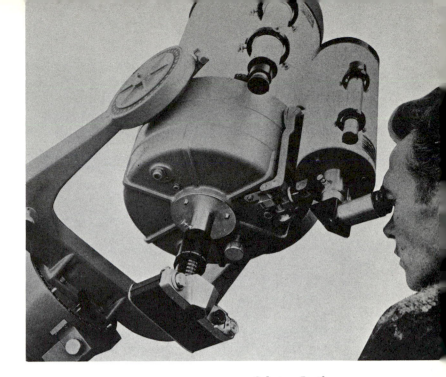

A 10-inch Schmidt-Cassegrain in a fork mounting.

on the right ascension of the star. But if it is of the 0–6–0–6 type, set the pointer on a division whose time difference from the zero mark is the same as the star's right ascension. For example, for a star of RA 8h, set the pointer on the 4 following the first 6. Now set the hands of your clock on 12 o'clock. As we pointed out above, even a cheap alarm clock will keep reasonably accurate sidereal time over the average observing period. To find any other star, look up its coordinates and move the telescope until the right ascension circle reading coincides with that of the star, *plus* whatever your clock now reads. Now move the telescope to the proper declination reading. The new star should now be visible in the eyepiece. If it is not, small adjustments of the telescope in right ascension and/or declination will bring it into view. If you are fortunate enough to have a power-driven polar axis, you can dispense with the alarm clock, for your telescope will keep sidereal time for you.

A more traditional method of finding stars is to subtract the right ascension of the star from your local sidereal time to find the local hour angle (LHA) of the star you want to find. Here's how it works: Suppose your local sidereal time is 16 hours. This means that the vernal equinox passed overhead 16 hours before you started to observe and is now far to the west. Suppose also that you are interested in a star whose RA is 13 hours. This star is 13 hours behind the vernal equinox and therefore only 3 hours west of your position. In terms of local hour angle, its position is 3 hours west. Move the RA circle on its shaft until your local sidereal time is under the pointer. Then move the telescope 3 hours to the west, set it to the proper declination, and the star should be in the field.

In practice, if the sidereal time is *greater* than the RA of the star, the star will be *west* of your meridian. But if the sidereal time is *less* than the RA, the star will be *east*. In this case, subtract the sidereal time from the right ascension.

Aligning the Equatorial Mounting

This type of mounting requires an accurate alignment. The polar axis must point in a true north-south direction with the elevated end to the north and the whole axis set at an angle equal to your latitude.

First, be sure that the base plate of the tripod or other support is level. Most commercially made mountings have a spirit level for this purpose. The next step is to align the polar axis to a true north-south position. This can be done in several ways:

1. You can use the North Star. Unfortunately, Polaris is not a true pole star; it circles the pole at a distance of almost a degree. Photographs of star trails around the pole show Polaris as a tiny *circle*, not the *point* it would be if it were true north. Nevertheless, it indicates true north when it is either above or below the true pole. There is an easy way to determine this condition. The line which connects Mizar, Polaris, and Schedir (in Cassiopeia) can be used as an hour angle clock. When the line is vertical, the pole star is in true azimuth, *i.e.*, it is in line with the true pole. Using this fact as a guide, you can establish a north-south line at your observing site and align the polar axis with it.

2. You can also establish a true north-south line by using a good prismatic compass, corrected for variation. The variation of a compass is the amount it points to the left or right of true north. You can obtain this figure from a table of variations or a Coast and Geodetic Survey map. Don't use a cheap compass for this purpose though, and be sure there are no metal objects in its vicinity when you make your measurement.

3. Possibly the easiest way to lay out your meridian line is by using the shadow of a plumb line at noon, sun time. If you have a friend who knows navigation, ask him to determine the time of noon for you. It will *not* be 12 o'clock on your watch, except twice a year. If you can't find a navigator, directions for finding local apparent noon (when the sun passes your meridian) are included in the appendix of this book.

Now align the polar axis in altitude. Many telescopes have a latitude scale in the mounting. Set your own latitude on this scale and you are ready to observe. If the scale is lacking, you can use the pole star for latitude as well as azimuth. When the Mizar-Schedir line is horizontal, the altitude of the polestar is equal to your latitude. To make use of this fact, set the declination circle at 90° and elevate the polar axis until Polaris is on a horizontal line through the center of the field. Clamp the polar axis in this position. Check the accuracy of your alignment by turning the telescope in declination to a star near the celestial equator. If the reading on the circle checks with the known declination of the star, the instrument is well adjusted. If not, small changes in the angle of the polar axis will compensate for the difficulty.

Keeping Records

If you want to double your observing enjoyment as well as gain a feeling of real accomplishment, keep a logbook. At the beginning it may seem only a tedious chore, but as your records accumulate and you are able to compare your most recent observations and experiences with previous ones, you will recognize its value.

A log must contain all the obvious entries: date; UT of the beginning of the observation; its duration; objects observed, with notes on their appearance and characteristics; instrumental notes; and so forth. Drawings or sketches, even very rough ones, are invaluable. Some objects are difficult to find, even under good seeing conditions. But if you have a little sketch of the star pattern around, say, the Ring Nebula in Lyra, you will find your previous difficulties greatly simplified the next time you look for this elusive object. Your records also constitute a fine commentary on the acuity of your observations when you compare them with what you *should* have seen. Test yourself on the moons of Jupiter. Make a sketch of the positions of the Jovian moons for several successive nights, then check your accuracy with a corresponding *Sky and Telescope* diagram. You may be surprised at the result. Further, you may be one of those individuals lucky enough to spot a comet, a tremendous bolide, a brand-new artificial satellite, or even a nova. If so your records will help authenticate your observations.

In the long run, though, the record you keep of the conditions under which you make observations will be of the greatest benefit. The logbook should show transparency of the sky, haze, percentage of cloud cover, atmospheric turbulence (both at the observing site and at higher altitudes), the phase of the moon (if visible), humidity, temperature, and any other factor that may affect the observation. The mere fact that you record these things will help impress them on your memory, and the outcome will be almost an instinctive recognition of conditions that will make you want either to haul your telescope out for an evening's enjoyment or to spend the time with a good book.

CHAPTER V

The Sun and Moon

The Sun

The Sun's Vital Statistics

	As Compared to earth	Actual figures	
		Earth	Sun
Diameter	109.3	7,900 miles	864,000 miles
Mass	333,434	6.6×10^{21} tons	2.2×10^{27} tons
Volume	1,300,000	26×10^{10} cu mi	34×10^{16} cu mi
Density	0.26	5.5 (water)	1.41 (water)
Gravity	28.0	32 ft/sec^2	900 ft/sec^2
Inclination to ecliptic	0.31	23.5°	7.2°
Apparent Magnitude	—	—	−27

Strangely enough, in spite of its prominent position in the heavens, the sun is often completely overlooked by amateur observers. This may be because of the dangers involved in observing the sun —dangers that are very real but which can be minimized if proper precautions are taken—or because the sun seemingly has so little to offer. The latter reason is completely invalid; the apparently blank face of the sun is subject to a fascinating variety of changes, and time spent looking for them is far from wasted.

PROJECTING THE SUN'S IMAGE

By far the safest way to observe the sun, and in the long run probably the most convenient, is by projecting its image through an eyepiece on some sort of screen. The method is completely safe and the image produced is relatively large and easy to observe. But don't use an expensive orthoscopic eyepiece, or in fact any cemented eyepiece, for this purpose because so much heat is generated by concentrating the sun's rays that the balsam melts and the eyepiece is ruined. Instead, use a Huyghenian —old microscope eyepieces are of this kind—or a Ramsden. Use moderate magnifications, the highest that will render a complete disk of the sun on your screen. Solar objects are best observed in relation to each other when the whole surface is visible.

The screen, a piece of Bristol board or drawing paper tacked onto a firm backing, should be mounted at the distance that produces a 6- to 8-inch image. To orient the features of the sun in relation to one another, draw a circle on the screen, then add a suitable number of coordinates at right angles to one another. Too many, or too heavy, lines will clutter the screen and obscure fine detail. Space them an inch apart and use a very sharp pencil to make the lines as fine as possible.

The sun's axis is tipped at an angle of a little over 7° to the plane of the ecliptic. As the earth travels around it, the angle changes, varying 7° from maximum to minimum in each direction. Consequently, the axis of the sun will rarely be perpendicular to its east-west motion as seen through your eyepiece, and you must allow for this in your drawing. The *American Ephemeris and Nautical Almanac* provides information for this variation, enabling you to plot the poles and equator in their proper positions. *Stonyhurst Disks** make it possible to do this mechanically.

Ordinarily, a telescope of fairly good aperture—at least six inches or more—is needed to provide resolution of fine detail. Nevertheless, you can observe sunspots, faculae, even the granulations of the solar surface using a smaller telescope if "seeing" conditions are right. Focusing is critical; the least deviation from perfection obscures detail. Any focusing at all is difficult at the beginning of an observing period. The sun's heat changes the curves in the optical system. For a few minutes—until they reach a leveling-off temperature point—you may have trouble.

When no obvious features are present on the sun's disk, it is difficult to know when the instrument is in sharp focus. Tapping the telescope tube helps resolve this problem. Any object that moves is probably dirt on the field lens of the eyepiece; tiny ones that remain stationary are on the sun's surface. Use these for making adjustments in focus. Curiously enough, this intentional disturbance of the image often reveals unsuspected features you may have overlooked before. More detail in a specific object, such as a sunspot, can be brought out by increasing magnification. Of course this involves loss of light and a dimming of the over-all features of the object, and this condition is made even worse if sunlight from outside the telescope strikes the screen. Both sharpness and brightness can be increased by slipping a three-sided box arrangement over screen and eyepiece, especially if the fourth side is covered except for an opening large enough to permit observation of the screen.

Altazimuth mounted telescopes are difficult to use for solar projection. The image moves very rapidly off the screen, and half the observing time

is used in adjusting the instrument. If you are fortunate enough to have a well-adjusted equatorial with a drive, three quarters of this annoyance can be eliminated and only periodic adjustments in declination need be made.

How do we "find" the sun in the first place? Sighting along the tube of your telescope is dangerous since the eye is directed at the full glare of the sun. The best method—simple and safe—is to adjust the telescope tube until it makes the smallest possible shadow on the ground. The sun must now be nearly centered, and only small movements of the telescope will bring its image on the screen. One word of warning: If your telescope is equipped with a finder, remove the finder eyepiece and cover the opening with a bit of cloth. It is easy to forget that looking through a finder at the sun is every bit as dangerous as looking at it through the main optics.

DIRECT OBSERVATION OF THE SUN

The warning expressed in the last sentence must be repeated here. *The direct transmission of the sun's rays through any combination of objective and eyepiece can damage the human eye beyond repair.* The intensity of the incoming light and heat must be reduced by something between 99.9 and 99.99 percent before it can be safely viewed. (If it is cut below the latter figure, the solar image becomes too dim to show detail.)

Light intensity may be decreased in several ways. Any unsilvered glass surface reflects only 5 percent of incident light and transmits the rest. If such a surface is placed in the light train and its action reinforced by a neutral density filter, the intensity is cut to safe limits. The simplest way of doing this, of course, is to use an unsilvered mirror in a reflector, and some amateur telescope-makers resort to this device. But it is no help for the owner of a refractor, nor is it practical for most observers.

Less drastic approaches involve the use of a solar prism or a Herschel wedge. A right-angle prism with perfectly flat, polished surfaces is an almost perfect light transmitter. But if it is turned as in the diagram opposite it acts as a reflector. Since many reflectors use such prisms to turn the light train toward the eyepiece, it is a relatively simple matter to adjust the prism mounting so it may be used for solar observation. This adjustment decreases the light reaching the eyepiece by 95 percent, still well above the safe limit, and a neutral filter of density 1 to 1.3 must be used in front of the eyepiece. Better still, the Herschel wedge, a flat piece of glass whose opposite surfaces are not parallel, may be inserted in the eyepiece drawtube. The wedge is mounted in its own fitting, of which one end fits the drawtube and the other accommodates the eyepiece. Unwanted light and heat pass out a third opening so

* A set of eight drawings of the sun's coordinates for various relative inclinations of its axis. They may be obtained from the American Association of Variable Star Observers, Solar Division.

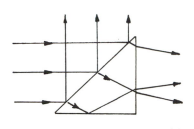 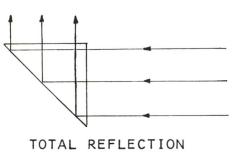

PARTIAL REFLECTION   TOTAL REFLECTION

A right-angle prism positioned for use as a sun diagonal (left); and for use as a substitute for a diagonal mirror (right).

that thermal currents are not set up in the telescope tube. The great advantages of the Herschel wedge are that it is adaptable to any type of telescope, it does not require any changes in other optical parts, and it can be quickly inserted and removed. Like the solar prism, however, it should be supplemented with a filter.

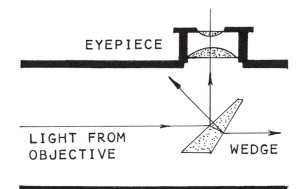

The Herschel wedge. Nearly 94 percent of the light and heat from the objective are reflected away from the eyepiece.

Another method of reducing light intensity is polarization. When a glass surface is placed so that light is reflected at an angle of about 57° (called Brewster's angle) the emergent rays are made up of waves moving only in one plane. Now if a second surface is placed so the polarized beam strikes it at this same angle, the light is almost completely cut off. By turning one of the surfaces slightly, the intensity of the light can be varied. This is the principle of the variable filter. The double reflection cuts the light to only .25 percent of its original value; the polarization makes it possible to reduce it almost to zero. One form of the variable filter consists of two Herschel wedges mounted so one can be turned. With this arrangement, no eyepiece filter is needed.

Finally, there are two other ways by which light intensity can be reduced, each of which has a se-

rious disadvantage. The first is to place a very dense filter (suncap) directly over the eye-lens of the eyepiece. Except when used with very small telescopes, suncaps are dangerous because the terrific heat assaulting them sometimes causes them to crack. (There are many recorded cases in which observers have suffered eye damage when a cracked suncap has allowed the full force of the sun's rays to strike their eyes.) The alternative is to place a filter in the front of the telescope and thus reduce the light before it enters the tube. A filter made for this purpose must be very dense and may often be partially silvered or aluminized to make it even safer. It is expensive, because to transmit rather than merely to reflect light, it must be made of high-quality glass with perfectly flat and parallel surfaces. To reduce its cost somewhat, a glass filter is usually made smaller than the aperture of the telescope with which it is used. (The remainder of the objective is covered with some opaque material.) This reduction in the effective aperture of the telescope cuts down on resolving power, however, and the resulting loss of detail is the most serious drawback of this type of filter.

It has probably become obvious by now that when you turn your telescope on the sun you are subjecting it to a great deal of heat. Whatever device is used to cut the sun's power is itself heated, as is the air inside the tube. Any change in temperature affects the definition of the image. Once the temperature is stabilized, however, the telescope will work well, even if not with the same efficiency that we expect when we view colder objects. The point is that solar viewing should not be an on again, off again process; once the telescope is "warmed up," observation should be continuous.

SOLAR FEATURES

What are the changes that occur on the sun's surface? The list is surprisingly long for a body whose surface is only a layer or two of incandescent gas.

The *photosphere* is the stratum of very hot gas

that makes up the visible part of the sun. Overlaying the photosphere are two layers of nearly transparent gas, the *chromosphere* and, outside it, the *corona*. These above-surface layers are clearly visible only when viewed through a coronograph or when the sun is in total eclipse. The chromosphere causes the darkening of the solar disk toward the limb. The explanation for this phenomenon is that the light from the sun's limb must travel a much greater distance through the chromosphere than the light from the center of the disk. The photosphere is a brilliant golden-yellow at first glance, but careful focusing will bring out some surface variation, such as a lemon-peel or granular pattern all over the disk, sometimes hardly detectable, occasionally pronounced. The granulations are assumed to be the tops of rising clouds of turbulent gas. They are rarely more than a thousand miles—more than one second of arc—wide. But sometimes they occur in clumps or groups; and then you can see them with only a small telescope. Once you have seen them at their highest intensity you will never forget them.

Occasionally, near the sun's limb, you will see bright, irregular patches showing up clearly against the darker background. These are called *faculae* and are supposed to be clouds of very hot gases that have risen well above the photosphere. They are not visible at the center of the sun's disk because of lack of contrast. In the center, however, you may see indistinct shaded areas only slightly darker than the background. If these are elongated, they are called wisps, but if they are small grayish blurs, they are called dark faculae, or veiled groups.

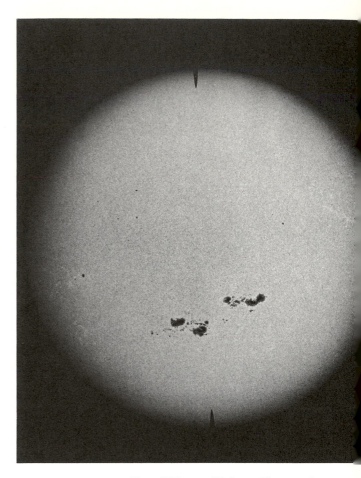

Mount Wilson and Palomar Observatories
The great sunspots of July 31, 1949. Note the "lemon peel" surface and the variation in the spots themselves. The sunspot at bottom center is over 33,000 miles wide.

SUNSPOTS

Most observers are fascinated by the ever-changing appearance and number of the sunspots. Following the life cycle of a sunspot group is a challenging and rewarding experience, especially if you keep records and make drawings of the event.

Sunspots start life as small dark dots near the equatorial region of the sun, usually between 5° and 30° north or south of the equator. Within a few days each black dot, or pore, develops into a full-sized group of spots made up of a leading and a following spot, separated by a few degrees of solar longitude. Lying in between are varying numbers of smaller spots spread in a line that roughly parallels the solar equator. If the group is well developed, the two principal members have a dark inner area, the umbra, surrounded by a lighter but well delineated border, the penumbra. The latter is usually marked by filamentous streaks that cross it from the umbra outward. The two principal spots separate until they may be as much as one hundred thousand

miles apart. The following spot grows more rapidly than its companion, at times becoming four or five times as large. The whole group may persist for several weeks, but when it starts to decay the following spot is the first to break up, first transforming itself into several smaller ones and then disappearing completely. Its companion shrinks, loses its penumbra, but may persist as a small round spot for another week or so. It too disappears, leaving behind it a region of faculae. Not all groups show this life cycle, and at sunspot maximum there may be a great variation in the development of sunspot areas.

No adequate explanation has yet been given for sunspot formation. One theory is that they consist of rapidly rising turbulent gases from below the photosphere, cooler and therefore darker than the surrounding areas. Another is that they are areas of calm; the charged (ionized) gas particles, being unable to pass through the magnetic field associated with the spot, therefore remain quiescent. Whatever

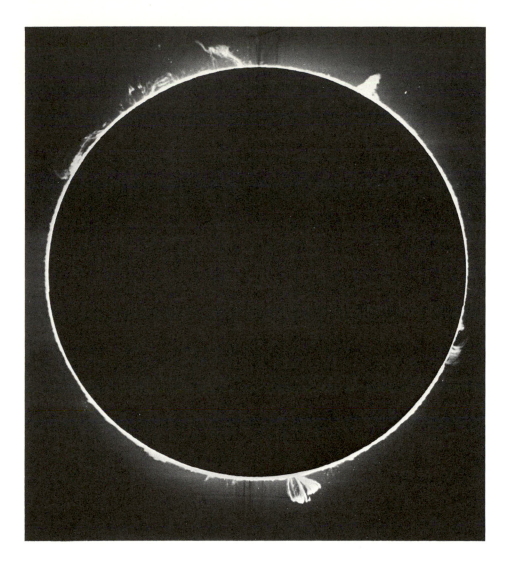

Two views, taken years apart, of the great solar prominences. Above, the whole edge of the sun, taken with the calcium K line on December 9, 1929. Below, 80,000-mile-high prominences photographed in the light of hydrogen on August 21, 1909.

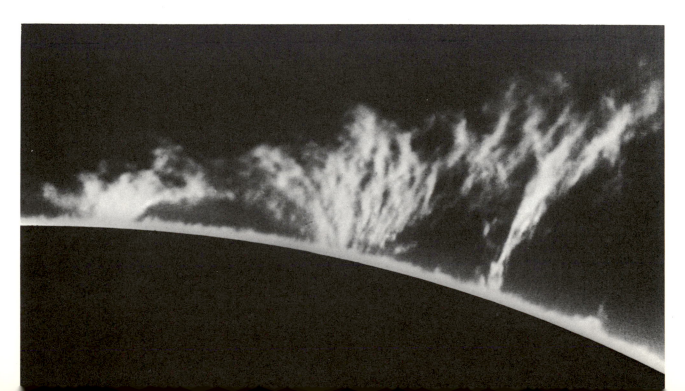

their origin, they show striking differences in appearance. Those near the limb are elliptical (explained only in part by the fact that they are viewed at an angle), in contrast with the mounded appearance of more centrally located spots. Sometimes they show color—dark violet in the umbra, rosy glows or browns of various shades and tints in the penumbra. Sometimes their shapes change rapidly. Some show considerable internal motion; others rotate slowly.

Considering the fact that the sun is our nearest star—we must travel almost 300,000 times as far to find the next one—it is surprising that so little is known about it. Its obvious characteristics—distance, size, mass, temperature, even the nature of its source of energy—are well known. But such phenomena as the sun's magnetic field, the fact that spots on one side of the solar equator are of opposite magnetic polarity to those on the other, and especially the sunspot cycle, are not well understood. We don't even know why sunspot maxima recur at 11-year intervals, taking 4 years to build to a maximum number, then 7 years to diminish to a minimum. Any one cycle may vary from these figures, sometimes by as much as 2 years, but the average is 11.

TELESCOPE ACCESSORIES FOR SOLAR WORK

Up to this point we have been talking about aspects of the sun visible through a small telescope. It is possible to see more exciting solar phenomena, but more sophisticated (and, unfortunately, more expensive) equipment is needed. The addition of a spectrohelioscope or a quartz monochromator brings out great detail on the sun's surface. When an occulting disk is added, the main disk of the sun is screened out and the beautiful solar prominences come into view.

The principle involved in either one of these devices is relatively simple. If we spread out the light of the sun by means of a slit and a diffraction grating or a prism, we obtain a band of bright colors crossed by dark lines. These lines only *appear* dark; actually, each is a source of light produced by an incandescent gas in the sun's atmosphere. There are many such gases, but for the purposes of this discussion we are concerned with only two, hydrogen and ionized calcium. The light produced by either may be used to view the solar disk. The colored band is called a *spectrum*. We can isolate any dark line in the spectrum by viewing it through a second slit. Now, since the line is really light from the sun, when both slits are lined up what we actually see is a narrow strip of the sun's surface. By moving the slits we can see other strips. If we make the slits oscillate back and forth we see, by the same kind

of persistence of vision as when we view a movie film, the whole solar surface.

The sun viewed through the calcium line appears very different than when looked at directly. It is broken up into mottled patches of ionized calcium gas called *flocculi* and, in the vicinity of sunspots, bright ragged blotches called *plages*. When viewed through the hydrogen line the flocculi show up as threadlike markings. Around sunspots the threads look something like an iron-filing arrangement near the poles of a magnet. There are also longer lines, called *filaments*, which may extend for thousands of miles across the solar disk.

Both the spectrohelioscope and its cousin, the quartz monochromator, make it possible to see actual motion in the solar gases. The flow of hydrogen toward a sunspot, the arching of masses of gases moving at velocities of hundreds of miles a second, and the brilliance of a flare near a sunspot are sights never to be forgotten. The views of the limb of the sun are even more spectacular. Here the great prominences thrust thousands of miles into space. They appear as loops, arches, eruptions, explosions, and are all the more breath-taking because they are silhouetted against the dark background of space. They may last for minutes, hours, even days, and during these periods travel incredible distances, sometimes as far as a million miles.

These marvelous telescope accessories have not only helped to reveal the true nature of our turbulent sun, but they are the source of unbelievably beautiful photographs of solar prominences. Not every amateur has the opportunity to use one, but even without them, the ever-changing face of the sun is well worth a large proportion of your telescope time.

The Moon

Looked over, then overlooked—this is the story of the moon as far as many observers are concerned. While it is true that practically all new telescope owners turn first to our natural satellite to marvel at its sweeping lava plains, its multitudinous craters, and its far-flung mountain ranges, few of us bother to make the more intensive observations that the moon deserves. One could study its roughhewn surface for decades and still not exhaust all its possibilities. In spite of intensive mapping, photographic studies, and work with spectroscopes, thermocouples, photometers, polarizing filters, radar—and even the marvelous photographs taken by the Ranger, Surveyor, and Orbiter satellites—the real nature of the moon's surface is still a matter of speculation. We know it is covered with a layer of basaltic rock, that it is airless, eternally silent, subject to intense heat and abysmal cold, and bom-

The Moon's Vital Statistics

	As compared to earth	Actual figures Earth	Moon		Distance from earth	At this distance the apparent angular diameter of the moon is
Diameter	.273	7,900 miles	2,160 miles	Nearest	221,463 miles	33′ 30″
Mass	.0123	6.6×10^{21} tons	8.1×10^{19} tons	Farthest	252,710 miles	29′ 21″
Volume	.0203	26×10^{10} cu mi	5.2×10^{9} cu mi	Average	238,857 miles	31′ 05″
Density	.604	5.5 (water)	3.33 (water)			
Gravity	.165	32 ft/sec^2	5.31 ft/sec^2			
Inclination to ecliptic	.281	23.5°	6.6°			

Inclination of orbit to ecliptic   5.1°
Noon surface temperature   212° F = 100° C = 373° K
Midnight surface temperature   −238° F = −150° C = 123° K
Synodic month   29d 12h 44m
Sidereal month   27d 7h 43m

barded with meteorites and all the radiation from which we are safely screened by our atmosphere. Yet an admission of our fundamental ignorance is implicit in the world's willingness to spend billions of dollars to put a man on its surface. Only then can we fill in the details that are merely guessed at now. In the meantime, our enigmatic neighbor in space is a rich source of enjoyment for anyone who owns even a small telescope.

GENERAL LUNAR FEATURES

There are many different kinds of lunar features, and several ways of classifying them, or placing them into general categories. The following is a relatively simple and somewhat abbreviated list, with examples to make the classification as clear as possible.

Flat Areas

1. Oceans — Only one of these, *Oceanus Procellarum*, the Ocean of Storms.
2. Seas — These vary in size from very large ones to small ones just a little bigger than one of the walled plains. *Mare Tranquillitatis*, the Sea of Tranquillity.
3. Bays — Usually indentations of the seas. *Sinus Iridum*, the Bay of Rainbows.
4. Lakes — More or less cut off from the seas. *Lacus Mortis*, the Lake of the Dead.
5. Marshes — Like lakes, but with a rougher surface. *Palus Nebularum*, Marsh of the Mists.
6. Walled plains — Large flat-bottomed craters. *Plato, Ptolemaeus.*

Circular Depressions
(usually classified by size and interior features)

1. Walled plains — 40 to 150 miles in diameter. Usually hexagonal or some form of polygon. Rarely contain interior mountains. *Clavius, Baily*
2. Ringed plains — 15 to 60 miles in diameter. Often circular. Rough interiors—mountains, ridges, etc. *Copernicus, Tycho, Alphonsus.*
3. Craters — 5 to 15 miles in diameter. Smaller and often appear deeper than the ringed plains. *Ariadaeus, Birt.*
4. Craterlets — 5 miles or less in diameter.

Mountains

1. Chain mountains	Lofty, up to 20,000 feet. *Pyrhenees.*
2. Block mountains	Broken-up plateaus. *Carpathians.*
3. Scarp mountains	Uptilted edge of large surface blocks. *Altai Scarp.*
4. Individual mountains	Appear on the maria. *Pico, Piton.*

Other Features

1. Rills	Includes clefts, cracks, rills. Narrow depressions, which may be straight, winding, or branched. Often have the appearance of dried-up river beds. *Hyginus Cleft, Ariadaeus Rill.*
2. Faults	Breaks in the maria surface. Similar to earthquake faults. *The Straight Wall in Mare Nubium.*
3. Valleys	Comparable to terrestrial features, although not, of course, of river origin. *Alpine Valley,* the long valley near Ptolemaeus.
4. Rays	Bright streaks emanating from certain craters. *Copernicus, Tycho, and Kepler ray systems.*
5. Domes	Swellings or blisterlike formations, sometimes with a tiny hole in the center. Range in size from 2 to 25 miles. *Dome inside Darwin.*
6. Ghosts	Vague outline of some lunar feature destroyed or covered up by later changes. *Ghost craters on Mare Nubium.*
7. Saucers	Depressed areas with no walls. They appear inside walled plains and on the maria. *Floor of Plato, Alphonsus.*
8. Bright spots	Origin uncertain. Especially prominent near full moon. *Area around Copernicus and around Linné.*

LUNAR GEOGRAPHY

Traditional usage for lunar directions has corresponded with the way the moon appears through an astronomical telescope: inverted, with north at the bottom, east at the right. This convention has caused much confusion because, although the moon rotates on its axis in the same direction as the earth, the sun rises in the *west.* The International Astronomical Union in 1961 adopted a resolution eliminating the words *east* and *west,* substituting *right* and *left,* and keeping south at the moon's top and north at the bottom. We use this system in this book.

The center of the moon's disk, on the average, lies near the center of Sinus Medii at a point about equidistant from the craters Schröter, Triesnecker, and Herschel. The lunar prime meridian is a line drawn through this point from Curtius to Timeaus. The equator also passes through the point as well as Rhaeticus and Landsberg. Latitude is measured north and south from the equator, as on the earth. The meridians of longitude increase to the right, from 0° to 360°.

We used the phrase *on the average* in locating the center of the moon's disk because, due to a phenomenon called libration, it is not always in the same place. As we see it from the earth, the moon apparently swings a little from side to side and also tips slightly up and down. The horizontal swing is called *libration in longitude;* the vertical tipping, *libration in latitude.* Even though our natural satellite keeps the same face toward us (since it rotates once on its axis each time it circles the earth), the librations make it possible for us to see a little more of its right and left areas, and of its top and bottom, than we could without them. Consequently, 41 percent of the lunar surface is *always* visible, another 18 percent is occasionally visible, and only 41 percent can never be seen.

Libration in longitude is caused by the variable speed of the moon around the earth. It travels fastest when closest to us in its elliptical orbit, slowest when farthest away. But it *rotates* at a constant rate. Thus, when it moves swiftly we see a little more on one side; when it moves slowly, we see the same amount more on the other side. Libration in latitude occurs because the moon's axis is tipped about 7° toward the plane of its orbit. Once a month we can see 7° of the surface beyond the north pole and fifteen days later an equal amount beyond the south pole.

There are also two other librations. Diurnal (daily) libration is due to the difference in size of earth and moon, but amounts to a difference of only 1°. The remaining negligible libration is caused by a slight tipping of the lunar axis from the plane of the ecliptic.

This shifting of the apparent central point of the moon caused by librations accounts for the fact that the shadow patterns near a crater when the moon is three days old in June are not exactly the same as those near the same crater when the moon is three days old in July. The librations create a slight change in position of the moon relative to the sun, and the shadows shift accordingly. As a matter of fact, the sun-moon relationship that creates a certain phase of the moon does not recur until fifteen lunations (the complete phase change from new moon to new moon, or 29½ days) later, and even then it will occur an hour earlier.

To determine precisely how the moon will be oriented at a particular time you must understand the concept of the sun's colongitude. You will see this term applied to many lunar photographs. It refers to the selenographic (lunar) longitude of the terminator. More specifically, the sun's colongitude is equal to the longitude of any lunar equatorial feature upon which the sun is rising. Although by definition it applies only to equatorial features, actually it is applicable to those lying on a wide belt on either side of the equator and becomes inaccurate only as the poles are approached. The *American Ephemeris* tabulates the colongitude of the sun for the beginning of each day of the year. If used with a lunar chart that shows lines of longitude, the position of the terminator may be found for any instant by using the following:

Sun's Colongitude		Position of the Terminator
Between		
0° and 90°		0° to 90°
90° and 180°	(add 180°)	270° to 360°
180° and 270°	(subtract 180°)	0° to 90°
270° and 360°		270° to 360°

For the waxing moon, the terminator outlines features upon which the sun is rising; for the waning moon, features upon which the sun is setting. As we see the surface through a telescope, afternoon shadows are thrown to the left of a feature, morning shadows to the right.

CONTRAST ON THE MOON'S SURFACE

The light reflected from any part of the lunar disk is measured in terms of albedo, the ratio of the amount of light reflected to that received. The average for the moon is about 7 percent, but this ratio varies from lunation to lunation. For example, a full moon at perigee (nearest to the earth) may be almost 30 percent brighter than one at apogee (farthest from the earth). Then too, some features are much brighter than others. Several scales have been devised to compare relative brilliance and, although none of these is comparable to photometric measurements, the one that follows—worked out by Beer and Madlow—is as good as any.

Brightness number	Color	Example
0	Black shadows	Crater interior when only rim is illuminated
1	Grayish black	Grimaldi floor
2	Dark gray	Sinus Iridum
3	Medium gray	Aristillus floor
4	Yellowish gray	Timocharis
5	Light gray	Interior of Tycho
6	Approaching grayish white	Kepler floor
7	Grayish white	Philolaus
8	White	Tycho central peak
9	Glittering white	Aristarchus interior
10	Dazzling white	Aristarchus central peak

OBSERVING THE MOON

Most observers are familiar with the waxing moon chiefly because it appears at the most convenient observing time—early in the evening. But a real acquaintance with lunar features requires observation throughout the entire lunation, including daylight observation. It is surprising how many otherwise obscure details can be seen by daylight, when the almost blinding glare of the gibbous moon is softened and diluted by the dispersion of sunlight in the atmosphere.

If you are not already familiar with lunar features it is best to start with an over-all examination, using low power. Pick out the most striking features first —maria, bays, large walled plains, mountain ranges, ray systems—and learn their names. This approach is not nearly as difficult as it sounds. Most of the lunar names are as striking as the objects themselves. Who could forget the name *Bay of Rainbows* once he has looked at the rainbow curve with the sunlight striking its mighty walls? Look at a variety of features under changing light conditions, especially at lunar sunrise and sunset. The changes in appearance are sometimes astonishing. When you have become familiar with the more obvious features, check each one under high power—300 or more—and note how details appear and disappear. The camera records its impressions for only a single instant of time, but the eye picks up small details as they change from instant to instant with the constant shifting of seeing conditions. Look for some

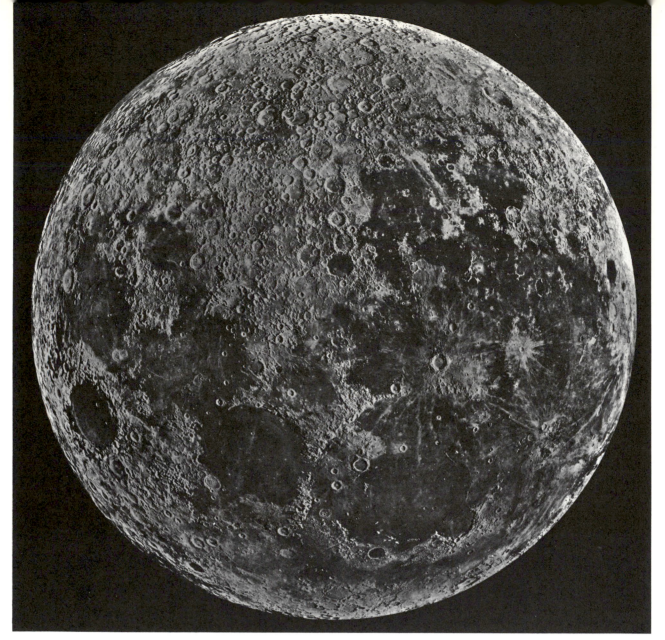

Above: A composite picture of the moon showing detail of the craters on all parts of the surface. Right: a map of lunar features.

1. Moretus	24. Guericke	47. Mutus	70. Hipparchus
2. Clavius	25. Letronne	48. Lilius	71. Delambre
3. Scheiner	26. Fra Mauro	49. Vlacq	72. Triesnecker
4. Maginus	27. Flamsteed	50. Cuvier	73. Maskelyne
5. Longomontanus	28. Grimaldi	51. Janssen	74. Taruntius
6. Schiller	29. Pallas	52. Stöfler	75. Appolonius
7. Phocylides	30. Reinhold	53. Maurolycus	76. Julius Caesar
8. Tycho	31. Landsberg	54. Fabricius	77. Manilius
9. Schickard	32. Hevelius	55. Walter	78. Plinius
10. Orontius	33. Copernicus	56. Rheita	79. Autolycus
11. Hainzel	34. Kepler	57. Furnerius	80. Posidonius
12. Lexell	35. Reiner	58. Aliacensis	81. Cleomedes
13. Wurzelbauer	36. Eratosthenes	59. Piccolomini	82. Aristillus
14. Regiomontanus	37. Marius	60. Stevinus	83. Geminus
15. Pitatus	38. Archimedes	61. Sacrobosco	84. Cassini
16. Doppelmayer	39. Timocharis	62. Frascastorius	85. Eudoxus
17. Purbach	40. Aristarchus	63. Petavius	86. Franklin
18. Arzachel	41. Plato	64. Catharina	87. Messala
19. Bullialdus	42. Mairon	65. Vendelinus	88. Hercules
20. Mersenius	43. Birmingham	66. Albategnius	89. Atlas
21. Alphonsus	44. Pythagoras	67. Cyrillus	90. Aristoteles
22. Gassendi	45. Curtius	68. Theophilus	91. Endymion
23. Ptolemaeus	46. Maginus	69. Langrenus	92. W. C. Bond

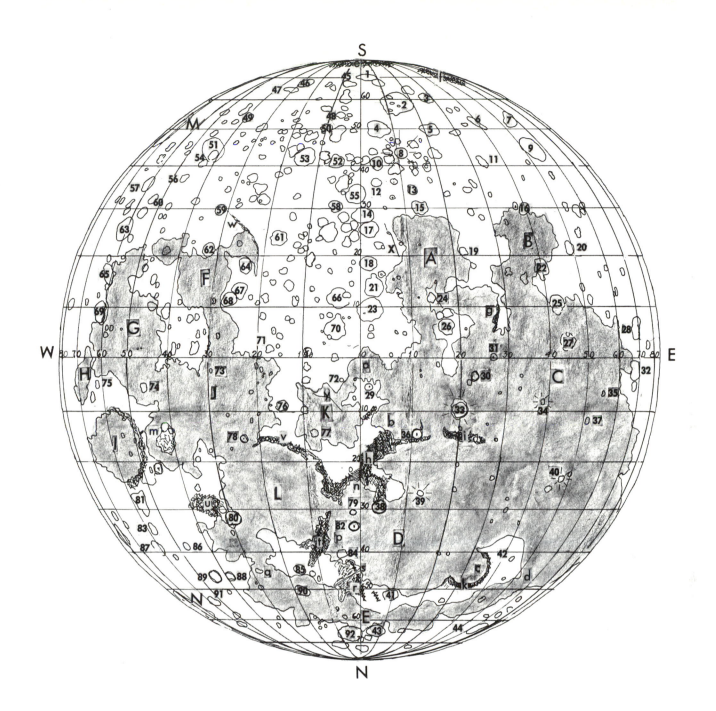

A. Mare Nubium (Sea of Clouds)
B. Mare Humorum (Sea of Moisture)
C. Oceanus Procellarum (Ocean of Storms)
D. Mare Imbrium (Sea of Rains)
E. Mare Frigoris (Sea of Cold)
F. Mare Nectaris (Sea of Nectar)
G. Mare Foecunditatis (Sea of Fertility)

a. Sinus Medii (Central Bay)
b. Sinus Aestuum (Seething Bay)
c. Sinus Iridum (Rainbow Bay)
d. Sinus Roris (Bay of Dew)
e. Leibnitz Mountains
f. Doerfel Mountains

g. Riphaean Mountains
h. Apennine Mountains
i. Carpathian Mountains
k. Jura Mountains
m. Palus Somnii (Marsh of Sleep)

H. Mare Spumans (Foaming Sea)
I. Mare Crisium (Sea of Crises)
J. Mare Tranquillitatis (Sea of Tranquillity)
K. Mare Vaporum (Sea of Vapors)
L. Mare Serenitatis (Sea of Serenity)
M. Mare Australe (Southern Sea)
N. Mare Humboltianum (Humbolt Sea)

n. Palus Putredinis (Marsh of Decay)
o. Lacus Somniorum (Lake of Dreams)
p. Palus Nebularum (Marsh of Mists)
q. Lacus Mortis (Lake of the Dead)
r. Alps (mountains)
s. Alpine Valley
t. Caucasian Mountains
u. Taurus Mountains
v. Haemus Mountains
w. Altai Scarp
x. Straight Wall
y. Hyginus Cleft

of the obscure lunar objects—the domes, tiny clefts and rills, the rolling hills on the maria, the saucers, the varying brightness of lunar spots. While it is impossible to list more than a few subjects for investigation, here are some you can have fun with.

LUNAR CHANGES

While few actual physical changes have ever been observed on the moon, they are still worth looking for. Most of the reported physical changes are in reality only variations in light values. Nevertheless there is considerable evidence that they do take place, and these "exceptions to the rule" make lunar observing really exciting. One of the most recent was the observation by Greenacre and Barr of Lowell Observatory of bright-colored spots in the area around Aristarchus and Schröter's Valley. The colors ranged from red-orange to red to pink to ruby. In one instance the color was so bright that it was described as like "looking into a large polished gem ruby." It is doubtful that this October 1963 observation could be duplicated with a small telescope, yet the possibility cannot be completely ruled out.

Another striking example of lunar change was the fogging of the floor of the crater Alphonsus, observed in 1956. The craterlets and the long rill at the lower left of the crater disappeared, even though neighboring areas still showed sharp detail. When the area was photographed in red light, the rill and craterlets reappeared. One explanation of this is that carbon dioxide gas was escaping from various points along the rill, a supposition confirmed (at least in part) two years later by the Soviet astronomer Kosyrev when the typical lines of carbon appeared on a spectogram of the crater. The gas was very thin—about a billionth of an atmosphere—nevertheless, it was dense enough to block ordinary light. Similar changes have been reported on the floor of Plato and other ringed plains.

The classic example of a lunar change is Linné, at the far right side of Mare Serenitatis. Linné was first observed as a definite crater formation and was indicated as such in the Schmidt drawings of the 1840's. In 1866 the crater apparently disappeared; by 1867 all that remained was a dome. But this dome itself underwent a change, for a craterlet appeared in its center in 1868 and now, nearly a hundred years later, is still evident. Today, Linné changes its appearance according to the light by which it is observed. Blue light shows only a bright spot; red light, a mound with a central craterlet. As in the case of Alphonsus, the change may be due to the evolution of carbon dioxide or to what astronomers call "residual outgassing."

There are also recorded instances of "flashes" in lunar shaded areas, possibly due to the impact of meteorites and the resulting heat. Finally, the progressive change in some of the variable spots on the moon may be due to some kind of physical change rather than differences in light value. In any event, it is peculiar that some brighten and others darken during the lunar day.

It goes without saying that any real change observed in a lunar feature should be reported.* All pertinent data, such as the simultaneous appearance of surrounding areas, the date and UT of the observation, the colongitude of the sun, seeing conditions, and telescope attributes (type of instrument, aperture, magnification, filters used, etc.), should be included.

THE SURFACE OF THE MOON

For years many astronomers argued that the moon was covered with a fine, sandy material many feet deep; others insisted there was only a thin layer of dust over solid rock or lava. The matter was settled when the astronauts landed: they found a mostly solid surface, overlain with several inches of a sticky, granular material that retained any impressions made in it. It is expected that in this cohesive material, lying in a near-vacuum, the footprints of the astronauts and the tracks of their vehicles will remain visible for thousands of years. So will their rubbish.

Most amateur lunar observers—and some professionals—formerly believed that the mountainous regions were extremely rugged and craggy, dominated by sharp peaks with precipitous slopes. From the small area now explored, however, it is evident that although there are vast rough areas strewn with huge boulders, most of the mountains are rounded, with gently rising shoulders. Conversely, some of the plains in the "sea" areas are smooth and flat. Perhaps the chief characteristic of the surface is its variability. You can demonstrate this for yourself by panning a telescope across the gibbous moon (before it gets too bright) and listing the different features as they come into view.

COMPARISONS

As we said earlier, the lunar craters can be classified by size and structure, and it is worth studying them from the point of view of differences and similarities. Here we might think a little bit about the crater origins. What must the shattering explosions have been like which produced the huge ringed plains, Aristarchus, Copernicus, Tycho, and Kepler? Notice that these craters are alike in their ray systems, central mountains, surrounding craterlets, and terraced external walls. They are almost circular in shape and show signs of having spewed out ash material, for they all brighten with the waxing moon. Now compare these with walled plains, such

A view of the crater Kepler, taken by Lunar Orbiter III. Although Kepler is 20 miles in diameter and more than 7,500 feet deep, it is an insignificant feature in the vast expanse of Oceanus Procellarum. (See pages 64 and 65, item 34.)

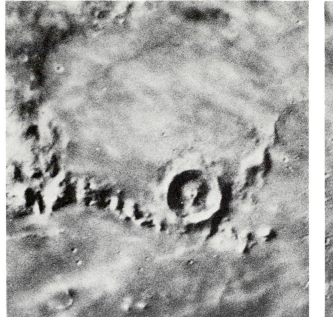 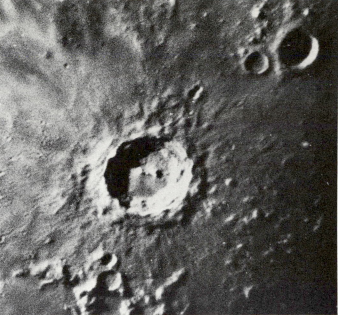

Questar Corporation

Copernicus (right) and Eratos-
thenes.

NASA

An Orbiter V view of Tycho, the
moon's most famous crater. At full
moon Tycho looks like the navel
of an orange; at other times it is
hard to find. It is a huge crater,
54 miles across and 14,000 feet
deep. Its central peak is 7,000 feet
high.

as Ptolemaeus, Clavius, and Hipparchus, which have smooth floors, low or no external walls, polygonal rather than circular boundaries, and (only rarely) central peaks. They are immense shallow areas, spreading over hundreds of square miles. Less spectacular, but just as interesting, are the ghost craters, such as Letronne, which show up with grazing light all over the floors of the maria. Have these craters drowned in a sea of lava? Have they sunk into the maria floors by their own weight? Or have they simply become inundated under tons of sandlike material?

THE RAY SYSTEMS

Among the most interesting lunar features are the rays, great systems of white streaks that were long the subject of controversy. Some observers thought they were chains of tiny craterlets; others, that they were created by gaseous materials or dust leaking from great faults; and still others, that they were layers of ashlike material blown from craters. This last supposition is now the accepted one. The rays can be seen clearly only at the gibbous and full phases of the moon because, like strips of paint, they have so little depth that they are almost invisible when viewed obliquely. Dinsmore Alter lists 108 different ray systems in his *Pictorial Guide to the Moon,* but even this extensive list does not include all of them. Some extend radially from craters (Tycho), some point only in one direction (Messier and W. H. Pickering), some seem to have no connection with the craters. They may extend for hundreds of miles, become broken or cut off, then continue in the same direction. One in particular seems to go all the way around the moon. This one starts at the south polar region, passes through Tycho, moves northward across the rough mountainous area to the left of Hipparchus, crosses Mare Serenitatis, and finally disappears over the northern horizon near the Humboldt Sea. Closer examination shows that it is not continuous; nevertheless, it appears almost like a meridian engraved on the lunar surface.

SOME INTERESTING LUNAR FEATURES

In addition to the general features discussed in the previous section, here are a few more very much worth looking for:
1. The Straight Wall in Mare Humorum
2. The Altai Scarp to the right of Mare Nectaris
3. The Triesnecker-Hyginus-Ariadaeus rill system between Mare Tranquillitatis and Mare Vaporum
4. The Alpine Valley between Mare Frigoris and Mare Imbrium

5. The great gash in the lunar surface to the right of the crater Ptolemaeus
6. The Rheita Valley between the craters Rheita and Metius
7. Schröter's Valley below Aristarchus
8. The mountains of the maria, Pico and Piton on Palus Nebularum
9. The great walled plain Schiller between Tycho and the Doerful Mountains
10. Sinus Iridum and the "waves" sweeping toward it from Mare Imbrium

DRAWING THE MOON

If you are one of those fortunate people who have some ability in drawing, try your skills on the moon. Line drawings become too fussy and cluttered; instead, try the method first devised by Russell Porter in 1930† and since brought to a high degree of precision by the lunar artists Alika Herring and Raymond Coutchie.

Use ordinary drawing paper, the pencil-sketching kind. You'll need a variety of pencils, from 2H to 6B, a rolled-up piece of blotting paper for an artist's stump, and some ruby erasers, one of which should be sharpened to a point. The artist's stump should have the dimensions of a cigar, with one sharp and one rounded end. You will use it for blending and grading shadows.

The paper must be prepared to represent a neutral background for the area around the lunar formation you wish to draw. Sprinkle with graphite scraped from the 2H pencil; rub this into the paper with the finger tip or a soft piece of cotton until an even texture has been produced. If you don't rub too hard or leave any excess, the result should be a soft, even gray color.

Start by drawing the outline of the object; then block in the heavy shadows. Next, use the eraser to produce the sunlit areas. Now, by alternately filling in and erasing to create differences in shading, work all around the drawing. Remember there are few *round* objects on the moon—look at Ptolemaeus, for example. At first glance it appears nearly circular; closer examination makes its hexagonal shape apparent.

Practice with a few features copied from photographs, then work from the moon itself. You will have only about half an hour for any lunar feature; over longer periods the shadows will change too much for your work to be accurate. Remember that accuracy, not art, is your prime objective, although it would be pleasant if you could combine them. Be sure you are comfortable when you begin. Arrange the support for the drawing and a small light near the eyepiece so your movements from eyepiece

---

* Thomas Y. Crowell Company, New York.

† *Scientific American,* October 1930.

to paper will be as limited as possible. The illumination on the paper should be of the same brightness as the lunar background observed through the eyepiece.

For this sort of work, a telescope drive is very important. If you must constantly adjust your telescope to keep the moon centered, you will waste your time, temper, and technique.

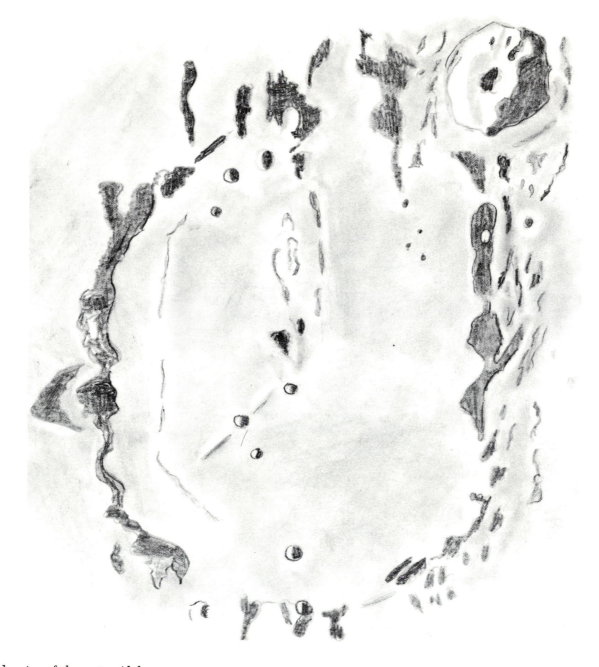

A drawing of the crater Alphonsus. Compare it with the photograph on page 64 (item 21).

CHAPTER VI

Occultations, Appulses, Eclipses

Occultations

As the moon moves eastward among the stars it can pass in front of all objects within 6½° of the ecliptic. Its path includes all the planets and many of the major stars and star groups; the Pleiades, Hyades, Regulus, Spica, Pollux, Aldebaran, Antares, Alhena, Dschubba, and Elacrab are just a few examples. If an object passes behind the east limb of the moon, its disappearance is called immersion. Similarly, its reappearance from behind the west limb is called emersion.

Timing occultations comes under the heading of useful fun for amateurs. Enough accurate reports on a given occultation provide a real addition to astronomical knowledge, since this is one of the most convenient and accurate methods of determining the moon's position. One might think that centuries of lunar observation would have evolved an accurate table for determining where the moon may be found for any instant of time, yet differences between its calculated and observed positions still exist.

For timing occultations, telescopes of any size or type may be used. The only other required equipment is an accurate timepiece, since the instant of immersion or emersion must be determined to the nearest second. The observer must also know the latitude and longitude of his observing site and its height above sea level.

Occultations, like eclipses, can be predicted well in advance, and there are many sources for this information.* Lists of occultations give the time of the event for a "standard" station. To find the time for your own location, you can use this formula:

Your time = Standard Time at the standard station
$$a(\lambda - \lambda_0) + b(\phi - \phi_0)$$

Here, λ_0 and ϕ_0 are your own longitude and latitude, and λ and ϕ are those for the standard station. The quantities a and b are correction factors, also included in the occultation list. To use the formula, fill in the information given in the list, making sure to apply the correct algebraic sign for each term.

The Standard Stations†

Station		Longitude	Latitude
A	(Massachusetts)	72°.5	42°.5
B	(Montreal)	73°.6	45°.5
C	(Washington, D.C.)	77°.1	38°.9
D	(Toronto)	79°.4	43°.7
F	(Illinois)	91°	40°
G	(Texas)	98°	31°
H	(Denver)	105°	39°.7
I	(New Mexico)	109°	34°
J	(Edmonton, Alberta)	113°.1	53°
K	(California)	120°	36°
L	(Oregon)	121°	32°.5
M	(Vancouver, B.C.)	123°.1	49°.5

† If you plot the positions given in the right-hand column of this list, you will find that only a few actually coincide with a large city. This is why some of the station locations are listed only as being within a state.

* See bimonthly issues of *Review of Popular Astronomy;* December issues of *Sky and Telescope;* and annual issue of *The Observer's Handbook.*

Even after you have applied the formula, the time found may be as much as a minute on either side of the actual event, so it is well to make preparations several minutes in advance. As the moon drifts across the field diameter of your telescope, note the east-west axis as well as the time required for the moon's passage across the field. Then, at *half* this time before the predicted time of occultation set the telescope to place the star at the field edge. The occultation will now occur near the center of the field. To time the event, set a stop watch by some accurate source of time or tune a short-wave radio to one of the standard time signals.

The data in your logbook should include:

1. Designation of the star (use a catalog number, map designation, or the system given in the occultation prediction)
2. Date and UT of occultation to 1-second accuracy
3. Longitude, latitude, and elevation of your observing point
4. Stellar magnitude, whether the occultation occurred at the dark or bright limb, and whether observed at immersion or emersion
5. Seeing conditions
6. Instrumental details: type and aperture of telescope, magnification used, etc.*

Appulses

When a planet approaches a star closely, the event is called a planetary appulse. This is a rare happening, and the actual occultation of a star (ninth magnitude or brighter) occurs even less often. The planets take up very little space in the sky; even mighty Jupiter has an angular diameter of only 50 seconds of arc when closest to us. The chance of such a tiny area shutting off the light from a bright star is indeed slight. Yet it does happen. Venus occulted Regulus in 1959, and in the period 1959 through 1964 Saturn has twice occulted stars, once in 1960 and again in 1962. These rare occasions are of course of considerable astronomical interest and receive a good deal of attention.

Eclipses

The earth revolves around the sun in the plane of the ecliptic; the moon travels around the earth in a plane tipped about 5° from the ecliptic. This 5° tip is all-important; it is the reason that we do not have eclipses of both sun and moon once each month. Solar eclipses occur only when a new moon passes

through the ecliptic; lunar eclipses occur only when a full moon passes through the ecliptic. The northward passage of the moon through the ecliptic is called the ascending node; the southward passage, the descending node.

Understanding the mechanics of an eclipse depends on your ability to put together several geometric variables. Predicting its *time* is an even more complex operation. Nevertheless, understanding the fundamentals will make the actual observation of eclipses much more enjoyable.

TYPES OF ECLIPSES

In a lunar eclipse, the moon swings behind the earth, relative to the sun. Therefore the darkening of the moon is caused by the earth's shadow. Solar eclipses, on the other hand, are caused by the actual passage of the moon in front of the sun, as seen from the earth. If the moon is at perigee (221,000 miles from earth), the eclipse will be total and may last as long as 7½ minutes. Partial eclipses may occur with the sun as much as 18½° on either side of the nodal point. Annular eclipses, where the moon does not completely cover the sun's surface, occur at apogee (253,000 miles from earth). In an annular eclipse the edge of the sun shows as a ring, or annulus, all around the rim of the moon.

ECLIPSE PATHS

The moon moves eastward around the earth, and because of the great difference between the distance of sun from the earth and that of the moon from the earth, the shadow of the moon races eastward faster than the earth turns. If the moon were to move in front of the earth and then stop, its shadow would move westward because of the earth's rotation. The speeding shadow is only a spot of darkness, never more than 167 miles in cross section, which traces a curved path across the globe. Inside this path, the eclipse is total, outside it is partial. Lunar eclipses, however, can be seen from widely separated vantage points because the earth's shadow is very large—nearly three times the moon's diameter—at the point where it reaches the moon. For example, the total eclipse of the sun of July 1963 could be seen only from a path about 60 miles wide stretching from Alaska to Maine, but the total lunar eclipse that occurred in December 1963 was visible all over North America.

ECLIPSES DURING THE YEAR

A synodic month, from full moon to full moon, is 29.53 days long, and six synodic months equal 177 days. The interval during which the sun moves from one node to another is 173 days. These figures are

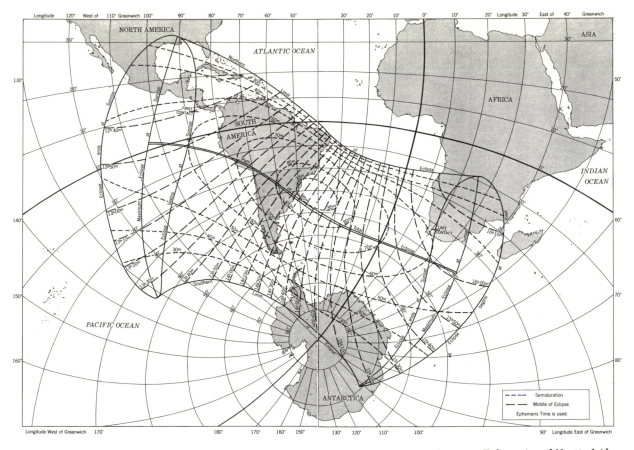

American Ephemeris and Nautical Almanac

A map showing the path of the total eclipse of the sun that occurred on November 12, 1966.

important because they determine how many eclipses can be seen during a year.

Suppose a solar eclipse occurs exactly at a node. In six synodic months there would be another solar eclipse at this node, but it would occur about 4° away from the node; in another six months it would occur 8° away. This would mean that the full moon must have been only 7° away fifteen days earlier—and therefore in eclipse. So it is possible that pairs of such eclipses could occur every six months. But it is also possible, if the distance from the nodes is just right, for one or two groups of solar-lunar-solar eclipses to occur within a single solar month. As the distance changes, one of the solar eclipses is eliminated, followed by a lunar one. The solar eclipse that remains brings us back to the original condition. The complete cycle covers four years. In any given year of the period, then, we will have a minimum of two eclipses, both of the sun, or a maximum of seven, of which five can be solar and two lunar, or four solar and three lunar.

PERIODIC ECLIPSES

Again let's assume that the sun is at one of the nodes and that an eclipse has occurred. As the

earth swings in its orbit, this node will not point toward the sun again for 346.62 days (a period called the eclipse year). As we have already seen, the synodic month is 29.53 days. An eclipse similar to

Millbrook School Observatory

Sequence showing the solar eclipse of October 2, 1959. The sun rose eclipsed just before 6:00, Eastern Standard Time; this series covers the period between 6:08 and 6:42.

73

the first cannot occur again until sun, moon, and earth are in the same relative positions, and this cannot happen until a whole number of synodic months nearly equals (within a day or two) a whole number of eclipse years. There are many such possibilities, most of which involve very large numbers, but two of the shorter ones are of interest. For example:

$$47 \text{ synodic months} = 4 \text{ eclipse years}$$
$$223 \text{ synodic months} = 19 \text{ eclipse years}$$
$$(18 \text{ earth years, } 11\tfrac{1}{3} \text{ days}).$$

The second possibility, called a *saros,* is especially interesting because of its history. Without knowing anything of the factors that produced the saros, the Chinese, the Babylonians, the Chaldeans, and the Greeks all used it to predict eclipses. In the saros, as in other possibilities, a series of eclipses start near the pole, then move toward the equator, and finally disappear at the opposite pole. They move southward if the original eclipse occurs at the ascending node, northward if the eclipse occurs at the descending node.

One other fact should be mentioned: The best total eclipses occur at perigee. The time elapsed from one perigee to another is called the *anomalistic* month. If an eclipse cycle contains an almost exact number of anomalistic months there will be a succession of total eclipses followed by a similar succession of annular eclipses. This condition applies to the saros (19 eclipse years equals 239 anomalistic months) and is perhaps the reason for its discovery by the ancients.

ECLIPSE SHADOWS

A single point of light casts very sharp shadows beyond an object placed in front of it, but an extended light source, such as the sun, creates two shadows. In the *umbral* shadow all light is cut off; in the *penumbral* shadow only part of the light is cut off. If you are familiar with these shadow patterns, you will have a better understanding of what happens in an eclipse. No part of the sun will be visible to an observer located in the dark part of the shadow (the umbra) and a total eclipse of the sun results. Some of the sun will be visible to an observer located in the partial shadow (the penumbra). It might be thought that an observer on earth would see no part of the moon while it is in the earth's shadow, but actually the moon is almost always visible even in total eclipse because the earth's atmosphere acts like a lens and refracts sunlight toward the lunar disk. The rays at the violet end of the spectrum are completely absorbed by the thick layers of air near the earth's surface. The more penetrating red rays, however, are bent just enough to focus on the lunar surface and we see the moon under this feeble illumination. This explains the reddish color so often commented on in a lunar eclipse; it also explains why the edge of the earth's shadow is not sharply outlined as it crosses the moon. Often it is difficult to tell where the umbra leaves off and the penumbra begins.

OBSERVING ECLIPSES

Few of us have the opportunity to view more than two or three eclipses during our lifetime, and the chance of seeing a total eclipse is very slim. If we were to choose any point on the earth at random, the inhabitants of that area could count on seeing a total eclipse only once every three hundred years! But if we expand our base to take in, say, the whole of North America, our chances are greatly improved. In the period 1959 through 1965, for example, North Americans had the opportunity to see two total and three partial eclipses of the sun, and six total and four partial eclipses of the moon.

SOLAR ECLIPSES

The dangers of solar observation are just as great during an eclipse as they are at any other time, and they should be emphasized because a great many inexperienced observers watch eclipses. It is hard to make people believe that the friendly sun has suddenly become a hazard and that looking at it with anything less than the most opaque neutral density filter or welder's goggles can have dire results. If you have set up your telescope for projection purposes, never leave it untended, for some misguided person may attempt to steal a quick peek through the eyepiece.

Projection of the image is the safest and simplest way to follow the early stages of a total eclipse or to follow the whole sequence in a partial one. Set up your telescope as described in chapter V.

The eclipse starts with a small crescent, or "bite," in the western edge of the sun's disk; in about forty minutes it progresses to the point when the bite reaches the center of the disk. If totality is expected, most of the following can be observed:

1. The moon continues across the sun until only a thin crescent of light remains. At any point during this period you can make an interesting nontelescopic observation of one of the most unusual phenomena associated with an eclipse. Hold a large sheet of cardboard, in which you have previously punched a dozen or so small holes, several feet above the ground. The crescent sun will project an image of itself through each hole, and you will see as many images as there are holes. Their size and intensity may be varied by moving the cardboard to different distances from the ground. If there is thick foliage nearby, the same effect will be produced by the small spaces between the leaves.

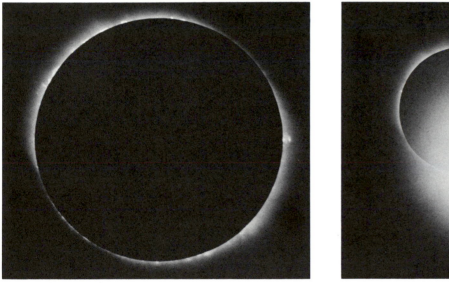

Charles Cuevas

The total solar eclipse of July 20, 1963. Top, the sun in total eclipse with prominences and corona showing. Lower left, detail of the prominences; the prominence large on the right is over 36,000 miles high. Lower right, the "diamond-ring" aspect of the eclipse, resulting because the sun is just beginning to emerge from behind the moon. In all three photographs north is at upper right.

2. As the solar crescent narrows, the quality of the sunlight changes. The surrounding landscape becomes bathed in an unnatural illumination, almost impossible to describe. The light is now coming from the solar limb and is made up almost completely of the rays from the red end of the spectrum.

3. During the last minutes before totality, the remaining section of the sun seemed almost constant in width; it now begins to decrease in length. If you are at a high altitude and look to the west at this point, you will see the approaching umbral shadow.

But you must look quickly because it will be traveling at close to three thousand miles an hour.

4. As the length of the crescent decreases, it will very likely break up into Baily's beads, bright points of light caused by the sun shining through points of low elevation on the rim of the moon. This is followed by the "diamond ring," a narrow band of light all the way around the rim of the moon, broken at one point by a brilliant spot of light.

5. Now you will see the chromosphere, reddish pink in color, followed by the solar prominences at various points around the black disk, and finally the corona. This is the *only* period during the whole spectacle when it is safe to view the sun directly through binoculars or other optical aids. The beautiful corona will vary in width and shape according to the state of the sunspot cycle. It has been variously described as "pearly," "fluorescent," or just "glowing," but none of these terms does it justice. It remains visible from about 1 to 7½ minutes.

6. During this period, if the sky is clear, it may become very dark. Stars and planets may appear in the area immediately surrounding the sun and a lunar occultation may even occur.

7. With the reappearance of the rim of the sun, you may be able to see the western edge of the shadow disappear into the sky as a cone-shaped area of darkness. Other than this, all of the eclipse phenomena previously described will repeat themselves, but in reverse order.

LUNAR ECLIPSES

You can watch eclipses of the moon most satisfactorily with your naked eye or with a telescope fitted with a low-power eyepiece. As mentioned earlier, the edge of the earth's shadow is not sharp as it moves across the moon; only the central part of the umbra is really dark. It is impossible to recognize the penumbral phase at the instant it begins. The mathematics of lunar eclipses tells us that this part of the phenomenon has begun, but we cannot detect any difference in the appearance of the moon until perhaps a quarter of an hour before the umbral phase, when a slight darkening of the eastern limb or an intensification of the shading on the maria occurs. But once the umbral part of the eclipse has begun, there are many interesting phenomena to watch for:

1. **Duration.** Whereas a solar eclipse can never last longer than 7½ minutes, a lunar eclipse may continue for as long as two hours, depending on how centrally the moon is located in the earth's shadow.

2. **Change in coloration.** The interior of the umbral shadow shows many color gradations—dark grays, reds, browns, oranges. The edge of the shadow may show variations of yellow, green, or blue.

3. **Darkness.** Again dependent on the passage

Don Strittmatter

Sequence of nine photos showing the total lunar eclipse of December 30, 1963, between 4:22 P.M. and 5:26 P.M. Eastern Standard Time. Photos 1–4, on Plus-X Pan, ¹⁄₁₀₀ second; 5, Plus-X, ¹⁄₅₀ second; 6–9, Tri-X Pan, ¹⁄₅₀, ¹⁄₂₅, ½, and 1 second respectively.

of the moon through a particular section of the shadow, lunar eclipses may vary from the very dark, in which the moon is almost completely obscured at mid-totality, to the very light, in which the only perceptible change is the appearance of copper-red or orange tints. The complete disappearance of the moon is very rare; it probably occurs only when the upper atmosphere contains a large amount of dust from a volcanic explosion. This phenomenon was actually observed in the early morning eclipse of December 30, 1963, when the author had difficulty believing his eyes and was only convinced after a neighbor reported that he had risen early to view the eclipse, but couldn't find the moon and so went back to bed again!

4. The sky. Some observers consider the change in the sky's brightness even more remarkable for lunar than for solar eclipses. The pre-eclipse full moon is bright enough to obscure anything dimmer than fourth-magnitude stars. At mid-totality, the sky has darkened so that all stars visible to the naked eye blaze out in their full glory. Perhaps one of the best indications of this change is the evidence of camera settings. Before the eclipse, an f/8 camera using film of ASA rating 160 requires an exposure of about $\frac{1}{500}$ second, but at deep eclipse it may require 15 seconds or more. Of course this great difference in exposure is for shooting the moon itself, but it also demonstrates the loss of light throughout the whole sky.

5. Timing. The size of the umbral shadow can be calculated for any given eclipse. In practice, however, the calculated value turns out to be somewhat too small. Part of the discrepancy may be explained by the bending of sunlight through the earth's atmosphere, but since it varies from one eclipse to another, the true cause is still a matter of conjecture. Once again the amateur may make a contribution to astronomical knowledge by timing the passage of the umbra over a few of the more obvious craters. The shadow edge is usually sharp enough so that timing for a small crater such as Kepler can be accurate to within five or six seconds. It is more difficult to estimate the passage over the center of a large formation—Plato, for example—so it is usually better to average the time interval between first contact with the crater rim and the moment when the crater is in complete shadow.

CHAPTER VII

The Planets

Although of incredible dimensions—over seven thousand million miles across—the solar system still occupies only an infinitesimal spot in the immensity of space. The farthest planet is about one two-thousandth of a light-year from the sun, while the nearest star is 4.2 light-years away, and the distance to the farthest quasi-stellar object, or quasar, visible in our largest telescope is measured in billions of light-years. Within this planetary speck in the universe are a variety of objects: tiny meteoroids, boulder-sized asteroids, tiny moons, larger moons —the size of the small planets—large planets, and even comets.

Conditions on the planets vary considerably. There is scorching heat on the sun side of Mercury, abysmal cold on Pluto; clear atmosphere on earth, dense clouds on Venus, frozen asphyxiants on Saturn and Jupiter. The year on Mercury lasts only 88 earth days, but almost 2½ centuries on Pluto. Jupiter spins like a top in its orbit; Uranus "rolls" around the sun. A hundred-pound earthling would weigh 27 pounds on Mercury, 140 pounds on Neptune, and 264 pounds on Jupiter. These are only a few of the more striking differences between the planets; there are many more. But there are many similarities as well. It is very likely that all are composed of many of the same elements found on earth. It is only the relative abundance of each element and the combinations in which they occur that vary from planet to planet. For example, nitrogen exists in the atmospheres of earth and Mars as an uncombined and harmless gas, while on Saturn it has united with hydrogen to form the noxious gas ammonia.

All of the planets are nearly spherical in shape, although those which rotate rapidly bulge at their equators. All move in the same direction around the sun, all rotate.

Planetary Orbits

Most of the planets revolve around the sun in orbits which are nearly circular in shape, although all are actually ellipses. The orbits of Venus and Neptune are so nearly round that if they were reduced to fit this page the eye could not distinguish either from a circle. Mercury and Pluto move in

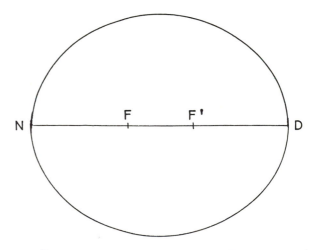

The ellipse. If F and F_1 are the foci and ND the major axis, then the eccentricity is equal to FF_1/ND.

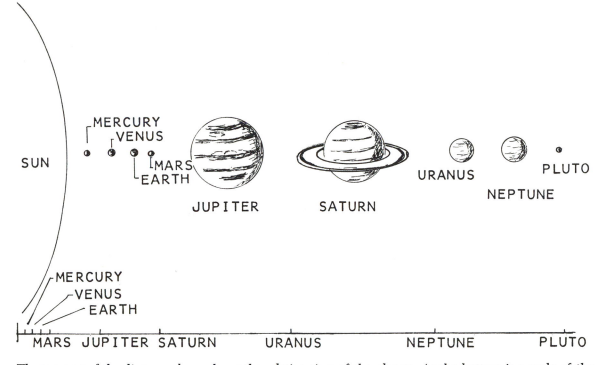

The top part of the diagram above shows the relative sizes of the planets. At the bottom is a scale of the relative distances of the planets from the sun.

obviously elliptical paths. The flattening of an orbit from a circle to an ellipse is called its *eccentricity*. This is the ratio of the distance between the foci of the ellipse to the length of its major (long) axis. If this ratio is very small, the ellipse is nearly circular. When the ratio approaches unity, the ellipse flattens until it becomes nearly a straight line. In general, an orbit in which the eccentricity is .005 or less is almost a circle; when the eccentricity is .250 or more, the orbit is more nearly an oval than a circle. This is important in understanding the eccentricity figure given with each planet later on.

Planetary Distances

An easy way to remember the relative distances of the planets from the sun is to use Bode's Law,*

a simple formula based upon a sequence of numbers. After starting with zero, suppose we write the progression:

0 3 6 12 24 48 96 192 384 768

If we add 4 to each of the above, we have

4 7 10 16 28 52 100 196 388 772

Dividing each number by 10, the series becomes

.4 .7 1.0 1.6 2.8 5.2 10.0 19.6 38.8 77.2

This final series of numbers gives the approximate distance of each planet from the sun, measured in astronomical units. One AU is 93 million miles, the average distance of earth from the sun. The correlation of these figures with the actual measured distance is striking out as far as Neptune.

	Mercury	Venus	Earth	Mars	Asteroids	Jupiter	Saturn	Uranus	Neptune	Pluto
Bode's Law Prediction	.4	.7	1.0	1.6	2.8	5.2	10.0	19.6	38.8	77.2
Actual Distance	.39	.72	1.0	1.52	2.77	5.2	9.54	19.2	30.1	39.5

* Bode's Law is not a law and it was not discovered by the German astronomer Johann Bode. The relationship given above had been well known before 1772, the year in which Bode gave it prominence.

By simple subtraction you can use Bode's Law to find the approximate distance between any two planets when both are on the same side of the sun. Saturn's distance from earth found this way is about

9 AU, or 837 million miles. Of course, these are only approximate distances. Actually, the planets approach each other at varying distances, depending upon where they are in their orbits. The mean distance of Mars, for instance, is .52 AU, or 47.4 million miles, but when Mars is closest to the sun and the earth farthest in their respective orbits, the distance of closest approach shrinks to only 35 million miles.

Relative Positions of the Planets

Venus revolves about the sun in 225 days, the earth in 365.25 days, and Jupiter in 11.86 years. Thus Venus continually outraces the earth in the "Solar Derby," and both practically leave Jupiter at the post. All the planets constantly change positions relative to the earth and the sun, and certain of these positions, or aspects, have been given names. Since Mercury and Venus (the inferior planets) have orbits inside that of earth, and the remainder (the superior planets) outside, the names are slightly different for the two groups. Let's use one planet from each group as an example.

When Venus is on a line between earth and sun, we say it is in *inferior conjunction*. Positions to the east or west of the sun are called *elongations*. At its greatest eastern elongation Venus is 48° east of the sun and sets after sunset. At its greatest western elongation the planet is 48° west of the sun and rises before sunrise. The ancients believed there were *two* planets and called the rising Venus *Phosphorus* and the setting, *Hesperus*. When Venus is on the opposite side of the sun from earth, it is in *superior conjunction*. Both Venus and Mercury show crescent, gibbous, and full phases because of their positions relative to earth and sun. The crescent phase occurs before and after inferior conjunction, the gibbous after the planets pass greatest elongation, and full at superior conjunction.

Mars, of course, can never pass between the sun and earth. Mars can have only gibbous and full phases, and can attain any elongation from 0° to 180°, relative to the sun. When Mars passes behind the sun as seen from earth, it is in *conjunction*. When the sun and Mars are in opposite directions from earth, the planet is in *opposition*. *Quadrature* occurs when a line drawn from earth to the sun forms a right angle with a similar line drawn between Mars and the sun. These terms are important because they tell us approximately where the planet can be found in the sky. Just before Mars is in conjunction it sets after sunset; just after conjunction it rises before sunrise. At opposition it rises when the sun is setting. At western quadrature it is overhead

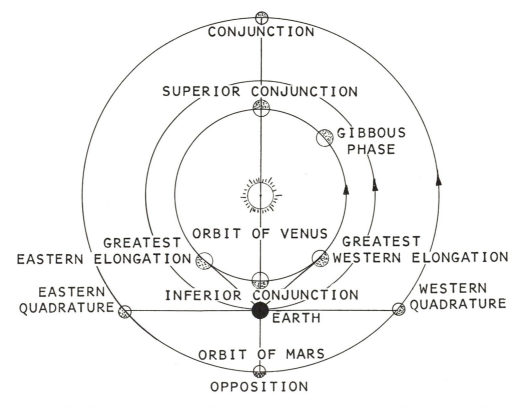

Aspects of the planets: the positions shown for Venus are characteristic of the inner (inferior) planets. Those shown for Mars are typical of the outer (superior) planets.

Planetary Motions

at sunrise; at eastern quadrature it is overhead at sunset. All of the superior planets behave in the same way.

In general, the planets appear to move eastward among the stars. The motion is hard to detect for the outer planets, but Mercury, Venus, and Mars noticeably change position from one night to the next. A phenomenon which greatly puzzled the ancients is that occasionally a planet appears to hesitate in its eastward flight through the stars, then actually begins to move backward (westward). After a period of time (which varies from planet to planet) it once more resumes its eastward motion. This apparent change of heart on the planet's part is called *retrograde motion*. The same thing happens when, in an automobile on a long, straight road, you catch up to and pass another car. For a moment the other auto seems to be moving backward. After it has dropped astern, however, it once again appears to move in your direction. So it is with the planets. We catch up with Mars at opposition and our greater speed makes Mars appear to drop back relative to the background of the distant stars. Quite the reverse is true at conjunction. Now Mars is traveling in the *opposite* direction and at this time has the greatest apparent speed through the stars.

Mars's retrograde motion may cover nearly 20° of the heavens and last as long as eighty-one days. As we catch up with Jupiter, however, its retrograde motion is only about half as great, and the effect is progressively less pronounced for Saturn, Neptune, Uranus, and Pluto. This backward motion is not easy to observe for Mercury and Venus since they are in the direction of the sun (at inferior conjunction) when the motions are most marked. The sky is not dark and there are no visible stars for reference points.

Because of the varying motions of the planets, they are not usually plotted on star charts. But you can find their positions for any date in astronomical magazines or almanacs. The charts in this book have been designed so you can plot planetary motions easily. Just use an easily erasable crayon or pencil and mark their positions on the overlay which accompanies each chart. The positions of Uranus and Neptune change only moderately from year to year because they are so far from the sun and take such long periods to complete a single revolution. Once you have plotted Neptune, for example, your positions will give you a rough approximation of where to find it on corresponding dates for the following year. On August 1, 1966, Neptune's position was RA 15h 10m, Decl. −15°53′; a year later, RA 15h 19m, Decl. −16°29′, probably well within the range of your finder. For Uranus the change in position is about twice as great.

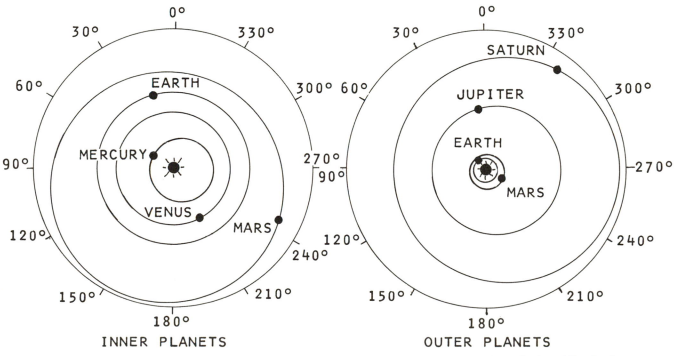

Review of Popular Astronomy

Heliocentric chart of planetary positions for November 1963. The position of the earth relative to the other visible planets is easy to find from diagrams of this type.

Heliocentric Charts

Heliocentric charts provide possibly the best way to understand the motions of the planets because the orbits of the planets are drawn to scale. Each ellipse is shown with its proper eccentricity and the position for each planet is indicated for a certain date. Using these charts, you can easily see the changes in the planetary configurations such as oppositions, elongations, perihelions and aphelions, heliocentric longitudes, etc. Charts like these are published in several periodicals and are a fine source of information in capsule form.

Observing the Planets

There are several cardinal rules to keep in mind for all successful planetary observations.

1. Don't attempt observations beyond the capabilities of your telescope if you wish to avoid being disappointed. Many drawings and photographs do not include the aperture of the telescope through which they were made. You need a 12-inch instrument to see any markings on Jupiter's satellites or fine detail on Mars. It is hopeless to look for such features through a telescope of smaller aperture.

Restrict your observations to what you have a reasonable expectancy of seeing.

2. Casual observations, no matter what aperture and magnification are employed, are almost useless unless you are content to limit your observing program only to the identification of various objects. For one thing, your eye must be trained to differentiate among subtle gradations of shading and color. For another, seeing conditions usually vary from moment to moment. Of half an hour's observations, possibly only a very few minutes will be really productive. Yet those brief moments are worth waiting for. This is why visual observations over a long period of time result in drawings much more detailed and complete than innumerable photographs of the same object. In planetary observations, the camera can rarely catch that moment of clarity when minute details leap out; the eye is there waiting for it.

3. Don't neglect a variety of optical and mounting accessories. Use filters; vary the type as well as the power of your eyepieces. A drive for your telescope permits you to view the planets as stationary objects rather than elusive apparitions drifting across the field of view. Make use of your finder or setting circles so your time is spent looking *at* an object rather than looking *for* it.

Mercury

Mercury's Vital Statistics		Mercury compared to earth	
Mean distance from sun	36 million miles (.39 AU)	Surface gravity	.36
		Diameter	.39
Nearest approach (perihelion)	29 million miles	Mass	.056
Farthest distance (aphelion)	43 million miles	Volume	.055
Eccentricity of orbit	.206	Density	.93
Inclination of orbit to ecliptic	7°		
Synodic period	116 days		
Sidereal period	88 days		
Rotation period	58.65 days		
Mean sidereal daily motion	4° 5'.4		
Angular diameter	Varies from about 5″ to about 13″		
Magnitude	Approaches at maximum −1.9		

Mercury is perhaps the most difficult of the planets to observe successfully. This smallest planet, never farther than 28° from the sun at greatest elongation, is hidden in the solar glare except at dusk and dawn. Even at these times it is difficult to get a good look because it must be viewed through the dense blanket of the earth's atmosphere.

The synodic period of the little planet is 16.5 weeks, and during 11 of them Mercury is visible

telescopically. Western elongation occupies 6 of the 11, eastern elongation the remaining 5. At these times the planet varies in brightness from −1.9 to about 1, in angular diameter from 13 to 5 seconds of arc, and in phase from crescent to full. The best time to view Mercury is at favorable elongations, when it is farthest from the sun yet relatively near the earth. The most suitable elongations occur when Mercury is an evening star (eastern elongation) in the fall and a morning star (western elongation) in the spring. Probably the minimum telescope aperture is 3 inches, used at a power of about 120. Experienced observers of Mercury don't agree very well on instrumental details, however. If you are looking for detail, fairly high power (150 to 350) and aperture (6 inches to 12 inches) are necessary. Even so, observing anything more than very faint and nebulous markings is a matter of good fortune under the best seeing conditions. Eyes trained by many patient observations may glimpse images similar to the detailed drawings which appear in textbooks and astronomical journals, but the average observer will see little more than an occasional dusky area or what might be interpreted as lines.

Our ideas about Mercury have been changed drastically since 1965 by the discoveries of astronomers using the great dish antenna at Arecibo, Puerto Rico, and by photographs taken in 1974 by Mariner X. For hundreds of years it was supposed that Mercury's sidereal period of 88 days coincided with its rotation time, that the planet had no atmosphere, and that its sunward surface was incredibly hot. It is now known that the rotation time is only 58.65 earth days; that there is a thin atmosphere present; and that, while the surface is undoubtedly hot, it is not uniformly so. (However, an 800-mile crater aptly named Caloris may be one of the hottest places in the solar system.) Mariner X explorations have also revealed that, contrary to expectations, Mercury has a heavy iron core, a

weak magnetic field, and a rather sandy surface. It is heavily pockmarked as a result of meteor impacts, and in this respect it bears a striking resemblance to our moon. As a matter of fact, all the planets out to Jupiter have this characteristic. The great exception is the earth, whose craters are insignificant in size and number.

Viewed against a dark sky, the glare of reflected light from the planet obscures faint markings especially at low magnifications. Increasing the magnification cuts down on glare but it also reduces contrast. For serious observers, therefore, daytime observations are the best. These require well-adjusted setting circles as well as reference to an almanac for the right ascension and declination of the planet.

TRANSITS OF MERCURY

Mercury occasionally passes in front of the sun and appears as a black spot against the solar disk. These events are of great interest astronomically, for they serve as a check on our time-keeping devices, as well as the distance scale of the solar system. The times of four "contacts" are recorded: two when Mercury is tangent externally to the limb of the sun, and the other two when it is tangent internally. These are rare events; there will be only three more Mercurian transits in this century. They will occur on November 13, 1986, November 6, 1993, and November 15, 1999.

Venus

Venus's Vital Statistics		Venus compared to earth	
Mean distance from sun	67.2 million miles (.72 AU)	Surface gravity	.90
		Mass	.81
Nearest approach (perihelion)	66.7 million miles	Volume	.88
Farthest distance (aphelion)	67.6 million miles	Density	.90
Eccentricity of orbit	.007	Diameter	.97
Inclination of orbit to ecliptic	3°24′		
Synodic period	584 days		
Sidereal period	225 days		
Rotation period	243 days *		
Mean sidereal daily motion	1°.6		
Angular diameter	Varies from 10″ to 61″		
Magnitude	−4.4 to −3.3		

* Retrograde, i.e., opposite to that of the earth.

The figures above show why Venus is considered the earth's twin. Any resemblance to our planet, however, ends with these physical characteristics; in all other respects there are vast differences. Most of the information we have about Venus, even now, is largely intelligent guesswork based on telescopic,

spectroscopic, and radar observations, as well as data returned by the Mariner and Venus space probes. Great radio telescopes, such as that at Arecibo, Puerto Rico, are especially useful with respect to Venus because, using radar techniques, they can "see" through its optically impenetrable

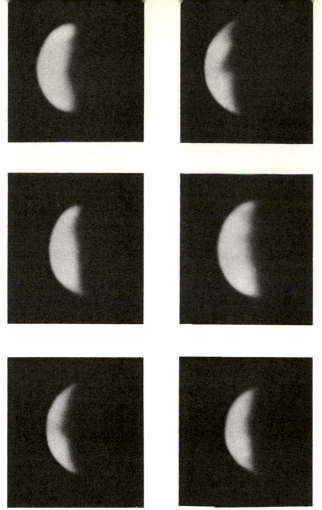

Venus, showing the changes that occur along the terminator.

atmosphere. They show a rough, pockmarked surface, with craters up to 600 miles in diameter, mountains as high as 3,000 feet, and depressions that appear to descend more than 1,500 feet.

Perhaps the most fascinating aspect of Venus is its atmosphere, which is unique in the solar system. Estimates of the surface temperature range from 700° F to 900° F. (In spite of this, ultraviolet photography reveals a brilliant polar cap, usually surrounded by a dark band.) The planet is shrouded with a dense layer of carbon dioxide, which makes up possibly 97 percent of the entire atmosphere. Above that is a mixture of other gases, including carbon monoxide, carbonyl sulfide, hydrogen sulfide, sulfur dioxide, hydrochloric and sulfuric acids, and a small amount of water vapor. Winds circle the planet in four to six days at speeds between 170 and 250 miles an hour. The foregoing estimates are based on information from two Mariner probes that flew past the planet and three Russian satellites that penetrated its atmosphere.

Unlike all other planets, which rotate counterclockwise, Venus turns in the "wrong" direction, taking 243 days for a complete rotation. Furthermore, the planet always presents the same face when it is closest to us. Its slow rotation indicates

an extremely weak magnetic field, a supposition borne out in information supplied by the instruments of passing or impacting satellites.

Venus is never more than 48° from the sun. Because of this it can appear as a morning star and a few months later decorate the evening sky. In the northern hemisphere, Venus remains above the horizon until after midnight in the spring (eastern elongation), but it shines with greatest brilliance when about 35° east or west of the sun. At such times its apparent magnitude approaches −4.4, brighter than any other object except the sun or moon, and can be a naked-eye object even in the daytime. The author once saw an amusing instance of this daytime visibility. During World War II, the gun crews of an Atlantic convoy actually opened fire on our twin planet, mistaking her for a high-flying enemy aircraft. They continued until the escorting battleship signaled that the convoy was in very little danger from this particular "enemy." The writer, who should have known better, was taken in as much as any of the gunners.

Venus's angular diameter varies greatly. Near inferior conjunction the planet appears as a long, thin crescent, 60 seconds of arc from tip to tip. When on the other side of the sun this figure shrinks to 10 seconds of arc and the shape changes from crescent to gibbous to full. The half-phase is called *dichotomy*. Curiously enough, although the relative positions of earth, sun, and Venus are well known and can be predicted accurately for any instant of time, the dichotomous phase does not always appear when expected. It may occur as much as two weeks early or late. The reason for the discrepancy is still not known.

WHEN TO OBSERVE VENUS

Our sister planet can be seen for seven months at each elongation. For the observation of "surface" features, choose the period halfway between western elongation and superior conjunction and, later, between superior conjunction and eastern elongation. When Venus is brightest, the glare of reflected sunlight from the cloud surface makes the planet very difficult to observe. As in the case of Mercury, the eye is flooded with too much light and it is almost impossible to see any detail. The glare can be diminished by several means. The easiest is the use of deep blue or violet filters (Wratten 47B or 48A) or similar low-transmission screens which reduce light scattering and increase contrast. You can also reduce the light-gathering power by decreasing the aperture or by using Herschel wedges or solar diagonals. Try looking at the planet when there are high clouds or generally hazy conditions. You may be surprised at how much more detail becomes apparent.

Lowell Observatory

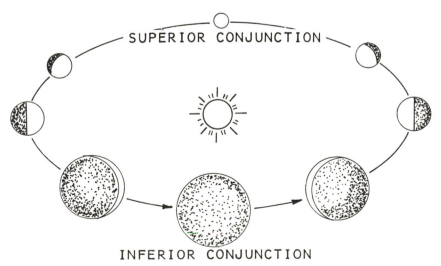

SUPERIOR CONJUNCTION

INFERIOR CONJUNCTION

Top: The various phases shown by the planet Venus. Venus appears brightest near inferior conjunction, when it is a thin crescent. At superior conjunction, Venus appears round in the telescope, but much fainter. Bottom: diagram of the various phases of Venus.

WHAT TO LOOK FOR ON VENUS

Any minute detail is of course impossible; it simply doesn't exist. After all, when observing Venus you are looking at the tops of clouds and any variations are bound to be nebulous. Nevertheless, there are some changes and features that are fun to look for.

1. At the crescent phases, look for changes or irregularities in the cusps. Sometimes they brighten until they take on the appearance of polar caps—almost like those on Mars.

2. At any time the terminator may show bumps, dents, or serrations. Most of these effects are due to our own atmosphere because the irregularities appear and disappear too rapidly to be the result of cloud motion on Venus herself. It is significant that the camera does not record them with as much clarity as the human eye.

3. Bright patches, grayish or dusky shadings, hazy areas, and darkening toward the terminator are often observed on nights of good seeing.

4. The "Ashen Light," a faint luminosity of the dark area beyond the terminator, is always worth looking for. Its nature has never been satisfactorily explained although it may be caused by sunlight reflected from the dense inner cloud layer of the planet.

5. Look for unusual effects of any kind—bright points of light, dark spots, any indication of lines, enlarging of the crescent tips, and persistent changes in the terminator line. Be sure the aberrations you record come from the planet itself; don't be misled by optical illusions or instrumental defects. As Patrick Moore, one of the greatest observers of the moon and planets, once pointed out, "the only observers to record sharp linear markings on Venus are those equipped with inadequate telescopes."

DRAWING VENUS

Before you attempt any drawings of Venus you should become thoroughly familiar with the changing apparent diameter of the planet as it progresses through its phases. Although you can make the drawings all the same size, it is just as instructive (and much more fun) to attempt to draw each phase to scale. If, for example, you decide a ½-inch disk represents "full" Venus, then the crescent phase will be nearly 3 inches from cusp to cusp. Your drawings, when placed side by side, will give you a vivid idea of the changing apparent size of Venus as she whirls in her 225-day trip around the sun.

TRANSITS OF VENUS

Venus, as well as Mercury, can pass between earth and the sun. These transits are extremely rare—the remaining years of the twentieth century will not see even one. The next Venusian transit will occur in June 2004. Those who watch it will find it fascinating because of a curious optical illusion—the atmosphere of the planet seems to draw a strip of blackness behind it as it crosses the sun's limb.

Mars

Mars's Vital Statistics		Mars compared to earth	
Mean distance from sun	142 million miles (1.52 AU)	Surface gravity	.38
		Mass	.108
Nearest approach (perihelion)	129 million miles	Volume	.15
Farthest distance (aphelion)	155 million miles	Density	.72
Nearest approach to earth	35 million miles	Diameter	.53
Eccentricity of orbit	.09		
Inclination of orbit to ecliptic	1°51′		
Synodic period	780 days		
Sidereal period	687 days		
Rotation period	24h 37.3m		
Inclination of axis	24°		
Mean sidereal daily motion	.52°		
Angular diameter	Varies from 4″ to 25″		
Magnitude (maximum)	−2.8		

Exciting to the imagination because of the possibility of some form of living material on its chilly surface, Mars is also the most interesting visually of all the planets. At nearest oppositions its ruby glow outshines everything in the sky except the sun, moon, and Venus. At conjunction it fades to a dull orange, matching the first-magnitude star Aldebaran in both appearance and brightness.

Opposition occurs, on the average, every two years and fifty days, but only at perihelion oppositions can the full glory of Mars be appreciated. Due to the orbital eccentricity of both earth and Mars, these oppositions occur every fifteen and seventeen years. At such times (1954 and 1956, 1971 and 1973, etc.) astronomers point their largest telescopes in the direction of the red planet, for it is only about 35 million miles from the earth, shines with a brilliance of nearly −2.8, and its angular diameter approaches 25 seconds of arc. Mars may, of course, be observed at any opposition for a period of about six weeks before and after the event, but since the difference in distance between opposition at perihelion and that at aphelion is nearly 28 million miles, about all that can be obtained from observations made at the latter is a nodding acquaintance with the planet. In 1965, for example, Mars was about 62 million miles away from the eye-

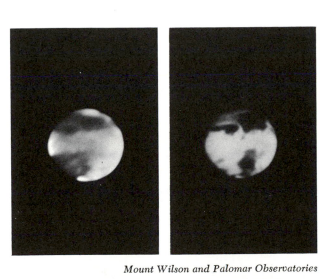

Mount Wilson and Palomar Observatories

Jack Eastman, Jr.

Top: two views of Mars as photographed through the 200-inch Palomar telescope. Bottom: remarkable clarity in photographs taken by an amateur. Syrtis Major and Mare Acidalium are clearly visible in these views of Mars taken on November 13, 1958.

pieces of our telescopes, even though it was in opposition at that time.

TELESCOPE DETAILS

You can see Mars best through 6-inch to 12-inch telescopes. Small telescopes give disappointing views because of their lack of resolution and light-gathering power. A 3-inch telescope, used at 30 to 40 magnifications per inch of aperture, reveals some of the larger surface features of the planet but does not bring out smaller details. Because of the tremors in the earth's atmosphere there is little point in using instruments larger than 12 inches; as far as Mars is concerned the other good qualities of these big telescopes are largely wasted. For serious study of the red planet you will need a good equatorial mounting equipped, if possible, with a drive mechanism. A varied supply of filters is invaluable in bringing out detail. These are discussed below in connection with certain of the Martian features.

THE MARTIAN "CANALS"

Until the explorations of the Pioneer and Mariner spacecrafts in the late 1960's and early 1970's, almost all drawings of Mars depicted a network of straight lines on its surface. These markings, which never showed up in telescopic photographs, were first reported in 1877 by the Italian astronomer Giovanni Schiaparelli. He referred to them as *canali*, or "channels"; but the word also means "canals," and other astronomers who "confirmed" the sightings (notably Percival Lowell, founder of the great observatory at Flagstaff, Arizona) propagated the idea that the lines were irrigation ditches constructed by intelligent beings. Many skilled observers never saw the lines at all, and those who accepted them as real proposed a number of alternatives to the notion of canals. Some said they were fault lines, similar to the Straight Wall on the moon; to others they were tracks made by grazing meteor impacts, or ray systems like the moon's, or line structures formed in the Martian crust early in the planet's history. But in the wealth of photographs and data provided by a succession of space probes, including the close-flying Mariners VI, VII, and IX, there is nothing to support any of these theories. There is certainly no evidence of canals, and in fact there seem to be no straight lines at all. The nature of the often-reported markings remains a mystery.

SURFACE FEATURES

The Pioneer and Mariner flights have, however, given us as complete a picture of the Martian landscape as can be gained without an actual landing

NASA-Jet Propulsion Laboratory

Mariner IX photographs of Mars. Above, a mosaic of pictures of the equatorial region, with the great chasm running horizontally across a superimposed outline of the United States. The chasm is about 2,500 miles long and nearly five miles deep (between three and four times the depth of earth's Grand Canyon). The huge volcano Nix Olympica is below and to the left of the Seattle label.

Left, a part of the great chasm, near the Tithonius Lacus region. The area shown is about 235 by 300 miles.

Lower left, a sinuous valley, which may be an age-old river bed. The valley resembles an arroyo of the western United States, and it has "horseshoes" similar to those of our slow-moving eastern rivers.

Lower right, another of the many ancient "river beds" is shown in a composite photograph of the Rasena region. The valley seen here is 435 miles long.

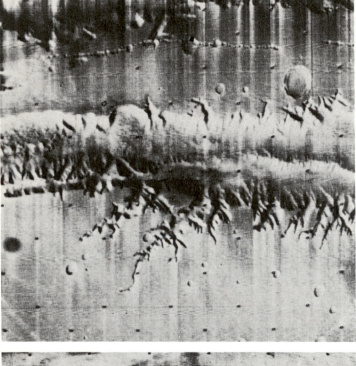

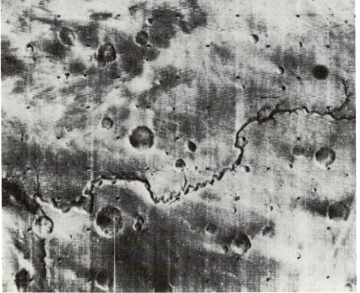

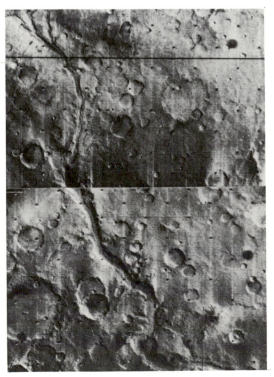

on the surface. They have revealed a surprising variety of features that, despite their enormous size, had gone undetected by earth's most powerful telescopes. Photographs have confirmed suggestions that the planet must be pockmarked by the impacts of meteorites and asteroids; they show craters similar to those on the moon, some with diameters of hundreds of miles. Some areas on Mars are seen to be rather flat and uninteresting, but there are also incredibly rough "badlands," and great basaltic plains in the northern hemisphere that are covered with old craters and still older volcanoes. Some of the volcanoes show signs of continuing activity. One of the largest of them, Nix Olympica, towers 15 miles above the surrounding plains and has a diameter of 335 miles at its base; it would cover most of the region from Portland, Maine, to Lake Ontario. Another, almost unbelievable feature is a great canyon lying along the equator: it is nearly five miles deep, and so long that it would stretch almost across the United States. None of these features can be seen through small telescopes except as varicolored patches and shaded areas, but there are others that show up clearly. Most striking are the polar caps, which seem to be made up of ice with a thin covering of frozen carbon dioxide. When Mars is at aphelion, the north pole is tipped toward the sun; at perihelion, the south pole is in sunlight. As on earth, the polar caps recede during the hemispheric summer, when the ice melts and the carbon dioxide sublimates (passes from the solid to the gaseous state without becoming liquid). The northern polar cap, although smaller, persists longer than the southern cap. Yet there is very little water in the atmosphere of Mars. All of it, if condensed on the surface, would form a layer only 10 to 20 microns deep—less than the thickness of tissue paper.

There is strong evidence that there must have been much more water in the past. The Martian channels, although dry now, are winding and branched, very much like river canyons on earth. One theory of the origin of the vast amount of water necessary to cut the great channels is that the planet must once have been heavily glaciated. Like earth, Mars wobbles on its axis. In the 50,000-year period of a full wobble, the caps would have built up, first at one pole, then at the other. In between, it is suggested, the overall climate of the planet became warmer, the caps melted, and the water evaporated into the thin Martian atmosphere and then fell in torrential rainstorms that deeply eroded the surface.

A supplement to this theory has to do with Mars' orbit. In each of two cycles, one of 95,000 and the other of 2 million years, the planet swings in toward the sun. If either of the inward swings coincided with the warming trend of a precessional

(wobble) cycle, a great deal of water would have been thereupon released to augment the "normal" flooding.

The face of Mars changes constantly. There are some areas which are reasonably constant, such as the formation called *Syrtis Major,* which has a strong resemblance to the great wedge of India. *Mare Acidalium,* in the northern hemisphere, retains its form but not its color. Many of the Martian features depend on the seasons. The color changes, for example, are almost continuous, which is what would be expected if the primitive vegetation is influenced by moisture from the melting polar caps. Observations started when a polar cap has begun to disappear usually show a darkening toward the temperate regions. Mare Acidalium is tan or gray during the winter season, changing to an olive green, then a darker green, as spring progresses into summer. The changes are not uniform, and the eastern half of the sea varies more than the western. As on the moon, the word *mare* is a misnomer. These seas contain no water, at least not on the surface, and their varied colors are the result of sandy deposits of several ores of iron and other materials. The predominating hues, especially in the equatorial regions, are reds, dusky oranges, and browns. Variety of color is, in fact, one of the distinguishing characteristics of Mars, as are the changing hues as the seasons progress.

Most drawings of Mars show well-defined markings. A typical chart includes many names of what appear to be permanent features. Many amateurs are bitterly disappointed when they turn their telescopes toward the dusky planet, having been misled by the detail which appears on the charts. What actually appears in the eyepiece is a series of ill-defined smudges. Yet continued observation reveals more and more detail. The fact is that observing Mars is a matter of practice and of chance. Practice trains the eye to register detail; chance determines what detail is possible at any given observation. The use of filters enhances contrast and aids in the resolution of detail. For a beginning, use an orange (Wratten 21) filter, or a deep yellow (Wratten 15) to enhance the possibility that you may catch a momentary glimpse of canali, which darkens the sea areas. A red filter (Wratten 25) will sharpen the contrast between the seas and the surrounding areas but it will also absorb the green color of the maria surfaces. To see this most clearly, try a light yellow (Wratten 8) filter.

THE MARTIAN CLOUDS

Mars's escape velocity (3 miles per sec) is low compared to earth's, and the fast-moving molecules of the lighter gases have long since departed. In addition, most of the oxygen has combined with surface materials. The atmosphere is unquestionably very thin—about as thick as ours at 55,000 feet. Spectroscopic evidence shows carbon dioxide, a small amount of water vapor, and almost no oxygen. It is likely that a great percentage of the Martian air is nitrogen. A man might exist in such thin air from the point of view of sufficient pressure on his body, but he would have to wear an oxygen mask. He would not need as much of this life-giving gas as on earth because the low surface gravity— a two-hundred-pound man would weigh only about seventy-five pounds—requires correspondingly less exertion and a lower metabolic rate.

THE MARTIAN MOONS

Certainly the strangest little objects in the whole solar system, the two moons of Mars will rarely be seen by the amateur unless he possesses a 16-inch telescope, and then only at favorable oppositions. The closest satellite, Phobos, appears at a maximum angular distance of only 25 seconds of arc from the parent planet. Deimos is just over 62 seconds away. Phobos is 14 miles in diameter and Deimos only six; each shines with a magnitude of about 12. Phobos, at a distance of about 3,700 miles above the surface, rises in the west and sets in the east 4½ hours later. Deimos is much more leisurely be-

Two sketches of Mars using 12½-inch Newtonian, 120X, with yellow filter. Left: August 26, 1956. Right: August 31, 1956.

However thin the atmosphere, it certainly contains clouds. Some twelve to fifteen miles above the surface are the "blue" clouds—not really blue but designated this way because they are best seen in blue light. These are probably made up of ice crystals, like our cirrus clouds. Dark blue filters (Wratten 39) show these very well. Ordinarily, when you use a blue filter on Mars only the clouds can be seen, for the atmosphere seems to be opaque to blue light. Sometimes, though, you can see all the way to the surface for periods which may last as long as ten days. Such "holes" in the Martian atmosphere seem to coincide with oppositions, for reasons which are not understood. Below the blue clouds, yellow-gray ones are seen periodically. These are dust storms, with winds of up to 250 miles an hour that may blow for weeks. A massive storm, repeatedly photographed by Mariner X in November 1971, gave scientists an unexpected opportunity to study at close range the circulation patterns of the Martian atmosphere. Dust appears everywhere on Mars, and seems to be thicker there than on any other planet. In some of the older craters it forms dunes as high as 1,000 feet.

cause of its greater distance (12,500 miles). Its period is about 30 hours, or 5½ hours longer than it takes the planet to turn on its axis. Thus the little moon (from Mars it would appear only a little brighter than Venus does to us) remains in the sky for 2½ days. The earth may one day have its own Phobos and Deimos, but these will be home-made, not natural satellites as are the Martian moons. Compared to our own moon these little objects are indeed insignificant. Both could be dropped into one of the smaller Martian craters, like marbles into a heel-print in the mud.

DRAWING MARS

In spite of the detailed and extensive drawings made by professional and amateur alike, there is still much to be learned about the main features of the planet. The Mariner IV photographs gave us more information in its short passage across the planet than had been learned in all of the forty-five close oppositions since the invention of the telescope. There is still wide variation in what observers think they see on its dusky surface. Recording variations in the appearance of the larger features can be an interesting and rewarding hobby. Because close oppositions occur only every fifteen and seventeen years, the hobby should be more active at these times. Yet in these brief periods, you can record changes in color, size, shape, obscuration of detail due to clouds, or any other significant departure from the usual appearance. Mars turns on its axis only 37 minutes slower per day than earth. A surface feature that appears in the center of the Martian disk on one night will therefore appear at the same place 37 minutes later the following evening. This means that the same feature will be visible each night over a period of about two weeks. After this it will disappear, but again become visible about three weeks later. Thus an observer has plenty of opportunity to become familiar with the characteristics of any feature and can spot any marked changes which occur.

The angular diameter of the planet varies considerably as Mars swings around the sun, but at opposition is large enough so that a 2-inch drawing is about the right size for recording detail. In making a drawing, the same techniques used in lunar drawings can be employed. It is usually most convenient to indicate the position of the terminator first (if the planet is in the gibbous phase) then sketch in the main features, and finally include detail. Color is a problem. Making a colored sketch while at the eyepiece of a telescope is almost impossible. One way out of the dilemma is to mark in abbreviations for color variations as long as a consistent and unvarying system is used.

Since the same features will appear night after night, you will end up with a series of drawings of one particular aspect of the Martian surface. Each one should have notations showing date, time of beginning the sketch, time of ending, magnification used, seeing conditions, the type and aperture of your telescope, and the Martian longitude and latitude of the area under observation.

The Asteroids or Minor Planets

Bode's Law predicts a planet 2.8 AU from the sun. Instead, circling the sun at varying distances in the space between the orbits of Mars and Jupiter are several thousand chunks of matter known as the asteroids, or minor planets. Varying in size, none is large in the astronomical sense. Nobody knows their actual diameters (except in a few cases), except for estimates based upon the amount of light they reflect. The largest, Ceres, is supposed to be between 425 and 480 miles in diameter, while the smallest known are less than a mile thick, too small even to have assumed spherical shapes. If the asteroids are the debris from a ruptured planet, it too must have been very small for their total mass has been estimated to be only about $\frac{1}{1,600}$ of that of the earth. They could all be piled up on the state of Texas with some overflow into the surrounding area.

There are about thirty asteroids whose magnitudes are brighter than 10, but only one, Vesta, can be seen with the naked eye. Unless you know exactly where to look, finding them is difficult. As an example, after the first four had been discovered in the early 1800's the German astronomer Hencke searched for fifteen years before finding another. Now they number in the thousands. At first each was named upon its discovery, then as the list grew too long they were assigned numbers. When the officially numbered list grew beyond 1,623, astronomers more or less gave up in disgust. They are still being found—a few visually, most as streaks on photographic plates exposed for other purposes. In this connection they have become such a nuisance that they are sometimes referred to as the "vermin of the heavens."

Although they are nothing much to look at once found, searching for asteroids can be an enjoyable pastime. Information concerning the positions of the four brightest (Ceres, Pallas, Juno, and Vesta) can be found in the *Observer's Handbook* and in the *Nautical Almanac*. Ephemerides for many others are occasionally published in the current astronomical journals or can be obtained directly from the Cincinnati Observatory Minor Planet Center.

The great majority of the minor planets are found between Mars and Jupiter. Most of them have orbital eccentricities less than that of Mercury, inclinations to the ecliptic of less than 10°, and periods of three to eight years. The exceptions are interesting. There are two groups of asteroids which move in the orbit of Jupiter, one leading and one following the great planet. Because these were originally given Homeric names, they are called the Trojan asteroids.

The nearer asteroids are even more interesting. Pallas darts above and below the ecliptic at an inclination of nearly 35°. Icarus has a very eccentric orbit. When closest to the sun it is only 19 million miles away, but then moves from this scorching position to one well beyond Mars at aphelion. Hidalgo never comes as close to the sun as Mars, and when farthest away shifts to a point in the orbit of Saturn. Some of the more eccentric asteroids miss the earth by only an astronomical whisker at perihelion. In 1936 Adonis passed the earth at a distance of only 1.34 million miles, and the following year Hermes skimmed past only a half million miles away. It is even possible for one or more of the asteroids to pass between earth and the Moon on their way around the sun. In case these figures sound alarming, the chance of an actual collision is only about a million to one.

The First Ten Minor Planets
(*In order of brightness*)

No.	Name	Magnitude	Diameter*	Period (years)	Eccentricity of orbit	Inclination of orbit
4	Vesta	6.1	240	3.63	.089	7.1°
1	Ceres	6.8	480	4.60	.076	10.6°
2	Pallas	8.0	280	4.61	.234	34.8°
7	Iris	8.4	104	3.68	.231	5.5°
6	Hebe	8.5	106	3.78	.204	14.8°
15	Eunomia	8.6	145	4.30	.187	11.8°
8	Flora	8.8	77	3.27	.157	5.9°
9	Metis	8.9	135	3.70	.124	5.6°
29	Amphitrite	9.0	113	4.08	.074	6.1°
20	Massalia	9.2	112	3.74	.144	0.7°

* The actual size of the asteroids is based upon their brightness and is uncertain. The figures given here are estimates.

Jupiter

Jupiter's Vital Statistics		Jupiter compared to earth	
Mean distance from sun	484 million miles (5.2 AU)	Surface gravity	2.66
		Mass	318
Nearest approach (perihelion)	460 million miles	Volume	1,312
Farthest distance (aphelion)	507 million miles	Density	.24
Nearest approach to earth	372 million miles	Diameter	
Eccentricity of orbit	.0484	equatorial	11.2 (88,700 miles)
Inclination of orbit to ecliptic	1°18′	polar	10.4 (82,800 miles)
Synodic period	399 days		
Sidereal period	11.86 years		
Rotation period			
System I (equatorial regions)	9h 50m 30s		
System II (temperate and polar regions)	9h 55m 41s		
Inclination of axis	3°		
Mean sidereal daily motion	4′.8		
Angular diameter (opposition)			
equatorial	47″		
polar	44″		
Magnitude (maximum)	—2.5		

Jupiter is often called the "amateur's delight" because of its everchanging surface, its large angular size and brightness, and the never-ceasing variations in the positions of its moons. Its greatest attraction, perhaps, is that it is almost as enjoyable when viewed with small instruments as with larger ones.

The great planet takes almost twelve years to make a complete circuit around the sun, and so is in opposition approximately every thirteen months. Even at the most favorable opposition it is over a third of a billion miles away. Yet the surface features as well as its oblateness can be clearly seen at any opposition. The flattening of the great ball gives some idea of the tremendous rotational speed.

You will become very conscious of Jupiter's rapid spin when you attempt to sketch its features. In twenty minutes the planet will have turned enough to make you wonder if you are still drawing the same object.

As with Venus, we see only the upper atmosphere of Jupiter. But whereas the Cytherean atmosphere is a comparatively thin shell of gases, the Jovian one may extend all the way to the core, varying only in density. It is fairly certain that what we see in our telescopes are shifting bands of methane (CH_4) and ammonia (NH_3), mixed rather liberally with hydrogen and helium. The first two are very

The expanded equatorial region of Jupiter shows up well in this photograph, taken at the gibbous phase. The Red Spot is at the left; the dot to the right is the shadow of the moon Io.

Jupiter through a 12½-inch reflector, focal length 113 feet. An amateur photograph, this view shows excellent detail.

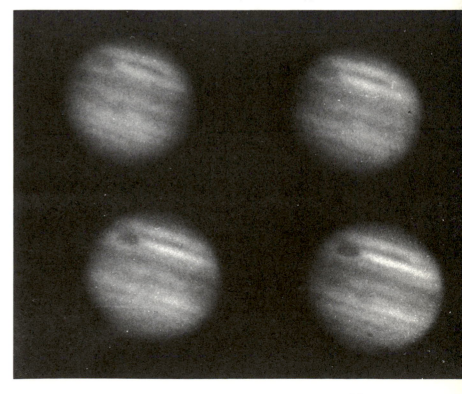

likely in the frozen state, although there are probably some quantities of their vapors in a sort of snowflake form, like the cirrus clouds in our own atmosphere. The surface is very cold, about −200° F, and the interior very hot (the tremendous pressures inside the planet create temperatures as high as 18,000° F). The area in between seems to be in constant turmoil. Jupiter produces more energy than it receives, and constantly emits powerful radio waves.

SURFACE FEATURES

The observer is first impressed by the presence of dark bands which circle the planet. Close observation reveals three to eight of these bands, depending upon the seeing conditions, the aperture of the telescope, and the apparent conditions on the surface of the planet. Astronomers refer to the dark bands as *belts* and the lighter areas in between as *zones*. Nomenclature of belts and zones is that used on earth, equatorial, tropic, temperate, and polar, with subdivisions of each zone. The most conspicuous belt is the heavy one just below (north of) the equatorial zone. Belts and zones alike are irregular—pocked with light and dark spots, streaks, and patches. Sometimes they are very prominent; sometimes hardly visible.

The belts are elongated clouds produced by the rapid rotation of the planet. Certainly there is little solid material present, for the equatorial regions of Jupiter rotate a little more rapidly than those to the north and south. The Jovian "day" at the equator is about five minutes shorter than elsewhere. The difference in rotational period is the basis for a further classification: the temperate and polar regions are called *System II*, and the more swiftly rotating equatorial regions, *System I*. Each system has its own longitude measurements in order to keep track of the relative positions of the everchanging planetary features.

Embedded in the south tropical region is the Great Red Spot, an oval area some 20,000 miles long and 8,000 miles wide. The Spot, which was definitely red in 1878, is no longer highly colored. Now it appears more as an indentation in the planetary surface, darker than the surrounding area and containing an even darker hollow, visible only at good seeing conditions with relatively large telescopes. The Great Spot also changes markedly in appearance and position. In 1961 its normally pale color deepened to a dark orange; a year later it appreciably lightened. Its longitude in System I has been increasing in recent years, and its size and shape vary as well. There is much speculation about the nature of the Great Red Spot. Having persisted for at least a century—possibly longer—it is probably made up of solid material floating in the highly compressed gases below the Jovian clouds.

Three large white oval areas which appeared in the south temperate zone in 1939 are conspicuous because their edges create shallow bays against the dark line of the south temperate belt. Their average length is about 20° of Jovian longitude and they are roughly about one third as wide as they are long. These are very nearly the dimensions of the Great Red Spot. The white ovals rotate faster than other System II objects, having circled the globe at least seventeen times more than other features of the belt since their discovery.

Few of the surface features of Jupiter persist for very long. The longest on record (exclusive of the Great Red Spot) was the South Tropical Disturbance, a dark area which lasted for thirty-eight years (1901–1939). It is unusual for any features to remain visible for more than two years; some last for only a few hours.

OBSERVING JUPITER

1. Telescopic details. You can do useful and interesting work with almost any telescope that is

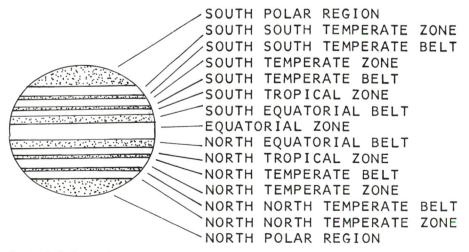

Jupiter's belts and zones.

3 inches or more in diameter. Of course the larger the aperture, the greater the resolving power and amount of detail which can be spotted. For low powers, orange (Wratten 21) or yellow (Wratten 8–12) filters reduce glare and increase contrast. Sometimes a blue filter (Wratten 82A) helps with the limb areas. It is best to start with low power to give the "general" view of the planet, then increase the magnification up to the limit of your telescope and the seeing conditions. Daylight observation of Jupiter is possible, provided that you use a deep red filter to reduce light intensity. Under these conditions you can use high magnifications and still retain good definition. Polaroid filters are also effective when the planet is at quadrature.

2. Transits. Systems I and II differ in rotation by about five minutes, but this difference is far from uniform for all the belts. Because each belt and zone has its individual features—dents, bumps, light or dark spots and patches, and so on—the period of the belt can be found by timing the appearance of an object from one transit to the next across the central meridian. If you keep a log which has spaces for time entries, the belt or zone observed, and a description of each object, the periods of several belts can be determined simultaneously. The average period of the planet is about 9h 53m, so you will probably not observe two successive transits of the same object on the same night. You will therefore have to wait for some multiple of the rotation period before observing again. For example, if you let one night and one hour (a total of about 49 hours) pass before your next observation, the planet will have rotated five times during the interval and the objects will again be near the central meridian. Now you need only divide the total time elapsed between observations by five in order to obtain the period for any given object.

3. Color. Compared to Mars, most observers fail to notice any striking color differences on the Jovian surface. Yet color variations do exist, although on a more subdued scale. The planet itself has a yellow-orange tinge, the larger belts often appear brownish-red, and the dusky shading of the polar regions is bluish. Any individual belt will exhibit changes of color with changes in longitude, usually variations of brown-red and gray. From time to time reddish streaks will appear; the edges of depressions or other features or markings will show orange tints a bit darker than the surrounding areas.

4. Changes in the surface features. Jupiter is in constant turmoil. Spots, streaks, colors, and patches appear and disappear on its vast surface. The belts, although they retain their relative positions, vary in intensity and width. Irregularities continually modify the belt and zonal edges. This is why Jupiter is perhaps the most fascinating of the planets to watch, and why keeping a consistent record of any changes is so important.

5. Drawings. Because Jupiter is definitely elliptical in shape, drawings of the planet must be done on blanks which duplicate the ellipse. The shape of the planet, while difficult to do consistently in free-hand sketches, is easy to reproduce mechanically.

Make a loop of thread such that when it is stretched into a double strand it is exactly 1.35 inches long. Now imbed two pins .75 inch apart in a heavy piece of cardboard. Place the loop of thread over the pins. Using a sharp pencil and keeping the thread taut at all times, draw a line around the pins. The result will be an ellipse whose major (long) axis will be just over two inches in length. The ratio of major to minor axes will be 14 to 15, which duplicates the relative dimensions of Jupiter as it appears in your telescope eyepiece. Using sharp scissors, carefully cut along the line. You can use this elliptical form to inscribe ovals on your drawing pad.

Shade the ellipse carefully as for a moon drawing. A sharpened ruby eraser can be used to create zones; the remaining shaded areas represent the belts. Darkening certain areas and lightening others gives a good rendition of the spots, patches, and streaks of the planet's surface. Drawings of Jupiter must be done quickly because of the rapid rotation, so you cannot spend too much time on detail. Twenty minutes is perhaps the maximum for any one drawing; half this time is even better for complete accuracy. Before attempting to draw the whole planetary surface, practice by working on sections—an individual belt or two.

6. Jupiter's satellites. Four of the thirteen satellites of Jupiter are observable in amateur telescopes. Of the remaining nine only one, Amalthea, has a name. The rest are designated only by Roman numbers. A few hundred miles in diameter, they are visible in large telescopes only.

Visible Moons of Jupiter

Satellite number	Name	Diameter (miles)	Mean magnitude	Synodic period
I	Io	2,020	5.5	1d 18h 29m
II	Europa	1,790	5.7	3d 13h 18m
III	Ganymede	3,120	5.1	7d 4h 0m
IV	Callisto	2,970	6.3	16d 18h 5m

With a little practice you can learn to recognize and follow each of the four visible moons. Callisto, the dimmest, is a dull bluish gray; it is farthest from the planet. Ganymede, the largest and brightest of the four, is distinctive because of its rosy orange hue. Io, a straw-colored dot near the parent planet, is probably the easiest to find. And Europa, smallest of the four, is readily identified because it is the only one which appears white in the telescope. Of course none can be identified by its apparent distance from Jupiter since they all transit the planet's disk. But when spread out in a line on one side of the planet the sequence is usually (but not always) Io, Europa, Ganymede, and Callisto.

The owners of large telescopes (12 inches and up) can pick up markings on Ganymede, whose appearance is something like that of Mars even to "polar caps." When seeing conditions are at their best, smaller telescopes sometimes reveal a dark equatorial belt on the little moon. The remaining three satellites show no markings at all in amateur-sized instruments.

The rapid motion of the Jovian satellites, rather than color or features, is their main attraction. They cross Jupiter's vast face, swing away at varying distances, then disappear behind the great planet. When outlined against a dark belt they can easily be seen in transit, but when the planetary background is a zone they are difficult to pick out because of lack of contrast. Often both the satellite and its shadow can be seen. Before opposition, the

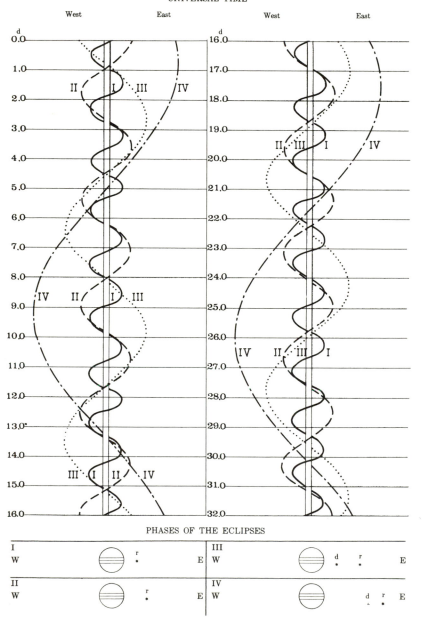

CONFIGURATIONS OF SATELLITES I–IV FOR DECEMBER

UNIVERSAL TIME

PHASES OF THE ECLIPSES

American Ephemeris and Nautical Almanac

Configurations of Jupiter's Galilean satellites for December 1974. I, Io; II, Europa; III, Ganymede; IV, Callisto.

shadow precedes the satellite across the disk, while the reverse is true after opposition. As seen in an inverting telescope from the Northern Hemisphere, the motion is from right to left, which corresponds to their westward direction of motion. Of course when they are on the far side of Jupiter, the moons move from west to east, or left to right.

Following the Jovian satellites from night to night is a pastime which has been enjoyed by multitudes of amateur observers ever since the time of the greatest amateur of all, Galileo. Various publications print diagrams showing the configurations of these whirling balls of matter from night to night. (See the diagram opposite.)

Saturn

Saturn's Vital Statistics

Mean distance from sun	886 million miles (9.54 AU)
Nearest approach (perihilion)	835 million miles
Farthest distance (aphelion)	938 million miles
Nearest approach to earth	742 million miles
Eccentricity of orbit	.056
Inclination of orbit to ecliptic	2°29′
Synodic period	378 days
Sidereal period	29.46 years
Albedo	.42
Rotation period (equatorial)	10h 14m
(temperate regions)	10h 38m
Inclination of axis	27°
Mean sidereal daily motion	1′.8
Angular diameter (opposition)	
equatorial	19″.5
polar	17″.5
Magnitude (maximum)	−.2

Saturn compared to earth

Surface Gravity	1.14
Mass	95.2
Volume	763
Density	.12
Diameter	
equatorial	9.5 (75,100 miles)
polar	8.5 (67,200 miles)

Ring system (each ring is about 10 miles thick)

Name	Diameter	Width
Ring A (outer)	169,300 miles	20,000 miles
Cassini's Division	149,000 miles	3,500 miles
Ring B (middle)	145,500 miles	33,000 miles
Ring C (Crepe Ring)	112,500 miles	20,000 miles

Distance from planet surface to Crepe Ring— 9,000 miles

Second largest and perhaps most spectacular of the planets, Saturn is so distant that opposition occurs only two weeks later each year. Distances of a few million miles can be visualized by most observers, but when we consider the vast reach of space that separates us from Saturn—nearly three quarters of a billion miles—we are surprised that we can see any detail at all on the ringed planet.

Saturn is similar to Jupiter in many respects. Its atmosphere is composed of methane, ammonia, hydrogen, and helium, as is Jupiter's. But because of a lower temperature (−300° F as compared to −200° F), the ammonia is mostly in the solid state

and does not appear so distinctly in our spectroscopes. Both planets whirl rapidly; Saturn takes about twenty-five minutes longer for a rotation. Both are oblate because of the terrific tangential velocity of particles in the equatorial regions, Saturn being the flatter of the two. Each has many satellites—thirteen for Jupiter, ten for Saturn. Neither is very dense. Jupiter would sink slowly in an earth-ocean large enough to contain it, Saturn would float. Both planets are banded by elongated clouds and, compared to earth, both are huge.

Saturn, again like Jupiter, has varying speeds of rotation for different zones. North tropical zone

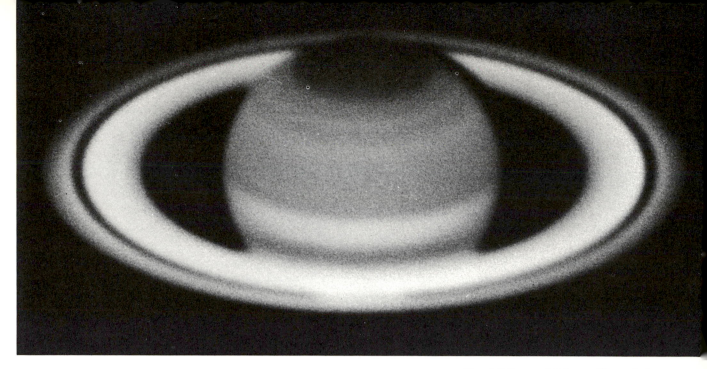

Mount Wilson and Palomar Observatories

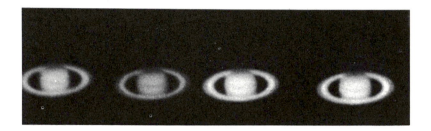

Jack Eastman, Jr.
Above: Saturn photographed through the 100-inch telescope at Mount Wilson. Left: Saturn photographed through a 12½-inch amateur telescope.

objects seem to rotate in a period of about 10h 38m while those of the equatorial region move more swiftly, the accepted figure being 10h 14m. None of these figures is exact since different features in the same zone vary in rotation time by as much as thirty seconds. The assumption is that the Saturnian atmosphere is in a fluid state.

Saturn is unique among the planets in one most important aspect. Nowhere else in the solar system do we find flat surfaces; curves are the rule. Saturn's rings have billions of square miles of perfectly level surface. The outer ring (Ring A) alone covers about 6 billion square miles. The composition of the rings has been a subject of debate since their discovery; the latest evidence suggests they are made up of ice (mostly water, with some ammonia), in chunks that may vary from less than an inch to 140 feet in diameter. Although the rings are thousands of miles wide, their average thickness is believed to be less than ten miles.

SURFACE FEATURES

There is not much detail to be seen on the globe itself. Part of it is obscured by the ring system, but in the visible sections there are somewhat the same features as on Jupiter—light oval spots, belt irregu-

larities, projections, dark areas, and curiously intertwined lines called festoons. These objects are faint compared to similar features on the larger planet. There are no large semipermanent markings such as Jupiter's Great Red Spot.

THE RINGS

There are two main rings, easily distinguishable and separated by a relatively narrow interval called Cassini's Division. This is a true space, not just dark obscuring material, for stars shine through it with undiminished brightness. Another, much narrower band, Encke's Division, is sometimes visible in the outer ring. Look for it about seven tenths of the distance from inner to outer edge. The middle ring (Ring B) is the widest and brightest area in the ring system. Almost obscured between it and the bright ball of the planet is the third or Crepe Ring. This one, called Ring C, is so unsubstantial that the globe shows through it. It is often missed by observers; small wonder when one considers that astronomers looked at Saturn through their telescopes for 140 years before anyone noticed it was there.

The rings, like Saturn's equator, are tipped at an angle of 27° to the plane of the ecliptic. The sidereal period of Saturn is nearly thirty years, and as the planet moves around the sun it moves around the earth also. This has the effect of changing the inclination of the rings relative to us. At one point in the orbit we see them tipped up, fifteen years later they have changed until they are tipped down at the same angle. At the middle point of the gradual change we view them from the side, or edge on. At this point they nearly disappear. This is not surprising because we are looking at the edge of a disk about ten miles thick from a minimum distance of three quarters of a billion miles. At these times more of the surface of the planet is exposed to view, its oblateness becomes very apparent, and we can see Saturn's moons more clearly since the rings now reflect no light. Edge-on views occur at fifteen-year intervals dating from 1966.

OBSERVING SATURN

Almost any telescope will disclose that Saturn has a ring system. To see any detail in the ring system or on the surface of the planet at least 3 inches of aperture are needed. Many observers, having seen drawings and photographs made using much larger instruments, are disappointed when viewing the Saturnian rings through their own telescopes. Wide variation in the image is the rule, not the exception. Galileo, looking through a 2½-inch, 30-power refractor thought he saw *three* planets, while Cassini, using a telescope of the same aperture but at 90 power, discovered the ring division which made him famous. Today's amateur-built telescopes are better in all respects than these historic instruments, and some fine drawings are possible with four- to six-inch reflectors. In general, however, the larger the aperture, the more interesting Saturn becomes to watch.

It is best to begin your viewing with low powers and work up to the highest which can be usefully employed. The filters suggested for observing Jupiter will increase the contrast of delicate shadings.

Accurate transit timing is quite difficult because of the vague surface details on Saturn. Here is another area of service for the patient amateur, who in this case must be ready for disappointment. Objects seen clearly at one observation may be nowhere in sight the next time you look for them, only to reappear at some subsequent time. At this point you must convince yourself that you are looking at the same feature, especially if there is some discrepancy in the expected time.

SATURN'S MOONS

Unlike Jupiter's satellites, Saturn's moons all have names. Moon-hunting around Saturn is as much fun as the same sport near Jupiter—perhaps more so because of the greater challenge. The list given below may help in your search, particularly if you supplement it with information from current astronomical magazines, the *American Ephemeris*, and,

American Ephemeris and Nautical Almanac

SATELLITES OF SATURN, 1974

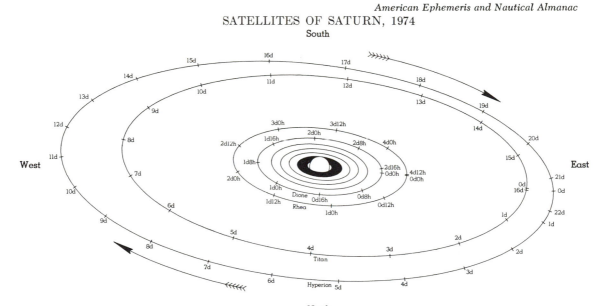

APPARENT ORBITS OF SATELLITES I–VII, AT DATE OF OPPOSITION, DECEMBER 23, 1973

	NAME	MEAN SYNODIC PERIOD			NAME	MEAN SYNODIC PERIOD	
		d	h			d	h
X	Janus	0	18.0	V	Rhea	4	12.5
I	Mimas	0	22.6	VI	Titan	15	23.3
II	Enceladus	1	08.9	VII	Hyperion	21	07.6
III	Tethys	1	21.3	VIII	Iapetus	79	22.1
IV	Dione	2	17.7	IX	Phœbe	523	15.6

after you have tried it for a few months, your own logbook. The chances are that you will not be able to find all of them, but at least five of the nine satellites can be picked up in telescopes of modest aperture and are easy to identify. Mimas, Hyperion, and Phoebe are very difficult because of their faintness. You may catch a glimpse of Enceladus when it is farthest from the parent planet.

DRAWING SATURN

Sketching the flattened globe and ring system can be rather difficult unless you have a good sense of perspective. The relative dimensions of the planet itself are 112 to 110, *i.e.*, the major axis of the ellipse is this much longer than the minor axis. The rings vary from almost straight line objects (1966) to reasonably fat ellipses (1973). Their dimensions for every four days throughout the year are given in the *American Ephemeris*. In 1962, for example, when the rings were about half open, the planet could be represented by a 60° ellipse (1 × ⅞ inch), while Ring A was more nearly a 15° ellipse (2¼ × ⁷⁄₁₆ inches). Plastic stencil ellipses can be obtained readily from any shop which deals in artist's supplies or mechanical drawing aids.

Ring B is always the brightest, Ring A almost as brilliant, but the Crepe Ring is practically indistinguishable except against the ball of the planet. Be careful that you don't confuse the shadow of the rings on the globe with surface markings. The highest powers your telescope and the atmospheric conditions will permit are necessary for detail either on the planetary surface or in the rings.

Saturn's Moons

Number	Name	Diameter (miles)	Distance from Saturn (miles)	Inclination of orbit to plane of the rings	Period (days)	Magnitude	Comment
I	Mimas	300	116,000	1°31′	.94	12.2	Not easily seen.
II	Enceladus	460	148,000	0°1′	1.37	11.9	Difficult, but possible
III	Tethys	600	183,000	1°6′	1.89	10.5	Easy in 3″ telescope
IV	Dione	600	235,000	0°1′	2.74	10.6	Easy in 3″ telescope
V	Rhea	810	327,000	0°21′	4.52	10.0	Easy in 3″ telescope
VI	Titan	2,980	759,000	0°20′	15.9	8.4	Any telescope
VII	Hyperion	100(?)	920,000	0°10′	21.3	14.3	Very difficult
VIII	Iapetus	500(?)	2,213,000	14°33′	80	10.8–12.3	Brightest when west of the planet
IX	Phoebe	100(?)	8,053,000	150°4′	550	14.0	Difficult. Moves in retrograde motion.
X	Janus	250	99,500	0°1′	.85(?)	13.0	On edge of Ring A; seen only when rings are invisible.

Uranus

Uranus's Vital Statistics		Uranus compared to earth	
Mean distance from sun	1.78 billion miles (19.2 AU)	Surface gravity	1.07
Nearest approach (perihelion)	1.70 billion miles	Mass	14.6
Farthest distance (aphelion)	1.87 billion miles	Volume	59.0
Nearest approach to earth	1.61 billion miles	Density	.28
Eccentricity of orbit	.047	Diameter	3.9 (29,900 miles)
Inclination of orbit to ecliptic	46′.3		
Synodic period	369.7 days		
Sidereal period	84 years		
Albedo	.93		
Rotation period	10h 45m		
Inclination of axis	98°		
Mean sidereal daily motion	0′.60		
Angular diameter	3″.8		
Magnitude (maximum)	5.7		

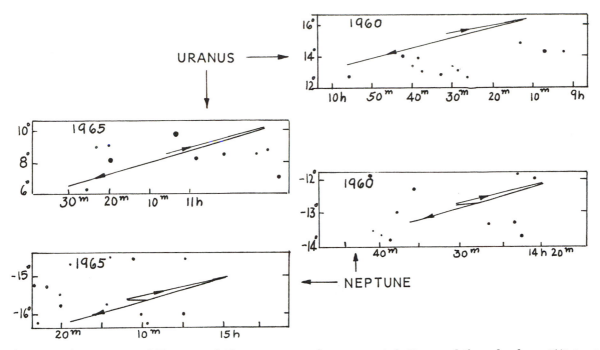

Change in the positions of Uranus and Neptune over a five-year period. Uranus shifts only about 1½° in right ascension, 5½° in declination; the shift for Neptune is even less.

Uranus is of very little interest telescopically. No detail is apparent on its pale greenish surface; the observer sees only a tiny disk of about 4 seconds of arc in diameter. Once its position has been determined, however, it is easy to locate and can be seen with the naked eye on a dark, clear night.

But as an exercise for the imagination Uranus is perhaps the most fascinating of the planets. Lying on its side, so to speak, it rolls along its orbit for part of the long journey around the sun, gradually seeming to turn its axis forward until one of the poles points in the direction of motion. This change takes place over a period of 21 years, one quarter of Uranus's orbit. In another 21 years the planet completes another quarter turn and is halfway around the sun in its long trek; 42 years and a half turn later it is back at its starting point. Of course this "turning" of Uranus is only apparent; actually its axis always points in the same direction and only *appears* to turn relative to its position in its nearly circular orbit around the sun.

During the 84-year journey the polar regions experience four 21-year seasons; a long winter of complete darkness, a spring in which the sun rises in the west and sets in the east (another peculiarity of Uranus is that it rotates in the "wrong" direction), a summer of constant daylight and an autumn which duplicates the spring season. The summer daylight might be a little disappointing to earth dwellers, for the sun shines on Uranus only about

⅟₃₆₈ as brightly as it does on our planet. It would have the appearance of a very brilliant star shining against a dark blue sky. The Uranian atmosphere seems to be mostly methane, a gas which absorbs all of the solar spectrum except the blue rays. If blue is the color of coldness, it is particularly fitting for Uranus because the temperature here is probably well below −300° F.

THE MOONS OF URANUS

Uranus has five satellites, all of which revolve in the plane of the planet's equator. Only two of them, Titania (III) and Oberon (IV) are bright enough to be seen in an 8-inch telescope. The remainder require much larger apertures. When Uranus presents its equator instead of a pole toward us, the moons appear in a vertical line. For those who have the patience to wait, the satellite orbits turn with the planet; the satellites describe concentric circles around Uranus whenever the planet presents a pole. This unique arrangement will next occur in 1987.

The moons Ariel (I), Umbriel (II), and Miranda (V) are distinguished by beautiful names and small diameters. It is small wonder that amateur-sized telescopes cannot pick up these tiny objects; like the larger members of the Uranian system they are so far away that light takes 2½ hours to cross the gulf separating us at opposition.

Neptune

Neptune's Vital Statistics		Neptune compared to earth	
Mean distance from sun	2.8 billion miles (30.1 AU)	Surface gravity	1.4
		Mass	17.3
Nearest approach (perihelion)	2.77 billion miles	Volume	60
Farthest distance (aphelion)	2.82 billion miles	Density	.41
Nearest approach to earth	2.68 billion miles	Diameter	3.5 (27,700 miles)
Eccentricity of orbit	.008		
Inclination of orbit to ecliptic	1.8°		
Synodic period	367.5 days		
Sidereal period	164.8 years		
Albedo	.84		
Rotation period	14(?)		
Inclination of axis	29°		
Mean sidereal daily motion	0'.36		
Angular diameter	2".5		
Magnitude (maximum)	7.6		

Neptune is even less interesting than Uranus telescopically, which is indeed faint praise. It can be seen as a point of light with small instruments, but at least 6 inches of aperture are needed to show a planetary disk, and then only under high magnifications and good seeing conditions. Of course no surface details can be seen. In composition, size, and temperature it is practically a twin of Uranus. But it rotates more slowly and its axial inclination, only about 30°, is closer to earth's than that of its "twin."

Neptune's moons are more interesting than the planet itself. Triton is the largest satellite in the solar system, so large (about 2,300 miles) and so massive that it may even have an atmosphere. It circles close to the parent planet, completing a revolution every six days, but it goes in the "wrong" (clockwise or retrograde) direction. Nereid is tiny, perhaps only 200 miles in diameter, and is distinguished by a very eccentric orbit. Its farthest distance from Neptune is over six times its closest approach. Nereid of course cannot be seen in an amateur's telescope, but Triton may sometimes be glimpsed in an 8-inch as a speck of light close to the planet.

Pluto

Pluto's Vital Statistics		Pluto compared to earth*	
Mean distance from sun	3.66 billion miles (39.6 AU)	Surface gravity	.30
		Mass	1.10
Nearest approach (perihelion)	2.8 billion miles	Volume	.18
Farthest distance (aphelion)	4.6 billion miles	Density	.46
Eccentricity of orbit	.25	Diameter	.59
Inclination of orbit to ecliptic	17°		
Synodic period	366.7 days		
Sidereal period	247.7 years		
Rotation period	6d 10h		
Mean sidereal daily motion	0'.24		
Magnitude (maximum)	14.5		

* Rough estimates based on inconclusive data.

A pale yellow planet which is so small and so far away that it requires at least 10 inches of aperture even to see it at all. Only the Palomar giant telescope can reveal the disklike appearance of the little planet; others show a starlike spot of light. But the enthusiastic amateur who wants to see all the planets might spot this fifteenth-magnitude object in the constellation Leo. It moves through the stars at a rate of 14.4 seconds of arc a day or 1°.5 a year. This is indeed a leisurely pace, for it will not return to the point where it was discovered in 1930 until the year 2178. For those who prefer time on their hands, living on Pluto might satisfy the requirement. The day is almost 6½ times as long as ours, and the Plutonian year lasts through some 14,200 of these long days.

CHAPTER VIII

The Stars—
Single, Double,
Variable

We have already discussed stars in general. Now we must talk about them in more detail and explore the things you can expect to see with your telescope.

In the first place, no matter how large the telescope, how carefully it is focused, or what magnification is used, no star ever appears as a disk. Indeed it would require some thirty feet of aperture to show anything more than a point of light for even the nearest stars. Many amateurs lose interest in individual stars because they think there is nothing to be seen except color and brightness. Yet these are the very things which excite the great majority of observers. The stars do yield a rich variety of colors: glittering blue-white, emerald-green, turquoise, orange, ruby, red, or just plain yellow. Some are so bright they produce dazzling diffraction patterns all over the field of view; others can hardly be detected except on nights of special seeing. Still others amaze us with their changes of intensity over periods of time. They appear singly, in pairs, multiples, clusters, or great masses which completely fill the eyepiece. On nights when the atmosphere is turbulent, they may dance in the field like animated jewels; a few hours later they may shine in still and brilliant clarity.

The number of really bright stars is surprisingly small. Only twelve are brighter than magnitude 1, and when the limit is increased to magnitude 3 or brighter, we can add only 131 more to the list. The ancients—Chaldeans, Arabs, Greeks, Romans—knew all these bright stars as old friends, gave them names and descriptions, and recognized many hundreds of them, both bright and dim. Many of the names and their meanings are lost now, but some

still remain. Of course, since astronomers have extended the list of known stars to some 500,000 of magnitude 10 or brighter—perhaps two billion of all magnitudes—it is impossible to name them all.

Knowing the name of a star and, if possible, the meaning of the name,* changes our whole attitude toward it. The star is no longer just a bright twinkle in the sky, but it becomes an old friend. We can refer to it as 225550 if we are interested only in its position, or as 32000 if we wish to imply that we know where to find it in a star catalog, or as Alpha Piscis Austrini if we are picking it out of constellation. But if we think of it as *Fomalhaut* (The Fish's Mouth), somehow we are making astronomy a matter of personal interest rather than a mere cataloging of heavenly objects. This is why the list of 234 stars in the star atlas starts with the names of the stars instead of their numbers.

Double Stars

Throughout history it was believed that most stars were single. Stars consisting of two or more associated bodies were thought to be rare. But now, far from the belief that double stars are a rarity, some authorities think that probably half the stars are of this kind.

What is a double star? Actually there are two different kinds. Those which simply *appear* close

* The delightful book called *Star Names and Their Meanings* has been reprinted by Dover Publications. It was written in 1899 by Richard Hinckley Allen, and has lost none of its charm through the years.

together but are not because one is farther out in space than the other, are called *optical doubles;* such pairs have no physical connection with each other. Stars which actually revolve around one another, or around a common center of gravity, are called *binaries.* There are three categories. Those which can be distinguished from one another by telescopic means are called *visual binaries.* If the pair is so close together that their dual nature can be determined only by the spectroscope, they are called *spectroscopic binaries.* Finally, if the stars revolve around their common center in such a way that they eclipse one another, they are known as *eclipsing binaries.*

The visual binaries vary tremendously in their apparent separation. Some are several minutes of arc apart, some only fractions of a second. All appear as single stars to the naked eye, but they can be separated telescopically if the aperture is great enough and the seeing conditions are sufficiently good. The resolving power of a telescope, as measured by the Dawes' limit formula—the smallest angular separation of two stars that a given telescope can resolve—equals 4.56 seconds of arc divided by the aperture in inches. For a few typical small-telescope apertures, the values are:

Aperture (inches)	Resolving power (seconds of arc)
2	2.28
3	1.52
4	1.14
5	.91
6	.76
8	.57
10	.46
12	.38

These figures are based upon exceptionally good seeing conditions, moderate brightness of the component stars, and about equal magnitude. You will be indeed fortunate if your telescope performs as well as this.

Most double-star observers are too ambitious at the start, choosing pairs close to the resolving power of their telescopes. You should begin with pairs whose separation is about double this figure, then attempt to narrow the gap. Use all the magnification your telescope will yield—at least fifty per inch of aperture. The definition of the image is of no concern. If you have a Barlow lens, use it. Otherwise, to obtain the required magnification you will have to use short-focal-length eyepieces, which are hard on both eyes and patience.

Double-star observing is a favorite pastime of many amateurs because it provides a test of the theoretical resolving power of the mirrors they have ground and polished so painstakingly. Their claims tend to sound like those of fishermen except that the size of the object captured is in the opposite direction. "Splitting" a double star means separating the components to the point where you see two apparent disks barely touching one another. If, instead, all you can see is a shape like a figure eight or an ellipse, give up and try again when the seeing is better. Maybe this time you will see two cleanly separated bodies, to your infinite satisfaction.

Another area of possible exaggeration lies in the reported colors of double stars. The writer, who is not color blind, has difficulty in seeing most of the brilliant hues described in some catalogs. The contrasting colors are very lovely under any circumstances, but don't be disappointed if you see only a reddish tinge when one of the components is listed as a "gorgeous ruby," or a faint blue when the book tells you to look for sapphire. Many color effects are physiological instead of real, as you can demonstrate for yourself. Hold a bright red object in a good light and stare at it for fifteen seconds or so. Then look at a sheet of plain white paper. You "see" the same shape, except that now it is green. Perhaps this is why the faint companion star of red Antares looks green—but on the other hand, maybe it *is* that color.

MEASURING THE SEPARATION OF VISUAL BINARIES

The period of revolution of a double-star system can be used to determine the masses of its components, and so these stars are of great interest to astronomers. The relative distances and positions of the secondary star (the *comes,* or fainter companion) with respect to the primary describe an ellipse when plotted, and this leads to the eventual determination of the mass of each star. Separation and relative position can be found by means of the *filar micrometer.* It is an expensive addition to your telescope at present-day prices—more than $200—because it must be highly precise in its operation. For this reason, too, it is perhaps beyond the skill of most amateurs to construct. The principle is simple: The instrument consists of two fine filaments, one fixed and one movable, placed in front of the field lens of the telescope eyepiece. Change of position of the movable filament is controlled by a calibrated drum-and-screw arrangement so the separation of the two filaments can be read to fractions of seconds of arc, thus indicating the separation of the components of the binary. The filaments can also be rotated. When the fixed filament is turned to bisect each star simultaneously, their relative positions may be read on another scale. If a series of position angles and corresponding distances is taken over a period of time, the orbit

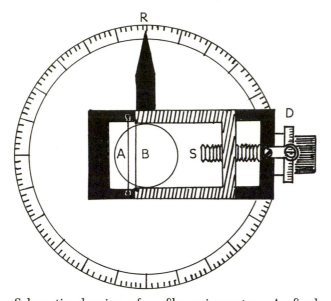

Schematic drawing of a filar micrometer: *A*, fixed thread; *B*, movable thread; *S*, screw; *D*, scale on drum; *R*, relative position scale.

of the secondary around its primary becomes known. To be of any value, these measurements must be very precise and undertaken only when seeing conditions are at their best. Nevertheless, it is a field where the amateur can be of great value, provided he has a fairly large (10 inches of aperture or more) solidly mounted telescope equipped with an accurate clock drive. The large aperture is necessary because the filar micrometer is used with binaries of small separation—2 seconds of arc or less. Photographic measurements work with more widely separated stars, but break down with the close ones because the stars tend to fuse together on the photographic plate.

Filar micrometers are, of course, useful for measurements other than double-star separation. The distance of a comet from a known star, the angular size of a planet or a lunar crater, the angular distance of satellites from their primaries—Jupiter's moons, for example—are only some of them.

DOUBLE STAR LISTS

It is obviously impossible to include a list of any significant number of visual binaries, so we have compromised by listing a sufficient number to provide the observer with a variation of brightness differences, separations, and colors. The positions given will make their location easy in the sky or on the charts at the back of the book.

Variable Stars

For those who tire of simple stargazing or casual observation of moon and planets, variable stars pro-

vide exciting and productive subjects. The sky is full of variables, especially in the region of the Milky Way. There are several types, but most observations are confined to a single class—the long-period variables.

What is a variable star? Essentially it is one whose light intensity changes, periodically in some cases, unpredictably in others. For those that have reasonably regular cycles, we measure the change in brightness from maximum to minimum. For the unpredictable ones, we simply observe the brightness at any given time.

Not all stars whose brightness changes are variables in the sense it is used here. Eclipsing binaries, for example, change in brightness because, as they revolve around one another, the nearer star cuts off the light from the farther one. Algol, in Perseus, is a case in point. Its magnitude changes from 3.2 to 2.1 and back to its original value regularly. The whole cycle takes 2 days, 20 hours, and 48 minutes.

To measure brightness without precise and expensive equipment, we use the human eye, together with nearby stars whose magnitudes have already been measured accurately, and make comparisons. For most of the known variables the American Association of Variable Star Observers (AAVSO) publishes charts of the variable and its surrounding stars with their magnitudes. We shall say more about these charts later.

Why should the amateur be interested in variable stars? First, because this is a field where almost any telescopic equipment, from binoculars to the latest model catadioptric instruments can be used. And second, because a study of the variable stars is an area in which the amateur can make a real contribution to astronomical knowledge. Except in a few cases, all that is known about variables is that they pulse; exactly why is still a matter of speculation. Even those stars whose periods are known still exhibit variations within the cycles themselves. The brightness changes by a sort of "start and stop" progression, and when we plot the change in intensity against time, we get a jagged line instead of a smooth curve. The irregular variables behave even more erratically, flaring and dimming without any apparent rhyme or reason. In short, variable-star observing is full of surprises, and completely "normal" behavior is the exception rather than the rule.

TYPES OF VARIABLES

1. Long-period variables. These have an average period of 280 days from maximum to maximum, although some require only half this time to complete a cycle and some much more. Differences between maxima and minima average six magnitudes, but again the individual differences are great. For the most part, these stars are reddish or orange in color. But when the variable is very faint, color is some-

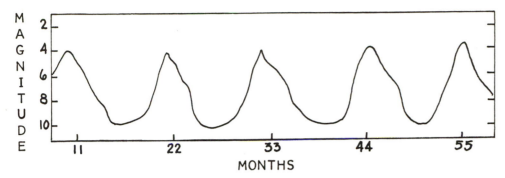

Changes in brightness of the long-period variable star Mira (Omicron Ceti).

times hard to distinguish, so this cannot always be used as an identifying characteristic.

2. Short-period variables. Cepheid variables take their name from Delta Cephei, the first one of this class discovered. There are two subclasses: the "classical" type in which the period averages 5.6 days and the "cluster" type (so named because they appear often in globular clusters) whose period averages 13½ hours. Again, these times are only the mean of rather large variations. Cepheids do not change in magnitude as much as the long-period variables; the difference in brightness is usually about one magnitude. These stars are of unusual interest because there is a relationship between their periods and their distance from us, and so they can be used as the "measuring sticks" of the universe.

3. Nonperiodic variables. This group contains all the "peculiar" stars, from those which merely behave a little strangely to the awe-inspiring novae, whose changes in brightness must be of cataclysmic origin. Some stars in this group are ordinarily faint, but may flare up at irregular intervals as SS Cygni does. A reversal of such behavior is an attribute of stars like R Coronae Borealis, ordinarily bright, but subject to fading. These stars change through about six magnitudes very rapidly, take a few months to recover, then after a period of several years of steady light, do the same thing again.

Novae are the most spectacular of all variables. An eleventh-magnitude star may, in the space of three days, increase its brilliance seventy thousand times until it shines with a magnitude of −1.5, possibly brighter than any other star in the heavens at that time. Overnight it may start to fade, rapidly at first, then in a period of a few years return slowly to its original dimness. Novae occur frequently in the heavens, but most of them are so far away they attract little attention except among astronomers.

IDENTIFYING VARIABLES

All variables have identifying numbers of six digits to show right ascension and declination, but they also have special letter designations which identify them as variables. The letters are assigned them in the order of their discovery in a constellation, starting with the letter R. Thus the first varia-

ble found in a constellation is designed R ——— (Example: R Andromedae), the next S ———, and so on. After Z has been reached, there are usually still more variables to be named. So astronomers then use double letters, RR ———, RS ———, until all double-letter combinations are used up. If this, too, proves to be inadequate, variable-star namers go back to the beginning of the alphabet, start with AA and work through to QZ. The whole system provides 334 possibilities, but in some constellations even this number is exhausted. At this point the next variable discovered is listed as V335 and subsequent ones are numbered in order. One variable in Sagittarius has the number V1175, and even this is far from being at the bottom of the list! This system of identification is called the Harvard designation because the original work on variable stars was done at Harvard College Observatory. It is now the practice to use both position numbers and Harvard designation when referring to a variable. Thus 001726 T Andromedae means that the position of this star is RA 0h 17m, Decl. 26° N, and that it is the third variable which was found in the constellation Andromeda.

Published lists of variables now include a wide variety of stars from which to choose.* The observer is limited only by the aperture of his telescope. Since there are few other factors to be considered, you can make a list of the variables which fall within the range of your geographical position and the size of your telescope, and start observing. Setting circles are desirable, but not necessary. If you have a good finder and a set of the variable star charts which can be obtained at cost from the AAVSO chart division, you need nothing else.

The AAVSO Charts

There are several types of these charts designed for telescopes of varying aperture, each drawn to its own scale and orientation.

---

* The AAVSO, 187 Concord Avenue, Cambridge, Mass., publishes a list of some 400 variables in their yearly bulletins. They also publish detailed charts by which the variables may be identified and located. *The Observer's Handbook* also contains a selected list of variables.

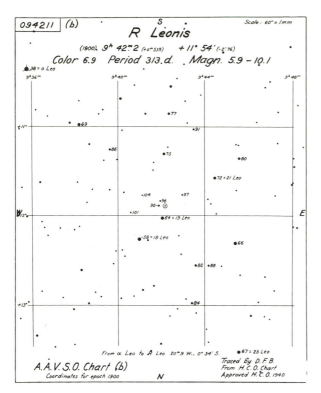

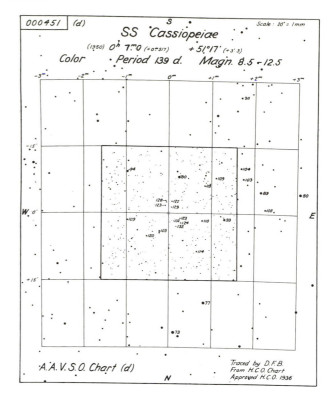

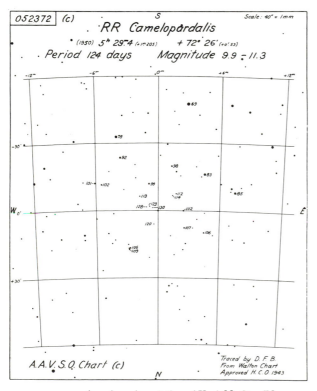

American Association of Variable Star Observers

Examples of charts of variable stars obtainable from the AAVSO.

1. Finder charts. For use with finders in locating the fields in which the variables occur. They include stars down to eighth magnitude but have no comparison stars.

Chart size:	4.5 inches × 6.5 inches
Scale:	1° = 10 mm (about ⅖ inch)
Area covered:	10° × 12°

2. Type *a* charts. For use with field glasses. The stars appear on the charts as they do to the naked eye, *i.e.*, the field is not inverted for telescopic use. Comparison stars are included.

Chart size:	8 inches × 10 inches
Scale:	1° = 12 mm (about ½ inch)
Area covered:	15° × 15°

3. Type *b* charts. For use with small telescopes (3-inch aperture or less). They include stars as dim as tenth or eleventh magnitude and have comparison stars. The field is inverted for telescopic use.

Chart size:	8 inches × 10 inches
Scale:	1° = 60 mm (about 2⅖ inches)
Area covered:	3° × 3°

4. Type *c* charts. For use with telescopes of 3-inch–4-inch diameter. They show stars to fourteenth magnitude. Inverted field; many comparison stars.

Chart size:	8 inches × 10 inches
Scale:	1° = 90 mm (about 3⅗ inches)
Area covered:	2° × 2°

5. Type *d* charts. For use with larger telescopes: 4 inch-aperture and up. Characteristics are the same as for *c* charts except for scale and area.

Chart size: 8 inches × 10 inches
Scale: 1° = 180 mm (about 7⅛ inches)
Area covered: 1° × 1°

6. Type *e* charts. For use with large telescopes when variables are faint and fields congested. Otherwise similar to *c* and *d* charts.

Chart size: 8 inches × 10 inches
Scale: 1° = 360 mm (about 14⅖ inches)
Area covered: 30′ × 30′

Note the change in scale from type *b* through type *e*. The *b* charts cover a relatively large area of the sky compared to that of the *c*, *d*, and *e* charts. In order to get the most from the charts, you will want to adapt the field of view of your telescope to the field covered by the charts. In other words, use low power (wide field) with type *b* charts, and succeedingly higher powers (smaller fields) with charts of smaller scale.

The orientation of the field is also very important. It can be confusing, for it varies with the optical arrangement of your telescope. But there is a simple rule which will help you orient any chart with any telescope, provided, of course, that the fields of telescope and chart are not reversed. After you have located the field of the variable, usually by means of a bright star in the vicinity, pick out a distinctive configuration of stars as you see them in the eyepiece, then hold the chart in such a way that the same configuration appears in a similar position.

The charts in the back of this book show only a few variables, and these are designated only with a "V." (Using a scale in keeping with the page size prohibited inclusion of variable star designations.) But, if you become interested in observing and recording variable stars, you can mark the designating letters directly on the charts. Thus they will contain only those variables in which you are interested.

FINDING THE VARIABLES

The easiest way to begin observing variables is to start with relatively bright ones such as R Leonis, 094211, so you can use a *b* chart. Let's say it is 1963, when this variable had a magnitude of about 5.8.

The *b* chart shows a fairly bright star, Omicron Leonis, in the upper left-hand corner. Its magnitude is 3.8 (the chart indicates this as 38 to avoid the use of decimal points which might be mistaken for stars), so it is easy to pick up in your finder. The field of your telescope, if you are using low power (about 50) and an eyepiece of apparent field of 50°, is approximately 1°. This means that if you center Omicron Leonis in the eyepiece, the variable will be outside the field. So you move away from the guide star until you have the distinctive flattened parallelogram which appears below R Leonis centered in the finder. Now, when you look through the main eyepiece again, the parallelogram should just about be centered in the field. Three of the four stars of the parallelogram are nearly the same magnitude; the fourth is about 2 magnitudes dimmer. The chart shows that R Leonis is on the opposite side of the figure from this dim star and is part of a small triangle, two points of which are relatively faint, magnitude 9 and 9.6 respectively. You will recognize R Leonis now because it is brighter than the other two and has a reddish tinge.

Now you must decide on its magnitude. Is it brighter than 19 Leonis (6.4) and less bright than 18 Leonis (5.8)? Nobody can say except you. Your final estimate may be that it is much closer in magnitude to the brighter of the two comparison stars. So you enter the data below in your log.

The entries in the log are self-explanatory except the one under the heading "Julian Day." This is a system used for calendar entries for variable stars as well as other purposes. It is based on the number of days which have passed since January 1, 4713 B.C. From the entry in the log, you can see that the number is very large, almost 2½ million. In practice, only the last four digits are used. Julian Day dates are easy to find from tables or calendars prepared for their use. Like other systems (except local time) the Julian Day starts at Greenwich. To adapt local time to a Julian Day system you must first convert your local time to Universal Time. In the example given above, 8:30 P.M. EST is 0130 UT, August 9, which is Julian Day 2438251, August 9. But what about the decimal? For timing variables, which change magnitude so slowly, a tenth of a day is close enough. All this sounds complicated but is really simple in practice—if you are good at arithmetic.

Designation	Julian Day	Date	Magnitude	Comparison Stars	Sky
094211 R Leonis	2438251.1	8 August 8:30 P.M.	5.9	5.8–6.4	Clear

Because variable stars comprise such a vast and ever-changing field, variable-star observers can make a real addition to our knowledge of the processes going on in the universe. These peculiar stars are a manifestation of the evolutionary processes by which stars are born, grow, and eventually die.

The star atlas contains a short list of some variables to use for practice. Try your hand on some of the short-period ones first, then move to those which change more slowly. If you find you would like to pursue this interest further, write to the American Association of Variable Star Observers. This organization will send you all the information you need to become a full-fledged contributor to astronomical knowledge

Quasars, White Dwarfs, Pulsars, and "Black Holes"

These objects are of little interest to many amateur observers because they are beyond the range of small telescopes, but they are so different from the rest of the phenomena in the heavens that they deserve mention.

Quasars (short for *quasi-stellar radio sources*) are very faint, intensely blue galaxylike formations that emit vast outputs of energy and strong radio signals. They were first discovered in the late 1950's with radio telescopes; later, optical images were found that matched the positions of the radio sources. The extraordinary emission lines of quasars puzzled astronomers for a time, but in 1963 it was found that the lines were atypical because they were very radically shifted to red, the longest wavelengths. This extreme red shift has been interpreted as a Doppler effect, that is, an increase in wavelength which indicates the quasars are traveling away from us at incredible speeds. The shifts of some quasars suggest they are receding at about 90 percent of the speed of light, and if this is true, they are about 12 billion light-years away. To be visible at such a great distance they would have to have almost unbelievable brilliance; yet they seem to be little larger than a star.

When the nature of their strange spectra was first explained, quasars seemed the most distant objects ever identified, and their existence was cited as support for the "Big Bang" theory of cosmology —the notion that all the components of the universe were formed at the same time, in the explosion of a great primordial mass. Most astronomers still believe that quasars are very remote, but some have argued that their great speed is illusory and that they are not as distant as was first thought. In fact, there is no really satisfactory explanation of the properties of these mysterious bodies; their real nature is a matter of controversy.

White dwarfs, on the other hand, are well known. They are very small, incredibly dense stars with high surface temperatures but low luminosity; they seem to be surrounded with gas about 60 miles thick, which dims their brilliant light. In a star's life cycle the white dwarf stage corresponds to extreme old age, but it is the fate only of stars whose mass is no larger than 1.2 times that of the sun. As the white dwarf evolves it shrinks to about the size of the earth, and its interior may be a million times more dense than that of the sun. About 3 percent of the stars in our galaxy are white dwarfs; two examples are the dark companions of Sirius and Procyon.

Pulsars, the first of which was discovered in 1967, are rapidly rotating neutron stars, very small but many millions of times denser than our sun. This high density is believed to be the result of a cataclysmic explosion which generated pressure so tremendous that the negative electrons of the atoms were forced into the positive protons of the atomic nucleus, creating neutrons that packed together in an incredibly small mass. Pulsars give off bursts of energy in the form of X-rays, each burst corresponding to one rotation of the star. The rate of rotation is very rapid, varying from two seconds to as much as thirty times a second. The latter speed is that of the pulsar at the center of the Crab Nebula. This star is believed to be one that exploded as a supernova, the light of which reached the earth in the year 1054. Such explosions are rare, and so are pulsars; the few that have been discovered are all in our own galaxy.

The strangest of all celestial objects are the collapsed stars called "black holes." These are composed of densely packed neutrons and have gravitational fields so powerful that no matter, or even light, can escape from them. Obviously, nobody has ever seen a black hole, but they can be detected by their immense gravitational fields and as sources of X-rays. These unusual objects seem usually to be part of an eclipsing binary system—one star visible and a measurable distance from us, the other the black hole itself. The heavy star, with its awesome gravity, pulls gas from the visible star, and the gas emits intense X-rays as it is sucked into the black hole. One such powerful source of X-rays is in the constellation Cygnus. Here the visible star, known as HDE 226868, eclipses its dark companion, periodically interrupting the flow of X-rays.

CHAPTER IX

Celestial Showpieces

Scattered throughout the starry background are thousands of objects for which the amateur and the professional alike search in the dark of the moon. For the most part these objects are relatively faint, which is why a dark, clear sky and the absence of moonlight is important in their location and identification.

It is obviously a waste of time to list all of the celestial showpieces, if for no other reason than that many of them cannot be seen through amateur instruments. Further, most of us are interested only in those which have distinctive characteristics. The groups that follow include as much variety as possible, but the list is not exhaustive. They are grouped and described according to type. Classification of individual objects includes as much detail as possible as to location, size, distance, brightness, on which map they may be found, and the month in which each appears on the observer's meridian.

The Open Clusters

The open clusters are concentrations of stars which appear as loosely arranged groups. They have no particular pattern, but are a distinct unit within the surrounding stars. One characteristic of open clusters is that their member stars all seem to have a common motion. Because they all appear within our own galaxy they are known as *galactic clusters*. The astronomer Otto Struve thinks there are possibly five hundred of these objects in the galaxy, many hidden from our view by dust clouds. Several

Stephen A. Walther

Amateur photograph of the Pleiades (top) and Hyades (bottom). This 15-second exposure was taken on September 28, 1962.

111

The beautiful globular cluster (M.5) in Serpens, photographed through the 200-inch telescope at Mount Palomar.

catalogs list as many as three hundred, of which 70 percent are visible from latitude 40° North.

No two open clusters are alike. They vary in size, distance from earth, number and concentration of stars, and brightness. Some spread over several degrees of arc; the diameters of others can be measured only in minutes. They range from a few hundred light-years from us to a hundred times this distance, sprinkled throughout the vast reaches of the galaxy. Some have less than a dozen stars, others have as many as 350. Several of the open clusters show a very dense concentration of stars. For example, the star density in M.11 (NGC 6705) is about twelve hundred times that of the area of the Milky Way surrounding the sun. On the other hand, some clusters are so spread out that they can be identified as clusters only because their individual stars appear to have a common motion.

A few of the bright, wide-spread galactic clusters can be easily seen with the naked eye, even in bright moonlight. You can always find the Pleiades, Hyades, Praesepe (the Beehive), or the double cluster in Perseus because they are made up of bright, gemlike stars, well spaced and easily distinguished. Some are best seen with slight telescopic aid such as binoculars or wide-field tele-

scopes used at low power. But at least half of the total require high power in varying degrees for the most satisfactory viewing. Many of this latter group are bright, but buried in the glowing background of the Milky Way and thus difficult to find. Still others are so distant and the light from each star so faint you may have trouble resolving them into clusters. In this case, follow the general rule for any indistinct object: wait for the darkest night and the best seeing conditions, be sure your eyes are completely dark adapted, and "sneak up" on the object using averted vision. Looking for faint clusters takes practice. Yet you may be pleasantly surprised at how quickly you can become adept at locating an elusive cluster, and at how much detail you can pick up once you have found it. A list of 62 open clusters is included in the star atlas.

The Globular Clusters

The globular clusters are closely packed, ball-shaped groups of stars. Unlike the open clusters, in which the stellar population may be counted in the scores or hundreds, globular clusters are made up of scores or hundreds *of thousands* of stars. The figure most often quoted as an average is 100,000 stars per cluster. These stars, moreover, are of a different kind than the blue and white members (Population I) of the open clusters. They are old, reddish stars of a class called Population II. It is generally considered that these spherical star groups were formed before the main part of the galaxy.

Again unlike the galactic clusters, the globulars are found outside our galaxy, arranged in a huge,

roughly spherical arrangement which surrounds the plane of the galaxy. Thus they are vastly more distant than the galactic clusters. Some are as far away as 250,000 light-years; none is closer than 7,500. Yet even at these great distances, they shine with considerable brilliance. This is not surprising when we consider that a tenth of a million stars are packed into a ball so tightly that the stars in the central area are perhaps less than a quarter of a

Mount Wilson and Palomar Observatories

M.27, the Dumbbell Nebula in Vulpecula. The photograph, above, was taken through the 100-inch telescope at Mount Wilson. Compare the detail with that of the drawing, below, which was done using a 12-inch reflector.

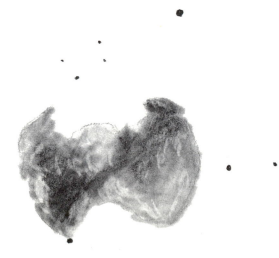

light-year apart. By way of comparison, our nearest stellar neighbor is over four light-years away, and the average distance between the stars in our arm of the galaxy is eight light-years.

The globulars are relatively easy to find. In fact, almost all of the hundred now known were discovered before the end of the eighteenth century. Considering the quality of the telescopes of those days, it should be easy for today's amateur to duplicate the achievement of the early astronomers. The list given in the star atlas includes globulars of the eleventh magnitude or brighter. Some are naked-eye objects: M.13 in Hercules, M.4 in Scorpius, and Omega Centauri in the southern sky are examples.

A glance at photographs of some of the globulars might leave the impression that if you have seen one of them you have seen them all. But this is far from true. They vary in size, in brightness, in stellar concentration, and even in shape. Most of them appear round, but a closer look shows an equatorial bulge somewhat similar to that of the larger planets. Some are very difficult to resolve into individual stars even at the edges where the stellar concentration is less. And although most of them have a bright central nucleus in which it is impossible to distinguish individual stars, a few show separation even at the center.

Owners of small telescopes will find it difficult to convince themselves that the more distant globulars look like anything more than slightly out-of-focus stars. But they will find that the loosely packed, wide-spread balls of stars in the nearer reaches of the heavens are very much worth looking for. For those who have telescopes with 10 inches of aperture or more, globular clusters which in smaller instruments are round, featureless objects will appear to have star streams reaching into space, dark areas, and irregular outlines.

Planetary Nebulae

Once you have located the relatively easy-to-find open clusters and the more obvious globulars, the planetary nebulae will offer a real challenge to the acuity of your vision and your skill in hunting for elusive objects.

These are dim objects, made up of gas excited into luminescence by the radiations from a central star. Their name comes from their planetary appearance since most of them shine with a dim greenish glow, have definite outlines, and are round or elliptical in shape. It is generally accepted that the planetaries are made up of expanding gases from stellar explosions. Indeed, this supposition is borne out by the fact that one of them, the famous Crab Nebula, is the remnant of a great supernova observed by the Chinese in A.D. 1054. The gases in the Crab are still spreading out at the rate of 600 miles per second.

The central star of planetaries is usually very dim. It rarely is brighter than eleventh magnitude, and it is the exception that it can be seen at all. The body, or expanded gas, of the nebula is also faint and has a tendency to blend into the sky background. But once you become accustomed to this you will find it increasingly easy to locate these small remnants of stellar wreckage.

Magnitudes range from 6.5 for the large Helical Nebula in Aquarius, NGC 7293, to 12 for the Little Dumbbell in Perseus. Those dimmer than magnitude 12 are almost impossible to pick up in amateur telescopes unless they are of large aperture.

It is possible that several thousand planetaries exist, even though only a few hundred have been recorded. Most of them are too dim to be seen or are obscured by the great dust clouds of intragalactic space. They are all galactic objects and are usually found quite close to its plane. As might be expected, their distance range is great, from a few hundred to many thousand light-years from us.

Detail in the planetaries is hard to detect. This may be surprising to those whose acquaintance with them is limited to the exquisite photographs taken through the great telescopes of the world. We hope to see the same intricate structure when we peer through our own eyepieces, but for the most part we must expect disappointment. Yet it is possible to see shapes, colors, and some structural detail in many of the planetaries listed in the star atlas. The Ring Nebula in Lyra is an inspiring sight as we look at it across more than two thousand light-years of space whether or not we can see its delicate interior shading or its faint central star. To the author, the Dumbbell Nebula has always looked more like a thickened bone from some prehistoric monster than the shape usually ascribed to it, but this has not lessened its fascination. The Saturn Nebula appears as an indescribably distant replica of its planet namesake, and this is a satisfying view even though more powerful telescopes show up little corpuscles of light here and there over its surface.

Of the planetaries listed in the star atlas, none requires a telescope of more than 4-inch aperture for a satisfactory view, and several can be picked up easily in 7 × 50 binoculars. Only a few of the smaller ones need high power, and for the most part you will be quite happy looking for the whole list through your medium- or low-power eyepieces.

Diffuse Nebulae

Unlike the relatively small planetary nebulae of the last section, the diffuse nebulae are composed

Mount Wilson and Palomar Observatories

Only large instruments will show the intricate detail of the Crab Nebula, M.1. The photograph above was taken through the 200-inch telescope at Mount Palomar, while the drawing below was made through a 12½-inch telescope at 200 power.

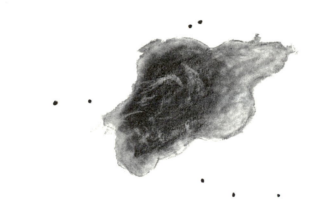

of vast, shapeless clouds of very rarified gas. Hydrogen is the most abundant, but other gases—nitrogen, oxygen, helium—may also be present. These clouds spread through the vast space between the stars in our galaxy. When they are spurred into luminescence by the radiations from the very hot nearby stars or shine because they reflect light from such stars, they are known as bright diffuse nebulae. The word "bright" gives an exaggerated notion of the amount of light they give off, for many are so indistinct that long hours of exposure are needed for their images to register on sensitive photographic emulsions. Only a few are brilliant enough for visual observation through a telescope.

In some cases the gas takes the form of very fine "dust" (for lack of a better word) which is apparently as widely dispersed as the gas clouds, and intermingles with them. When this "cosmic smog," as it is sometimes called, is thick enough, it can completely block off the light from stars lying beyond it. Early astronomers thought the resulting dark patches of sky were holes through the star fields, but actually they are the silhouettes of the obscuring masses of cosmic matter. In this form they are known as dark nebulae. Perhaps the outstanding example is the Horsehead Nebula (NGC 1434) in the constellation Orion.

Some of the most beautiful celestial photographs

115

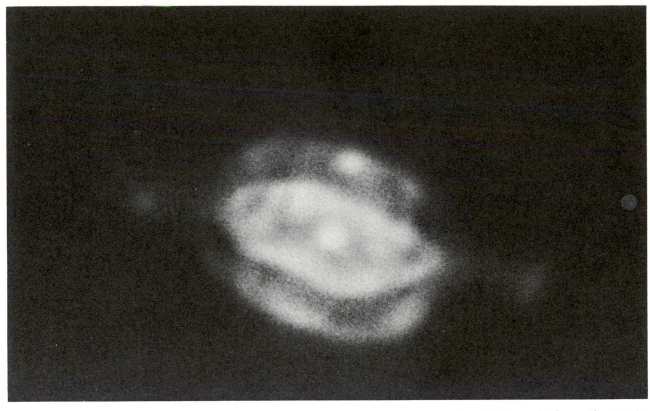

Mount Wilson and Palomar Observatories

The Saturn Nebula in Aquarius, NGC 7009. Photographed with the 60-inch telescope at Mount Wilson.

One of the most spectacular objects in the sky is the Horsehead Nebula in Orion, just south of the star Zeta Orionis. This view was taken through the 200-inch telescope at Mount Palomar.

Mount Wilson and Palomar Observatories

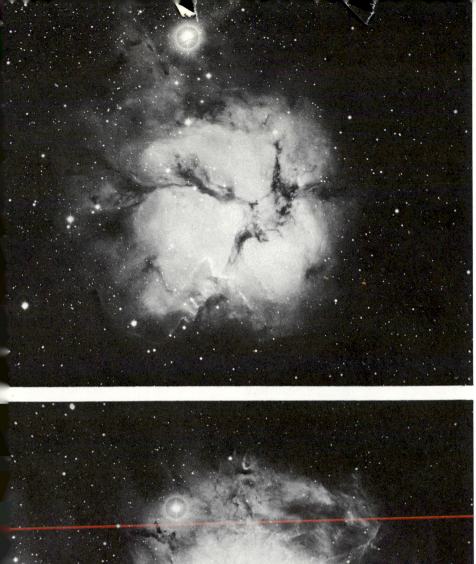

Mount Wilson and Palomar Observatories
A favorite among amateur astronomers, the Trifid Nebula, M.20, can be found in the constellation Sagittarius. This picture was taken through the 200-inch Hale telescope at Mount Palomar. The photograph on page 193 shows this nebula as a part of the star clouds in Sagittarius.

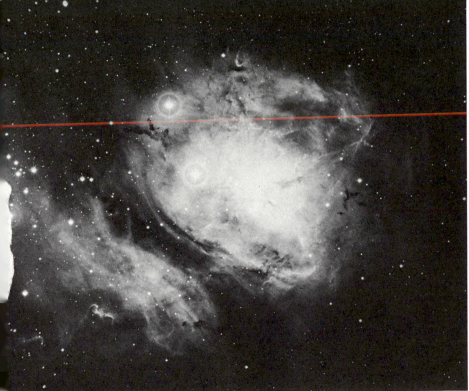

Mount Wilson and Palomar Observatories
The lovely Lagoon Nebula in Sagittarius, M.8. This photograph was taken through the 200-inch telescope at Mount Palomar.

ever taken have the diffuse nebulae as their subjects.* Unfortunately these objects, which appear in such splendor in photographs, require large aperture and wide fields to be seen visually, and even then they cannot compare to their photographs. The lovely colors which appear on the photographic emulsion cannot be seen by the eye. Nevertheless

* "First Color Portraits of the Heavens," by William C. Miller, *National Geographic Magazine*, May 1959.

there are several diffuse nebulae which are very much worth your attention: the Great Nebula in Orion and the Lagoon and Omega nebulae in Sagittarius, among others. A list of the diffuse nebulae is included in the star atlas.

The diffuse nebulae are very large, both in size and in their angular diameter as seen through your telescope, compared to other celestial objects. Most of them are best seen through low-power—wide-

Mount Wilson and Palomar Observatories

This photograph of the famous Whirlpool Nebula in Canes Venatici, taken through the Hale telescope, shows remarkable detail. Note the thin arm of stars extending from the parent galaxy to the smaller one. Although the two separate parts are visible through small telescopes, this connecting arm is very difficult to see.

field telescopes or binoculars—but in some, such as the Trifid and Lagoon nebulae, the intricate detail brought out by higher powers is worth pursuing.

Extragalactic Nebulae—The Galaxies

In the eyepiece of your telescope other galaxies appear as fuzzy patches of light, showing little form and even less detail. Why then do many amateurs seek the distant galaxies with so much enthusiasm? For some, it is the pleasure of overcoming the technical problem of locating and identifying objects so evanescent they can hardly be seen against the sky background, even on dark nights. For others, it is the enchantment of distance and time—the realization that these little patches of light are so far away

that one is looking back through millions of years of history to be able to see them at all.

These indistinct blobs are so far away that their distances are measured in megaparsecs (a parsec is 3.26 light-years and the prefix *mega* means "millions of"). Their light has been traveling across space for more years than have passed since the first forms of life came into being in the primordial ooze of our planet. Each is so large that it contains as many stars as we can count in our Milky Way. Each is a separate universe, separated from all the others by incalculable distances. There are so many their numbers must be counted by many millions, and even then we see only some of them. The remainder are beyond the range of our greatest telescopes.

In spite of the great distances involved, even a moderate-sized telescope (6 inches or less) can

118

Not as spectacular as the Whirlpool Nebula, this spiral in Pisces, M.74, is still a lovely sight. 200-inch photograph.

reveal great numbers of these objects, not of course in the detail shown in time-exposure photography, but certainly enough for you to recognize the various types.

There are at least a thousand galaxies of magnitude 13 or brighter. For the most part, they are the "look-alikes" of the heavens. Because of this, some observers consider it a fruitless task to attempt to find objects whose main difference is their position in the heavens. Yet there are a few whose difference in appearance is great enough to make their visual pursuit a rewarding one.

There are four main classes of galaxies, each divided into subclasses. These are described in the star atlas, together with a representative list of individualists in the family of galaxies.

The Milky Way Star Clouds

Earth and the sun are located about 27,000 light-years from the center of our galaxy, and roughly 13,000 light-years from its edge. The galaxy is disk-shaped, 80,000 light-years across and possibly 10,000 thick on the average. Whenever we look in any direction along the *plane* of the galaxy, we should expect to see star clouds of varying density. Conversely, at right angles to the plane the stars

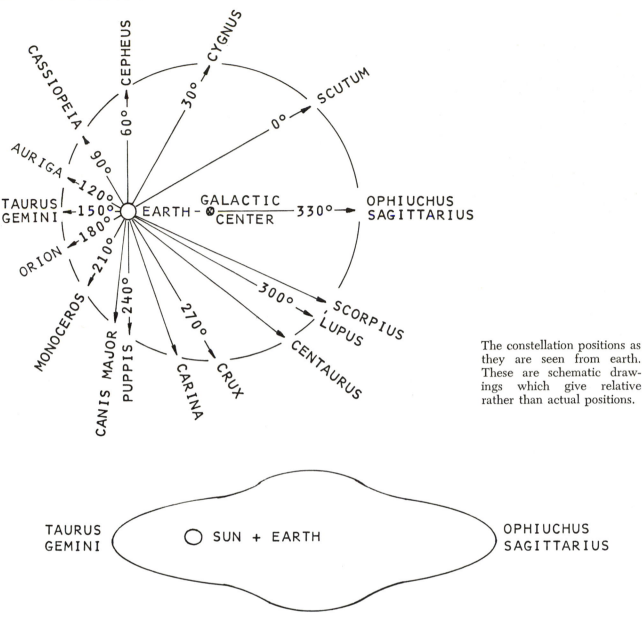

The constellation positions as they are seen from earth. These are schematic drawings which give relative rather than actual positions.

should be sparse and much more widely separated. The greatest concentration of stars is the great band we call the Milky Way. If we look toward Sagittarius, which lies in the direction of the galaxy's center, we see a greater concentration of stars than in any other direction. Taurus is located directly opposite Sagittarius; when we look this way we are facing the edge of the galaxy nearest us. Here, too, we see the Milky Way, although not nearly as great nor as dense as the view toward the center of the galaxy.

Thus the summer Milky Way, as seen from the Northern Hemisphere, is much more spectacular than that of the winter Milky Way. In the evening from June to September we see a long luminous band of stars beginning in the northeast in Perseus

and stretching across the sky through Cygnus to Scorpius in the southwest. The cold winter nights bring the edge of the galaxy into view as a less brilliant band of stars passing through Auriga, Taurus, Gemini, Orion, and finally Canis Major. Unfortunately for northern viewers, the most beautiful part of the Milky Way lies in the southern constellations—Lupus, Centaurus, Crux, Carina—hidden from their view by the bulge of the planet. Here too are found the most intriguing, and certainly the loveliest, star clouds in the heavens, the subgalaxies called the Large and Small Magellanic Clouds (Nubecula Major and Nubecula Minor). These are not part of the Milky Way; they lie outside of our galaxy at a distance of about 170,000 light-years.

The stellar concentration in the Milky Way would

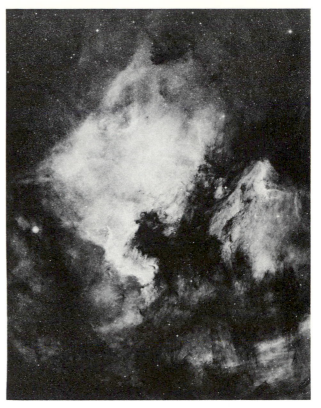

Mount Wilson and Palomar Observatories
The view toward the center of the galaxy: the beautiful star clouds in Sagittarius.

Mount Wilson and Palomar Observatories
Copyright National Geographic Society
The North America Nebula in Cygnus. This wide-field photograph was taken with the 48-inch Schmidt telescope at Mount Palomar.

be even heavier if it were not for the vast expanses of obscuring matter, the cosmic smog mentioned earlier. Sometimes the cosmic dust clouds appear as great dark rifts which cut through the bright background of stars; sometimes they outline the star masses and their attendant glowing gas clouds. In the latter case we observe great patterns which have familiar outlines—the North America Nebula in Cygnus or the California Nebula in Perseus, for example.

The great star clouds of the Milky Way are wonderful objects for binoculars or low-power, wide-field telescopes. On dark, clear nights they are of

endless interest because of their great variety. Vast forms such as the North America Nebula are difficult to see because of their size—several degrees —and because the delineation between light and dark areas is not sharp. But the star clouds are treasure troves of smaller objects—open clusters, multiple-star systems, patches of dark and bright nebulosity, planetary nebulae. A telescopic sweep of the Milky Way from horizon to horizon is an adventure into the immensity of our galaxy, for no other observation really brings home the fact that the stars are literally countless.

CHAPTER X

Wanderers of the Heavens

With the exception of the planets and asteroids, all the objects we have discussed up to now show so little motion across the sky they seem to be fixed in space. Their apparent motion across the sky is due almost entirely to the revolution and rotation of the earth. Moreover (and again with an exception—the variable stars), their appearance changes very little from day to day or year to year.

But there are three types of heavenly bodies whose motion across the sky is appreciable and whose appearance changes constantly: comets, meteors, and artificial satellites. We know, of course, that certain comets return at definite intervals, but at any time we might see a new and previously unobserved comet. We do not even know what the familiar ones will look like when they come back from their long journey through the solar system. We are sure that at fixed times of the year the earth passes through areas of cosmic debris, and at such times we expect a meteor "shower" as a result. But we have no real basis for estimating the number of meteors we may see, and although we know in what part of the sky to look, we are constantly surprised by meteors from unexpected directions. Finally, though many might not consider this a true astronomical pursuit, the ever-changing number of earth satellites comprise a separate field. Watching one of the Echo satellites travel across the sky just after sunset is as much fun as following any other heavenly body. The writer will never forget the excitement of a group of schoolboy astronomers as they watched one of the early Russian satellites (Sputnik II) trace a fiery path across the heavens

on its way to final extinction in the waters of the Caribbean Sea.

Here is another area of astronomy where the amateur is nearly on a par with the professional. Comets are almost exclusively amateur "property" since so many of them have been discovered and recorded by amateurs. Comet Ikeya-Seki of 1965 was discovered by, and named for, an amateur. Meteors, too, are easy to count and record on your charts. With the exception of repeating comets, you have the satisfaction of viewing objects never seen before.

Comets

Even though they are rarely seen, there are millions of comets. The sun, as it plunges through space toward Hercules and Lyra, carries with it a vast cloud of them. This cloud of comets may extend almost to the nearest star, over four light-years away.

Comets are loosely packed knots of matter made up of relatively small amounts of solid material impregnated in fluffy masses of frozen gases. The gases are mostly methane, ammonia, water molecules in icy crystalline patterns (like snowflakes), and what the chemists call "free radicals" composed of carbon, oxygen, hydrogen, and nitrogen atoms arranged in various combinations. In addition, there are very likely heavier materials—chunks of matter ranging in size from fine dust particles to larger rocklike

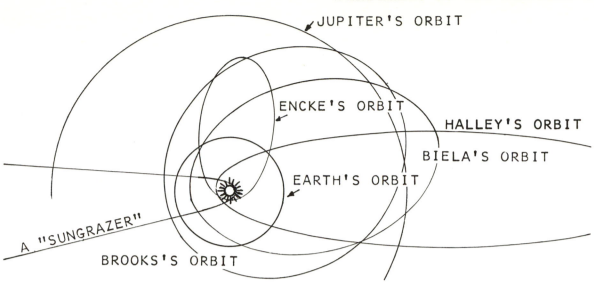

JUPITER'S ORBIT

ENCKE'S ORBIT

HALLEY'S ORBIT

BIELA'S ORBIT

EARTH'S ORBIT

A "SUNGRAZER"

BROOKS'S ORBIT

A few characteristic comet orbits.

objects. These are made up of iron, nickel, manganese, silicon, magnesium, and possibly others.

These knots of matter are in constant motion. As the sun and its family of planets move with and through the great cloud, occasionally one of the cometary masses plunges toward the sun as it is sucked into the solar gravitational field. On the way, it may be influenced by the field of one of the planets, so its approach to the sun may be from any direction. If the comet is traveling very fast, it passes around the sun in a hyperbolic curve. At slower speeds its path is a parabola; at slower speeds still, an ellipse. Most comets travel in either parabolic or elliptical paths, favoring the former by a ratio of about 4 to 3; only a few are hyperbolic. Since parabolas and hyperbolas are open-ended curves, comets following these paths never return. The ellipse is a closed curve and comets with elliptical orbits are likely to be repeaters. But this is not always true, for reasons we give later. In any event, at perihelion the comet passes very close to the sun, usually within the orbit of the earth and sometimes even inside that of Mercury. In the case of elliptical orbits the aphelion distance may be well beyond Neptune or even Pluto. Some of the ellipses may be greatly flattened; others are nearly circular.

Why do we not see more comets? Supposedly there are millions of them in the great cloud, yet recorded history lists only 1,600 sightings, and of these only 670 have been observed closely enough to plot their actual path through the heavens. One reason is that a comet usually does not become luminescent until it is within one or two astronomical units of the sun. The solar radiations are great enough at this distance to warm the frozen gases, and the excited atoms and molecules driven off not only produce their own light, but also reflect that

of the sun. Even then, unless the comet is approaching at a favorable angle as viewed from earth, its faint light may never be seen. Very few comets are naked-eye objects; some of them are even too faint for visual telescopes and are unsuspected until they appear on the photographic plates of the big observatories. So, instead of seeing a great many representatives of the comet cloud, we can count on catching sight of only five or six comets a year, on the average.

It has been estimated that the original cometary body as it emerges from space and heads for the sun may be only a few thousand yards in diameter and may weigh as little as a cubic mile of water. This "tiny" mass remains as the nucleus of the comet, but under the warming influence of solar radiation the outside frozen gas layers expand to tremendous distances, forming a glowing envelope called the *coma*. At the same time, chemical reactions taking place among the free radicals mentioned earlier create heat within the comet itself. The heated gases expand rapidly into the vacuum of space and become extremely tenuous. As the comet streaks toward the sun, the pressure of light and the particles—mostly protons—which constantly stream from the sun force the gas away from the main body of the comet and a tail is formed. This is why the tail constantly points away from the sun.

The comet has now grown to many times the diameter of the earth and its tail may extend for millions of miles. Within the coma, the glowing nucleus may be clearly visible but it is not always so. The expansion of the cometary material decreases its density almost to the vanishing point. In fact, comets at this stage have been described as the "nearest thing to nothing." One evidence of this

Donald J. Strittmatter

Comet Seki-Lines. This 40-second exposure was taken on April 10, 1962.

is that even dim stars can be clearly seen through the tail. In 1886 a comet passed right through Jupiter's moon system without damage to the comet or the moons. However, a direct collision can be disastrous. In 1908 a comet apparently exploded as it entered the earth's atmosphere above a remote section of Siberia, leveling every tree over an area of twelve hundred square miles. At first, the widespread damage was thought to be the result of a large meteorite impact, but data collected by three expeditions to the locality* seem to indicate that the colliding body was a comet. The striking power of a comet must of course be concentrated in its nucleus, for the earth passed right through the tail of Halley's Comet in 1910. However, the chance of a direct collision with a comet nucleus is so remote as to be negligible.

In their passage around the sun, comets leave a wake of meteoric material behind them as long as the luminescent stage lasts. Once around the sun, they recondense and again become invisible unless their entire orbits are close to the sun. In such a case, they are permanently visible. Because of the loss of mass, no comet can ever be considered a permanent member of the cosmos. Even so, some of them return again and again. Halley's Comet, for example, has been observed twenty-nine times; Encke's Comet, forty-five times. In general, comets live uncertain lives. In addition to dissipating their own matter as they swing around the sun, they are also subject to the gravitational field of any planet they may pass near. Thus they may be deflected from a "normal" orbit when passing inside the planet's orbit. Biela's Comet made six successful passes around the sun at intervals of 6.62 years. But during its last two orbits, it broke into two constantly separating parts, each part becoming dimmer as the interval between them increased. Its fragments still remain, for each time the earth passes through what was once its orbit, a meteor shower occurs. Any comet which passes too close to the sun

* "Did a Comet Collide with the Earth in 1908?" Kirell P. Florensky, *Sky and Telescope*, November 1963.

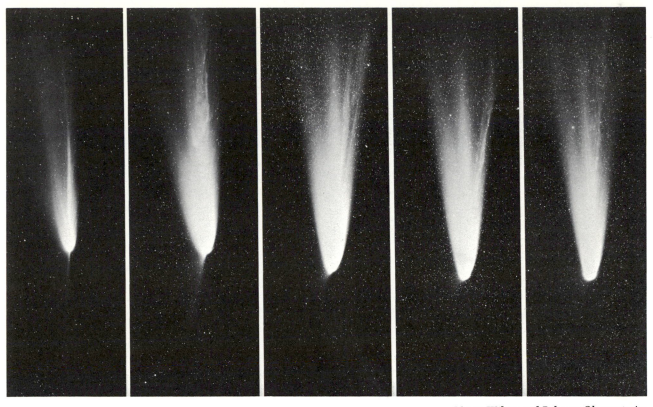

Mount Wilson and Palomar Observatories

Comet Arend Roland, 1957. This series of photographs, taken with the 48-inch Schmidt telescope, shows changes that occurred over a six-day period. (Left to right: April 26, April 27, April 29, April 30, May 1.)

is likely to be broken up because of the terrific forces imposed upon it.

OBSERVING COMETS

Most comets are dim and require some sort of telescope aid to be seen at all. Because they are extended objects, however, low-power wide-field instruments are best. If properly mounted on tripods, 25×100 binoculars are ideal instruments, as are the apogee Moonwatch telescopes used by satellite spotters. These telescopes are 20×120 refractors with a very wide field; 7×50 binoculars work fine, too. Lacking any of these, use your own telescope at its lowest power to obtain as wide a field and as much contrast as possible.

Since comets do not become visible until they are close to the sun, the obvious time to look for them is just after sunset or just before sunrise when the sky is still completely dark. Some of them approach the sun so closely they must be looked for very close to the actual time of sunrise or sunset, and at these times are very difficult to find. Many of those who looked for Comet Ikeya-Seki were disappointed for this reason—the glare of the rising sun obscured the comet completely. Yet the closer a

comet gets to the sun, the brighter it becomes; the length of the tail is also dependent on the comet's distance from the sun. At a distance, the comet may look like an out-of-focus star, a planetary nebula, or an elliptical galaxy. Nevertheless, some comets when first discovered have had well-developed tails and been instantly recognizable.

As comets move toward the sun, the coma around the nucleus expands and the nucleus itself may become brightly visible. At the same time the tail becomes more extensive, possibly splitting into streamers or even separating into blobs of gas. The tail may be straight, curved, or irregular, or (rarely) even have a projection *toward* the sun, as did Comet Arend-Roland in 1956 and Comet Wilson in 1961. As the comet passes around the sun and moves away, the tail disappears, the coma shrinks, the magnitude dims, and finally nothing can be seen. This may take place over a period of weeks or months, depending upon the orbit.

The magnitude of a comet is important but, unfortunately, hard to estimate. However, it can be judged with reasonable accuracy by racking the eyepiece out of focus until the comet and any nearby comparison stars have the same appearance. For such comparisons, the charts of the American

Association of Variable Star Observers are invaluable.

Comets are named in several ways. They usually bear the name of their discoverer or, if old repeaters, the name of the man who first computed the orbit. They are also designated by the year in which they are found. To distinguish them from other comets of the same year, a letter is added which indicates the order of appearance. The comet is given an official designation, once its orbit has been determined, according to the year of its perihelion passage, plus a Roman numeral to show its position in the sequence for that year. Thus the bright comet discovered in 1956 is known as Comet Arend-Roland, 1956h (the eighth comet of 1956) and 1957 II (the second comet to pass around the sun in 1957).

What are the chances of seeing a comet in any given year? On the average, pretty high. 1960 was a great year for these remarkable objects: eight previously reported, nine of the returning-period type, two whose nearly circular orbits made them visible throughout the year, and four new discoveries. Not many years even approach this record, but if you are determined to see a comet, go out and look. Possibly your efforts may be rewarded if you are persistent; you may see a previously reported comet or, if you are very lucky, even discover a new one. But be sure your discovery really is a comet before you telephone the nearest observatory to give its position (in right ascension and declination, or relative to some nearby star). If the most careful examination under all powers of your telescope is unable to convince you that you are looking at a comet, wait twenty-four hours and look again. If the object has not moved during the interval, it is not a comet.

Meteoroids, Meteors, Meteorites

This section deals with objects that are usually not good subjects for the telescope. They are so fleeting that they appear in your eyepiece only as an accidental streak across the field. Yet they are true members of the solar system and, as impressive naked-eye objects, deserve their share of space in any book dealing with astronomy.

Meteoroids are chunks of matter in space ranging in size from tiny particles to boxcars. When one of the smaller particles, the size of a grain of sand or smaller, darts into our atmosphere and is heated to incandescence, we see a streak in the sky called a *meteor*, or "shooting star." Part of the light may come from the glowing meteoroid, but most of it comes from the ionized air particles with which it has collided. At the height above the earth where meteors appear—forty to eighty miles—the atmosphere is very thin and is easily ionized into a

glowing streak. *Bolides* are particles large enough to produce a brilliant flash and leave a trail which persists for some time. Sometimes these are accompanied by an actual explosion which sounds very much like thunder. Finally, if a large chunk gets all the way through the atmosphere and strikes the earth, the object is called a *meteorite*.

METEORS

Because meteors are caused by debris left from the passage of a comet, the tiny particles are moving in an orbit just as the parent comet was and with approximately the same speed. Through the ages, some comet trails have become so widely diffused that their residue fills much of interplanetary space, especially along the ecliptic. On any dark night, then, an observer can expect to see half a dozen meteors as the tiny wandering objects plunge into the earth's atmosphere. But the *total* number that might be seen in any twenty-four-hour period from all points on the earth reaches the unbelievable figure of 90 million. Most of these are *sporadic* meteors in the sense that they don't come from any particular point in the sky. Ordinary meteors vary in brilliance from 5 to 0, but if they are bolides they may appear as brilliant as Venus or even the full moon.

Usually more meteors can be seen after midnight than in the early hours of the evening. As the earth travels around the sun it rotates in the same direction it revolves. When you see a meteor shortly after sunset it is overtaking the earth, whereas before dawn it is meeting the earth head on. Relative to the earth, the pre-dawn meteors are traveling at high speeds—some as high as 45 miles a second—while the post-sunset meteors may be traveling at only 10 to 20 miles a second. Our planet speeds around the sun at 18.5 miles a second, so any meteor moving at a speed less than this would never catch up.

Radiant meteors all seem to come from a specific sky area and are seen when the earth intersects the path of a comet. These meteors may also appear in any part of the sky and seem to have no connection with one another. Yet, if their paths are traced backward, they all intersect in a small area called the *radiant*. You can demonstrate this for yourself. Hold a ruler up against the sky background so that its edge coincides with the path taken by the meteor. There is always enough residual glow so you can do this with accuracy. Check the paths of several meteors and you will become convinced that all have the same origin. This is just what we would expect if the earth were charging through an area littered with cometary debris, and of course the number of meteors seen on one of these occasions should increase greatly. Instead of six or eight a *night*, the

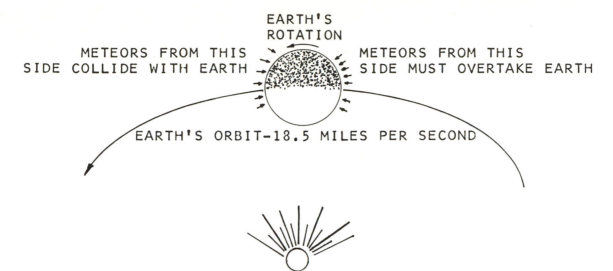

EARTH'S
ROTATION

METEORS FROM THIS
SIDE COLLIDE WITH EARTH

METEORS FROM THIS
SIDE MUST OVERTAKE EARTH

EARTH'S ORBIT—18.5 MILES PER SECOND

SUN

Why we see more meteors after midnight than before.

rate may rise to sixty an *hour*. Some of the great meteor showers of the past have had as many as one thousand an hour.

Meteor showers are usually named for the constellation in which the radiant lies, but sometimes may take the name of the comet which caused them. The meteors which originate in Draco in June are called Draconids. In October there is another shower from the same constellation; these meteors are named for the parent comet and are called Giacobinids. Some meteor showers are very brief, lasting only a single night, but many extend over a period of several days or even weeks. Some occur in the daytime and can be "seen" only on radarscopes. As might be expected, long-lasting meteor showers result when the earth passes through a wide band of debris, and in such cases we should also expect the radiant to shift from night to night. Most of these prolonged showers reach a peak of activity about the middle of the period.

METEORITES AND BOLIDES

Although sand-sized grains of matter burn in the atmosphere, pieces larger than this seem to get through without destruction. These fall to the earth as meteorites. There seems to be no upper limit to their size. The Hoba West meteorite in South Africa weighs 60 tons; the Ahnighito meteorite now on display in the Hayden Planetarium in New York weighs 34 tons. But meteorites many thousand times heavier than this have struck the earth from time to time. The object which created the Barringer crater in Arizona must have weighed at least 12,000 tons (some estimates put its weight at 63,000

tons). Yet the Barringer Crater (4,100 feet across, 600 feet deep) is a baby compared with the three-mile-wide Chubb Crater in Ungava. Strangely enough, medium-sized meteorites survive their impact with the earth, while the monsters are completely destroyed. The smaller ones have a larger surface-area-to-weight ratio, and the atmosphere serves as a cushion to slow their rate of fall. The great ones plunge through with very little decrease in speed, and the heat of impact vaporizes them completely. The resulting explosion must be very similar to that of a fission bomb. Fortunately these are very rare—one estimate is that the chance of a really large meteorite striking a city is less than 1 in 100,000,000. Yet what might happen if one struck a populated area is beyond imagination.

Meteorites fall roughly into three main classes, but there are many subgroups of the primary divisions.

1. Aerolites—the stony meteorites. Aerolites are rarely very large and are made up of earthy materials, silicates, and compounds of magnesium. Imbedded in them are tiny particles of nickel-iron alloys called chrondules. These little particles provide a rough test to determine whether the "stone" you pick up is a meteorite or just a garden-variety rock. Hold it against a grinding wheel for a few moments, then examine the ground surface with a magnifier. If specks of metallic material appear, you may be reasonably sure you have found a meteorite. Aerolites are black when they first arrive on earth, but become brownish after they have weathered. They differ from ordinary stones of the same color by their weight—they are heavier—and their

The Soviet satellite Sputnik II passing through Perseus. The dashed line was produced by holding a card in front of the telescope for 5-second intervals.

smooth surfaces which are similar to pebbles. Most meteorites—95 percent—are of the stony variety.

2. Siderites—the metallic meteorites. Composed of 80 to 95 percent iron, 5 to 15 percent nickel, and occasionally small amounts of cobalt, the siderites pepper the earth in all sizes. The great craters in Africa, Canada, the United States, Russia, and Australia were all gouged out by siderites, yet they also may be as small as an ounce or two. They are usually rough and irregular, with pocked or pitted surfaces. When they first fall they are black, but rust to a mottled brown after being exposed to terrestrial weather. Siderites are always heavy because of their metallic content, but the key to their meteoritic origin is the crystalline markings which appear when a surface is first ground and then etched with acid. The markings are called Widmanstätten figures—patterns of straight lines that intersect to form triangles, parallelograms, and other geometric figures.

3. Siderolites—the iron-stone meteorites. Much rarer than the other two types, the siderolites are spongy arrangements of iron ores in which the spaces are filled with minerals. They have a mottled, often pitted appearance. Like the others, newly fallen specimens are black, but become a yellow-brown upon exposure to the weather.

Any of the three kinds of meteoric material may appear as bolides, and are of the greatest scientific interest when they do because this type of fiery meteoritic display is so rare. The average sky-watcher is lucky if he sees only one of these in his lifetime. Yet meteorites themselves are far from rare; about ten tons of these objects fall on the earth in an average day. At widely separated times in the earth's history, great showers of meteorites have fallen. These rare events have caused greater terror and consternation than a major earthquake.

MICROMETEORITES

On the lower side of the size-weight scale, the tiny particles called micrometeorites can also penetrate our atmosphere without damage. These are literally without number, and fall continually upon the earth to the extent of ten thousand tons daily. It might appear from the size of this figure that the earth is gradually becoming buried under such a smothering mass of material. But this great quantity when spread out over the surface of the earth becomes considerably less impressive. It amounts to four ounces per square mile per year!

Micrometeorites are too small to be seen with the naked eye unless they occur in clumps or groups. Their diameters range from .005 to .0005 inch, and they appear in all conceivable forms and shapes. Yet you can prove their presence very easily. Collect several gallons of rain water or melted snow from your roof. Allow the water to evaporate until only a pint or two is left, then pass a strong magnet through the water. Place the scrapings from the magnet on a piece of glass and examine them under a magnifying lens or low-power microscope. The number and variety of tiny particles you find may be a surprise.

THE ORIGIN OF THE METEOROIDS

It made sense at the beginning of this section to connect comet debris and meteor showers and to suppose that the former supplied material for the latter. But how to account for the giant meteorites? If the description of a comet as a "fluffy mass" is correct, it is hard to visualize it as containing objects weighing many thousands of tons. A reasonable explanation is that there must be *two* kinds of meteoroids. One supposition turns to the asteroids to find the second kind. Here it is presumed that a planet, with a composition similar to earth's, once existed in the space between Mars and Jupiter. If such a planet—a nickel-iron core surrounded by a mantle of rocky material—broke up, the materials for the three main types of meteorites were present ready-made. The explosion (or possibly collision with some other solar system body) would send fragments of matter in every direction. Such a theory could account for the meteorite showers, the pockmarked surfaces of Mars and the moon, the great holes in the earth's surface, and even for the micrometeorite dust.

There may also be another reasonable explanation for *some* of the meteorites. From whatever source, the moon has certainly been subjected to a merciless rain of chunks of matter, even more so than the earth since there is no lunar atmosphere to destroy or retard them. Some authorities think it possible that meteorites which strike the moon a glancing blow might chip off fragments which themselves become meteorites. If these chunks fly away from the moon at only 1.5 miles per second, they could escape the lunar gravitational field completely and, if headed in the right direction, could even strike the earth. In fact, it turned out that the lunar explorers brought back samples of the lunar surface which match almost exactly the composition of the stony and glassy meteorites already "mailed" to us by our obliging neighbor.

OBSERVING METEORS

Meteors are naked-eye objects and any attempt to use telescopes for them is usually fruitless. At the time of a meteor shower it is sometimes fun to catch the flash of one in your telescope eyepiece. But even if you are successful, the effect is not nearly as rewarding as the naked-eye view.

1. Finding the radiant of a meteor shower is an interesting experience, if only to find out how closely it coincides with the predicted point of origin. Even during showers, meteors appear all over the sky, not just at the radiant point. The earth is heading toward the spot from which they originate, and the meteors are streaming past on almost parallel paths on all sides. These paths will appear to be shorter near the radiant. Of course, if a meteor is approaching head-on, it will not appear as a streak in the sky; only as a short-lived point of light.

2. The brilliance of meteors is interesting to check and compare. If the night is dark, you can easily see meteors as dim as fifth magnitude. In a good shower, such as the Leonids, they will range from very dim streaks to flashes brighter than first magnitude. For comparison purposes, use the stars. The table given below may help you make estimates to within half a magnitude of a meteor's true brightness.

Representative Stellar Magnitudes

−2.0	Jupiter
−1.5	Sirius (Alpha CMa)
− .06	Arcturus (Alpha Boo), Capella (Alpha Aur), Vega (Alpha Lyr)
0.5	Procyon (Alpha CMi)
1.0	Altair (Alpha Aql), Aldebaran (Alpha Tau)
1.5	Deneb (Alpha Cyg), Bellatrix (Gamma Ori), Alioth (Epsilon UMa)
2.0	Kaus Australis (Epsilon Sgr), Menkalinan (Beta Aur), Mirzam (Beta CMa)
2.5	Dschubba (Delta Sco), Mirach (Beta And), Phekda (Gamma UMa)
3.0	Haris (Gamma Boo), Kaus Borealis (Lambda Sgr), Alcyone (Eta Tau)
3.5	Maasym (Lambda Her), Ain (Epsilon Tau), Coxa (Theta Leo)
4.0	Muliphein (Gamma CMa), Sceptrum (53 Eri), Sadalachbia (Gamma Aqr)
4.5	Taygeta (19 Tau), Sham (Alpha Sge), Pherkard (Delta UMi)
5.0	Mesarthim (Gamma Ari), Kuma (Nu Dra), Diadem (Alpha Com).

3. Compare the frequency of flashes for 10-minute periods before and after midnight. Some observers have noticed that meteors often occur in

close-interval pairs or triads. Do your observations check with this?

4. Bolides (any meteor brighter than magnitude −2) should be checked as carefully as possible for brightness, color change, length of path in degrees, altitude above the horizon, persistence of the trail, and time (to the nearest second) of occurrence. As an example of the importance of amateur reports on bolides, Dr. Charles P. Olivier, Director of the American Meteor Society, was able to establish from them the path and altitude of the bolide of March 25, 1963, from the moment it appeared over central Pennsylvania until it fell into the Atlantic Ocean near Newport News. If you are lucky enough to see a bolide, report your observations to the nearest observatory or direct to the American Meteor Society.

Earth Satellites

For countless ages the earth has had only one satellite, the moon. In 1957, the launching of the first Soviet satellite changed this condition. Now the earth is orbited by many of these whizzing objects, some reaching, at apogee, almost halfway to the moon and some even impacting her surface.

The life of most satellites is brief, but there is an ever-increasing number that may last for years. The requirement for "permanence" is simple: The orbit of the satellite must be far enough outside our atmosphere, both at apogee and perigee, to reduce air friction to a minimum. If put into orbit at an average height of 150 miles, a satellite may remain aloft for about eight days, but at five times this height, its life can be measured in years.

The visibility of any satellite depends upon its size, the reflectivity of its surface, its distance from the earth, and finally, the angle its orbit makes with the equator of the earth. If this angle is small, observers in far northern or southern latitudes may not see the satellite at all, even though it may be very bright. The 100-foot balloon satellite Echo II, for example, was seen as a bright object all over the world because it reflected sunlight from a large surface area and its orbit, inclined about 86° from the equator, took it nearly over the poles while the earth rotated beneath it. On the other hand, the Copernicus telescope satellite has a much smaller reflective surface and its path is inclined only 35° from the equator. Such a satellite can be seen in tropical regions, but in the middle latitudes it would be very difficult to spot because it hardly rises above the southern horizon. Only satellites whose orbits incline more than 60° from the equator are visible everywhere on earth. Just how visible depends, of course, upon the other factors mentioned above.

Once launched into orbit, satellites obey all the laws which govern celestial objects. Their orbits are ellipses, with the center of the earth at one of the foci. The orbit may be nearly circular like that of the Meteor 12 satellite of June 30, 1972, whose perigee is 556 miles and apogee 576 miles. Or it may be a highly eccentric ellipse. Molniya I, for example, comes within 300 miles of the earth's surface, but at apogee it is 24,700 miles away—a tenth of the way to the moon. Some satellites, such as the Transits, orbit directly or nearly over the poles. Others, like Intelsat 4, follow around the equator. This satellite has a nearly circular orbit within 1° of the equator, and it moves around the center of the earth once in 1,440 minutes. But in spite of its speed it is almost parked in the sky, for our planet rotates beneath it once every 1,436 minutes in the same direction. Such "stationary" orbits are typical of communications satellites, which bounce radio or television signals from one part of the earth to another; circumpolar orbits are typical of satellites that record weather conditions or are used to survey features of the earth's surface.

The periods and speeds of satellites depend upon the size of their orbits. The moon, still our best satellite, moves around the earth in 27.3 days. Its linear speed is 2,287 miles an hour at its average distance of 240,000 miles. Compare this with a satellite that is 500 miles above the earth. Obeying the same laws of distance, speed, and period, it will make a complete revolution in about 100 minutes, moving at a speed of just under 17,000 miles an hour. As a satellite moves closer to the earth its period decreases and its speed increases. We can use this information to predict how long a satellite will last once it moves close, using its period as a measuring stick. When the period decreases to 87 minutes, the satellite has come within 100 miles of the surface; it is flying in dangerously thick atmosphere and will soon burn up.

Theoretically, the orbit of a satellite is fixed in space; in practice, this is not true, for there are several factors which influence it. High-flying, very light satellites like Echo II are pushed off course by the pressure of sunlight. Those with small inclinations to the equator are affected by the gravitational pull of the equatorial bulge. This has two effects: It makes the whole orbit turn in a direction opposite to the motion of the satellite and it causes the perigee point to shift in the satellite's direction. These disturbing effects, plus the rotation of the earth and the period and inclination of a satellite, make accurate predictions of the time and place of its appearance very difficult unless you are computer-minded. Fortunately, for some of the brighter satellites, some newspapers, as well as some astronomical magazines, regularly print predictions of their positions.

The average telescope is not a good instrument for observing the satellites because of its small field and the difficulty of moving the instrument smoothly enough to follow swiftly moving objects. A satellite will skip across a fairly wide field in from one to five seconds. Even if you are able to keep the elusive object in view, wrestling with a telescope mounting is likely to distract your attention from the satellite itself. If you feel badly about not being able to use your cherished instrument for this purpose, remember that no telescope will reveal details of a satellite's structure; all you can ever see is a swiftly moving point of light.

The best instruments for satellite hunting are 7×50 binoculars, Moonwatch apogee telescopes, or hand-held, rich-field reflectors. You need low power, wide field, and bright images for this kind of observing. Although some of the satellites are easily followed with the naked eye, using some sort of optical aid adds a new dimension to the experience. Your visual impression will be stereoscopic because the satellite will be seen against a background of distant stars, and watching the bright object slip across them also heightens your sense of the tremendous speed with which they move.

Finding satellites if you have been given a time, an approximate position, and the direction of travel is easy since many of them are naked-eye objects or become visible with only slight optical aid. Locating the others is a matter of chance. Because many of them are launched with inclinations greater than 45°, they move across the sky from northwest to southeast or, when the earth has turned 180° under their orbits, from southwest to northeast. A slow sweep of the northern or southern skies, well above the horizon, may increase your chance of finding these fascinating little objects.

CHAPTER XI

Sky Glows

When conditions are right, observers living in certain areas can see strange and beautiful glows in the sky: the cone of dim illumination called the zodiacal light, the nebulous spot of light opposite the sun called the counterglow or *Gegenschein*, the flash of green light following sunset or preceding sunrise, and, most spectacular of all, the auroras.

These are naked-eye phenomena for the most part; the telescope does little for them. But since they are exciting and sometimes exceedingly lovely to watch, they deserve a place in this book even though it is devoted mainly to telescopic objects.

Auroras

If you live in the latitude of 39° North (about the latitude of Washington, D.C.) you may see auroras on five to ten nights during the year. In Maine, or the northern rim of the United States in general, there will be as many as twenty-five nights when the sky is lit by the auroral glow. Along a line which passes through the southern part of Hudson Bay and Alaska the number increases to one hundred, but only a few hundred miles to the north (through northern Labrador and Alaska) two out of three clear nights will be marked by auroras. The number then decreases as the pole becomes nearer. Roughly the same count at the same latitudes is observable in the southern hemisphere, with a maximum again, 25° from the south magnetic pole. Perhaps the poorest area for auroral observations is the tropics, where you will be fortunate if you see the beautiful colors once in ten years.

Auroras occur in many colors and forms. Colors vary through the whole spectrum: shades of red, yellow-green, yellow, and blue. Sometimes, as in the great auroral display of February 1958, the red colors may be so brilliant as to give the impression of a monumental fire beyond the horizon, but the normal color is yellow-green.

Auroral displays often seem to dance along the horizon. Actually, the lower edge is normally about seventy miles above the earth, and is often much higher than this. Laterally, the spread may extend for hundreds of degrees around the sky and in some cases it may completely surround the observer, rising upward all the way to the zenith. Such displays are once-in-a-lifetime experiences, at least for those who live in temperate latitudes.

Usually the display begins as an arc across the northern sky (hence the name, Aurora *Borealis*). This early stage has few distinguishing features and appears only as a homogeneous band of light. The band stretches toward the south as the aurora develops and begins to show ray structure, thin streamers that look like great pencils of light. The streamers seem to stay in the same position, appearing and disappearing within a few seconds. If the display grows from this stage into a "spectacular," the rays may develop into draperies, curtains, and crowns of light, and various colors appear. Bright red patches come and go; green rays near the horizon turn to dull red higher in the sky and to brilliant red near the apex. Pearly white areas may be shot through with lavender bands, the whole panoply of colors shifting and dancing in the sky.

What causes the aurora? The most popular theory

The Aurora Borealis as projected on the sky dome of the Hayden Planetarium.

attributes it to solar emanations—protons and electrons—striking the atmosphere and causing the thin upper gases to glow, just as a stream of electrons shot through rarefied neon gas in an advertising display produces a bright light. The red auroras seen high in the sky are produced by excited oxygen atoms while the red that occurs at lower altitudes is due to ionized oxygen molecules and probably also to nitrogen. The most common auroras (yellow-green) come from oxygen gas under low pressure, bombarded by the incoming particles. Nitrogen molecules which have lost an electron from impact glow blue. The theory which ties the aurora to solar activity is based on the observation that solar flares are often followed by auroral displays after a lapse of a day. This indicates that the particles thrown out by the sun travel at about a thousand miles a second. But it is unlikely that protons and electrons traveling at this speed could penetrate the atmosphere to within seventy miles of the earth's surface, so there is some doubt that a cause-and-effect relationship between solar activity and the aurora is a complete explanation for these beautiful displays. The great magnetic storms which disrupt telephone and radio communications are usually accompanied by auroras, but the exact relationship of the two has yet to be established. In fact, the truth of the matter is that the cause of auroral displays has yet to be found.

The Zodiacal Light

The zodiacal light is a dim, wedge-shaped glow which can be seen thrusting above the western horizon about an hour and a half after sunset. It can also be observed in the east at the same interval before sunrise. It slants up from the horizon in the direction of the ecliptic. Since the zodiacal constellations are strung along the ecliptic, this dim but beautiful glow was named for them.

Amateur observers rarely see the zodiacal light because of its lack of brilliance. Moonlight obscures it completely, so it can be seen in the evening only in the interval between three days after full moon to three days after new moon, or in the morning three days before new moon to three days before full moon. For northern observers, February and March are the most favorable months for viewing the zodiacal light after sunset, and September and October are best for watching the elusive glow before dawn. These are the times when it is most nearly perpendicular to the horizon. Thus there are only about twenty-eight days in the year for watching the western aspect of the light and another twenty-eight to look for it in the east. At other times it slants up from the horizon at such a low angle it is very difficult to distinguish from the ordinary sky background. Southern hemisphere observers should look for it at the reverse periods from those given

133

The zodical light as seen at Palermo, Italy, on April 1, 1872. (From a sketch by Professor Piazzi Smyth.)

above, *i.e.*, the dawn light occurs in March and the evening light in October.

Even at its best and brightest, the zodiacal light fades into the sky background so gradually it is difficult to see any boundaries. But once you spot the glow, which first appears as a second twilight, move your head back and forth as though you were watching a ping-pong match; this increases the contrast between the dim light and the sky background. The light now appears as a broad cone, widest at the horizon and tapering into the sky in the general direction of the Pleiades.

What causes the zodiacal light? One explanation is that the region of the ecliptic is filled with tiny dust particles, spread out into a huge disk which lies almost in the plane of the ecliptic. The light from the sun is reflected from, or refracted by, these particles. When the sun sets or rises, the section of the disk which is illuminated appears as a band of light shaped like a spindle, or two cones placed base to base. The earth occupies a spot approximately in the center of the spindle. Thus from any place on earth at sunset we see one cone of the spindle and at dawn, the other.

The Gegenschein or Counterglow

The spindle shape of the zodiacal light creates still another effect. At midnight, the end of the cone opposite the sun produces a spot of light called the Gegenschein or counterglow. This is indeed a very faint patch of light centered on the ecliptic opposite the position of the sun. It has an irregular shape, some 20° by 30° in size. Much more difficult to spot than the parent zodiacal light, it can be seen only on clear, very dark nights when the moon is well below the horizon. Such nights occur during a period which extends from about three days after the moon's last quarter to three days before first quarter.

Locating the Gegenschein is a triumph for any amateur astronomer. It is a test for the sensitivity of your vision, for even the brightest section is little more illuminated than the rest of the sky and its borders are almost indistinguishable, so gradually does it blend into surrounding areas. Look for it shortly after your local midnight on the section of the ecliptic that is on your meridian. Make sure your eyes are completely dark-adapted—twenty to thirty minutes in a dark room are a guarantee of this. If you find that direct gaze at the sky produces no results, try averted vision.

Both the zodiacal light and the counterglow are of great interest, not only to astronomers but to space travelers. One explanation of the mysterious light is that it may be an extension of the sun's corona and therefore an aspect of radiation effects rather than a simple reflection of light by dust particles.

The Green Flash

If you live in a locality where sunsets are spectacular, especially if the sun disappears behind water or a low, sharply defined horizon, you may want to spend some entertaining (or perhaps frustrating) moments looking for the solar "green flash."

Watch the sun during the final moments of sunset. As the last thin crescent approaches the horizon it will appear to flatten into a short, straight line. At this moment look at it through moderate-power binoculars (7 × 50 binoculars present no danger to the eye if used for solar observation *only* at this final moment). If conditions are right, the thin line of the sun seen through the binoculars resolves itself once more into a crescent, but above the yellow crescent a green or green-blue fringe may appear. The ends of the fringe, where they touch the horizon, are brighter than the central portion, but as the sun continues to sink the bright spots move toward one another. When they meet, a brilliant flash of color appears, lasting for about two thirds of a second. This is the "green flash."

In practice, there may be considerable variation from the description given above. The colors may be blue, blue-green, yellow-green, or some other combination according to the color perception of the observer. The time for the final stage may be several seconds, but the flash itself is short: less than a second. Sometimes the flash is so brilliant it may be seen without optical aid.

Don't expect to see the green flash every time you look at a sunset, for it can be observed only under certain conditions. These are a sharp horizon, a clear atmosphere, and an inversion layer of air. The latter occurs when there is a sharply defined stratum of air whose temperature is higher than it should be according to its distance above the earth. Ordinarily, air temperature decreases with increasing height; in this case the reverse is true and a blanket of warm air lies over the colder air near the surface of the earth. In some localities this occurs rather often; in others it is comparatively rare. You may see flashes on two successive evenings, then look every night for a month without seeing another.

Although the green flash is most often reported from tropical areas, it may occur anywhere in the world as long as conditions are favorable. The author has seen it in the South Pacific and also across the waters of Casco Bay in Maine. Moreover, it can be seen at sunrise as well as sunset. In either case the effect is so startling many observers may want to "waste" some time looking for it.

CHAPTER XII

Celestial Photography

Perhaps you have wanted to try your hand at celestial photography, but have held back because of imagined technical difficulties. While it is true that some objects in the heavens are hard to photograph satisfactorily, there are many others as easy as the landscape around you.

Let's start with a rough outline of what you need for the various types of celestial photography in the order of their difficulty, both as to technique and equipment. Later we shall go into more detail, but this preliminary list will show you what you can expect to do with the equipment you have on hand. You may find you need little more.

1. Large constellations, the aurora, bright comets, satellites, star trails.

Easy, because almost any camera will do, provided you mount it on a sturdy tripod and use very fast film (Royal-X Pan or its equivalent). A 35-mm camera with a 50-mm lens of speed f/2.8 works beautifully for these objects. So do the popular reflex 2¼ × 2¼-inch cameras. The camera is fixed in position and exposures are of the order of 10 seconds.

2. Small constellations such as Lyra, Sagitta.

Same requirements as above except that lens focal length should be 3 to 6 inches instead of the 50-mm (2-inch) size.

3. Coarse open clusters such as the Pleiades, Hyades, or even Praesepe; star clouds, like those in Sagittarius or Scutum.

These are a little more difficult since the camera must be mounted equatorially and guided to follow the object; exposures are longer. Ideal for those who have equatorial mounts for their telescopes since the camera can be clamped to the telescope tube. Lenses of 3- to 6-inch focal length are needed, but slower film may be used.

4. Large nebulae, open clusters, wide areas of the moon, and so on.

Now you will use the optical system of your telescope. If it is of short focal length, attach the camera lens (set at infinity) directly to the eyepiece of the telescope. For longer-focal-length telescopes, remove both camera lens and telescope eyepiece and use the camera as a plateholder at the prime focus of the telescope. A guide telescope of the same focal length as the main instrument is needed, for exposures are longer and the object must be kept centered on the film.

5. Planetary nebulae, planets, lunar detail, globular clusters, galaxies.

The image is projected through the telescope eyepiece to the plateholder or camera (minus its lens). Other requirements as above.

Photography with a Fixed Camera

Let's start with the easiest objects on the list—the large constellations. With fast films of ASA

Stephen A. Walther

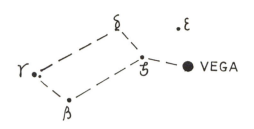

The constellation Lyra.

have shorter exposures since their relative speed across the film is greater.

CAMERAS AND FILMS

Before we go any further we must straighten out a difference in terminology which is sometimes confusing. To a camera buff a 6-inch lens means 6 inches of *focal length;* to the astronomer the term means 6 inches of *aperture.* The camera enthusiast often stops down (reduces the aperture) of his lens, and his f-number changes with every reduction. Thus a 5-inch focal length, f/4.7 lens has a useful diameter of a little over an inch (5 ÷ 4.7 = 1.06). If the same lens is used at f/8, the lens aperture has been reduced to ⅝ inch by closing the diaphragm opening. The camera owner, therefore, uses f-numbers to describe the useful aperture of his lens, and is really talking about light-gathering power.

What cameras are suitable for astrophotography? The real authorities on the subject, such as Dr. Henry Paul of New York State and the famous California amateur Alan McClure, say that no one camera can be used for all phases of astronomical work. Short-focus cameras are fine for wide areas of the sky, but as the apparent diameter of the object to be photographed becomes smaller, the camera focal length must increase and the plate scale becomes larger. Thus a 35-mm camera is useful for astrophotography in focal lengths up to possibly 6 inches. Beyond this, larger film size is necessary. Reflex 2¼ × 2¼-inch cameras or the old-fashioned 4 × 5 cameras give good results. These latter have slow lenses, but when used with fast films often produce negatives which make excellent 8 × 10 enlargements. The point is reached eventually where even the longest-focal-length lenses will not yield sufficient plate scale for heavenly bodies of small angular diameter, and then the telescope must be used in place of the camera lens.

ratings of 1,000 or more, exposure times are so short the stars literally "stand still" for your camera. If the camera lens is at least an inch in aperture and has a speed of at least f/4.5 (f/2.8 is still better—most 35-mm cameras satisfy these requirements) you can prepare your own photographic atlas of the heavens.

Wait for a dark, moonless night. Load your camera with Kodak Royal-X Pan (or its equivalent), mount it on a sturdy tripod, and try a ten-second exposure of the Big Dipper. You may be pleasantly surprised at the result, especially if you blow your prints up to 8 × 10 size.

Even easier, try a Polaroid camera. If you don't have one of your own, borrow your neighbor's. He will probably be delighted at the opportunity to add a whole new area to his photographic repertory. The 3,000-speed, type 47 film plus a Polaroid camera produces wonderful photographs of constellation-sized sky areas. Start with a ten-second, f/4.7 exposure and allow the film to develop for two minutes instead of the one-minute period usually recommended. The longer development yields greater contrast in your print. If the stars don't appear as bright as you might like, lengthen the exposure time. This on-the-spot development of prints is what makes stellar photography with a Polaroid so exciting. Your darkroom is in the back of the camera, so you can experiment until you get the exposure time just right. How long this can be is limited by background light in the sky and the motion of the stars. Stars near the polar region can be exposed for about thirty seconds before they begin to "trail"; those near the celestial equator must

Stephen A. Walther

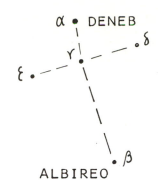

The Northern Cross.

Camera lenses suffer from the same defects as telescope lenses: spherical aberration, astigmatism, coma. These result in malformed images at the edge of the field and it is sometimes necessary to reduce the aperture by one or two stops especially if the lens is fast (f/1.4 to f/2.8). This usually results in improving definition, but at the same time cuts down on light and makes longer exposures necessary.

For astronomical photography, you will want to use the slowest film which will do the job properly. "Snapshots" of the stars require the very fastest film. But these films are subject to grain (where isolated clumps of the light-sensitive emulsion react faster than others), and are less sharp. When you expose longer you can use slower films which are less subject to grain and give more contrast. For very long exposures, you must use antihalation film. Halation occurs when light passes through the film and is reflected, causing a ring or halo around a star image. Eastman Kodak* produces a series of films for astronomical work designated by the letter *a*, as 103*a*0. Besides their antihalation qualities, these films vary in sensitivity to color and, used with the proper filters, will bring out features which do not register on ordinary film. But this does not mean that stock panchromatic films cannot be used for

---

* Kodak Photographic Plates for Scientific and Technical Work, 50 cents.

astrophotography. They are excellent general-purpose films because they record the whole spectrum with nearly equal sensitivity. Sometimes their performance can be improved by using a weak yellow filter to reduce background light and to eliminate the blue rays which do not focus at the same point as other light.

If you develop your own prints, astronomical photographs are very little different from terrestrial ones as far as the developers are concerned. You probably won't go far wrong if you stick to those with which you are familiar. Overdevelopment is helpful in increasing contrast with the slower films, but with the fast ones normal development is safest. Be particularly careful in handling negatives, for the dark background of astronomical photos brings out film scratches and other blemishes with disastrous clarity.

PHOTOGRAPHING "SPECIAL EVENTS"

Some heavenly phenomena such as the aurora, the brighter comets, and satellite passages can be photographed without special equipment.

The Aurora Borealis is a wonderful subject for color photography. High-speed color film such as Eastman ASA 160 and lenses in the range of f/2.8 or faster can be used with exposures of five seconds or so. Black-and-white films above 200 ASA permit exposures of one half to one second, and even medium-speed films require only thirty to sixty seconds. The aurora usually extends over very large areas of the sky, so if you are fortunate enough to own a wide-angle lens, this is the time to use it.

Bright comets are also a good subject for fast-film, fast-lens combinations. Unless the comet is moving rapidly through the stars, exposures up to sixty seconds are possible. Beyond this, both comet and stars will show appreciable motion on the film. The latter is unimportant if you obtain a good photo of the comet, so this is one occasion where you will want to try a variety of exposures.

Perhaps as much fun as any type of photography is attempting to "catch" the satellites. The two Echoes and the Pegasus satellites (these are espe-

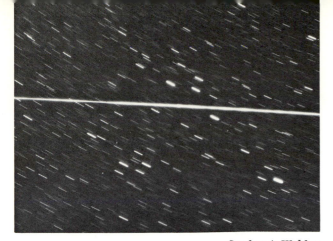

Stephen A. Walther

Echo I passing through Hercules.

Stephen A. Walther

Star trails around Polaris.

cially good for observers in southern latitudes) are easy to photograph with almost any camera, using moderate-speed film. Since newspapers publish predicted times and altitudes of the easily visible satellites, you can lie in wait for them. Mount your camera on a solid tripod and aim it at the part of the sky through which the satellite is expected to pass in the highest part of its orbit. Set the camera on bulb, and open the lens as the satellite approaches. Even if you miscalculate a little in aiming the camera you will still get a picture because the average camera lens covers an area of about 40° of the sky. In your photo the satellite will appear as a streak across "trailing" stars. Some photographers think the record is more interesting if the satellite's track is interrupted periodically. You can do this by placing your hat over the lens at regular intervals: ten seconds off, five seconds on—whatever separation seems most striking after you have tried it once or twice.

STAR TRAILS

Except for the satellites, in fixed-camera photography we have tried to stop the motion of the objects mentioned above. Wonderfully effective photographs may be obtained by doing just the opposite. If, for example, you center the North Star in the field of your camera and open the shutter for periods of thirty minutes to four hours, you will obtain a striking photograph of star trails around the true north point of the heavens. The longer the exposure, the longer the trails. If you point the camera at stars near the ecliptic, they will trail in long, graceful arcs across the photograph. Photographs such as this can be enlarged to any size you wish. You can decide how long the trails may be for any length of time by using the formula

$$\text{length of trail on film (inches)} = \frac{\text{focal length of lens (inches)} \times \text{time (minutes)}}{229}$$

There is a limit to this kind of exposure, depending upon the amount of nonstellar light which reaches the film. Any kind of background light—

the crescent moon, distant city lights, automobiles on a highway and so on will soon fog even a slow film. There are other hazards, too. Anything which moves the camera in the slightest degree will cause a jog in the star trail; high winds, accidental jarring of the tripod, even backlash in the shutter mechanism. You must also watch out for the lights of passing airplanes, dew forming on your lens, clouds, wind-whipped branches of trees. This formidable list of precautions applies not only to attempts to photograph star trails, but to any long-exposure photography.

Photography with a Moving Camera

Short-focus lenses and fast film serve very well for objects of large angular diameter. But small constellations and star patterns require longer focal length in your lenses, for otherwise the stars are bunched together on the film. You can still use a fixed camera for these if your lenses are 3 to 6 inches and are used with fast film. But if you want to photograph objects as small as the Pleiades, you need not only longer-focus lenses, you must also guide your camera to follow their motion. It may interest you to see why.

The actual size of the image on your film may be found by the following formula:

$$\text{image diameter (inches)} = \frac{\substack{\text{angular size of}\\\text{object}\\\text{(minutes of arc)}} \times \substack{\text{focal length}\\\text{(inches)}}}{57.3 \times 60}$$

Stephen A. Walther

Ceres (in white circle) on February 22 (top) and one month later on March 18, 1963 (bottom).

Now let's try to photograph the Pleiades, whose angular diameter is 100 minutes of arc, with a 35-mm camera whose lens is 50 mm (2 inches). If you measure the image on the negative you will find it only six hundredths of an inch in diameter.*

* Diameter in inches $= \dfrac{100 \times 2}{57.3 \times 60} = .058$

Obviously you will have to change to a longer-focal-length lens. But when you do this you must also lengthen the exposure to several minutes and now the stars will trail badly on the film. The only way out of the dilemma is to move the camera at the same rate as the apparent motion of the stars.

Fortunately, there is a relatively easy solution to the problem if your telescope has an equatorial mount. You attach your camera firmly to the telescope tube, find a guide star in the planned photographic field upon which you can center the telescope, and start your clock drive. But like many procedures which sound very simple, this one has some built-in difficulties. To keep a guide star centered in the field, you must have an eyepiece equipped with a reticle or cross hairs. The cross hairs must be very fine; otherwise the star has a tendency to "hide" behind them. If you aren't fortunate enough to have this kind of eyepiece, use an out-of-focus star for a centering device by racking the eyepiece inside focus until the enlarged image just fills the field. Now keep the edges of the expanded star on the outside of the field by compensating for any variations in the rate of the telescope motion. Most telescope drives have their own idiosyncrasies, the most common of which is too fast or too slow rate in right ascension. Either variation causes the stars to trail. You must compensate for this by hand-guiding, either using slow-motion adjustments (if you have them) or by gently tapping or pushing the telescope tube. Here is a case where a smoothly operating, vibration-free mounting is worth its weight in gold.

You must also be sure that the polar axis of the telescope points true north. If it doesn't, you will find that star images near the center of the field are round and true, but that those on the edge trail badly. Extra time spent in making sure your telescope is properly aligned pays large dividends.

The advantages of using a moving camera outweigh any trouble you may have in setting the system up by a very large margin. Now you can use slow film with its consequent gain in contrast and lack of grain. Exposure times of up to thirty minutes or more and corresponding film speeds may be used. Exposure time is limited only by your ability to guide the camera, the background light in the sky, and the reciprocity law, which is a measure of emulsion efficiency. Most films are made to operate best at exposures of about one fiftieth of a second. For long exposures they become less efficient with increase in time. For example, to improve on a washed-out negative which has been exposed for two minutes, your next attempt should be for three or four times as long instead of twice the original exposure.

The combination of longer focal lengths, larger plate scale, and a camera that moves makes it pos-

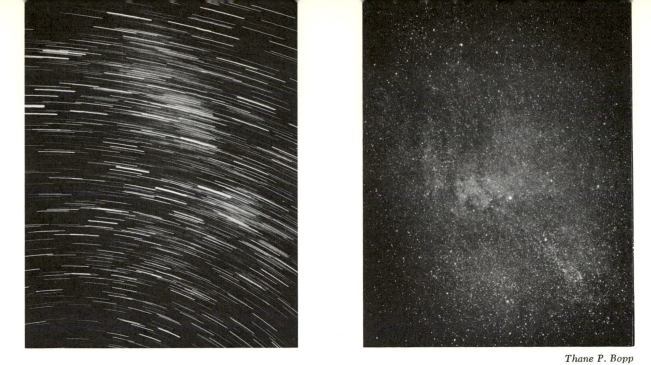

These two views of Cygnus were taken with a Polaroid 110A camera and ASA 3000 film. Left: Cygnus star trails; right: star clouds in Cygnus.

sible for you to obtain beautiful photographs of coarse clusters, the star fields of the Milky Way, and similar expanded views of the heavens. These are the objects that show up well in low-power binoculars. For objects with angular diameters smaller than these, however, you must adapt your photographic equipment to the telescope itself.

Photography Through the Telescope

As the objects we wish to photograph become smaller, we must find some means of magnifying them to an acceptable image size before we can record them on film. We saw that the Pleiades photographed through a 2-inch camera appeared on the film as a blob of stars only .06 inch wide. The moon through the same camera would have a film diameter of .02 inch. Now suppose we try a very simple expedient to increase the film scale. Let's remove the lens from the camera and the eyepiece from our telescope, and couple the camera to the eyepiece tube so that the image from the telescope objective falls directly on the film. If the telescope has a focal length of, say, 50 inches, the arrangement we are now using is a camera with focal length 50 inches. The Pleiades will appear on the film emulsion with a diameter of 1.5 seconds of arc and the moon has grown to almost half an inch. This is called prime-focus photography and is the simplest and easiest way of photographing objects of small angular diameter.

There are several other methods for increasing magnification besides using the prime focus of the telescope.

1. Using a Barlow lens. The Barlow is what is known as a negative lens; it causes light rays to spread out instead of converging, as a positive lens does. The rays from the telescope objective converge, of course, but if a Barlow lens is placed in their path they converge *less,* and this increases the focal length of the objective. The result is a larger image. In practice, the Barlow is placed in the eyepiece drawtube just inside the focal length of the objective.

2. For short-focus spotting scopes, binoculars, etc., you can attach the camera *with* its lens directly to the eyepiece of whatever instrument you are using. In this arrangement, the focal lengths of instrument and camera are combined into what is called *equivalent focal length.* You can find this by multiplying the magnification of the telescope by the focal length of the camera lens, or

$$\text{EFL} = \frac{f_o}{f_e} \times f_c$$

where the subscripts represent objective, eyepiece, and camera. As we have seen before, the f-number of a telescope is the focal length of the objective divided by the aperture. Similarly, the f-number of a telescope-camera combination in which both eyepiece and camera lens are used is the equivalent focal length of the combination divided by the aperture of the telescope. Combined into one expression, it is

$$\text{f-number} = \frac{f_o \times f_c}{f_e \times A}$$

Suppose, for example, that you couple the eyepiece of a 15-power spotting scope to the 2-inch

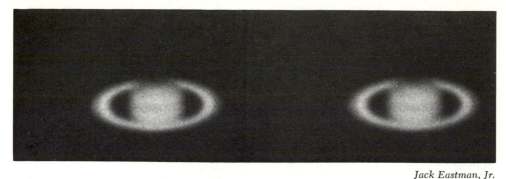

Jack Eastman, Jr.

Saturn—taken on Super Hi Pan, 8-second exposure with an effective focal length of 170 feet; developed in D-19.

focal length lens of your 35-mm camera. The combination has an equivalent focal length of 30 inches. If the aperture of the spotting scope is 3 inches, the f-number of the whole arrangement is f/10. This combination will produce an acceptable ¼-inch image of the full moon on your film, large enough for a very good print when enlarged. Both camera and telescope should be focused on infinity, with the camera lens close to the eyepiece of the telescope. If your camera has a single reflex lens, you can determine just how close the lens and eyepiece should be by moving the camera back and forth until you get a sharp image.

3. Eyepiece projection. For long-focus telescopes of 50 inches or more you can remove the camera lens and project the image from the eyepiece directly on the film. There are two variables in this arrangement: the image becomes larger with short-focal-length eyepieces and also as the distance of the eyepiece from the film increases. In practice, you arrange eyepiece and camera (or plateholder) until you get a sharp image at the film plane. Now if the film plane is moved away from the eyepiece the image expands. The relationship of this distance to f-number and also to plate scale is given by the formula

$$\text{f-number} = \left(\frac{L}{f_e} - 1\right) \times \frac{f_o}{A}$$

where L is the distance of the eyepiece from the film plane, and the other symbols are the same as in the formulas above.

Use your best orthoscopic eyepieces for eyepiece projection, because the quality of the image depends upon the quality of the eyepiece.

Equipment

So far we have said nothing about the mechanical arrangements for coupling cameras to telescopes. Fortunately they are neither expensive nor difficult to obtain. Several companies supply camera frames, clamps, adapter tubes, adjustable sleeves, camera mounts, and so on. You can attach a camera to almost any reflector or refractor with these fittings. If you have been ingenious enough to build your own telescope, the problem of hitching up a camera will be a simple one, but here are a few hints.

1. **To attach the camera to the telescope tube:** For any equatorially mounted telescope, reflector or refractor, you will want to attach the camera as near the front of the telescope as possible. Make a flat plate of plywood or metal upon which to mount the camera. On the underside of the plate, attach a pair of curved supports which will fit the curvature of the tube. This plate and its supports may be bolted directly to the tube for a permanent installation, or attached for temporary use by means of a pair of thick leather straps which pass clear around the tube and can be tightened until the plate is completely immovable. The addition of a camera to a well-balanced telescope puts a strain on the drive mechanism, so it will be necessary to add counterweights on the side of the tube opposite the camera and also on the other end of the tube. This arrangement can be used for any photography where the camera must follow the stars. Since you will be using your telescope optical system to guide the camera, you should of course make sure that the camera axis is parallel to that of the telescope *i.e.,* that when an object is centered in the telescope eyepiece it is also centered on the film.

2. **To attach the camera to the telescope drawtube:** If the camera is light, it can be attached directly to and supported by the drawtube in which the telescope eyepiece fits. This requires an adapter tube, one end of which can be attached to the lens opening of the camera, the other of the proper outside diameter to slide smoothly into the drawtube itself. This is an excellent arrangement for prime-focus photography, for sharp focusing can be accomplished by sliding the whole unit in or out of the drawtube. Heavier cameras require independent

Don Strittmatter

Two views of the moon taken with a 6-inch reflector using eyepiece projection. Film was Royal Pan, ½₀₀-second exposure, and was developed for 30 minutes with Microdol.

support such as the plate described above. This of course must be located just in back of the eyepiece adapter for reflectors, and must have a perpendicular plate attached to it to support the camera. The actual coupling between camera and telescope can be a bellows-type piece of rubber tubing. Several arrangements are possible. If for prime focus (without eyepiece or camera lens), the rubber adapter fits over the drawtube at one end and the adapter tube (which has replaced the camera lens) at the other. For short-focus reflectors (where both eyepiece and camera lens are to be employed) the rubber adapter simply connects lens and eyepiece. And for eyepiece projection, it connects eyepiece and camera adapter tube.

For refracting telescopes the camera must be supported by a plate or pair of rods which are extensions of the telescope tube itself. Otherwise the arrangements are the same as in the reflector.

Using the Telescope-Camera

The various arrangements mentioned above have one thing in common: accurate and careful guiding is required for any degree of success. As plate scale increases, guiding becomes progressively more difficult and errors which might be tolerable at low powers must be corrected. The guide telescope should ideally have the same focal length as the main instrument, but since this is impossible in most cases, it should at least be used at the same magnification. If, for example, you have a 15-power guide telescope and are photographing an object at 150-power, motion which is almost undetectable in the guide telescope shows up with disastrous clarity on the film. Instead of the sharp, well-defined images you had hoped for, poor guiding results in streaks and trails, fuzzy blobs, or even double images.

As focal length increases, so does f-number and plate scale. High power requires large film size, so you must replace your 35-mm or 2¼ × 2¼ camera frame with a plate-holder housed in a light-tight box. The old box camera, minus lens, serves well for this purpose. But now focusing becomes a problem, since you can no longer use the reflex systems of the smaller cameras. Most amateurs solve this one by removing the plate-holder and substituting a piece of ground glass, examining the image on the ground glass with a magnifier to be sure the focus is sharp.

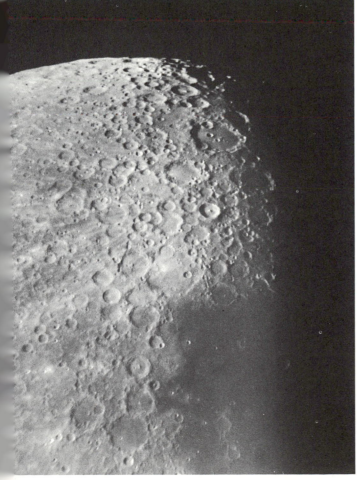

143

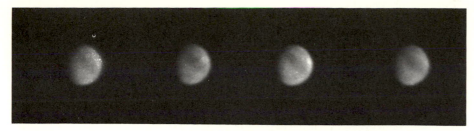

Jack Eastman, Jr.
Mars at gibbous stage.

Some Selected Objects

PLANETS

Most of us want to start celestial photography with the planets and small areas of the moon. Actually, these are the most difficult of all heavenly bodies to photograph.

Let us take the easiest planetary example, Jupiter, to see what difficulties are involved. The angular diameter of Jupiter at opposition is about 45 seconds of arc, which means that an ordinary camera will register it as only a dot on the film. For any hope of detail, we must use a 6-inch (or larger) telescope and eyepiece projection since we must have an equivalent focal length of about 200 inches. Even so, the image on the film will be only about .04 inch, but if we are accurate in focusing we can enlarge it to an acceptable size. We should use a fine grain film (Kodak Microfile, Plus X, etc.) and a fine grain developer. Assuming that the atmospheric conditions are good, the mounting is steady, and the exposure is short, we can obtain a good photograph of the planet.

Exposure times for the planets are difficult to calculate because there are so many variables: seeing conditions, the aperture of the telescope, film speed, etc. Roughly, it is in the range of 1 to 10 seconds, but the only way to find out for sure is by trial and error. Try taking several shots of the planet on the same plate at varying exposures to save time and money.

The requirements for successful photographs of the planets sound somewhat alarming, yet many amateurs have been able to cope with them successfully. The nearby planets vary greatly in angular diameter as they approach and recede from the earth. Mars' size changes from 4 to 25 seconds of arc, that of Venus from 10 to 61. Obviously, you will want to wait for the nearest opposition of Mars, although Venus makes an interesting photographic study through all angular diameters and phases.

THE MOON

For general views of the moon you can obtain fine results at the prime focus of your telescope. The moon reflects plenty of light (almost too much at full moon), so you can use slow, fine-grain film and still retain detail and contrast in your enlargements. Exposures are short, and guiding is not a problem because of the short exposure time. For the full moon, exposures vary between $\frac{1}{100}$ and $\frac{1}{25}$ second, depending upon film speed. This should be increased by a factor of 4 to 6 for the quarters and 8 to 10 for crescents.

Closer views require either short-focus telescopes used with eyepiece and camera lens or longer-focus instruments and eyepiece projection. Some of the most beautiful lunar photographs are those of Mr. and Mrs. Ralph Davis of Florida, using a 3½-inch Questar and eyepiece projection. Close-up views of the moon are tricky but exceptionally satisfying when you succeed with them.

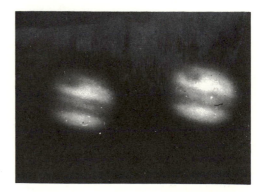

Jack Eastman, Jr.

Jupiter. Left: as photographed on July 1, 1959; right: June 28, 1961.

THE SUN

Before you consider solar photography you should reread the section on the hazards involved in any kind of solar work. Unless all the precautions listed there are carefully observed, solar photography can be dangerous both for the photographer and his equipment. Perhaps the safest way is to project the image of the sun on a screen placed at right angles to the eyepiece and to photograph the projected image. This requires some shielding around the screen to cut out as much extraneous light as possible, and involves some loss of detail. But if your object is a photographic record of sunspots, this is as satisfactory a method as any.

Because the sun has approximately the same angular diameter as the moon, direct photography of its surface can be accomplished most easily at prime focus, *provided adequate measures are taken to reduce the light and heat.* Dr. Henry E. Paul recommends covering the objective with neutral density filters after reducing the aperture to a minimum of 3 inches. This is a safe and simple method, provided enough filters are used to reduce the light and heat to $\frac{1}{10,000}$ or less of its value. The author has had very happy results using the Questar telescope previously mentioned, which has a very efficient and safe filter for solar work.

Fine-grain films work best for this type of photography if you wish to see any sunspot detail in your enlargements. Exposure time varies, of course, upon the density of the filters used, but is ordinarily in the $\frac{1}{100}$ to $\frac{1}{25}$ second range. At these speeds guiding is not necessary.

NEBULAE, GLOBULAR CLUSTERS, GALAXIES

These objects fall within a wide photographic range, some very easy, others extremely difficult. Large, bright nebulae such as M.42 (the Orion Nebula) can be photographed with a long-focus camera or at the prime focus of your telescope, but planetary nebulae and the galaxies require wide-aperture telescopes (to gather enough light), eyepiece projection, and long exposures. The most satisfactory prints of this latter group come from telescopes of 10 to 20 inches of aperture after very careful guiding through long exposures. Because of the exposure time, antihalation films sensitive to dim light should be used. Bright globulars like M.13 and M.5 fall in the medium-aperture range, but long exposures are still necessary unless ultrafast film is used.

Here again, as in planetary photography, careful guiding, rock-solid mountings, long-focus telescopes, and large film size are all requirements for successful work. Sounds impossible for an amateur? By no means. Pick up any copy of the popular astronomical journals and you will find beautiful examples of the "difficult" subjects mentioned above, all taken by amateurs.

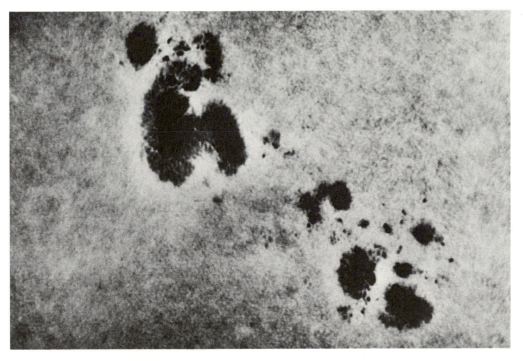

Questar Corporation

Sunspots of August 26, 1971.

The maps in the Star Atlas include those celestial objects which can be seen by the naked eye under good viewing conditions: that is, objects of the sixth magnitude or brighter. The transparent overlays, when smoothed flat over the maps, add those objects which can be seen only through a telescope.

STAR ATLAS

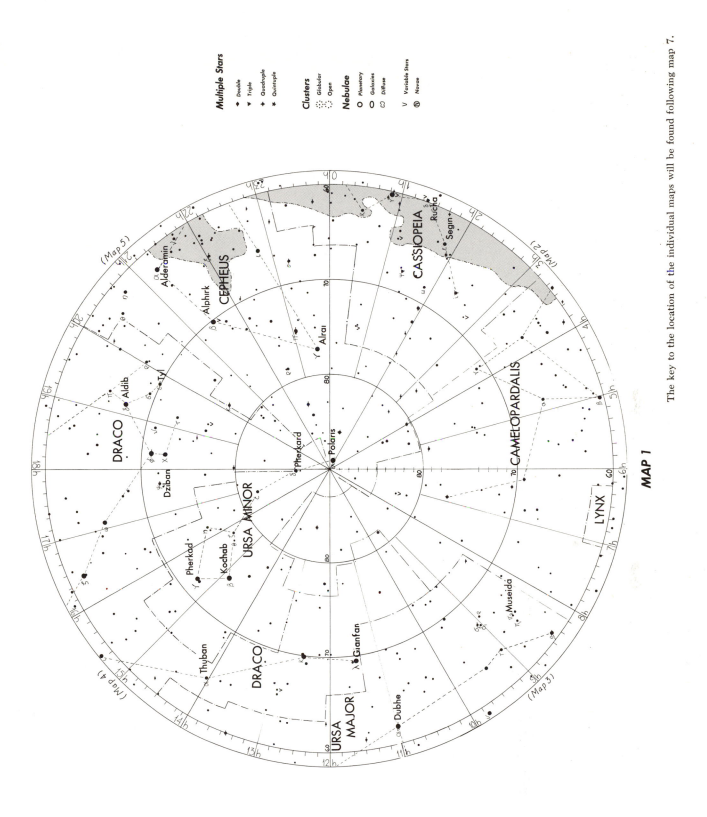

Star Magnitudes

>1 ●	4 •
1 ●	5 ·
2 ●	6 ·
3 ●	<6 ·

Milky Way Boundaries

Constellations ——·——·——
          ————————

Ecliptic ···············

Multiple Stars

◆ Double
▼ Triple
✦ Quadruple
✶ Quintuple

Clusters

⬭ Globular
⬚ Open

Nebulae

○ Planetary
⊂⊃ Galaxies
▱ Diffuse

V Variable Stars
Ⓝ Novae

MAP 1

The key to the location of the individual maps will be found following map 7.

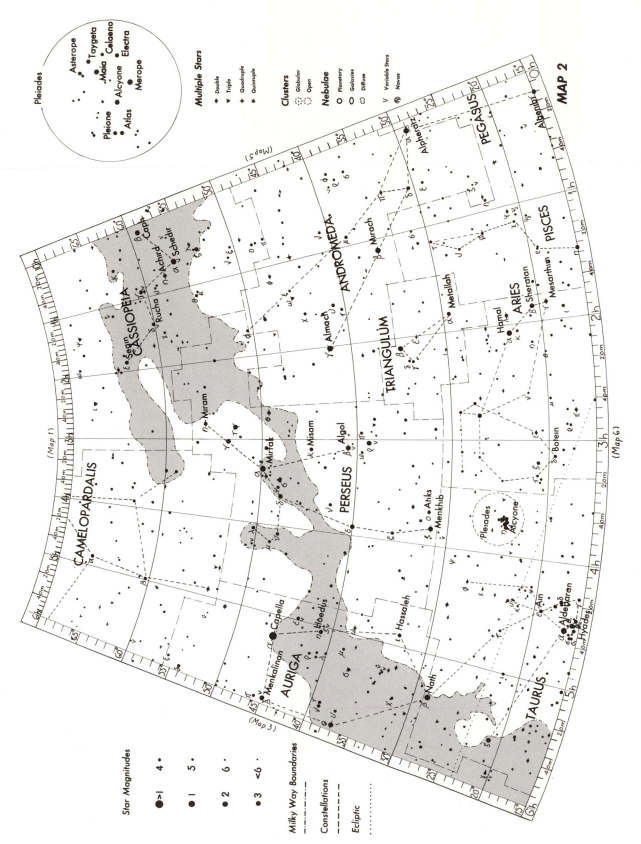

Pleiades

Asterope
Taygeta
Maia   Celaeno
Alcyone   Electra
Merope
Pleione
Atlas

Multiple Stars

• Double
▼ Triple
✦ Quadruple
✱ Quintuple

Clusters

⬡ Globular
○ Open

Nebulae

○ Planetary
◎ Galaxies
▢ Diffuse

V Variable Stars
⊕ Novae

MAP 2

(Map 5)

CAMELOPARDALIS

CASSIOPEIA

ε• Segin

ε• Segin   Caph
β•
Achird •α   Schedir
Ruchbah ν

Miram

Misam

Mirfak

Algol

Atiks

Menkhib

PERSEUS

ANDROMEDA

Mirach
β•

ω   ξ
Almach
γ• Almach

TRIANGULUM

Metallah

β•
γ• δ

ARIES

Hamal
α•   κ
β•
Sheratan

Mesarthim

Botein

Pleiades
η•   Alcyone

PISCES

PEGASUS

Alpheratz
δ•

Algenib
β•

0h

25°

30°

TAURUS

Ain
ε•
α• Aldebaran
Hyades

Nath
β•

Hassaleh

Haedus
η•

Capella
α• Capella

Menkalinan
β• Menkalinan

AURIGA

(Map 3)

(Map 1)

Star Magnitudes

● >1   • 4
● 1   • 5
● 2   • 6
• 3   · <6

Milky Way Boundaries ———

Constellations — — —

Ecliptic ··········

The key to the location of the individual maps will be found following map 7.

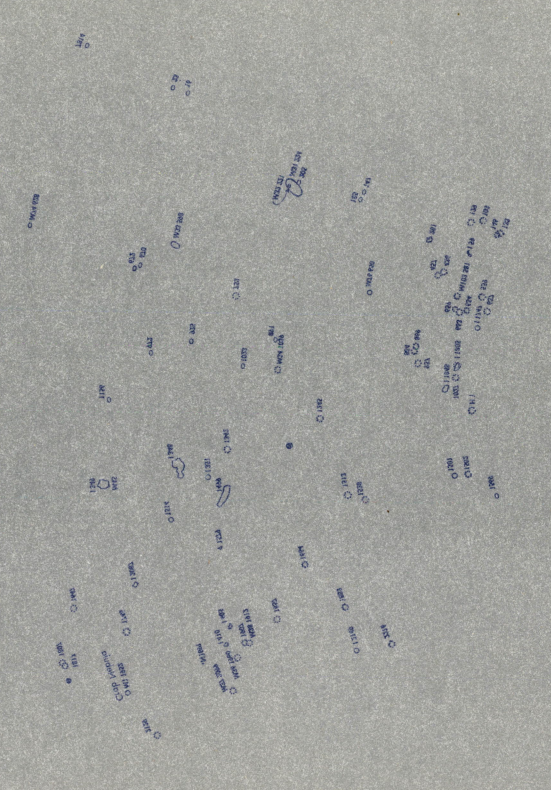

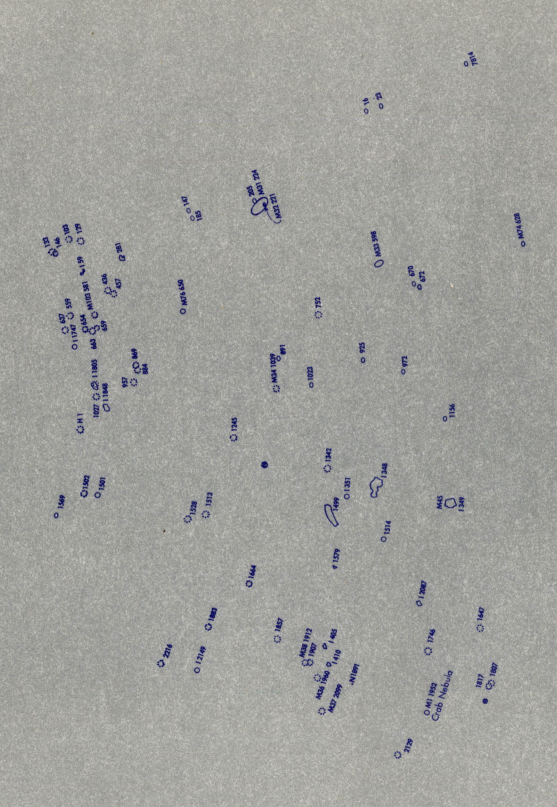

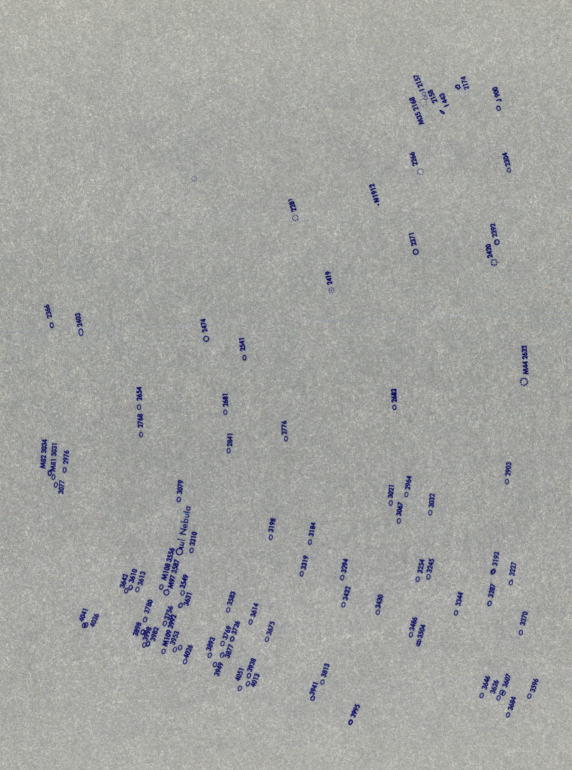

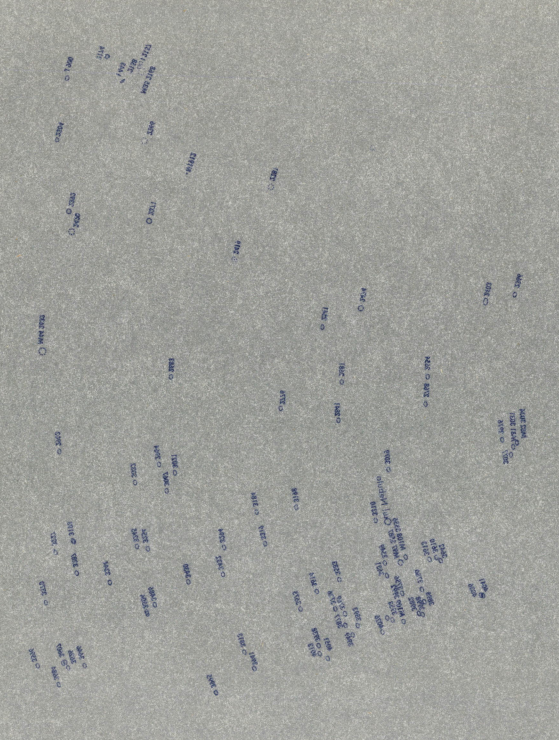

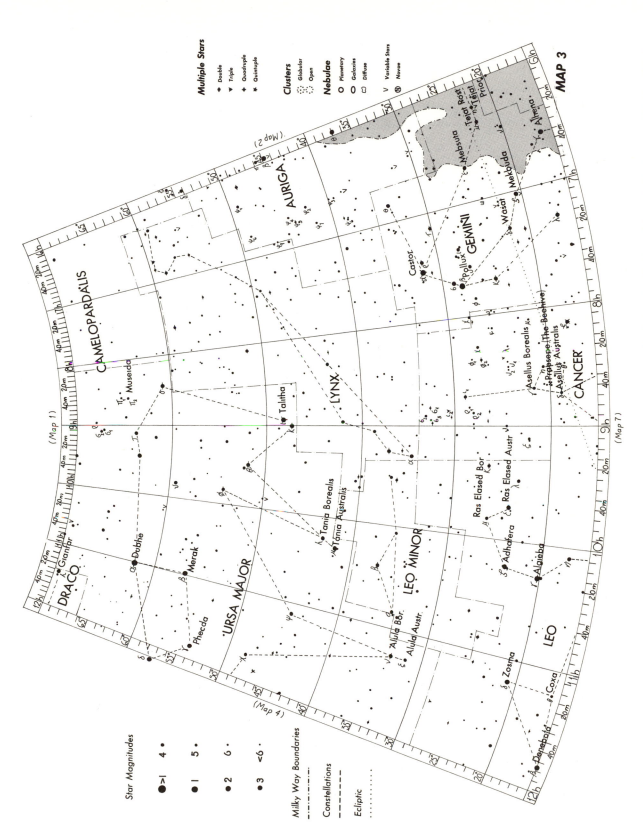

Star Magnitudes

⬤	>1
●	1
●	2
•	3
•	4
·	5
·	6
·	<6

Milky Way Boundaries — · — · —

Constellations — — — —

Ecliptic · · · · · · ·

Multiple Stars

◆	Double
▼	Triple
✦	Quadruple
✳	Quintuple

Clusters

⊙	Globular
○	Open

Nebulae

⊙	Planetary
◯	Galaxies
▭	Diffuse
V	Variable Stars
◐	Novae

MAP 3

DRACO

CAMELOPARDALIS

Giansar

κ

Dubhe

Merak

Phecda

URSA MAJOR

Museida

π₁ π₂

Talitha

LYNX

λ Tania Borealis

Tania Australis

AURIGA

ψ₅

ψ₃

ψ₁

ψ₇

ψ₂

Castor

Pollux

GEMINI

Mebsuta

Tejat Posti

Mejat

Prior

Mekbuda

Wasat

Alhena

Alzirr

Asellus Borealis μ

Praesepe-The-Beehive

Asellus Australis

CANCER

Ras Elased Bor

Ras Elased Austr

Adhafera

Algieba

Aljula Bor

Aljula Austr

LEO MINOR

Zosma

Coxa

Denebola

LEO

(Map 1)

(Map 2)

(Map 4)

(Map 7)

The key to the location of the individual maps will be found following map 7.

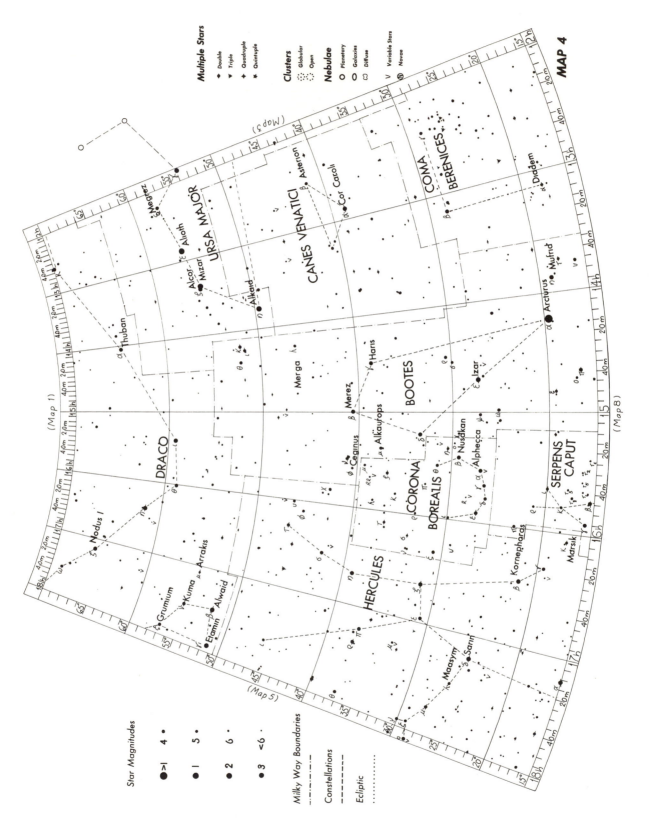

The key to the location of the individual maps will be found following map 7.

MAP 4

Star Magnitudes
- ● >1   · 4
- ● 1   · 5
- ● 2   · 6
- · 3   · <6

Milky Way Boundaries
Constellations
Ecliptic

Multiple Stars
- ◆ Double
- ▼ Triple
- ✦ Quadruple
- ✶ Quintuple

Clusters
- ⬭ Globular
- ◇ Open

Nebulae
- O Planetary
- 0 Galaxies
- ⊂⊃ Diffuse
- V Variable Stars
- ⊛ Novae

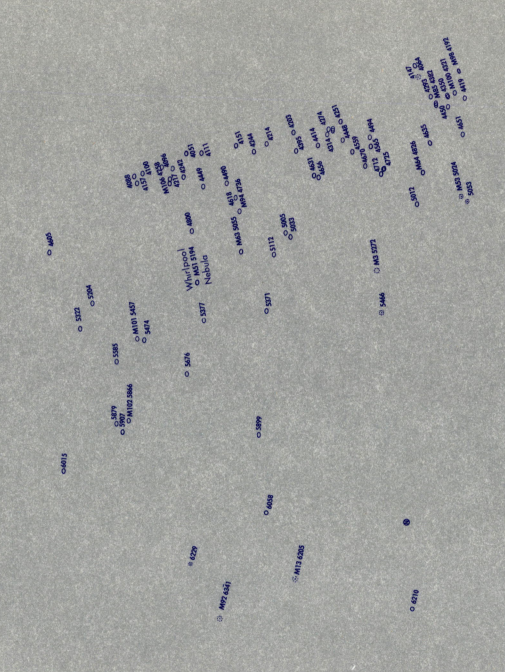

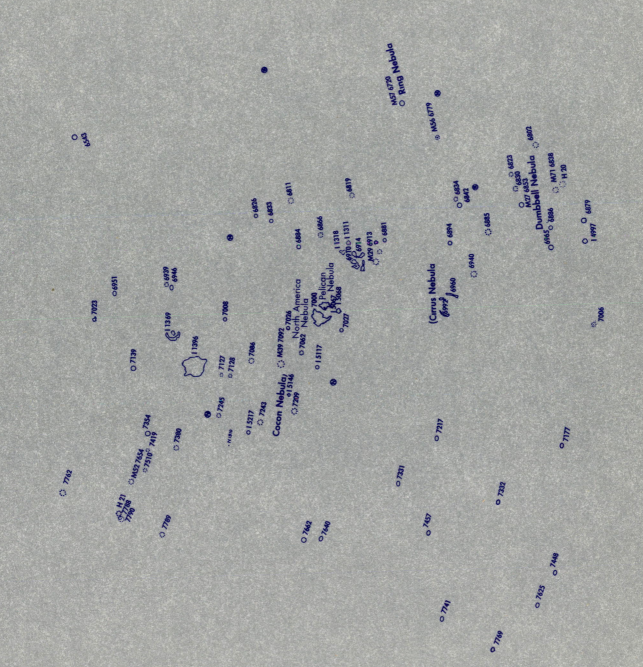

Ring Nebula

M57 6720

M56 6779

6543

6826
6833

6811

6819

6802
6830
6823

M27 6853

Dumbbell Nebula

M71 6838

H 20

6834
6842

6866

6884

11318
11311

6965 6886

6879

14997

6951

6939
6946

6881

M29 6913
6914

6894
6908

6940

6885

7023

11369

North America
Nebula

Pelican
Nebula

7000

M39 7092

7026

7027
7068

7062

7006

7139

11396

7008

Cirrus Nebula
6992
6960

7127
7128

7086

15117

Cocon Nebula
15146

7217

7245

15217

7209

7243

N 7090

7177

7354
7419

7331

M52 7654

7510

7380

7332

7762

H 21
7788
7790

7789

7457

7625

7448

7662

7640

7741

7769

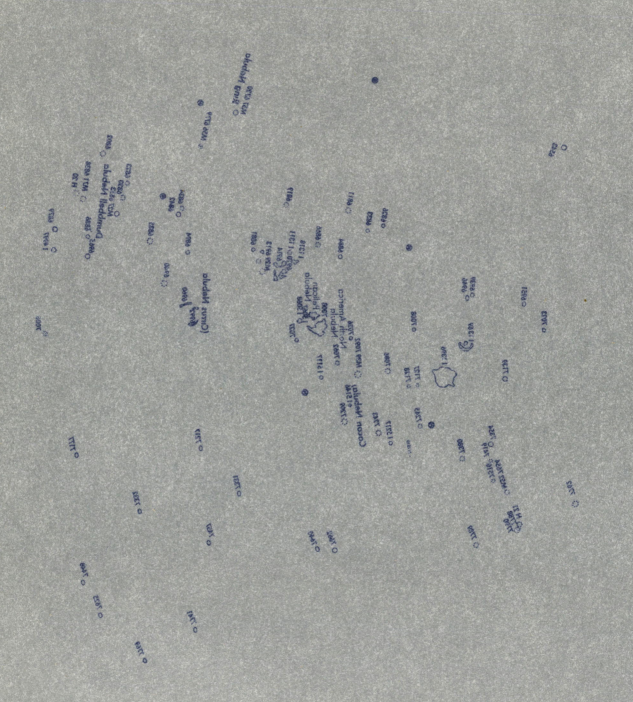

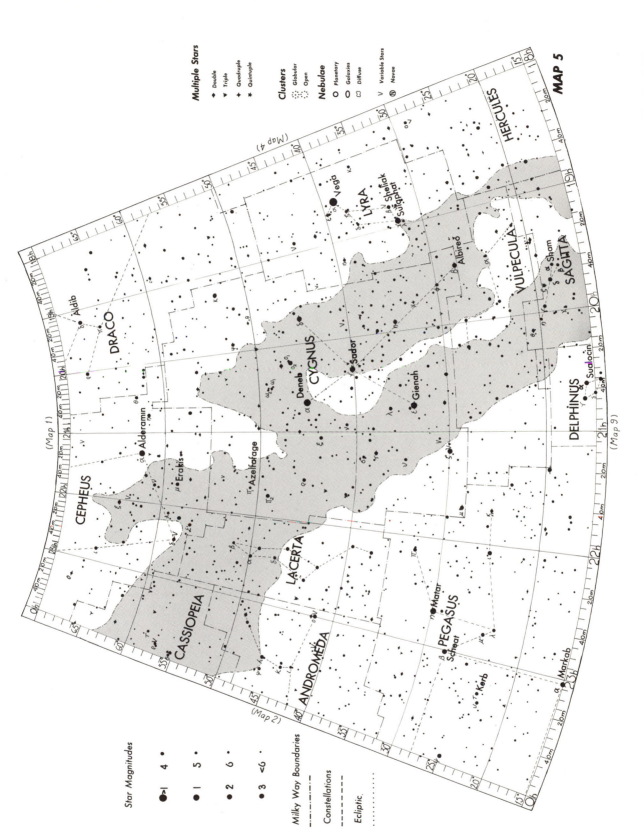

Star Magnitudes

- ● >1   4 •
- ● 1   5 •
- • 2   6 •
- • 3   <6 ·

Milky Way Boundaries — — —

Constellations — · — · —

Ecliptic ··········

Multiple Stars

- ♦ Double
- ▼ Triple
- ✦ Quadruple
- ✦ Quintuple

Clusters

- ⊙ Globular
- ○ Open

Nebulae

- ⊙ Planetary
- ◯ Galaxies
- ▭ Diffuse
- V Variable Stars
- ⃝ Novae

MAP 5

The key to the location of the individual maps will be found following map 7.

CEPHEUS

DRACO

CYGNUS

LYRA

HERCULES

VULPECULA

SAGITTA

DELPHINUS

PEGASUS

ANDROMEDA

LACERTA

CASSIOPEIA

Aldib

Alderamin

μ Erakis

π Azelfafage

π₁

π₂

Deneb

Sador

Gienah

ε

Vega

Sheliak

Sulaphat

δ β

Albireo

β

α Sham

δ

Matar

Scheat

β

Kerb

Markab

α

Sualocin

α

β

γ δ

(Map 1)

(Map 4)

(Map 2)

(Map 9)

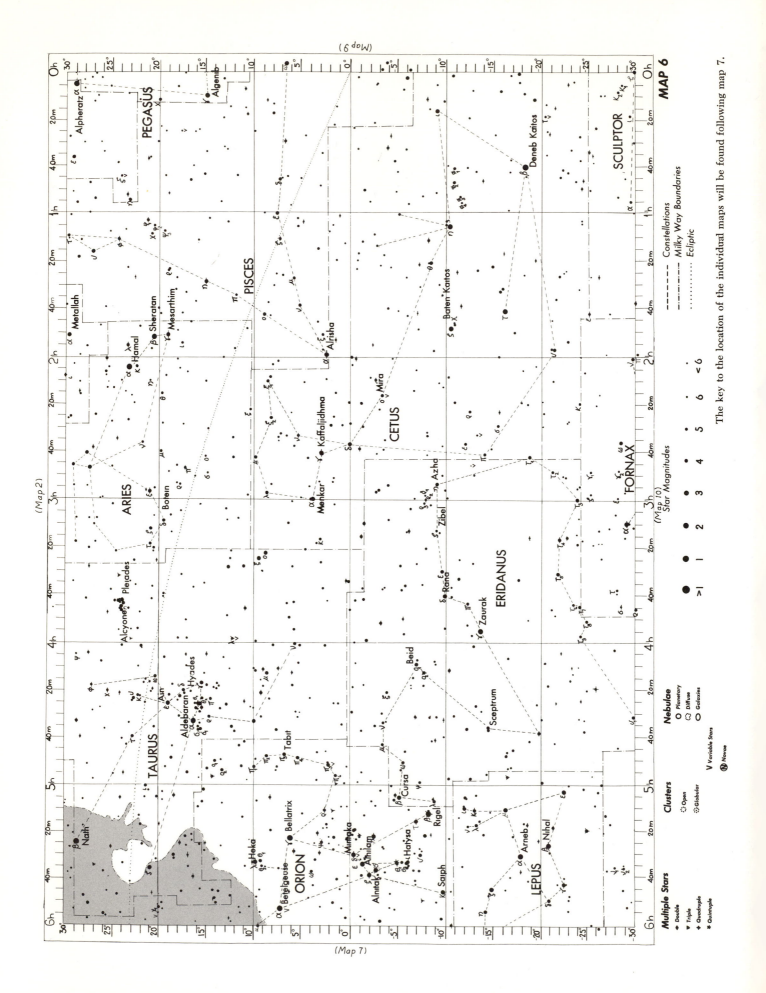

MAP 6

The key to the location of the individual maps will be found following map 7.

------	Constellations
–·–·–	Milky Way Boundaries
·········	Ecliptic

Star Magnitudes

● >1 ● 1 ● 2 ● 3 ● 4 • 5 · 6 · <6

Multiple Stars

+ Double
▼ Triple
✦ Quadruple
✳ Quintuple

Clusters

○ Open
⚬ Globular

Nebulae

○ Planetary
♋ Diffuse
○ Galaxies

V Variable Stars

Ⓝ Novae

(Map 9)

(Map 7)

(Map 2)

PEGASUS

Alpheratz α

Algenib γ

SCULPTOR

Deneb Kaitos β

PISCES

Metallah

Sheratan β

Hamal α

Mesarthim γ

Alrisha α

ARIES

Botein

Mira

Kaffaljidhma γ

CETUS

Menkar α

Baten Kaitos ζ

Azha

Zibel

Rana δ

ERIDANUS

Zaurak γ

FORNAX

(Map 10)

Pleiades

Alcyone η

TAURUS

Aldebaran α

Hyades

Beid

Sceptrum

Nath β

Heka

Tabit

ORION

Bellatrix γ

Betelgeuse α

Mintaka δ

Alnilam ε

Alnitak ζ

Hatysa

Saiph κ

Rigel β

Cursa β

LEPUS

Arneb α

Nihal β

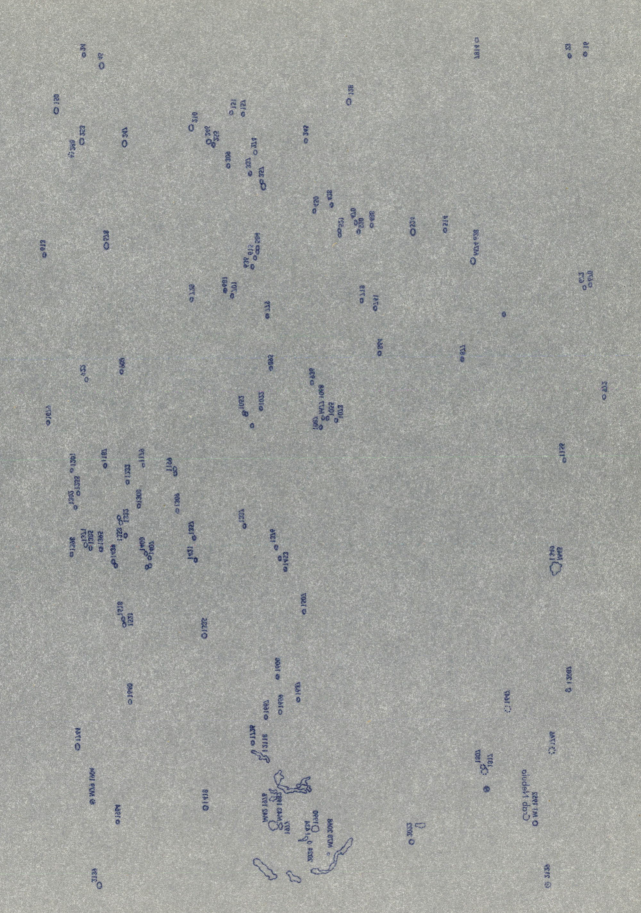

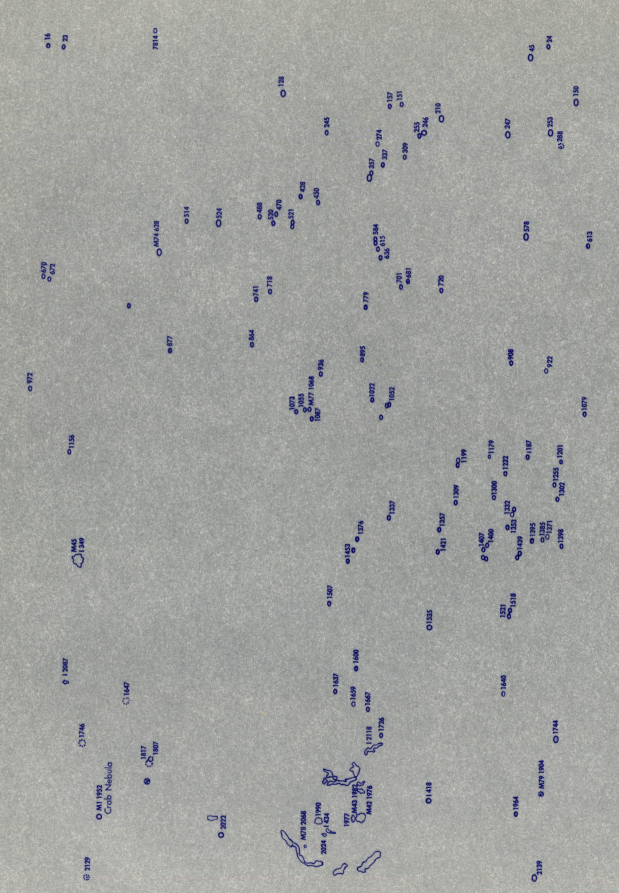

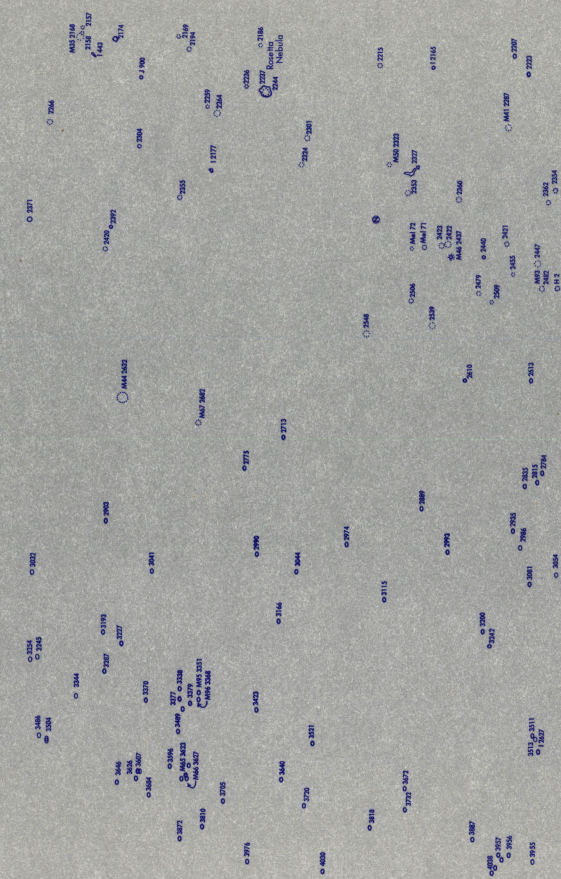

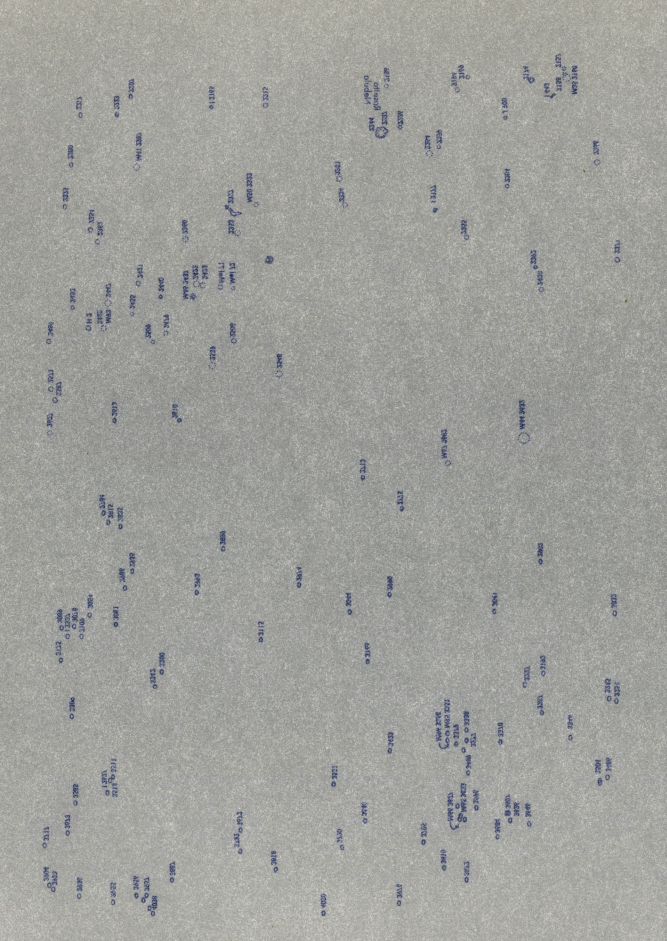

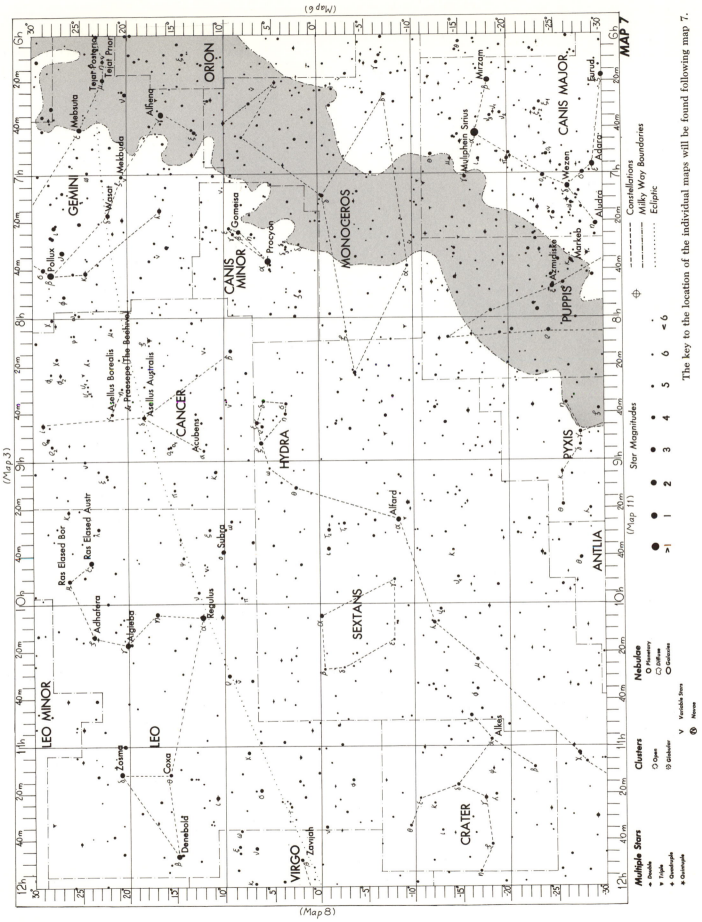

MAP 7

The key to the location of the individual maps will be found following map 7.

Constellations — — —
Milky Way Boundaries — · — · —
Ecliptic ···········

⊕

Star Magnitudes

>1   1   2   3   4   5   6   <6

Multiple Stars

✧ Double
▽ Triple
✦ Quadruple
✺ Quintuple

Clusters

◯ Open
⊕ Globular

Nebulae

◯ Planetary
◠ Diffuse
◯ Galaxies

∨ Variable Stars
Ⓝ Novae

(Map 6)

(Map 3)

(Map 8)

(Map 11)

ORION
GEMINI
CANIS MINOR
CANIS MAJOR
MONOCEROS
PUPPIS
PYXIS
ANTLIA
HYDRA
CANCER
LEO MINOR
LEO
SEXTANS
VIRGO
CRATER

Tejat Posterior
Tejat Prior
Mebsuta
Alhena
Mekbuda
Wasat
Pollux
Gomeisa
Procyon
Sirius
Mulphein
Mirzam
Wezen
Adara
Aludra
Markeb
Azmidiske
Furud
Ras Elased Bor
Ras Elased Austr
Adhafera
Algieba
Regulus
Subra
Acubens
Asellus Borealis
Praesepe (The Beehive)
Asellus Australis
Zosma
Coxa
Denebola
Zavijah
Alphard
Alkes

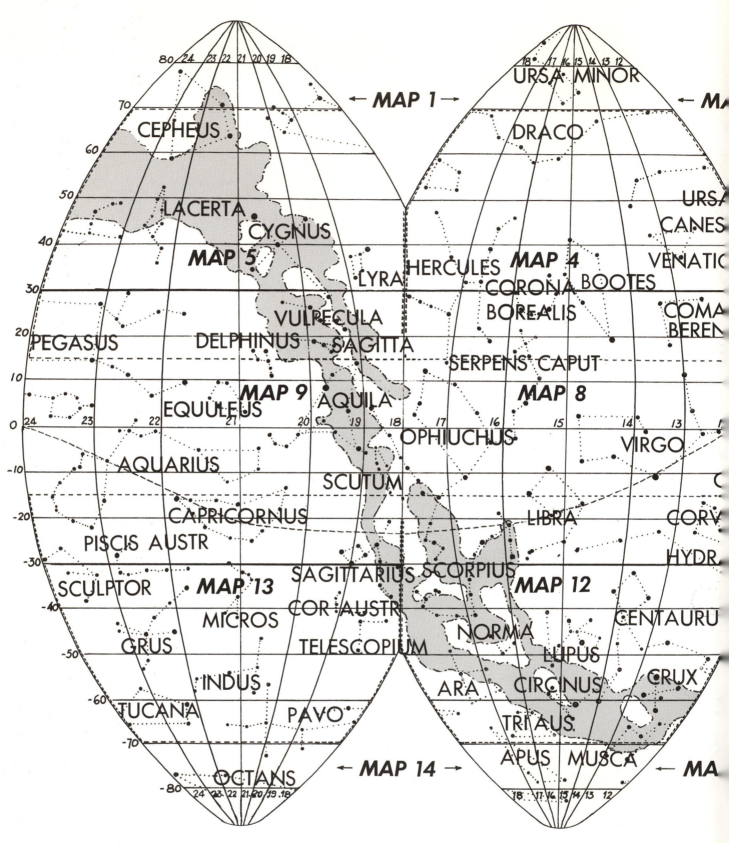

Ecliptic
- - - - -

CHART OF THE C

and

Key To Th

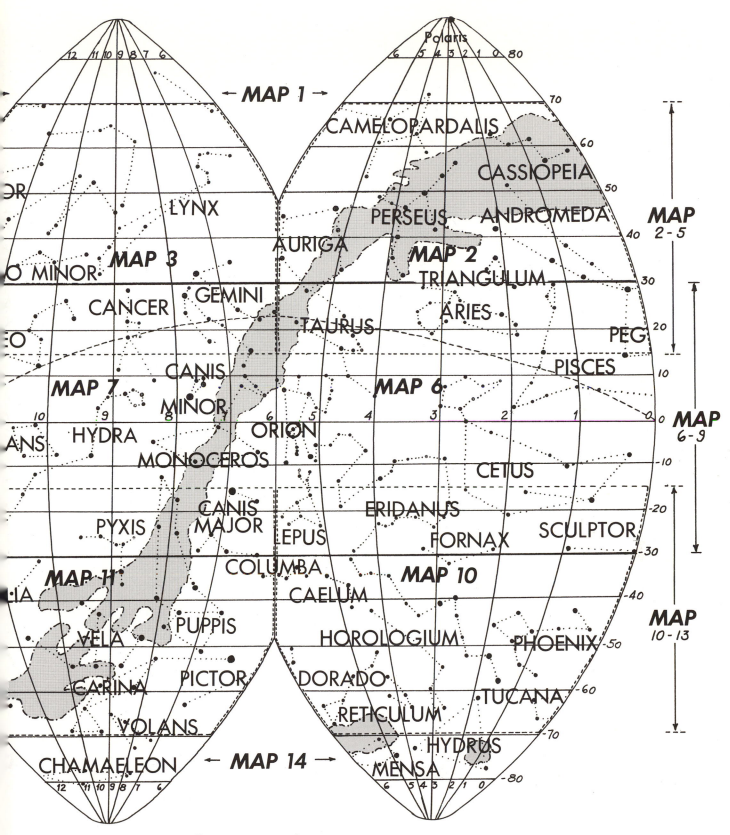

Polaris

← MAP 1 →

CAMELOPARDALIS

CASSIOPEIA

LYNX

PERSEUS   ANDROMEDA

MAP 2-5

AURIGA

MAP 3

MAP 2

O MINOR

TRIANGULUM

CANCER

GEMINI

ARIES

TAURUS

PEG

PISCES

CANIS

MAP 7

MAP 6

MINOR

MAP 6-9

HYDRA

ORION

ANS

MONOCEROS

CETUS

CANIS

ERIDANUS

PYXIS

MAJOR

LEPUS

FORNAX

SCULPTOR

COLUMBA

MAP 11

MAP 10

CAELUM

MAP 10-13

PUPPIS

VELA

HOROLOGIUM

PHOENIX

CARINA

PICTOR

DORADO

TUCANA

VOLANS

RETICULUM

HYDRUS

CHAMAELEON   ← MAP 14 →   MENSA

Milky Way Boundaries
— · — · — · —

LATIONS

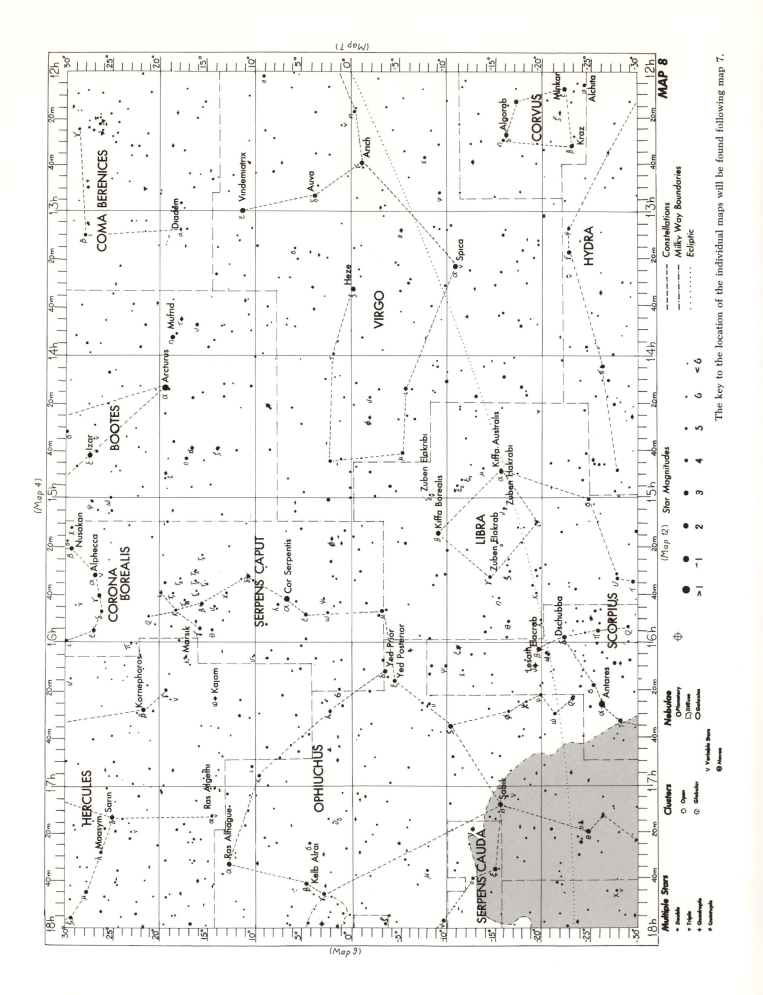

MAP 8

The key to the location of the individual maps will be found following map 7.

----- Constellations
––– Milky Way Boundaries
.... Ecliptic

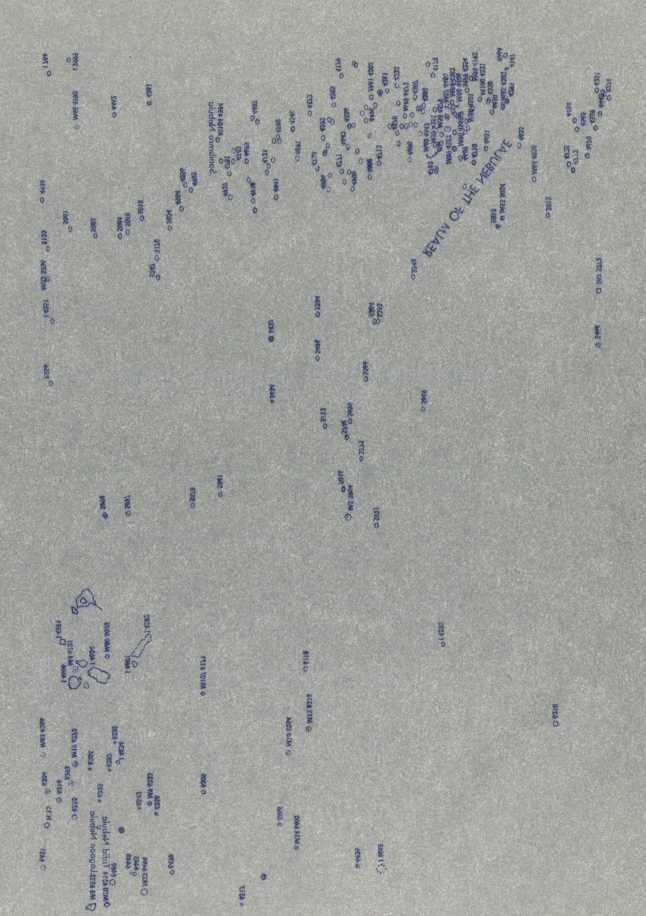

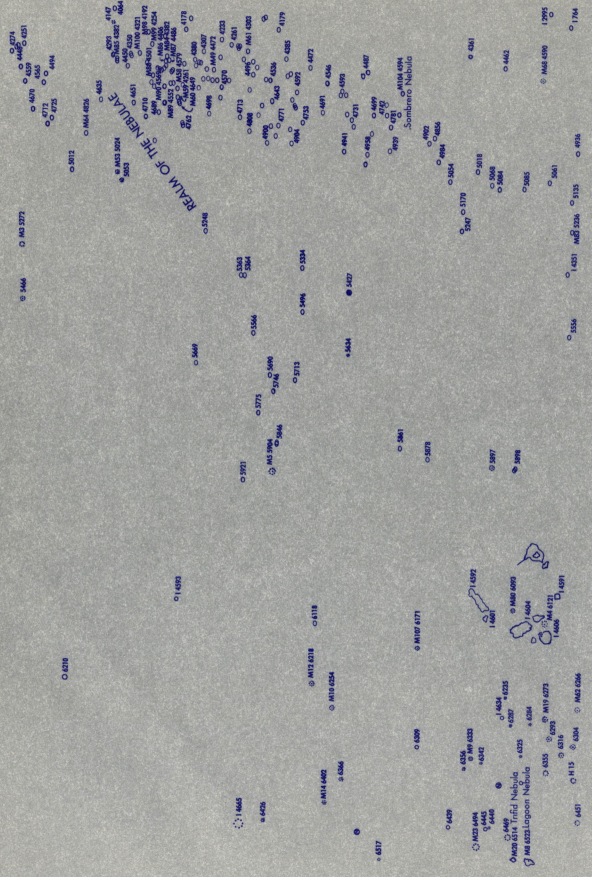

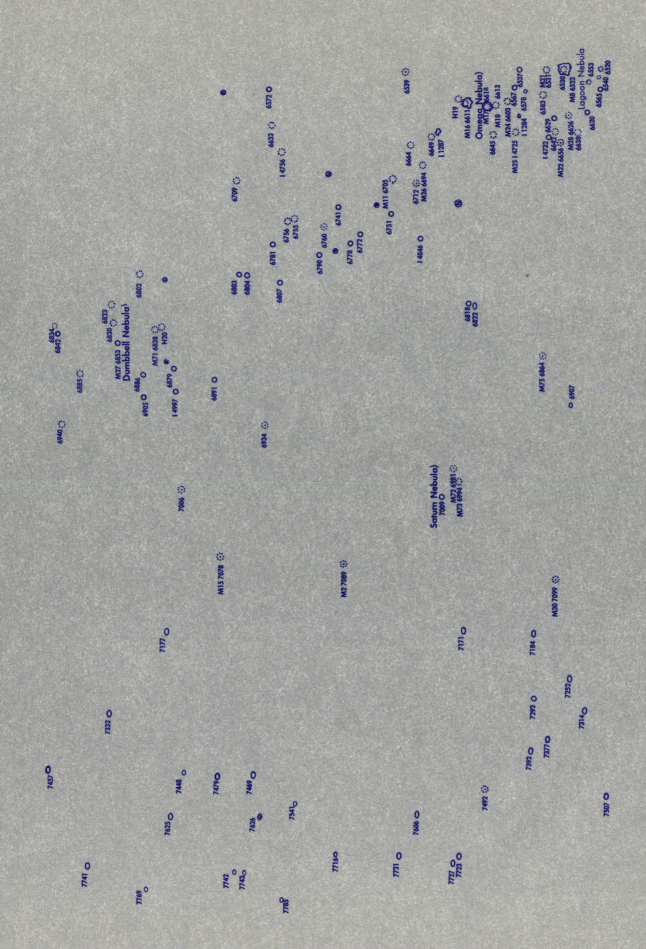

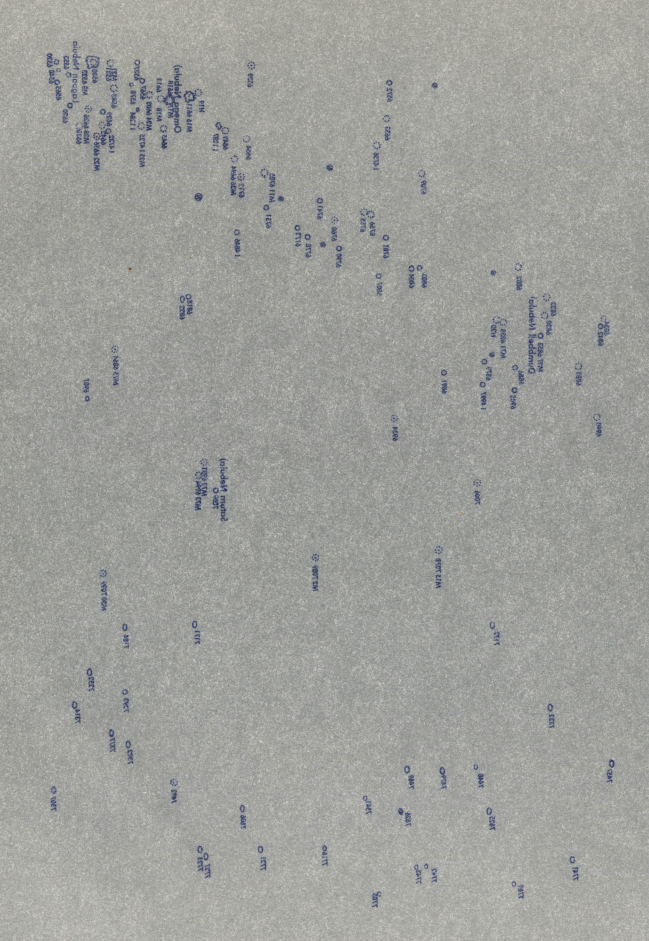

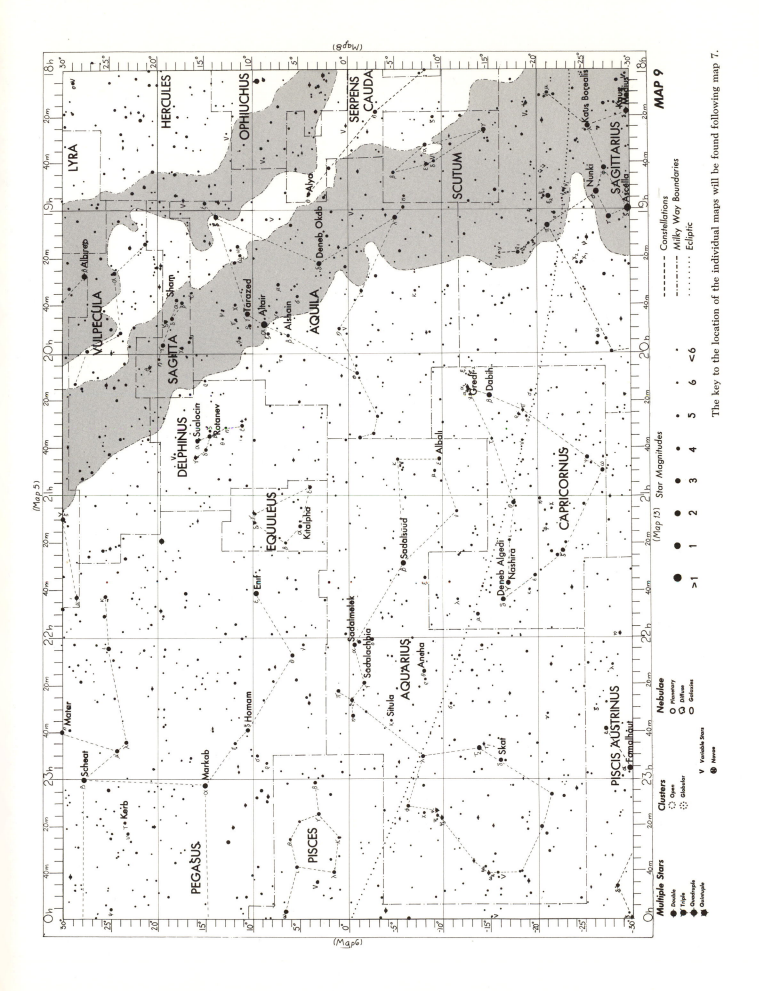

MAP 9

The key to the location of the individual maps will be found following map 7.

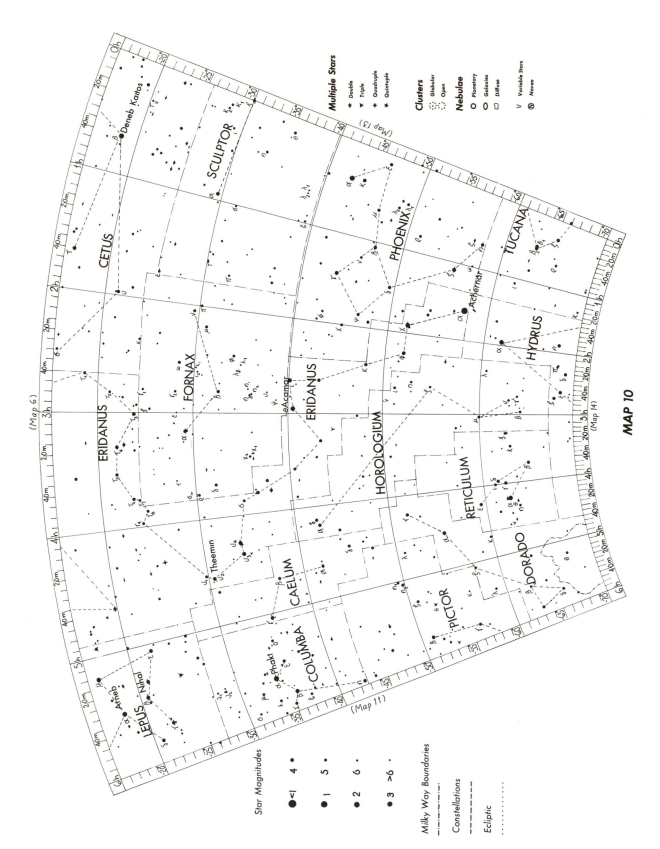

MAP 10

The key to the location of the individual maps will be found following map 7.

Star Magnitudes

<1 • 4 •
1 • 5 •
2 • 6 •
3 • >6 •

Milky Way Boundaries

Constellations

Ecliptic

Multiple Stars

♦ Double
▼ Triple
✦ Quadruple
✳ Quintuple

Clusters

⬡ Globular
⬭ Open

Nebulae

○ Planetary
0 Galaxies
▭ Diffuse

V Variable Stars
Ⓝ Novae

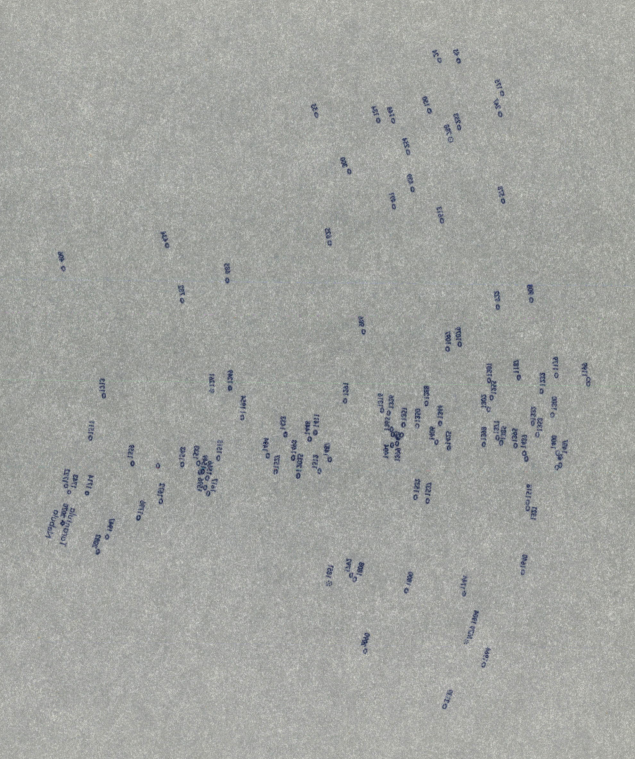

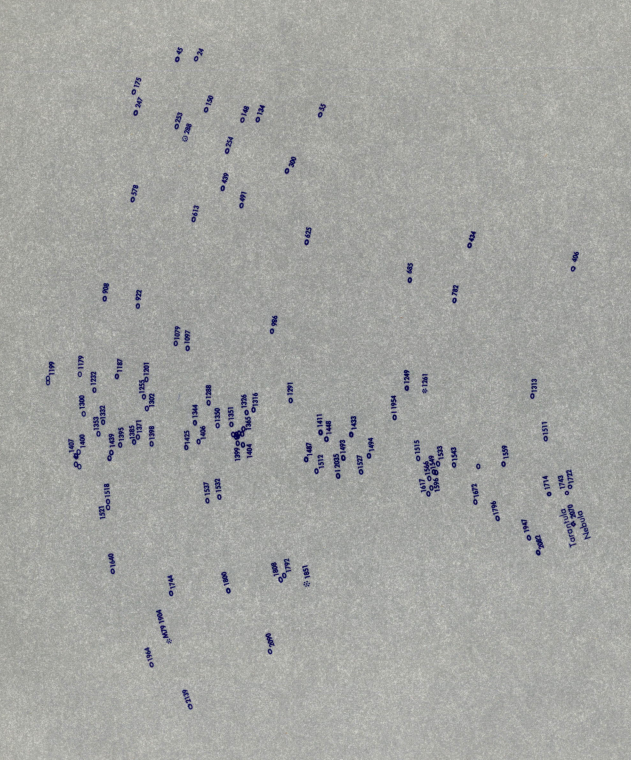

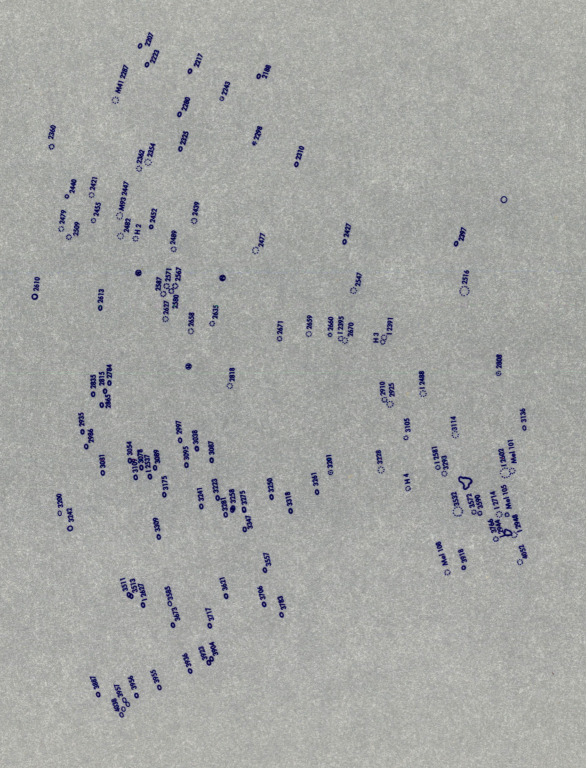

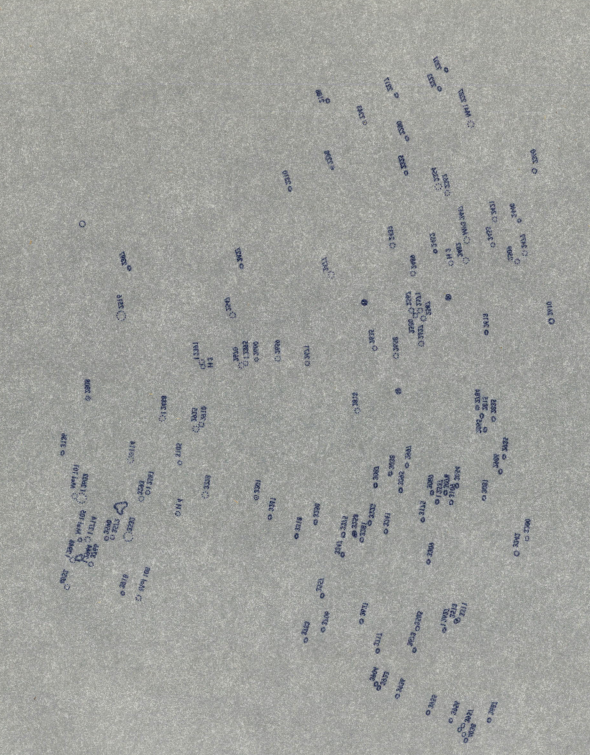

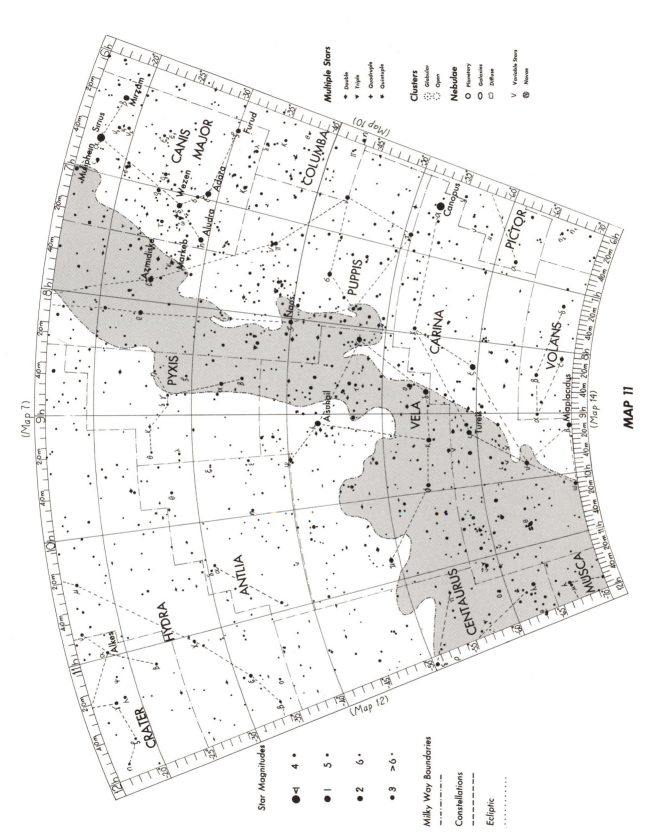

MAP 11

The key to the location of the individual maps will be found following map 7.

Star Magnitudes

● <1 4 ·
● 1   5 ·
● 2   6 ·
· 3   >6 ·

Milky Way Boundaries — — —

Constellations — — — —

Ecliptic ·········

Multiple Stars

◆ Double
▼ Triple
✦ Quadruple
✹ Quintuple

Clusters

⬡ Globular
○ Open

Nebulae

○ Planetary
◯ Galaxies
⊂⊃ Diffuse
∨ Variable Stars
🅝 Novae

CRATER
HYDRA
ANTLIA
PYXIS
CANIS MAJOR
COLUMBA
PUPPIS
CARINA
VELA
PICTOR
VOLANS
CENTAURUS
MUSCA

Sirius
Mirzam
Wezen
Adara
Aludra
Markeb
Azmidiske
Furud
Muliphein
Naos
Asohail
Canopus
Turais
Miaplacidus
Alkes

(Map 7)
(Map 10)
(Map 12)
(Map 14)

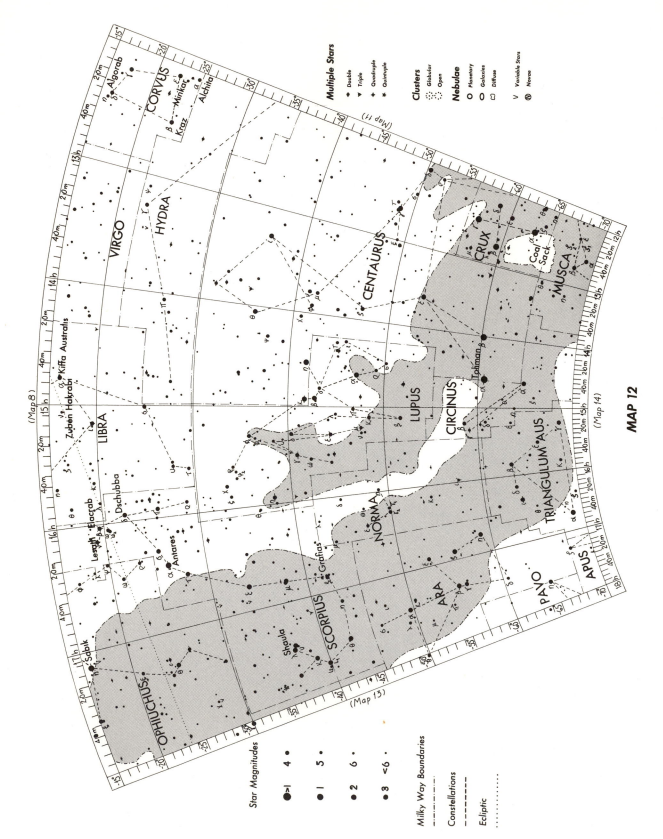

Star Magnitudes

- ● >1 ● 4
- ● 1 · 5
- ● 2 · 6
- · 3 · <6

Milky Way Boundaries

Constellations — — —

Ecliptic ·········

Multiple Stars

- ◆ Double
- ▼ Triple
- ✦ Quadruple
- ✱ Quintuple

Clusters

- ◌ Globular
- ◦ Open

Nebulae

- ○ Planetary
- ⊘ Galaxies
- ⊂⊃ Diffuse

- V Variable Stars
- Ⓝ Novae

VIRGO

HYDRA

CORVUS — Algorab, Minkar, Kraz, Alchiba

CENTAURUS

CRUX — Coal Sack

MUSCA

LIBRA — Kiffa Australis, Zuben Hakrabi

LUPUS

CIRCINUS — Lohman

NORMA

TRIANGULUM AUS.

ARA

APUS

PAVO

OPHIUCHUS — Sabik

SCORPIUS — Lesath, Elacrab, Dschubba, Antares, Grafias, Shaula

(Map 8)

(Map 11)

(Map 13)

(Map 14)

MAP 12

The key to the location of the individual maps will be found following map 7.

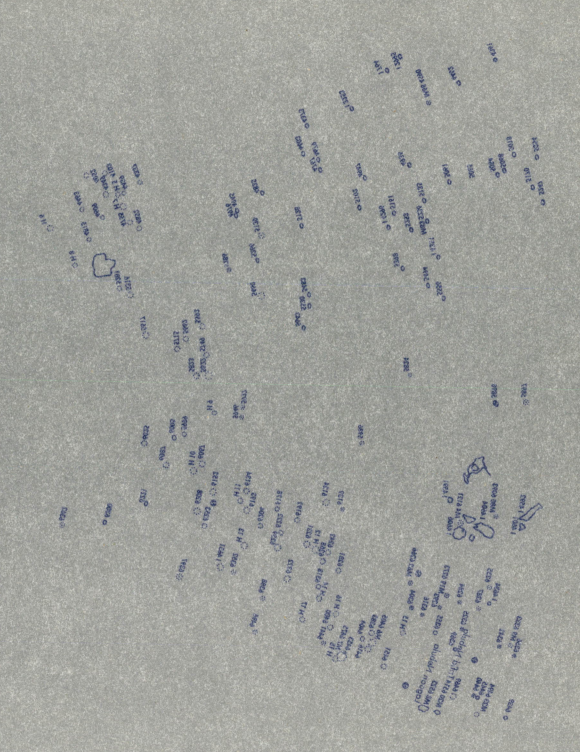

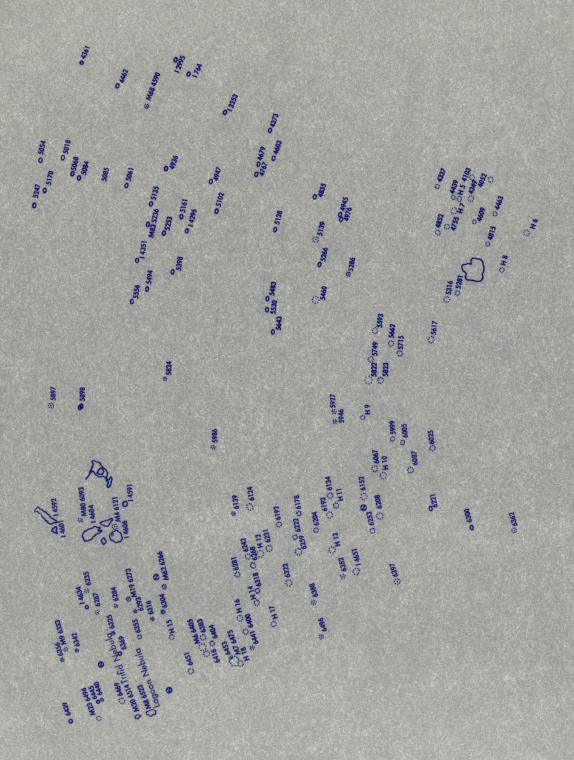

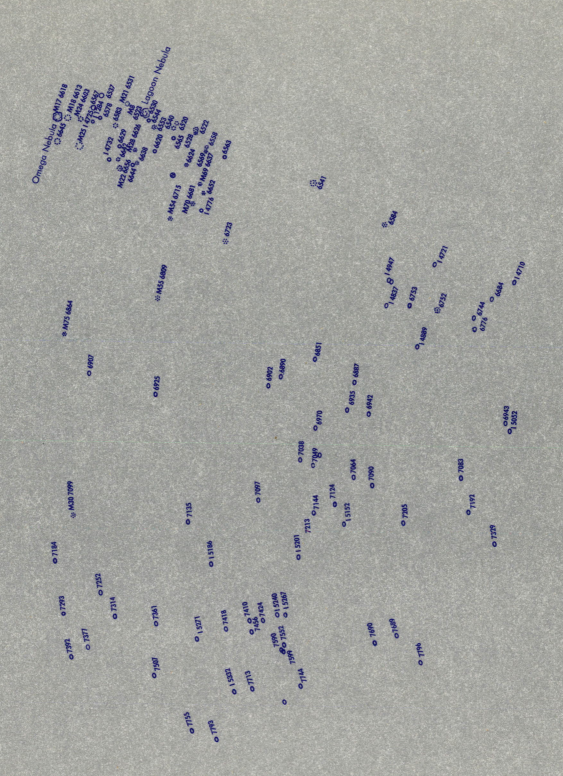

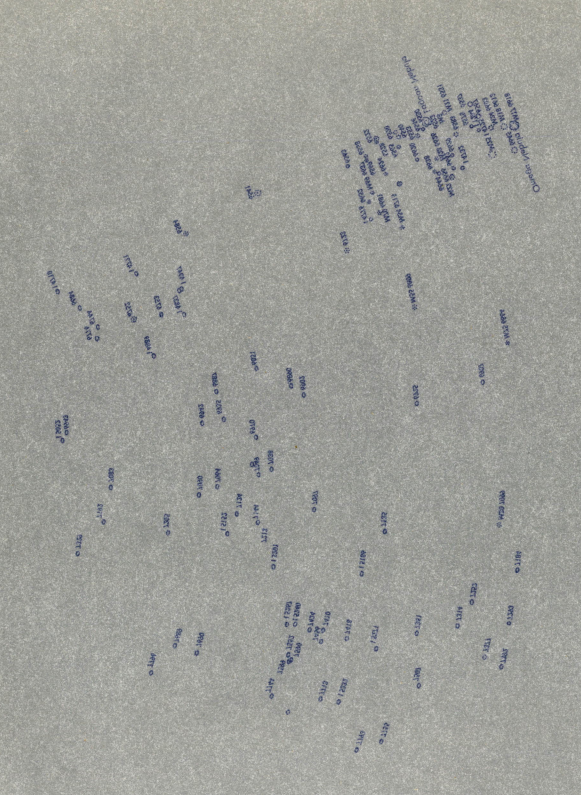

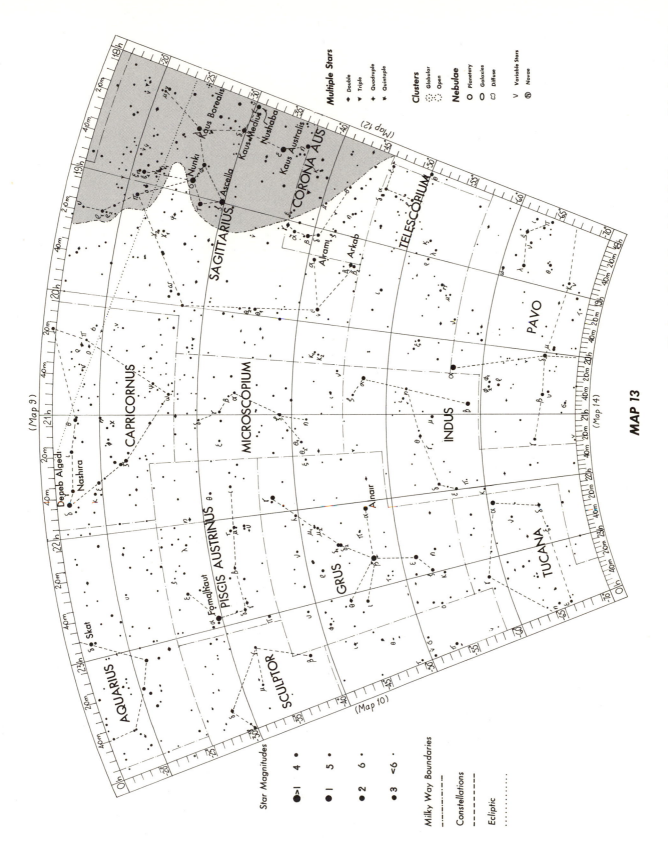

Star Magnitudes

●>1 · 4
● 1 · 5
● 2 · 6
● 3 · <6

Milky Way Boundaries
Constellations
Ecliptic

Multiple Stars

◆ Double
▼ Triple
✦ Quadruple
✴ Quintuple

Clusters

⬡ Globular
⬭ Open

Nebulae

○ Planetary
◯ Galaxies
⬭ Diffuse

V Variable Stars
Ⓝ Novae

MAP 13

The key to the location of the individual maps will be found following map 7.

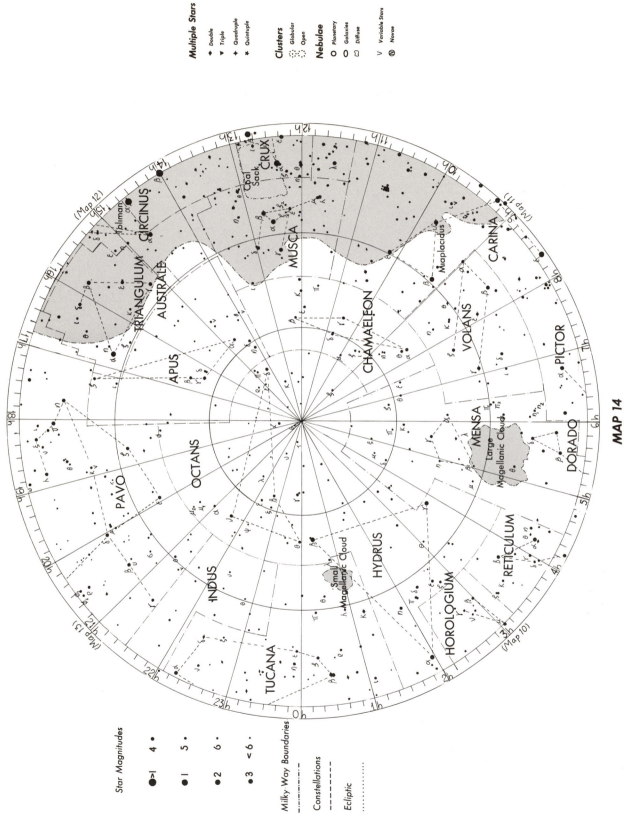

Star Magnitudes

● >1   ● 4
● 1   • 5
● 2   · 6
● 3   · <6

Milky Way Boundaries ―·―·―

Constellations ― ― ―

Ecliptic ....

Multiple Stars

♦ Double
▼ Triple
✦ Quadruple
✹ Quintuple

Clusters

⊙ Globular
∷ Open

Nebulae

○ Planetary
◯ Galaxies
⌘ Diffuse

V Variable Stars
Ⓝ Novae

MAP 14

The key to the location of the individual maps will be found following map 7.

(Map 12)
(Map 15)
TRIANGULUM AUSTRALE
CIRCINUS
Hbliman
MUSCA
Coal Sack
CRUX
(Map 11)
CARINA
Miaplacidus
CHAMAELEON
VOLANS
APUS
PICTOR
MENSA
Large Magellanic Cloud
DORADO
OCTANS
PAVO
INDUS
HYDRUS
Small Magellanic Cloud
RETICULUM
HOROLOGIUM
(Map 10)
TUCANA
(Map 13)

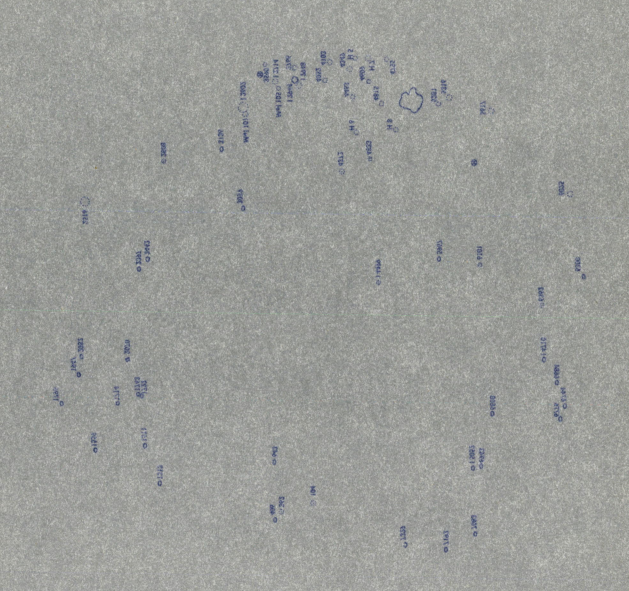

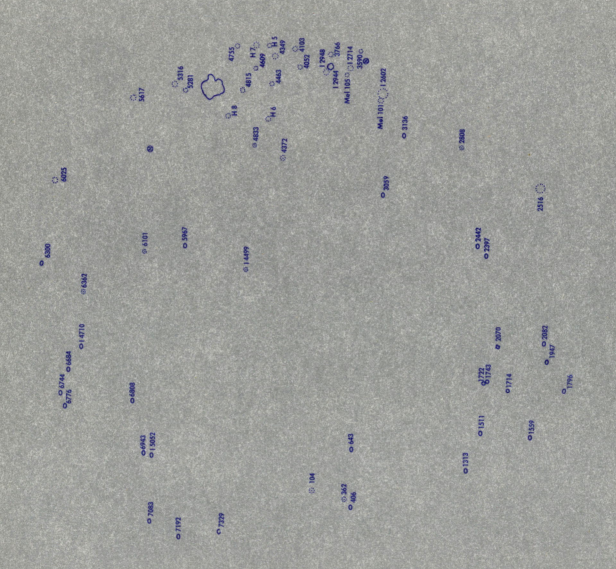

GAZETTEER

An Alphabetical List of 234 Named Stars

Name*	Designation†	Type‡	Apparent Magnitude	1970 Position RA (h/m)	Decl. (°/′)	Map No.	Distance
Acamar	θ Eri	A2	3.4	0257	−4026	10	
Achernar	α Eri	B5	0.6	0137	−5724	10	140
Achird	η Cas	F8	3.6	0047	+5738	2	
Acrab (Elacrab)	β Sco	B1	2.9	1603	−1943	8, 12	650
Acubens	α Cnc	A3	4.3	0857	+1159	7	
Adara	ε CMa	B1	1.6	0657	−2856	7, 11	680
Adhafera	ζ Leo	F0	3.6	1015	+2334	3, 7	
Ain	ε Tau	K0	3.6	0427	+1907	6, 2	
Albali	ε Aqr	A0	3.8	2046	−0936	9	
Albireor	β Cyg	A0, K0	3.2	1930	+2754	5, 9	
Alchita (Alchiba)	α Crv	F2	4.2	1207	−2434	8, 12	
Alcor	80 UMa	A5	4.0	1324	+5509	4	
Alcyone	η Tau	B5	3.0	0345	+2401	2, 6	541
Aldebaran (Palilicium)	α Tau	K5	1.1	0434	+1627	2, 6	68
Alderamin	α Cep	A5	2.6	2118	+6227	1, 5	
Aldib (Nodus II)	δ Dra	K0	3.2	1913	+6737	1, 5	

*Since many stars have several names, some alternates are included.

†The Bayer designation of Greek letter and constellation abbreviation. In a few cases, principally for the stars of the Pleiades, we have used the Flamsteed number.

‡Astronomers have classified many of the stars into types according to their spectra. The ten groups designated by the letters O, B, A, F, G, K, M, R, N, and S. Each main group has subdivisions from 0 to 9. Thus A2 means subtype 2 of group A. An easy way to remember the main types is by the mnemonic "Oh, be a fine girl. Kiss me right now, Susie."

Type	Example	Temperature (degrees Kelvin)	Most apparent elements	Color
O	Naos	30,000-60,000	Mostly helium	Blue-white
B	Spica, Rigel	12,000-25,000	Mostly helium	Blue-white
A	Vega, Deneb	8,000-11,000	Hydrogen and light metals	White
F	Procyon	6,200-7,200	Metals evident	Yellow-white
G	Sun, Capella	4,600-6,000	Many metals, especially iron	Yellow
K	Arcturus	3,500-4,900	Many metals, calcium	Orange
M	Antares	2,600-3,500	Heavy metals, titanium	Orange-red
R	Variable stars	2,000-3,000	Heavy metals, zirconium	Red
N	α Cygni			
	Variable stars	2,000-3,000	Carbon	Deep red
S	19 Piscium			

Name	Designation	Type	Apparent Magnitude	1970 Position RA (h/m)	1970 Position Decl. (°/′)	Map No.	Distance
Alfard (Cor Hydrae)	α Hya	K2	2.2	0926	−0831	7	94
Algenib	γ Peg	B2	2.9	0012	+1501	6, 2	570
Algieba	γ Leo	K0	2.6	1018	+1959	3, 7	90
Algol (Gorgona)	β Per	B8	2–3	0306	+4051	2	105
Algorab	δ Crv	A0	3.1	1229	−1621	8, 12	
Alhena	γ Gem	A0	1.9	0636	+1625	3, 7	105
Alioth	ϵ UMa	A0	1.7	1253	+5608	4	68
Alkaid (Benetnash)	η UMa	B3	1.9	1346	+4928	4	210
Alkaurops	μ Boo	F0	4.5	1523	+3729	4	
Alkes	α Crt	K0	4.2	1058	−1807	7, 11	
Almach	γ And	K0	2.3	0202	+4210	2	260
Alnair	α Gru	B5	2.2	2206	−4707	13	
Alnilam	ϵ Ori	B0	1.7	0536	−0113	6	1,600
Alnitak	ζ Ori	B0	2.0	0539	−0157	6	1,600
Alphecca (Gemma, Gnosia)	α CrB	A0	2.3	1533	+2649	4, 8	76
Alpheratz (Sirrah)	α And	A0	2.1	0007	+2855	2, 6	90
Alphirk	β Cep	B1	3.3	2128	+7026	1	
Alrai	γ Cep	K0	3.9	2338	+7728	1	
Alrami (Rukbat)	α Sgr	B8	4.1	1922	−4041	13	
Alrisha (Rescha, Kaitain)	α Psc	A2	4.3	0200	+0237	6	
Alshain	β Aql	K0	3.9	1954	+0620	9	
Alsuhail	λ Vel	K5	2.2	0907	−4319	11	750
Altair	α Aql	A5	0.9	1949	+0847	9	17
Aludra	η CMa	B5	2.4	0723	−2915	7, 11	
Alula Australe	ξ UMa	G0	3.9	1117	+3142	3	
Alula Boreale	ν UMa	K0	3.7	1117	+3316	3	
Alwaid	β Dra	G0	3.0	1729	+5219	4	
Alya	θ Ser	A5	4.5	1855	+0410	9	
Ancha	θ Aqr	K0	4.3	2215	−0756	9	
Antares (Vespertilio)	α Sco	M0, A3	1.2	1628	−2622	8, 12	520
Arcturus	α Boo	K0	0.2	1414	+1921	4, 8	36
Arich (Porrima)	γ Vir	F0	2.9	1240	−0117	8	32
Arkeb Posterior	β_2 Sgr	F0	4.5	1921	−4451	13	
Arkeb Prior	β_1 Sgr	B8	4.3	1920	−4431	13	
Arneb	α Lep	F0	2.7	0531	−1750	6, 10	900
Arrakis	μ Dra	F6	5.1	1704	+5435	4	
Ascella	ζ Sgr	A2	2.7	1901	−2955	9, 13	
Asellus Australis	δ Cnc	K0	4.2	0843	+1816	3, 7	

Name	Designation	Type	Apparent Magnitude	1970 Position RA (h/m)	Decl. (°/′)	Map No.	Distance
Asellus Borealis	γ Cnc	A0	4.7	0842	+2135	3, 7	
Asterion	β CVn	G0	4.3	1233	+4131	4	
Asterope	21 Tau	B9	5.8	0344	+2426	2	
Atiks	o Per	B1	3.9	0342	+3213	2	
Atlas	27 Tau	B8	3.8	0347	+2358	2	
Auva (Minelauva)	δ Vir	M0	3.7	1254	+0334	8	
Azelfafage	π₁ Cyg	B3	4.8	2142	+5103	5	
Azha	η Eri	K2	4.1	0255	−0901	6	
Azmidiske	ξ Pup	G0	3.5	0748	−2447	7, 11	
Baten Kaitos	ζ Cet	K0	3.9	0150	−1029	6	
Beid	o₁ Eri	F1	4.1	0410	−0655	6	
Bellatrix	γ Ori	B2	1.7	0524	+0619	6	470
Betelgeuse	α Ori	M0	0-1	0554	+0724	6	650
Botein	δ Ari	K2	4.5	0310	+1937	2, 6	
Canopus (Suhel)	α Car	F0	−0.9	0623	−5241	11	180
Capella (Alhajoth)	α Aur	G0	0.2	0514	+4558	2	45
Caph	β Cas	F5	2.4	0007	+5849	2	45
Castor	α Gem	A0	1.6	0733	+3157	3	45
Ceginus	φ Boo	G5	5.4	1537	+4207	4	
Celaeno	16 Tau	B7	5.4	0343	+2412	2	
Cor Caroli (Chara)	α CVn	A0	2.9	1255	+3829	4	
Cor Serpentis (Unuk El Haia)	α Ser	K0	2.7	1543	+0631	8	71
Coxa	θ Leo	A0	3.4	1113	+1536	3, 7	
Cursa	β Eri	A3	2.9	0506	−0507	6	78
Dabih	β Cap	G0, A0	3.2	2019	−1453	9	
Deneb (Arided)	α Cyg	A2	1.3	2040	+4510	5	540
Deneb Algedi (Scheddi)	δ Cap	A5	3.0	2145	−1616	9, 13	
Deneb Kaitos (Diphda)	β Cet	K0	2.2	0042	−1809	6, 10	57
Deneb Okab	δ Aql	F0	3.4	1924	+0303	9	
Denebola	β Leo	A2	2.2	1148	+1444	7	43
Diadem	α Com	F4	5.2	1309	+1741	4, 8	
Dschubba	δ Sco	B0	2.5	1559	−2232	8, 12	590
Dubhe	α UMa	K0	1.9	1102	+6154	1, 3	105
Dziban	ψ Dra	F5	4.9	1743	+7211	1	
Electra	17 Tau	B5	3.8	0343	+2401	2	
Enif	ε Peg	K0	2.5	2143	+0944	9	780
Etamin (Eltanin, Rastaban)	γ Dra	K5	2.4	1756	+5129	4	108
Erakis	μ Cep	M2	Var.	2142	+5839	5	
Fomalhaut	α PsA	A3	1.3	2256	−2947	9, 13	23
Furud	ζ CMa	B3	3.1	0619	−3003	11	
Gianfar	λ Dra	M0	4.1	1130	+6930	1, 3	

Name	Designation	Type	Apparent Magnitude	1970 Position RA (h/m)	1970 Position Decl. (°/')	Map No.	Distance
Gienah	ε Cyg	K0	2.6	2045	+3351	5	63
Gomeisa	β CMi	B8	3.1	0726	+0820	7	
Grafias	ζ Sco	K5	3.8	1653	−4219	12	
Gredi	α Cap	G0, G5	3.8	2016	−1237	9	
Grumium	ξ Dra	K3	3.9	1753	+5653	4	
Hamal	α Ari	K2	2.2	0205	+2319	2, 6	76
Haris	γ Boo	F0	3.0	1431	+3826	4	
Hasseleh	ι Aur	K2	2.9	0455	+3307	2	330
Hatsya	ι Ori	Oe5*	2.9	0534	−0556	6	2,000
Heka	λ Ori	Oe5	3.7	0533	+0955	6	
Heze	ζ Vir	A2	3.4	1333	−0027	8	
Hoedus I	ζ Aur	K0, B1	3.9	0500	+4102	2	
Hoedus II	η Aur	B3	3.3	0504	+4112	2	
Homam	ζ Peg	B8	3.6	2240	+1040	9	
Izar (Mirak, (Pulcherrima)	ε Boo	K0	2.7	1444	+2712	4, 8	103
Kaffaljidhma	γ Cet	A2	3.6	0242	+0306	6	
Kajam	ω Her	A2	4.5	1624	+1405	8	
Kaus Australis	ε Sgr	A0	1.9	1822	−3424	13	105
Kaus Borealis	λ Sgr	K0	2.9	1826	−2526	9, 13	
Kaus Medius	δ Sgr	K0	2.8	1819	−2951	9, 13	103
Kelb Alrai	β Oph	K0	2.9	1742	+0435	8	
Kerb	τ Peg	A5	4.7	2319	+2334	5, 9	
Kiffa Australis (Zubenelgenubi)	α Lib	A3	2.9	1449	−1555	8, 12	
Kiffa Borealis (Zebeneschamali)	β Lib	B8	2.7	1515	−0916	8	
Kochab	β UMi	K5	2.2	1451	+7417	1	105
Kornephoros (Rutilicus)	β Her	K0	2.8	1629	+2132	4, 8	103
Kraz	β Crv	G5	2.8	1233	−2314	8, 12	108
Kuma	ν Dra	A8	5.0	1732	+5512	4	
Lesath	ν Sco	B2	4.3	1610	−1923	8, 12	
Maasym	λ Her	K4	4.5	1730	+2608	4, 8	
Maia	20 Tau	B9	4.0	0344	+2415	2	
Markab	α Peg	A0	2.6	2303	+1502	9	
Markeb	κ₁ Pup	B8	4.5	0738	−2644	7, 11	
Marsik	κ Her	G4	5.3	1607	+1707	4, 8	
Matar	η Peg	G0	3.1	2242	+3004	5, 9	
Mebsuta	ε Gem	G5	3.2	0642	+2510	3, 7	
Megrez (Kaffa)	δ UMa	A2	3.4	1214	+5712	4	
Mekbuda	ζ Gem	G0	Var.	0702	+2037	3, 7	
Menkalinan	β Aur	A0	2.1	0557	+4457	2	88
Menkar	α Cet	M0	2.8	0300	+0358	6	
Menkhib	ζ Per	B1	2.9	0352	+3148	2	1,000
Merak	β UMa	A0	2.4	1100	+5635	3	78
Merez (Nekkar)	β Boo	G5	3.6	1501	+4030	4	

*Emission lines in spectrum.

Name	Designation	Type	Apparent Magnitude	RA (h/m)	1970 Position Decl. (°')	Map No.	Distance
Merga	38 Boo	F4	5.8	1448	+4615	4	
Merope	23 Tau	B5	4.2	0345	+2351	2	
Mesarthim	γ Ari	A0	4.8	0152	+1909	2, 6	
Metallah (Mothallah)	α Tri	F5	3.6	0151	+2926	2, 6	
Miaplacidus	β Car	A0	1.8	0913	−6935	14	
Minkar	ε Crv	K0	3.2	1209	−2227	8, 12	
Mintaka	δ Ori	B0	2.5	0530	−0019	6	1,500
Mira	o Cet	M5	2–10	0218	−0307	6	
Mirach	β And	M0	2.4	0108	+3527	2	76
Miram	η Per	K0	3.9	0248	+5546	2	
Mirfak	α Per	F5	1.9	0322	+4945	2	570
Mirzam	β CMa	B1	2.0	0621	−1756	7, 11	750
Misam	κ Per	G8	4.0	0308	+4445	2	
Mizar	ζ UMa	A2	2.4	1323	+5505	4	88
Mufrid	η Boo	G0	2.8	1353	+1833	4, 8	32
Muliphein	γ CMa	B8	4.0	0702	−1535	7, 11	
Museida	π₂ UMa	K2	4.8	0837	+6426	1, 3	
Naos	ζ Pup	Od*	2.3	0803	−3955	11	
Nashira	γ Cap	F2	3.8	2138	−1648	9, 13	
Nath	β Tau	B8	1.8	0524	+2835	2, 6	300
Nihal	β Lep	G0	3.0	0527	−2047	6, 10	
Nodus I	ζ Dra	B5	3.2	1709	+6545	1, 4	
Nunki	σ Sgr	B3	2.1	1853	−2620	9, 13	
Nusakan	β CrB	F0	3.1	1527	+2912	4, 8	
Nushaba (Nash)	γ Sgr	K0	3.1	1804	−3026	13	
Phakt	α Col	B5	2.7	0539	−3405	10	
Phecda (Phad)	γ UMa	A0	2.5	1152	+5351	3	
Pherkad	γ UMi	A2	3.1	1521	+7156	1	90
Pherkard (Yildun)	δ UMi	A0	4.4	1743	+8636	1	
Pleione	28 Tau	B8	Var.	0347	+2403	2	
Pollux	β Gem	K0	1.2	0743	+2805	3	35
Procyon (Elgomaisa)	α CMi	F5	0.5	0738	+0518	7	11.3
Rana	δ Eri	K0	3.7	0342	−0952	6	
Ras Algethi	α Her	M3	3.5	1713	+1425	8	
Ras Alhague	α Oph	A5	2.1	1734	+1235	8	
Ras Elased Australis	ε Leo	G0	3.1	0944	+2355	3, 7	
Ras Elased Borealis	μ Leo	K3	4.1	0951	+2610	3, 7	
Regulus (Kalb)	α Leo	B8	1.3	1007	+1208	7	84
Rigel	β Ori	B8	0.3	0513	−0814	6	900
Rotanev	β Del	F3	3.7	2036	+1429	9	
Rucha (Ksora)	δ Cas	A5	2.8	0124	+6005	1, 2	
Sabik	η Oph	A2	2.6	1709	−1541	8, 12	69

*Dwarf star.

Name	Designation	Type	Apparent Magnitude	1970 Position RA (h/m)	Decl. (°′)	Map No.	Distance
Sadalachbia	γ Aqr	A0	4.0	2220	−0132	9	
Sadalmelek	α Aqr	G0	3.2	2204	−0028	9	
Sadalsud	β Aqr	G0	3.1	2130	−0542	9	
Sador	γ Cyg	F8	2.3	2021	+4010	5	750
Saiph	κ Ori	B0	2.2	0546	−0941	6	2,100
Sarin	δ Her	A2	3.2	1714	+2453	4, 8	
Sceptrum	53 Eri	K4	4.0	0437	−1422	6	
Scheat	β Peg	M0	2.6	2302	+2755	5, 9	
Schedir	α Cas	K0	2.3	0039	+5622	1, 2	150
Segin	ε Cas	B3	3.4	0152	+6331	2	
Sham	α Sgr	F8	4.4	1939	+1757	5, 9	
Shaula	λ Sco	B2	1.7	1732	−3705	12	310
Sheliak	β Lyr	B8, B2	3.4	1849	+3310	5	
Sheratan	β Ari	A5	2.7	0153	+2040	2, 6	52
Sirius (Canicula)	α CMa	A0	−1.6	0644	−1640	7, 11	8.7
Situla	κ Aqr	K1	5.3	2236	−0424	9	
Skat	δ Aqr	A2	3.5	2252	−1559	9, 13	
Spica (Azimech)	α Vir	B2	1.2	1323	−1100	6	220
Sualocin	α Del	B8	3.9	2038	+1548	5, 9	
Subra	o Leo	F5, A3	3.8	0940	+1003	6	
Sulaphat	γ Lyr	A0	3.3	1858	+3239	5	
Tabit	π₃ Ori	F8	3.3	0448	+0655	6	
Talitha	ι UMa	A5	3.1	0857	+4810	3	
Tania Australis	μ UMa	K5	3.2	1021	+4140	3	
Tania Borealis	λ UMa	A2	3.5	1015	+4304	3	
Tarazed (Reda)	γ Aql	K2	2.8	1945	+1033	9	
Taygeta	19 Tau	B7	4.4	0343	+2422	2	
Tejat Posterior	μ Gem	M0	3.2	0621	+2232	3, 7	
Tejat Prior	η Gem	M0	3.4	0613	+2231	3, 7	
Theemin	μ₂ Eri	K0	3.9	0434	−3037	10	
Thuban	α Dra	A0	3.7	1404	+6432	1, 4	
Toliman	α Cen	G0	0.1	1438	−6043	12, 14	4.3
Tureis	ι Car	F0	2.2	0916	−5909	11	
Tyl	ε Dra	G3	4.0	1948	+7012	1	
Vega	α Lyr	A0	0.1	1836	+3836	5	26.5
Vindemiatrix	ε Vir	K0	2.9	1301	+1108	8	
Wasat	δ Gem	A8	3.5	0718	+2202	3, 7	
Wezen	δ CMa	F8	2.0	0707	−2621	7, 11	2,100
Yed Posterior	ε Oph	K0	3.3	1617	−0437	8	
Yed Prior	δ Oph	M0	3.0	1613	−0337	8	
Zaurak	γ Eri	K5	3.2	0357	−1336	6	
Zavijah (Alaraph)	β Vir	F8	3.8	1149	+0157	7	
Zibel	ζ Eri	A3	4.9	0314	−0856	6	
Zosma	δ Leo	A3	2.6	1113	+2042	3, 7	82
Zuben Elakrab	γ Lib	G6	4.0	1534	−1442	8	

Name	Designation	Type	Apparent Magnitude	1970 Position		Map No.	Distance
				RA (h/m)	Decl. (°/′)		
Zuben Elakribi	δ Lib	A0	Var.	1459	−0815	8	
Zuben Hakrabi	ν Lib	K5	5.3	1504	−1600	8, 12	

Visual Binaries

1970 Position (RA and Decl.)	Magnitudes of elements	Separation (seconds of arc)	Color	Designation or Constellation	Map No.
000166	6.0, 7.5	15.3	Yellow, blue	Cas	1, 2
001309	5.9, 7.6	11.8	White, purple	35 Psc	6
003534	4.4, 8.7	36.1	White, blue	π And	2
003821	5.6, 8.8	6.6	Yellow, blue	55 Psc	2, 6
004757	3.6, 7.5	10.1	Yellow, purple	η Cas (Achird)	2
010405	6.8, 7.6	33.3	White, blue	77 Psc	6
015289	2.5, 8.8	19.0	Yellow, pale blue	Polaris	1
015219	4.8, 4.8	8.2	White, gray	γ Ari (Mesarthim)	2, 6
015623	4.8, 7.4	37.4	White, blue	λ Ari	2, 6
020003	4.3, 5.2	2.1	Green, blue	α Psc (Alrisha)	6
020242	2.3, 5.1	10.0	Orange, greenish blue	γ And (Almach)	2
020939	6.1, 6.7	16.7	Yellow, blue	59 And	2
021102	5.7, 7.7	16.3	Topaz, violet	66 Cet	6
021130	5.4, 7.0	3.6	Yellow, blue	ι Tri	2, 6
022867 (triple)	4.7, 7.0, 8.2	2-7	Yellow, blue, blue	ι Cas	1, 2
023525	7.4, 6.6	38.7	Yellow, gray	30 Ari	2, 6
023927	5.4, 9.5	28.8	Topaz, blue	33 Ari	2, 6
024203	3.7, 6.4	3.0	Yellow, blue	γ Cet (Kaffaljidhma)	6
024956	3.9, 8.6	28.4	White, blue	η Per	2
031540	6.8, 7.8	3.4	Yellow, blue	Per	2
033501	6.0, 8.2	6.0	Gold, blue	Tau	6
034711	5.0, 9.3	9.2	Green, purple	30 Tau	6
041917	5.0, 8.7	52.1	Red, blue	φ Tau	2, 6
042940	6.9, 7.1	9.0	White, white	Per	2
044209	6.8, 6.7	9.2	Yellow, white	55 Eri	6
050828	6.0, 8.2	11.9	White, gray	Tau	2, 6
051213	4.5, 7.5	2.6	Yellow, blue	κ Lep	6
051203	4.6, 8.6	7.0	Yellow, blue	ρ Ori	6
052503	4.7, 10.0	2.6	Yellow, yellow	ψ Ori	6
053000	2.5, 6.9	52.8	White, blue	δ Ori (Mintaka)	6
053310	3.7, 5.7	4.4	Yellow, red	λ Ori	6
053731	5.5, 8.5	12.5	Yellow, blue	Aur	2
053902	2.1, 4.2	2.4	Yellow, blue	ζ Ori (Alnitak)	6
054323	3.8, 6.4	95.0	Yellow, red	γ Lep	6, 10
060949	6.8, 6.1	7.7	White, lilac	41 Aur	3
062205	4.5, 6.5	13.2	Gold, blue	ε Mon	7
065060	5.9, 7.1	0.3	Gold, purple	14 Lyn	1, 3
065514	5.2, 8.5	3.0	White, blue	μ CMa	7
071617	3.7, 10.0	10.0	Green, blue	λ Gem	3, 7

1970 Position (RA and Decl.)	Magnitudes of elements	Separation (seconds of arc)	Color	Designation or Constellation	Map No.
073332	2.0, 2.9	2.2	Both greenish white	α Gem (Castor)	3
074325	3.7, 3.7	6.8	Orange, blue	κ Gem	3, 7
081018 (quadruple)	5.7, 6.0, 5.1, 6.0	1.0, 6.0	Yellow-orange combination	ζ Cnc	3, 7
084529	6.6, 4.2	30.7	Yellow, blue	ι₁ Cnc	3, 7
091737	4.0, 6.0	2.9	Green, blue	38 Lyn	3
092204	6.7, 8.0	21.3	White, gray	Hya	7
092239	8.5, 9.2	82.5	Yellow, lilac	Lyn	3
101671	6.6, 7.2	16.7	White, white	UMa	1
101820	2.6, 3.8	4.3	Yellow, green	Leo	7, 3
111453	7.8, 6.3	12.6	Yellow, white	UMa	3
113745	8.2, 6.3	10.0	White, white	65 UMa	3
115447 (quadruple)	6.5, 6.8, 7.2, 8.3	63.0, 4.0	Yellow-white	65 UMa	3
121541	5.8, 8.9	11.5	Red, blue	2 CVn	4
122816	8.4, 3.1	24.0	Yellow, purple	δ Crv (Algorab)	12, 8
123419	6.7, 5.2	20.3	Orange, blue	24 Com	4, 8
124001	3.6, 3.6	5.2	Yellow, yellow	γ Vir	8
125222	5.1, 9.0	29.0	Purple, blue	35 Com	4, 8
125539	5.4, 2.9	19.7	Yellow, yellow	α CVn (Cor Caroli)	4
132355	2.4, 4.0	14.5	White, white	ζ UMa (Mizar)	4
141252	6.6, 4.6	13.2	White, blue	κ Boo	4
143917	4.9, 5.8	5.6	White, white	π Boo	4, 8
144427	2.7, 5.1	2.9	Orange, green	ε Boo (Izar)	4, 8
145019	4.8, 6.9	6.7	Yellow, purple	ξ Boo	4, 8
151120	4.7, 9.7	58.6	Yellow, purple	ι Lib	8, 12
151120	6.8, 7.7	24.2	Yellow, white	Ser	4, 8
153311	5.2, 4.2	3.9	White, white	δ Ser	8
153837	6.0, 5.1	6.0	White, blue	ζ CrB	4
160311	4.2, 7.2	7.9	White, gray	ξ Sco (Elacrab)	8
160420	2.9, 5.1	13.7	White, blue	β Sco	8, 12
161717	5.3, 6.5	29.4	Yellow, red	κ Her (Marsik)	4, 8
161019 (quadruple)	6.8, 7.8, 4.4, 6.4	2-41	Yellow-orange combination	ν Sco	8, 12
162423	5.9, 5.2	3.5	Yellow, blue	ρ Oph	8, 12
171314	3.5, 5.4	4.6	Orange, green	α Her (Ras Algethi)	4, 8
171326	5.3, 5.3	4.8	Yellow, red	36 Oph	8, 12
171425	3.2, 8.8	10.0	Green, purple	δ Her (Sarin)	4, 8
171624	6.9, 5.4	10.8	Blue, yellow	o Oph	8, 12
171913	4.4, 8.7	47.3	Green, lilac	ν Ser	8
172337	5.5, 4.5	4.0	Green, green	ρ Her	4
173155	5.0, 5.0	62.0	White, white	ν Dra	4
175903	3.9, 8.2	54.6	Yellow, red	58 Oph	8
180022	5.2, 5.1	6.5	Green, red	95 Her	4, 8

1970 Position (RA and Decl.)	Magnitudes of elements	Separation (seconds of arc)	Color	Designation or Constellation	Map No.
180403	4.3, 6.0	4.6	Yellow, red	70 Oph	9
183352	5.4, 9.0	25.8	Yellow, blue	Dra	5
184340 (quadruple)	6.0, 5.1, 5.1, 5.4	2.8-2.3	Yellow-orange combination	ϵ Lyr	5
184538	4.3, 5.8	43.0	Topaz, green	ζ Lyr	5
184501	5.7, 7.3	13.0	White, blue	5 Aql	9
185159	4.8, 8.2	34.0	Orange, green	o Dra	5
185504	4.5, 5.4	22.6	Yellow, yellow	θ Ser	9
190304	7.2, 5.5	38.0	White, lilac	15 Aql	9
192928	3.2, 5.4	35.0	Yellow, blue	β Cyg (Albireo)	5, 9
193916	5.5, 8.9	45.6	Yellow, blue	54 Sgr	9, 13
194534	5.0, 8.5	25.9	Red, blue	17 Cyg	5
194819	5.0, 5.8	8.0	Green, blue	Sge	5, 9
195308	5.8, 6.5	36.0	Yellow, green	57 Aql	9
200050	5.3, 9.1	42.0	Yellow, blue	26 Cyg	5
200609	6.5, 8.9	4.0	Yellow, purple	Aql	9
201078	4.2, 8.2	7.4	White, blue	κ Cep	1
201613 (quadruple)	4.6, 9.0	45.5	Yellow, yellow	α_1 Cap	9
	3.8, 10.6	7.1	Yellow, yellow	α_2 Cap (Gredi)	9
202619	5.2, 8.5	3.2	Yellow, blue	π Cap	9, 13
202718	5.0, 10.0	1.0	Yellow, purple	ρ Cap	9, 13
202819	6.6, 6.1	21.9	White, blue	o Cap	9, 13
204431	4.3, 9.6	6.0	Yellow, blue	52 Cyg	5
204516	5.5, 4.5	10.4	Yellow, green	γ Del	5, 9
205704	5.3, 6.2	0.9	White, blue	ϵ Equ	9
212870	Var., 8.0	13.7	White, blue	β Cep (Alphirk)	1
215156	7.3, 5.5	19.8	Green, blue	Cep	5
220364	6.6, 4.6	7.2	Blue, blue	ξ Cep	5
221070	5.5, 8.6	14.7	White, blue	Cep	1
211273	6.1, 8.5	29.0	Yellow, white	Cep	1
221421	5.7, 7.2	5.0	Yellow, blue	41 Aqr	9, 13
221838	6.1, 9.0	15.9	White, blue	Lac	5
222700	4.6, 4.4	2.0	White, yellow	ζ Aqr	9
222858	7.5, Var.	41.0	Yellow, blue	δ Cep	5
231409	4.5, 9.4	49.4	Yellow, blue	ψ Aqr	9
235856	5.1, 7.2	3.1	Green, blue	σ Cas	5

Short-Period Variables

Position 1900*	1970	Designation	Maximum	Minimum	Type	Period (days)	Map No.
005381	005982	U Cep	6.7	9.8	Eclipsing	2.49	1
030140	030640	β Per	2.1	3.3	Eclipsing	2.87	2
035512	035912	λ Tau	3.5	4.0	Eclipsing	3.95	6
184633	184933	β Lyr	3.4	4.3	Eclipsing	12.93	5
025838	030339	ρ Per	3.3	4.0	Semiregular	33–55	2
060822	061322	η Gem	3.1	3.9	Semiregular	233.0	3, 7
153738	154039	RR CrB	7.1	8.6	Semiregular	60.0	4
171014	171314	α Her	3.0	4.0	Semiregular	100.0	9
061907	062407	T Mon	6.4	8.0	Classical Cepheid	27.02	7
065820	070221	ζ Gem	4.4	5.2	Classical Cepheid	10.15	3, 7
194700	195101	η Aql	4.1	5.2	Classical Cepheid	7.18	9
222557	222858	δ Cep	4.1	5.2	Classical Cepheid	5.37	5
192242	192543	RR Lyr	6.9	8.0	Cluster Cepheid	0.56	5
083610	083910	VZ Cnc	7.6	8.3	Cluster Cepheid	0.18	7
154428	154728	R CrB	5.8	14.8	R Coronae Borealis	–	4, 8

* As listed on AAVSO charts.

Long-Period Variables

Position 1900*	1970	Designation	Maximum	Minimum	1964	Period (days)	Map No.
001755	002256	T Cas	6.7	12.7	7.8	445	2
001838	002238	R And	5.0	15.3	7.0	408	2
021403	021703	O Cet	2.0	10.1	3.4	332	6
022813	023213	U Cet	6.7	13.0	7.5	235	6
050953	051354	R Aur	6.6	13.8	7.7	459	2
054920	055420	U Ori	5.2	12.9	6.3	372	2, 6
061702	062102	V Mon	6.0	14.0	7.0	335	7
070122	070523	R Gem	5.9	14.1	7.1	370	3, 7
070310	070710	R CMi	7.0	11.8	8.0	313	7
081112	081512	R Cnc	6.1	11.9	6.8	362	7
094211	094612	R Leo	4.4	11.6	5.8	313	7
103769	104369	R Uma	6.2	13.6	7.5	302	1, 3
122001	122401	SS Vir	5.9	10.0	6.8	355	8
131546	131846	V CVn	7.0	8.2	6.8	192	4
143227	143627	R Boo	5.9	13.1	7.2	223	4, 8
151731	152032	S CrB	5.8	13.9	7.3	361	4
162119	162519	U Her	6.2	13.3	7.5	406	4, 8
170215	170616	R Oph	6.2	14.4	7.9	302	8, 12
171723	172123	RS Her	7.2	13.4	7.9	219	4, 8
183308	183709	X Oph	5.9	9.2	6.8	334	9
190108	190508	R Aql	6.2	12.1	6.1	300	9
191019	191519	R Sgr	6.6	13.3	7.3	269	9, 13
194032	195033	X Cyg	2.3	14.3	5.2	407	5
204405	204805	T Aqr	6.7	14.0	7.7	202	9
210868	210968	T Cep	5.2	11.2	6.0	390	5, 1
213753	214054	RU Cyg	6.9	10.2	8.0	234	5
230759	231159	V Cas	6.7	13.4	7.9	228	5
233815	234216	R Aqr	6.7	11.6	6.5	387	9, 13
235350	235751	R Cas	4.8	13.6	7.0	431	5
235715	000115	W Cet	6.5	14.5	7.6	351	9, 13

* As listed on AAVSO charts.

Open Star Clusters

NGC number	Constel- lation	Angular size (minutes of arc)	No. of stars	Class*	Magni- tude	Distance (light- years)	Date on meridian	1970 Position RA (h/m)	Decl. (°′)	Map No.
129	Cas	11	50	e	10	6,500	11/13	0028	+6004	1, 2
225	Cas	12	20		9	1,690	11/16	0042	+6138	1, 2
457	Cas	10	100	e	8	2,145	11/25	0117	+5810	2
559	Cas	7	60	e	7	8,940	11/28	0127	+6308	1, 2
581 (M.103)	Cas	5	60	d	7	3,740	11/29	0131	+6033	1, 2
663	Cas	11	80	e	7	2,570	12/2	0144	+6107	1, 2
752	And	45	70	d	7	3,410	12/5	0156	+3731	2
869	Per	36	350	f	4	4,310	12/10	0217	+5701	2
884	Per	36	300	e	5	4,310	12/11	0220	+5658	2
I 1805	Cas	20	20	d	7	2,140	12/14	0230	+6118	1, 2
1039 (M.34)	Per	18	80	d	6	1,430	12/17	0240	+4239	2
H 1	Cas	15	30	e	7	5,915	12/24	0308	+6308	1, 2
1245	Per	30	40	e	7	16,250	12/25	0312	+4708	2
1342	Per	15	40	c	7	2,700	12/29	0330	+3713	2
Mel 22 (M.45)	Tau	100	130	c	2	410	1/2	0345	+2402	2, 6
1513	Per	12	40	d	9	1,485	1/7	0408	+4926	2
1528	Per	25	80	e	6	2,830	1/8	0413	+5111	2
Mel 25	Tau	330	40	c	1	130	1/10	0418	+1534	2, 6
1545	Per	18	25		8	4,290	1/10	0418	+5011	2
1817	Tau	15	10	d	9	6,790	1/23	0510	+1640	2, 6
1857	Aur	9	45	d	9	5,400	1/25	0518	+3919	2
1893	Aur	12	20	d	8	2,570	1/26	0524	+3323	2
1907	Aur	5	40	f	10	6,690	1/27	0526	+3518	2
1912 (M.38)	Aur	20	100	e	7	3,580	1/27	0527	+3549	2
1960 (M.36)	Aur	12	60	f	6	3,780	1/29	0533	+3408	2
2099 (M.37)	Aur	20	150	f	6	4,700	2/2	0550	+3233	2
2168 (M.35)	Gem	40	120	e	5	2,570	2/7	0607	+2420	3, 7
2169	Ori	5	19	d	6	2,570	2/7	0607	+1358	7
2194	Ori	8	100	e	9	16,300	2/8	0612	+1250	7
2244	Mon	40	16	c	6	5,400	2/13	0631	+0453	7
2287 (M.41)	CMa	30	50	e	5	2,470	2/17	0646	−2044	7, 11
2281	Aur	17	30	e	7	5,400	2/17	0647	+4105	3, 7
2323 (M.50)	Mon	16	100	e	7	2,600	2/20	0702	−0818	7

*(c) Loose and irregular   (Hyades)
 (d) Loose and poor   (The Beehive)
 (e) Intermediate rich   (M.41 in Canis Major)
 (f) Fairly rich   (M.67 in Cancer)
 (g) Rich and concentrated (M.11 in Scutum)

NGC number	Constel-lation	Angular size (minutes of arc)	No. of stars	Class	Magni-tude	Distance (light-years)	Date on meridian	1970 Position RA (h/m)	Decl. (°/')	Map No.
2353	Mon	20	25	d	5	3,420	2/24	0713	−1014	7
2360	CMa	12	50	g	10	3,420	2/25	0716	−1535	7, 11
2420	Gem	7	20	e	10	10,800	3/1	0736	+2138	3, 7
2437 (M.46)	Pup	24	150	f	9	5,910	3/2	0741	−1445	7
2447 (M.93)	Pup	25	60	f	6	3,570	3/3	0743	−2348	7, 11
2506	Mon	10	50	g	11	7,440	3/7	0759	−1032	7
2539	Pup	21	150	f	8	5,910	3/9	0810	−1244	7
2548	Hya	30	80	f	5	3,420	3/10	0812	−0541	7
2627	Pyx	8	40	f	8	8,150	3/16	0836	−2950	7, 11
2632 (M.44)	Cnc	90	75	d	6	513	3/17	0838	+1948	3, 7
2682 (M.67)	Cnc	15	65	f	6	2,700	3/20	0849	+1155	7
Mel 111	Com	275	30	c	3	270	5/14	1224	+2617	4, 8
6405 (M.6)	Sco	25	50	e	5	1,850	8/1	1738	−3212	12
6475 (M.7)	Sco	60	50	e	5	1,240	8/5	1752	−3448	12
6494 (M.23)	Sgr	25	120	e	7	4,490	8/6	1755	−1901	8, 12
6531 (M.21)	Sgr	10	50	d	7	2,960	8/8	1803	−2230	9, 13
6603 (M.24)	Sgr	4	50	g	5	16,300	8/11	1817	−1826	9, 13
6611 (M.16)	Ser	25	55	c	6	5,400	8/11	1817	−1347	9
6613 (M.18)	Sgr	12	12	d	8	6,200	8/11	1818	−1708	9, 13
I 4725	Sgr	40	50	d	7	1,790	8/14	1830	−1916	9, 13
6694	Sct	9	20	f	9	12,700	8/18	1844	−0926	9
6705 (M.11)	Sct	10	200	g	6	5,650	8/19	1849	−0618	9
6709	Aql	12	40	d	8	2,570	8/20	1850	+1019	9
6913 (M.29)	Cyg	12	20	d	7	3,090	9/12	2023	+3825	5
7092 (M.39)	Cyg	30	25	e	5	815	9/29	2131	+4818	5
7243	Lac	20	40	d	7	2,570	10/10	2214	+4944	5
7380	Cep	10	50	d	9	2,570	10/18	2246	+5755	5
7654 (M.52)	Cas	12	120	e	7	3,800	10/28	2323	+6127	1, 5
7789	Cas	30	200	e	10	13,150	11/5	2356	+5633	5

Globular Star Clusters

NGC number	Constel-lation	Angular size (minutes of arc)	Class*	Magni-tude	Distance (thousands of light-years)	Date on meridian	1970 Position RA (h/m)	Decl. (°′)	Map No.
1904 (M.79)	Lep	3.2	V	8	43.0	1/27	0523	−2433	6, 10
4147	Com	1.7	IX	9	84.5	5/10	1209	+1842	4, 8
4590 (M.68)	Hya	2.9	X	8	37.4	5/17	1238	−2636	8, 12
5024 (M.53)	Com	3.3	V	8	65.0	5/25	1312	+1820	4, 8
5139	Cen	23.0	VIII	4	16.3	5/29	1325	−4709	12
5272 (M.3)	CVn	9.8	VI	6	45.0	6/2	1341	+2832	4, 8
5466	Boo	5.0	XII	9	47.0	6/8	1404	+2840	4, 8
5897	Lib	7.3	XI	11	45.0	6/26	1516	−2054	8, 12
5904 (M.5)	Ser	12.7	V	6	27.0	6/26	1517	+0212	8
6093 (M.80)	Sco	3.3	II	8	35.8	7/11	1615	−2255	8, 12
6121 (M.4)	Sco	14.0	IX	6	7.5	7/13	1622	−2627	8, 12
6171 (M.107)	Oph	2.2	X	9	97.5	7/15	1631	−1259	8
6205 (M.13)	Her	23.0	V	6	22.2	7/18	1641	+3630	4
6218 (M.12)	Oph	9.3	IX	7	18.8	7/19	1646	−0154	8
6235	Oph	1.9	X	11	51.3	7/20	1651	−2207	8, 12
6254 (M.10)	Oph	8.2	VII	7	16.2	7/21	1656	−0404	8
6266 (M.62)	Oph	4.3	IV	7	22.2	7/22	1659	−3005	12
6273 (M.19)	Oph	4.3	VIII	7	22.2	7/22	1701	−2613	8, 12
6284	Oph	1.5	IX	10	54.0	7/23	1703	−2443	8, 12
6287	Oph	1.7	VII	10	28.2	7/23	1703	−2240	8, 12
6293	Oph	1.9	IV	8	47.0	7/24	1708	−2632	8, 12
6304	Oph	1.6	VI	10	18.8	7/25	1712	−2926	8, 12
6333 (M.9)	Oph	2.4	VIII	7	26.0	7/26	1717	−1829	8, 12
6341 (M.92)	Her	8.3	IV	6	35.8	7/26	1717	+4311	4
6356	Oph	1.7	II	9	33.2	7/27	1722	−1747	8, 12

*The globular clusters are classified according to stellar concentration. Roman numerals from I (heavy concentration) to XII (sparse concentration) are used for this purpose. Thus M.55 in Sagittarius, noted for its loosely packed structure, is assigned the number XI, while M.2 in neighboring Aquarius, which is difficult to resolve into stars, is designated as II. An intermediate object, M.13 in Hercules, one in which there is a packed nucleus surrounded by a decreasing density of resolvable stars, is given the number V.

NGC number	Constel- lation	Angular size (min. of arc)	Class	Magni- tude	Distance (thousands of light- years)	Date on meridian	1970 Position RA (h/m)	Decl. (°/′)	Map No.
6402 (M.14)	Oph	3.0	VIII	8	23.4	8/1	1736	−0314	8
6626 (M.28)	Sgr	4.7	IV	7	15.0	8/12	1823	−2453	9, 13
6637 (M.69)	Sgr	2.8	V	8	23.4	8/13	1829	−3222	13
6656 (M.22)	Sgr	17.3	VII	6	9.8	8/15	1834	−2357	9, 13
6681 (M.70)	Sgr	2.3	V	10	65.0	8/17	1841	−3220	13
6712	Sct	2.1	IX	9	19.5	8/20	1851	−0845	9
6715 (M.54)	Sgr	2.1	III	7	49.0	8/20	1853	−3031	13
6779 (M.56)	Lyr	1.8	X	8	45.0	8/26	1916	+3007	5
6809 (M.55)	Sgr	10.0	XI	5	18.8	9/1	1938	−3100	13
6838 (M.71)	Sge	6.1		9	17.9	9/4	1953	−1836	5, 9
6864 (M.75)	Sgr	1.9	I	8	78.0	9/7	2004	−2201	9, 13
6934	Del	1.5	VIII	9	54.0	9/11	2033	+0718	9
6981 (M.72)	Aqr	2.0	IX	10	59.2	9/19	2052	−1239	9
7006	Del	1.1	I	10	195.0	9/21	2100	+1605	5, 9
7078 (M.15)	Peg	7.4	IV	6	49.0	9/29	2128	+1202	9
7089 (M.2)	Aqr	8.2	II	6	51.4	9/30	2132	−0058	9
7099 (M.30)	Cap	5.7	V	8	42.0	10/1	2139	−2320	9, 13
7492	Aqr	3.3	XII	10	95.5	10/23	2307	−1556	9, 13

Planetary Nebulae

NGC number	Constel-lation	Angular size (minutes)	Magnitude Nebula	Star	Distance (light-years)	Class*	Date on meridian	1970 Position RA (h/m)	Decl. (°′)	Map No.
40	Cas	1 × .6	10	11	3,250	3	11/8	0011	+7222	1
246	Cet	4 × 3.5	9	11	1,500	3	11/17	0046	−1203	6
650-1	Per	2.6 × 1.5	12	17	8,200	5	12/1	0140	+5125	2
(M.76, the Little Dumbbell Nebula)										
I 289	Cas	.7 × .5	12	15	8,500	4	12/24	0308	+6113	1, 2
1514	Tau	2 × 1.5	11	10	4,300	5	1/7	0407	+3041	2
1535	Eri	.3 × .3	9	11	2,140	4	1/8	0413	−1249	6
I 418	Lep	.2 × .2	12	11	7,450	4	1/25	0526	−1243	6
1952	Tau	6 × 4	8	16	910	6	1/29	0533	+2200	2, 6
(M.1, the Crab Nebula)										
2392	Gem	.8 × .7	9	11	1,360	3	2/28	0727	+2058	3, 7
2438	Pup	1.1 × 1.1	11	17	5,400	4	3/3	0741	−1439	7
2440	Pup	.9 × .3	12	17	6,500	5	3/3	0741	−1808	7, 11
3132	Ant	1.6 × .9	8	11	1,300	4	4/9	1006	−4017	11
3242	Hya	.7 × .6	9	11	1,800	3	4/13	1023	−1829	7, 11
3587	UMa	3.4 × 3.3	12	14	7,500	3	4/25	1113	+5512	3
(M.97, the Owl Nebula)										
4361	Crv	1.3 × 1.3	11	13	4,300	3	5/13	1223	−1836	8, 12
I 3568	Cam	.3 × .3	12	12	6,200	2	5/16	1233	+8244	1
6153	Sco	.5 × .4	12		5,950	1	7/14	1629	−4011	12
6210	Her	.3 × .2	10	11	2,580	2	7/18	1644	+2350	4, 8
6309	Oph	.3 × .2	12	14	6,200	3	7/26	1713	−1253	8
6543	Dra	.3 × .4	9	11	1,700	3	8/7	1758	+6638	1, 4
6572	Oph	.3 × .2	10	12	2,480	2	8/10	1811	+0650	9
6567	Sgr	.2 × .1	12	15	6,500	2	8/11	1812	−1905	9, 13
6720	Lyr	1 × 1.4	9	15	2,150	4	8/20	1853	+3300	5
(M.57, the Ring Nebula)										
6818	Sgr	.2 × .3	10	15	2,850	4	9/1	1942	−1416	9
6853	Vul	8 × 4	8	13	975	3	9/6	1958	+2238	5, 9
(M.27, the Dumbbell Nebula)										
6905	Del	.7 × .6	12	14	7,100	3	9/12	2021	+2001	5, 9
7009	Aqr	.7 × .4	8	12	1,430	3, 4	9/22	2102	−1130	9
(The Saturn Nebula)										
7027	Cyg	.3 × .2	10	17	3,600	6	9/23	2106	+4207	5
7293	Aqr	15 × 12	7	13	590	4	10/14	2228	−2100	9, 13
(The Helical Nebula)										
7662	And	.5 × .5	9	13	1,800	3, 4	10/28	2325	+4221	5

*Class 1. Starlike. Usually appears like a slightly out-of-focus star. (NGC 6153 in Scorpius)
Class 2. Oval, uniformly bright. (NGC 6210 in Hercules)
Class 3. Oval, irregularly bright. (NGC 3587, M.97, the Owl Nebula in Ursa Major)
Class 4. Ringlike. (NGC 6720, M.57, the Ring Nebula in Lyra)
Class 5. Irregular. (NGC 1514 in Taurus)
Class 6. Exceptions to any of the above. (NGC 1952, M.1, the Crab Nebula in Taurus)

Diffuse Nebulae

NGC number	Constel- lation	Angular size (minutes)	Distance (light- years)	Date on meridian	1970 Position RA (h/m)	Decl. (°/′)	Map No.
I 349 (Region around Merope)	Tau	30 × 30	410	1/2	0344	+2340	2, 6
I 1499 (California Nebula)	Per	145 × 40	1,950	1/6	0401	+3620	2
1976 (M.42, the Great Nebula in Orion)	Ori	66 × 60	975	1/30	0534	−0524	6
1982 (M.43)	Ori	20 × 15	975(?)	1/30	0534	−0517	6
I 434 (Horsehead Nebula)	Ori	60 × 10	1,300	1/31	0540	−0225	6
2024	Ori	30 × 30	1,300	1/31	0541	−0151	6
2068 (M.78)	Ori	8 × 6	(?)	2/1	0545	+0003	6
2237 (Rosetta Nebula)	Mon	64 × 61	3,850	2/15	0631	+0439	7
2264 (Cone Nebula)	Mon	60 × 30	3,260	2/15	0639	+0957	7
6514 (M.20, the Trifid Nebula)	Sgr	27 × 29	2,200	8/7	1800	−2302	8, 12
6523 (M.8, the Lagoon Nebula)	Sgr	35 × 60	2,500	8/8	1802	−2420	8, 12
6611 (M.16)	Ser	35 × 28	4,550	8/12	1818	−1347	8
6618 (M.17, the Omega Nebula)	Sgr	46 × 37	3,250	8/12	1818	−1611	8, 12
6960 6992 (The Veil Nebula)	Cyg	190 × 8	1,300	9/18	2044 2055	+3046 +3134	5
I 5067 (The Pelican Nebula)	Cyg	85 × 75	910	9/19	2048	+4415	5

NGC number	Constel-lation	Angular size (minutes)	Distance (light-years)	Date on meridian	1970 Position		Map No.
					RA (h/m)	Decl. (°/′)	
7000 (The North America Nebula)	Cyg	100 × 120	900	9/21	2058	+4412	5
I 5146 (The Cocon Nebula)	Cyg	12 × 12	5,500	10/4	2153	+4707	5

Extragalactic Nebulae

NGC number	Constellation	Angular size (minutes)	Magnitude	Date on meridian	Type*	1970 Position RA (h/m)	Decl. (°/′)	Map No.
55	Scl	3 × 25	8	11/9	S	0014	−3923	10
205	And	3 × 8	9	11/16	E	0039	+4132	2
221 (M.32)	And	2 × 3	9	11/16	E	0041	+4043	2
224 (M.31)	And	40 × 60	5	11/16	Sb	0041	+4107	2
247	Cet	18 × 6	11	11/18	S	0047	−2055	6, 10
253	Scl	6 × 22	9	11/18	Sc	0047	−2527	6, 10
300	Scl	20 × 15	11	11/20	S	0054	−3752	10
524	Psc	3 × 3	11	11/27	E	0123	+0922	6
598 (M.33)	Tri	40 × 60	8	11/30	Sc	0132	+3030	2
628 (M.74)	Psc	8 × 8	10	11/30	Sc	0135	+1538	2, 6
1068 (M.77)	Cet	2 × 2	9	12/17	Sb	0241	−0009	2
1291	Eri	8 × 8	10	12/26	SB	0316	−4113	10
1316	For	3 × 5	10	12/28	S	0322	−3713	10
1365	For	8 × 6	11	12/31	SB	0333	−3614	10
2903	Leo	5 × 11	9	3/28	Sc	0930	+2139	3, 7
2997	Ant	7 × 6	11	4/2	S	0945	−3103	11
3031 (M.81)	UMa	10 × 16	8	4/4	Sb	0954	+6912	1, 3
3034 (M.82)	UMa	2 × 7	9	4/4	I	0954	+6950	1, 3
3115	Sex	1 × 4	9	4/8	E	1004	+0733	7
3166	Sex	1 × 1	11	4/10	Sc	1012	+0334	7
3169	Sex	2 × 4	12	4/10	Sa	1013	+0337	7
3351 (M.95)	Leo	3 × 3	10	4/18	SBb	1042	+1152	7
3368 (M.96)	Leo	4 × 7	9	4/18	Sa	1045	+1159	7
3379 (M.105)	Leo	2 × 2	10	4/19	E	1046	+1245	7
3556 (M.108)	UMa	2 × 8	10	4/24	Sb	1110	+5551	3

*There are four main types of the galaxies, each divided into subclasses.

1. The elliptical nebulae (E) are featureless and smooth, perceptibly brighter in the center than at the edges. Nearly round examples of this class are designated E0, with numbers increasing as the ellipse flattens. Thus E7 is assigned to elliptical galaxies so spread out they are lenticular or lens-shaped.

2. Normal spiral galaxies (S) are made up of bright nuclei with spiral arms developing at a tangent from opposite points on the nucleus. Young spirals (Sa) have arms which are close in to the nucleus, middle-aged (Sb) spirals have more extended arms, and the oldest type (Sc) have widespread spiral arms.

3. Barred spiral galaxies look somewhat like the normal type except that the spiral arms extend from opposite ends of a band of glowing material which extends across the nucleus.

4. Irregular galaxies (I) follow none of the patterns mentioned above. There are two types, resolvable and unresolved. The former show some detail in the form of granulations, bright patches, dark areas, and the like. The latter are smooth-textured and featureless.

NGC number	Constellation	Angular size (minutes)	Magnitude	Date on meridian	Type	1970 Position RA (h/m)	Decl. (°/′)	Map No.
3623 (M.65)	Leo	2 × 8	10	4/26	Sb	1117	+1317	7
3627 (M.66)	Leo	2 × 8	9	4/27	Sb	1119	+1310	7
3992 (M.109)	UMa	7 × 7	11	5/6	SBc	1156	+5332	3
4192 (M.98)	Com	2 × 8	10	5/10	Sb	1212	+1504	4, 8
4254 (M.99)	Com	5 × 5	10	5/12	Sc	1217	+1435	8
4258 (M.106)	CVn	6 × 20	10	5/12	Sb	1218	+4728	4
4303 (M.61)	Vir	6 × 6	10	5/13	SBc	1220	+0438	8
4321 (M.100)	Com	5 × 5	10	5/13	Sc	1221	+1559	4, 8
4374 (M.84)	Vir	3 × 3	10	5/13	E	1224	+1303	8
4382 (M.85)	Com	2 × 4	10	5/13	E	1224	+1821	4, 8
4406 (M.86)	Vir	3 × 4	10	5/14	E	1225	+1306	8
4449	CVn	3 × 5	9	5/14	I	1227	+4415	4
4472 (M.49)	Vir	4 × 4	9	5/15	E	1228	+0809	8
4486 (M.87)	Vir	3 × 3	10	5/15	E	1229	+1233	8
4501 (M.88)	Com	3 × 6	10	5/15	Sc	1231	+1435	8
4526	Vir	1 × 6	11	5/16	Sa	1233	+0751	8
4552 (M.89)	Vir	2 × 2	11	5/16	E	1234	+1243	8
4565	Com	1 × 15	10	5/16	Sb	1235	+2609	4, 8
4569 (M.90)	Vir	3 × 6	11	5/16	Sc	1235	+1319	8
4594 (M.104)	Vir	2 × 7	9	5/17	Sa	1238	−1128	8
4621 (M.59)	Vir	3 × 2	11	5/18	E	1241	+1148	8
4631	CVn	1 × 12	9	5/18	Sc	1241	+3243	4
4649 (M.60)	Vir	3 × 4	9	5/18	E	1242	+1143	8
4736 (M.94)	CVn	4 × 5	8	5/21	Sb	1250	+4117	4
4826 (M.64)	Com	4 × 8	9	5/22	Sb	1255	+2141	4, 8
5055 (M.63)	CVn	3 × 8	10	5/26	Sb	1315	+4211	4
5128	Cen	8 × 10	7	5/28	I	1324	−4251	12
5194 (M.51)	CVn	6 × 12	8	5/30	Sc	1329	+4721	4

NGC number	Constellation	Angular size (minutes)	Magnitude	Date on meridian	Type	1970 Position		Map No.
						RA (h/m)	Decl. (°/ʹ)	
5195	CVn	2 × 2	8	5/30	I	1329	+4725	4
5236 (M.83)	Hya	8 × 10	10	6/1	Sc	1335	−2943	8, 12
5253	Cen	4 × 2	11	6/2	I	1338	−3130	12
5322	UMa	1 × 1	10	6/4	E	1348	+6020	1, 4
5457 (M.101)	UMa	22 × 22	10	6/7	Sc	1402	+5429	4
6643	Dra	1 × 3	11	8/12	Sb	1820	+7434	1
6822	Sgr	10 × 20	11	9/2	I	1943	−1450	9
7479	Peg	3 × 3	12	10/22	SBc	2303	+1209	9
7793	Scl	4 × 6	10	11/5	S	2356	−3244	13

Periodic Comets

Observed by or named for	Year of discovery	Period (years)	Perihelion (A.U.)	Will return
Gunn	1970	6.80	2.44	Feb. 1976
Wolf	1884	8.43	2.51	Feb. 1976
Harrington-Abell	1955	7.19	1.77	July 1976
Schaumasse	1911	8.18	1.20	Aug. 1976
Klemola	1965	11.0	1.76	Aug. 1976
d'Arrest	1851	6.23	1.17	Aug. 1976
Pons-Winnecke	1819	6.34	1.25	Nov. 1976
Kojima	1970	6.19	1.63	Dec. 1976
Johnson	1949	6.77	2.20	Jan. 1977
Dutoit-Neujmin	1941	6.31	1.67	Feb. 1977
Van Houten	1961	15.75	3.94	Feb. 1977
Kopff	1906	6.42	1.57	Mar. 1977
Faye	1843	7.39	1.62	Mar. 1977
Grigg-Skjellerup	1902	5.12	1.00	Apr. 1977
Encke	1786	3.30	0.39	Aug. 1977
Temple I	1867	5.50	1.50	Jan. 1978
Arend-Rigaux	1951	6.84	1.44	Feb. 1978
Temple II	1873	5.26	1.36	Feb. 1978
Wolf-Harrington	1924	6.55	1.62	Mar. 1978
Whipple	1933	7.47	2.48	Mar. 1978
Tsuchinshan I	1965	6.64	1.50	May 1978
Comas-Sola	1926	8.55	1.77	May 1978
Daniel	1909	7.09	1.66	June 1978
Tsuchinshan II	1965	6.80	1.78	Sept. 1978
Van Biesbroeck	1954	12.41	2.41	Dec. 1978
Halley	240 B.C.	76.1	0.59	May 1986

Annual Meteor Showers

Name	Usual dates	Position of radiant at maximum	Hourly rate (varies from year to year)	Associated comet
Quadrantids (Bootids)	January 3	152050	40	
Lyrids	April 20-22	181234	15	1861 I
Eta Aquarids	May 1-11	222400	20	1910 II (Halley)
June Draconids	June 28	131554	12	1951 VI (Pons-Winnecke)
Delta Aquarids	July 24- August 6	223617	20	
Perseids	August 12	030458	50	1862 III
Giacobinids	October 9	172854	10	1946 V (Giacobini-Zinner)
Orionids	October 15-25	062015	20	1910 II (Halley)
Taurids	October 26- November 16	033214	15	1953f (Encke)
Andromedids (Bielids)	November 14	013244	10(?)	1852 III (Biela)
Leonids	November 15-20	100822	15	1861 I (Tempel)
Geminids	December 9-13	073232	60	
Ursids	December 21-22	142876	15	1939 X (Tuttle)

Solar Eclipses 1976–1985

Date	Type	Duration (minutes)	Location
1976, 4/19	A	7	Algeria, Turkey, S. USSR, Tibet
1976, 10/23	T	5	Africa, Indian O., Australia
1977, 4/18	A	7	Venezuela, Atlantic O., S. Africa, Indian O., N. Pacific O.
1979, 2/26	T	3	N.W. United States, Canada, Greenland
1979, 8/22	A	7	S. Pacific O.
1980, 2/16	T	4	Zaïre, Kenya, Indian O., India, S.E. Asia
1980, 8/10	A	3	Pacific O., Peru, Brazil
1981, 2/4	A	1	S. Pacific O.
1981, 7/31	T	2	USSR, N. Pacific O.
1983, 6/11	T	5	Indian O., Java, New Guinea
1983, 12/4	A	4	Atlantic O., Zaïre, Somalia
1984, 5/30	A	1	Mexico, S.E. United States, Atlantic O., Algeria
1984, 11/2	T	2	New Guinea, S. Pacific O.
1985, 11/12	T	?	S. Pacific O.

Lunar Eclipses 1976–1985

Date	Complete duration (minutes)	Total phase (minutes)	Location
1976, 5/13	86	—	Mauritius
1977, 4/4	102	—	W. Brazil
1978, 3/24	218	90	Borneo
1978, 9/16	214	82	Maldive Is.
1979, 3/13	188	—	Somalia
1979, 9/6	206	52	Samoa
1981, 7/17	160	—	N. Chile
1982, 1/9	214	84	Pakistan
1982, 7/6	224	102	Easter I.
1982, 12/30	210	66	Hawaii
1982, 6/25	130	—	Pitcairn I.
1985, 5/4	212	70	Mauritius
1985, 10/28	204	42	Bay of Bengal

The Messier Catalog

The 104 objects of the famous Messier Catalog comprise a list notable for its historical interest, its even distribution throughout the heavens, and its variety. The Messier objects have long been favorites among amateur astronomers, but are rarely compiled separately. We have collected these objects and listed them on a day-to-day basis throughout the year.

Charles Messier was a comet hunter — without question the greatest of his time. Even though he also observed other astronomical phenomena — eclipses, occultations, transits, sunspots — his all-absorbing interest was the comets. From his tower observatory at the Hotel de Cluny in Paris he was able to discover, by his own count, 21 of them. During the period of his most intense work, from 1754 to 1770, he happened upon many other objects which might conceivably be mistaken for comets. To him these objects simply cluttered up the heavens, and in order to prevent other comet hunters from wasting time on them, he published a list of 45 of these non-cometary objects in 1771. This was the first installment of the now famous Messier Catalog.

It is perhaps a common impression that Messier discovered all of the objects in his remarkable list. Although this was true for some of them, for he was an indefatigable searcher of the heavens, his greatest contribution lay in the confirmation of objects reported by earlier observers: Hevelius, Huygens, Halley, Maraldi, and Kirch, among others. Several of the objects he listed are now considered as doubtful*, and at least one, M.40, simply does not exist. By the year 1784 his list had grown to 103 objects, and 6 more were added in 1786 by the astronomer Mechain.

Why is Messier's list of particular interest to amateurs? In the first place, anyone who owns a reasonably good telescope can see anything Messier did, and usually in more detail. Secondly, the Messier objects are favorably located for observers in the Northern Hemisphere. All of them can be seen from the United States, since they vary in declination from 35° South to 70° North. They are so evenly distributed in right ascension that only two of the hour circles, 4h and 22h, are not represented on the list. Thus you can find some of them on any night of the year. To make things even better, most of them (73 out of 104) appear in the spring and summer skies, when they can be observed in comfort. Finally, the list is fascinating in the variety of objects listed, their differences in complexity and brilliance, and, in many cases, the detail which becomes apparent under continued observation. They range from dim M.72, a globular cluster in Sagittarius, to brilliant M.7, an open cluster in neighboring Scorpius. They differ in size: the great spiral nebula M.33 in Triangulum is so large it covers an entire low-power field (and is often missed by the amateur because of this). In contrast, the Ring Nebula in Lyra (M.57) is only 1 minute of arc by 1 minute of arc in size.

The list which follows separates the Messier objects by season rather than by number. If you decide to include a complete list in your log, you can start on any day of the year, knowing that each subsequent object will appear on your meridian at 9 P.M., local time. All of them appear on the maps in the star atlas.

The Autumn Messier Objects

The autumn list has notable representatives of each type of object described earlier. Here are the beautiful Andromeda Galaxy (M.31), the brilliant globular cluster, (M.15) in Pegasus, the famous open double cluster (M.34) in Perseus, and the great spiral nebula (M.33) in Triangulum. The cool, crisp nights of autumn make observing of any kind fun; autumn is a fine time for you to start your hunt for the Messier objects.

Messier number	NGC number	Constellation	Angular size	Magnitude	Date on meridian	1970 Position RA (h/m)	Decl. (°/′)	Map No.
55	6809	Sgr	15	5	9/1	1938	−3100	13

Bright enough to be seen with the naked eye, this splendid globular cluster can be found by following an imaginary line drawn eastward through the center of the Milk Dipper. It lies 7½° from Ascella, the brightest star in the Dipper's bowl.

---

*M.40, M.47, M.48, M.91, M.102

Mount Wilson and Palomar Observatories

The spiral nebula in Triangulum, M.33.

Mount Wilson and Palomar Observatories

The great Nebula in Orion, M.42. A great cloud of fluorescent gas and dust, this is one of the best known nebulas. Note the dark nebula that obscures the lower right-hand corner.

Messier number	NGC number	Constel- lation	Angular size	Magnitude	Date on meridian	1970 Position RA (h/m)	Decl. (°/ ´)	Map No.
71	6838	Sge	6	9	9/4	1952	+1836	5, 9

Look in the Arrow of Sagitta for this small, lovely globular.

| 27 | 6853 | Vul | 8 × 4 | 8 | 9/6 | 1958 | +2238 | 5, 9 |

The Dumbbell Nebula. Difficult in small telescopes, its shape becomes more apparent with increase in aperture and power. A marvelous sight in large telescopes.

| 75 | 6864 | Sgr | 1.9 | 8 | 9/7 | 2004 | −2201 | 9, 13 |

A distant globular. It is small and its stars are difficult to resolve. It lies about halfway between the star Omega Sagittarii and Dabih (Beta Capricorni).

| 29 | 6913 | Cyg | 12 | 7 | 9/12 | 2023 | +3825 | 5 |

A small open cluster of about 20 stars, just south of Sador, the central star in the crossarm of the Northern Cross.

| 72 | 6981 | Aqr | 2 | 10 | 9/19 | 2052 | −1239 | 9 |

A small, fuzzy globular cluster which is difficult to resolve into stars even at the edge. Nevertheless, it stands out in southern Aquarius and serves as a guidepost to find a more interesting object, the Saturn Nebula, one of the objects Messier failed to record.

| 73 | 6994 | Aqr | − | − | 9/21 | 2057 | −1245 | 9 |

One of Messier's doubtful listings. A little asterism of only four stars.

| 15 | 7078 | Peg | 7.4 | 6 | 9/29 | 2132 | +1202 | 9 |

A famous globular cluster which contains over sixty variable stars. The edge stars show up well on nights of good seeing. On such nights this globular seems to have almost half the diameter of the moon.

Messier number	NGC number	Constel-lation	Angular size	Magnitude	Date on meridian	1970 Position RA (h/m)	Decl. (°′)	Map No.
39	7092	Cyg	30	6	9/29	2132	+4818	5

A large open cluster. Great in small telescopes at low power.

| 2 | 7089 | Aqr | 8.2 | 6 | 9/30 | 2132 | −0058 | 9 |

A lovely globular which is very similar to M.15. A fine object for the larger telescope (8 inches or more), but beautiful in any instrument.

| 30 | 7099 | Cap | 5.7 | 8 | 10/1 | 2139 | −2320 | 9, 13 |

A small globular about 4 degrees east of Zeta Capricorni, near an eighth magnitude star. It is resolvable in a 6 inch reflector, and appears to have streamers of stars to the north and west.

| 52 | 7654 | Cas | 13 | 7 | 10/28 | 2323 | +6126 | 1, 5 |

A poorly defined irregular open cluster. Look for the orange-red star it contains.

| 32 | 221 | And | 3 × 2 | 9 | 11/16 | 0041 | +4043 | 2 |

A small elliptical companion galaxy to M.31, the Great Spiral Galaxy in Andromeda. Often overlooked because of its famous neighbor in space.

| 31 | 224 | And | 160 × 40 | 4 | 11/16 | 0041 | +4107 | 2 |

The Great Spiral Galaxy in Andromeda. It appears as a fuzzy spiral and will at first be disappointing to those who expect it to look like its photographs. But further study under varying seeing conditions and magnifications reveals more and more detail in this beautiful object.

| 103 | 581 | Cas | 6 | 7 | 11/29 | 0131 | +6033 | 1, 2 |

An open cluster northeast of Rucha in Cassiopeia. Located on an imaginary line between Rucha and Segin (Epsilon Cassiopeiae). It contains a red star as the focus of a brilliant field.

| 33 | 598 | Tri | 60 × 40 | 8 | 11/30 | 0132 | +3030 | 2 |

A tremendous nebula whose spiral nature shows only in large telescopes. Because of its size and very poor contrast with the sky background, this object is hard to find. Use low power and search carefully with fully dark-adapted eyes. You will pick it up on a line drawn through Mirach in Andromeda and Hamal in Aries, halfway between the two stars, and about 4 degrees west of Metallah in Triangulum. Most amateurs consider finding this great spiral a minor triumph of good observing techniques.

| 74 | 628 | Psc | 8 × 8 | 10 | 11/30 | 0135 | +1538 | 2, 6 |

A broadside spiral. Small telescopes will not reveal the spiral arms, but a night of good seeing and an 8-inch telescope bring out the delicate structure.

| 76 | 650-1 | Per | 2 × 1 | 12 | 12/1 | 0140 | +5125 | 2 |

This is a small planetary nebula which appears as two faint patches of light in contact. Known as the Little Dumbbell Nebula, it lies northwest of the star Phi Andromedae.

The beautiful globular star cluster in Hercules, M.13. Notice that the cluster is elliptical rather than round in shape. Compare this globular with the cluster in Serpens shown on page 112.

A view toward Sagittarius, the densest concentration of visible stars in the sky. The Trifid Nebula (M.20) and the Lagoon Nebula (M.8) are clearly visible. (For larger photographs of these nebulas, see page 117.)

The Winter Messier Objects

Winter brings several beautiful open clusters into view, among them the Pleiades and Hyades in Taurus. In addition, the loveliest irregular nebula in the heavens, the Great Nebula of Orion, can be seen throughout the winter season. Perhaps less spectacular but of great historical interest because it was the first object in the Messier list, the Crab Nebula in Taurus will help liven your chilly observing sessions.

Messier number	NGC number	Constel-lation	Angular size	Magnitude	Date on meridian	1970 Position RA (h/m)	Decl. (°′)	Map No.
34	1039	Per	18	6	12/17	0240	+4239	2

A beautiful open cluster of more than ninety stars, spectacular under low power or in a wide-field telescope. Many of the stars are double. It is barely visible to the naked eye but you can pick it up easily in your finder by sweeping the area between Algol and Alamak.

| 77 | 1068 | Cet | 2 × 2 | 9 | 12/17 | 0241 | −0009 | 2, 6 |

Small, indistinct; don't waste too much time on this spiral nebula unless you have a very large telescope.

| 45 | | Tau | 100 | — | 1/2 | 0345 | +2402 | 2, 6 |

The Pleiades, or Seven Sisters. You can see at least a hundred stars in this magnificent open cluster, even with a small telescope. Look for nebulosity around the stars Merope, Electra, Maia, and Celaeno (see expanded view of the Pleiades on map 2) if your telescope is 6 inches or more.

Messier number	NGC number	Constel-lation	Angular size	Magnitude	Date on meridian	1970 Position RA (h/m)	Decl. (°′)	Map No.
79	1904	Lep	3	8	1/27	0523	−2433	6, 10

A small, globular cluster, very bright in the center. Placed at one corner of a flattened parallelogram, of which the other three corners are the stars Delta, Beta, and Epsilon of the constellation Lepus.

| 38 | 1912 | Aur | 18 | 7 | 1/27 | 0527 | +3549 | 2 |

Very lovely open cluster with about one hundred stars visible to the naked eye. Small telescopes may reveal a cross-shape which disappears with increasing aperture. Look for it between Capella and Nath.

| 1 | 1952 | Tau | 6 × 4 | 8 | 1/29 | 0533 | +2200 | 2, 6 |

The Crab Nebula, gaseous remnant of the nova first observed by Chinese astronomers over nine hundred years ago. It is now an indistinct planetary nebula which you will find just northeast of Zeta Tauri. Large aperture and good seeing conditions will bring out some detail, especially if red or orange filters are used.

| 36 | 1960 | Aur | 12 | 6 | 1/29 | 0533 | +3408 | 2 |

On the threshold of naked-eye visibility, this open cluster of about sixty stars is found on the edge of the Milky Way, about midway between M.38 and M.37.

| 42 | 1976 | Ori | 66 × 60 | − | 1/30 | 0534 | −0524 | 6 |

The Great Nebula of Orion. Clouds of swirling gas make up this diffuse nebula, which many observers think the most beautiful in the heavens. It surrounds Theta Orionis, a quadruple star called the Trapezium. Easy to find even with the naked eye, it appears as the middle star in Orion's Sword.

| 43 | 1982 | Ori | 20 × 15 | − | 1/30 | 0534 | −0517 | 6 |

This is the northeast wing of the Great Nebula, M.42.

| 78 | 2068 | Ori | 8 × 6 | − | 2/1 | 0545 | +0003 | 6 |

A wispy, filamentous nebula. Look for the tenth-magnitude star embedded in it. It is about 20 minutes west of Mintaka.

| 37 | 2099 | Aur | 24 | 6 | 2/2 | 0550 | +3233 | 2 |

One of the finest objects for small telescopes, this brilliant open cluster of about 150 stars offers variety in both brilliance and grouping of it member stars.

| 35 | 2168 | Gem | 40 | 6 | 2/7 | 0607 | +2420 | 3, 7 |

A naked-eye open cluster. Magnificent in telescopes over 8 inches of aperture; an excellent object for any telescope. It appears almost triangular in small instruments but has a diamond shape in larger ones. Look for it near Tejat Prior.

| 41 | 2287 | CMa | 32 | 6 | 2/17 | 0646 | −2044 | 7, 11 |

There are more than fifty stars of about eighth magnitude in this open cluster. Look for the bright red star near the center and the curved-line arrangement of the other stars. About 4 degrees southwest of Sirius.

Messier number	NGC number	Constellation	Angular size	Magnitude	Date on meridian	1970 Position RA (h/m)	Decl. (°/′)	Map No.
50	2323	Mon	16	7	2/20	0702	−0818	7

A straggling open cluster with a central red star located about one-third the distance between Sirius and Procyon.

| 46 | 2437 | Pup | 24 | 9 | 3/2 | 0741 | −1445 | 7 |

An open cluster of 150 stars. Less brilliant than M.35 or M.37, but well worth looking for.

| 93 | 2447 | Pup | 25 | 6 | 3/3 | 0743 | −2348 | 7, 11 |

A very lovely five-armed open cluster located just at the edge of the Milky Way rift in Puppis.

The Spring Messier Objects

Spring is an open season for nebula hunters. The sky abounds with galaxies, especially in the Coma Berenices-Virgo region. Most are dim and hard to find, but this makes them all the more challenging to the observer who wants to find all the Messier objects (and who has the patience to do so). Not all are difficult, though. You can easily find the magnificent Whirlpool Nebula in Canes Venatici, the Owl Nebula in Ursa Major, and even the "Black-eye" Nebula in Coma Berenices. And when you tire of looking at nebulae, there are some beautiful open clusters and globulars to divert you. For example, try the Beehive (Praesepe) in Cancer, or the globular clusters in Coma Berenices and Canes Venatici. But for the most part, in spring you will be waiting for those dark nights when the black sky background will allow the elusive nebulae to come dancing into your eyepiece.

Messier number	NGC number	Constellation	Angular size	Magnitude	Date on meridian	1970 Position RA (h/m)	Decl. (°/′)	Map No.
44	2632	Cnc	90	6	3/17	0838	+1948	3, 7

Praesepe, or the Beehive, is one of the loveliest open clusters in the heavens. The combinations of double and triple stars in a brilliant star field are exceptionally beautiful in a low-power field. The astronomer who coined the phrase "diamonds in the sky" for the stars must have had the Beehive in mind. There are more than sixty stars brighter than tenth magnitude in this cluster.

| 67 | 2682 | Cnc | 15 | 6 | 3/20 | 0849 | +1155 | 7 |

You can easily count sixty-five stars in this irregular open cluster and even more on a dark clear night. A wonderful object for low power.

| 81 | 3031 | UMa | 16 × 10 | 8 | 4/4 | 0954 | +6912 | 1, 3 |

A bright spiral nebula which appears even brighter because of its glowing nucleus. The spiral arms are very faint, however. You can pick up M.82 in the same area since the two nebulae are only about 45 minutes apart.

| 82 | 3034 | UMa | 7 × 2 | 9 | 4/4 | 0954 | +6950 | 1, 3 |

An irregular nebula which appears only as a curved splash of light in anything other than large telescopes. Look for both M.81 and M.82 at the apex of an isosceles triangle whose base is the line between Gianfar in Draco and Dubhe in Ursa Major.

Messier number	NGC number	Constel-lation	Angular size	Magnitude	Date on meridian	1970 Position RA (h/m)	Decl. (°/′)	Map No.
95	3351	Leo	3 × 3	10	4/18	1042	+1152	7

With M.96 only 4 minutes away this nebula makes a pair of spirals. In moderate-sized telescopes, M.96 is the brighter of the two although the difference is difficult to detect in small instruments.

| 96 | 3368 | Leo | 7 × 4 | 9 | 4/18 | 1045 | +1159 | 7 |

See M.95 above.

| 105 | 3379 | Leo | 2 × 2 | 10 | 4/19 | 1046 | +1245 | 3 |

A dim elliptical nebula located just to the northeast of M.96.

| 108 | 3556 | UMa | 8 × 2 | 10 | 4/24 | 1110 | +5551 | 3 |

Easily visible in low power, this spiral nebula appears as a moderately bright strip in which is embedded a faint star. It lies close to Merak on a line between Merak and Phecda.

| 97 | 3587 | UMa | 3 × 3 | 12 | 4/25 | 1113 | +5512 | 3 |

The Owl Nebula. A famous planetary southeast of Merak in the Big Dipper. Two dark spots in an otherwise uniform disk give this planetary its name. Although the Owl Nebula itself is easy to locate and observe with a small telescope, you will probably find it difficult to see the dark spots.

| 65 | 3623 | Leo | 8 × 2 | 10 | 4/26 | 1117 | +1317 | 7 |

M.65 and M.66 are "twin" spiral nebula since they appear in the same field in moderate apertures and magnifications. They are featureless but bright enough to be found without much difficulty if you look along a line passing through Zosma and Coxa and extended below the triangle in Leo.

| 66 | 3627 | Leo | 8 × 2 | 9 | 4/26 | 1119 | +1310 | 7 |

See M.65 above.

| 109 | 3992 | UMa | 7 × 7 | 11 | 5/6 | 1156 | +5332 | 3 |

A barred spiral, fairly bright, located just south of the Big Dipper star Phecda. You will probably find it to be brighter than the accepted magnitude indicates.

| 98 | 4192 | Com | 8 × 2 | 10 | 5/10 | 1212 | +1504 | 4, 8 |

A pale spiral nebula whose light is flooded out by the nearby fourth-magnitude star. Use the star as a focus, then move it out of the field and the nebula will appear to the west.

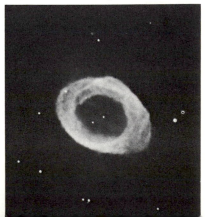

Mount Wilson and Palomar Observatories
M.57, the Ring Nebula in Lyra. Although it appears as a ring through the telescope, this nebula is actually a spherical shell of gas around a central hot blue star.

Messier number	NGC number	Constel- lation	Angular size	Magnitude	Date on meridian	1970 Position RA (h/m)	Decl. (°/′)	Map No.
99	4254	Com	5 × 5	10	5/12	1217	+1435	8

Although brighter than the accepted magnitude, this pale spiral is still a difficult object for the small telescope.

Messier number	NGC number	Constel- lation	Angular size	Magnitude	Date on meridian	RA (h/m)	Decl. (°/′)	Map No.
106	4258	CVn	20 × 6	10	5/12	1218	+4728	4

Another faint spiral, but like M.99, appears brighter than its accepted magnitude. Almost in the same field is another spiral, NGC 4217.

61	4303	Vir	6 × 6	10	5/12	1220	+0438	4, 8

There is a bright center in this faint spiral, but it still requires the light-gathering power of large aperture (8 to 10 inches) to be seen clearly.

100	4321	Com	5 × 5	10	5/13	1221	+1559	4, 8

One of the faint, very distant spirals of the Coma-Virgo group. You can be proud of your skill in finding elusive objects when you identify this one.

84	4374	Vir	3 × 3	10	5/13	1224	+1303	8

A dim elliptical nebula appearing in the same field as M.86, which is almost its twin. The two nebulae lie at right angles to one another.

85	4382	Com	4 × 2	10	5/13	1224	+1821	4, 8

Another dim elliptical nebula, the northernmost of the Coma-Virgo group.

86	4406	Vir	4 × 3	10	5/14	1225	+1306	8

See M.84 above.

49	4472	Vir	4 × 4	9	5/15	1228	+0809	8

Not difficult in any telescope over 3-inch aperture. An elliptical nebula which is nearly round. It has been described as ''pearly'' in color and is well defined. It lies between two sixth-magnitude stars.

87	4486	Vir	3 × 3	10	5/15	1229	+1233	8

Another of the roundish, dim galaxies of the Coma-Virgo group. Listed as an elliptical nebula.

88	4501	Com	6 × 3	10	5/15	1231	+1435	8

An elongated, pale spiral. It has no distinguishing features other than its shape.

89	4552	Vir	2 × 2	10	5/16	1234	+1243	8

A tiny, dim, almost perfectly round object. Listed as an elliptical nebula but looks more like a planetary.

Messier number	NGC number	Constellation	Angular size	Magnitude	Date on meridian	1970 Position RA (h/m)	Decl. (°/′)	Map No.
90	4569	Vir	6 × 3	11	5/16	1234	+1319	8

Another dim spiral, but easier to spot than M.89 because of its size.

| 58 | 4579 | Vir | 4 × 3 | 10 | 5/16 | 1235 | +1158 | 8 |

Although this one appears in the lists as a spiral nebula, it is not well defined and very difficult to spot. It is a real challenge.

| 68 | 4590 | Hya | 2.9 | 8 | 5/17 | 1238 | −2636 | 8, 12 |

A globular cluster lying just under Corvus in a sparse star field.

| 104 | 4594 | Vir | 7 × 2 | 9 | 5/17 | 1238 | −1128 | 8 |

The "Sombrero Nebula," a spiral. Some observers think it looks more like an edge-on view of an oyster. In any event it is not well defined in small telescopes.

| 59 | 4621 | Vir | 3 × 2 | 11 | 5/18 | 1241 | +1148 | 8 |

An elliptical nebula which often appears brighter than its assigned magnitude. Helpful in spotting M.58 above.

| 60 | 4649 | Vir | 4 × 3 | 9 | 5/18 | 1242 | +1143 | 8 |

Larger than M.59, it has the same magnitude. This is not a twin nebula; the other nebula in the field is a close spiral companion, NGC 4647.

| 94 | 4736 | CVn | 5 × 4 | 8 | 5/21 | 1250 | +4117 | 4 |

One of the three Messier objects lying between the end of the Big Dipper's handle and Cor Caroli (the other two: M.51 and M.63, see below). A spiral, but it looks like a luminous ball in small and medium telescopes.

| 64 | 4826 | Com | 8 × 4 | 9 | 5/22 | 1255 | +2141 | 4, 8 |

The famous "Black-eye" Nebula. Unfortunately the dark patch which gives it its name can be seen only in large telescopes.

| 53 | 5024 | Com | 3.3 | 8 | 5/25 | 1312 | +1820 | 4, 8 |

A beautiful globular which usually seems brighter than eighth magnitude. Look for a wide double star (Diadem), just below it. M.53, NGC 5053 (another globular), and Diadem form a flattened triangle.

| 63 | 5055 | CVn | 8 × 3 | 10 | 5/26 | 1315 | +4211 | 4 |

A spindle-shaped spiral with a bright nucleus. Easily visible in 3-inch instruments, it lies above the triangle of stars which make up the main figure of Canes Venatici.

| 51 | 5194 | CVn | 12 × 6 | 8 | 5/30 | 1329 | +4721 | 4 |

The Whirlpool Nebula. Don't expect it to look like its photographs, although you can see its dual nature even in a 3-inch telescope. Two balls of glowing gas are evident at all times, and continued study will bring out some of the beautiful detail if you use high power and wait for moments of good seeing.

The Summer Messier Objects

One might think Messier compiled his catalog solely for the satisfaction of summer observers in the Northern Hemisphere, for many of the most spectacular objects on his list appear at this time of year. The sky abounds in beautiful globular clusters, among them M.13 in Hercules and M.5 in Serpens. Some of the loveliest planetary nebulae are also present: The Ring Nebula (M.57) in Lyra, the Lagoon (M.8), Horseshoe (M.17), and Trifid (M.20) nebulae in Sagittarius, and the Dumbbell Nebula (M.27) in Vulpecula. Here, too, are brilliant open star clusters M.7 in Scorpius and M.23 in Sagittarius, to say nothing of the spectacular star fields in Scutum, Sagittarius, and Ophiuchus. Once you start searching for these fascinating objects, you will find yourself waiting patiently for the dark of the moon when you may examine them at your leisure.

Messier number	NGC number	Constellation	Angular size	Magnitude	Date on meridian	1970 Position RA (h/m)	Decl. (°/′)	Map No.
83	5236	Hya	10 × 8	10	6/1	1335	−2943	8, 12

A broadside spiral, easily visible in small telescopes. Look for it about halfway along a line drawn between Delta Hydrae and Theta Centauri.

| 3 | 5272 | CVn | 9.8 | 6 | 6/2 | 1341 | +2832 | 4, 8 |

A brilliant globular cluster lying between Arcturus and Cor Caroli. Easily resolvable in a 6-inch telescope at high power. This one is well worth spending some time on.

| 101 | 5457 | UMa | 22 × 22 | 10 | 6/7 | 1402 | +5429 | 4 |

An easy object for any telescope. Look for it just above the handle of the Big Dipper as the third vertex of a triangle in which the other two are Mizar and Alkaid. A spiral in big telescopes, you will probably see it as a large, pale object.

| 5 | 5904 | Ser | 12.7 | 6 | 6/26 | 1517 | +0212 | 8 |

The brightest globular in the northern skies. Its bright central area is surrounded by thousands of stars resolved into the pinpoints of light which make this splendid object so fascinating.

| 80 | 6093 | Sco | 3.3 | 8 | 7/11 | 1615 | −2255 | 8, 12 |

A small, bright globular lying near the long-period variable R Scorpii.

| 4 | 6121 | Sco | 14 | 6 | 7/13 | 1622 | −2627 | 8, 12 |

A globular so large it almost fills the field at medium powers. Look for it below a line drawn between Antares and Sigma Scorpii.

| 107 | 6171 | Oph | 2.2 | 9 | 7/15 | 1631 | −1259 | 8 |

A good test for moderate-sized telescopes, this globular cluster lies approximately halfway between Zeta and Phi Ophiuchi.

Messier number	NGC number	Constellation	Angular size	Magnitude	Date on meridian	1970 Position RA (h/m)	Decl. (°/′)	Map No.
13	6205	Her	23	6	7/18	1641	+3630	4

The famous Hercules cluster. Like M.5, it has to be seen to be believed. Look for it about one-third of the straight-line distance between Eta and Zeta Herculis. On good nights you can see it with the naked eye. At such times see if your telescope can pick up the dark lanes and star streams described by many observers. Note, too, its elliptical shape.

12	6218	Oph	9.3	7	7/19	1646	−0154	8

A beautiful globular cluster but relatively hard to find since it lies in a sparce star field. Of some help is the fact that it is one corner of a parallelogram formed by Upsilon, Delta, and Lamba Ophiuchi.

10	6254	Oph	8.2	7	7/21	1656	−0404	8

Very similar to M.12 but also hard to find. If you can locate M.12, M.10 lies just to the southeast, about 3 degrees away.

62	6266	Oph	4.3	7	7/22	1659	−3005	12

A fine, bright globular. Low in the sky, near RR Scorpii.

19	6273	Oph	4.3	7	7/22	1701	−2613	8, 12

Fairly bright, but small. This globular lies almost due east of Antares and due north of M.62, in the "blank space" north of Scorpius.

92	6341	Her	12	6	7/26	1717	+4311	4

Often overlooked because of its proximity to its famous neighbor M.13, this is a fine, bright globular although its stars are difficult to resolve.

9	6333	Oph	2.4	7	7/26	1717	−1829	8, 12

A small globular cluster with a very bright nucleus. The outlying stars can be resolved with a moderate-sized telescope.

14	6402	Oph	3	8	8/1	1736	−0314	8

Even though this globular lies in a sparse star field, it is not difficult to find since it forms the right angle of a triangle which includes Zeta Serpens Caudi and Mu Ophiuchi.

6	6405	Sco	26	5	8/1	1738	−3212	12

A very fine open cluster in the northeast corner of Scorpius. It is low in the sky for northern observers but when the atmosphere is clear near the horizon this cluster is well worth looking for.

7	6475	Sco	60	5	8/5	1752	−3448	12

Like M.6, this brilliant and extensive open cluster appears very low in the sky. Look for it in a six-star asterism northeast of Lambda Scorpii.

Messier number	NGC number	Constel- lation	Angular size	Magnitude	Date on meridian	1970 Position RA (h/m)	Decl. (°/′)	Map No.
23	6494	Sgr	27	7	8/6	1755	−1901	8, 12

A very fine open cluster for low-power viewing. There are at least 120 stars arranged in curved lines. The sixth-magnitude star on its western edge will help you find this beautiful cluster.

| 20 | 6514 | Sgr | 29 × 27 | − | 8/7 | 1800 | −2302 | 9, 13 |

The Trifid Nebula, so-called for the three dark rifts which meet at the center of this diffuse cloud of gas. Beautiful with high power, but the rifts are difficult with anything less than an 8-inch telescope.

| 8 | 6523 | Sgr | 90 × 40 | − | 8/8 | 1802 | −2420 | 9, 13 |

The Lagoon Nebula. A large irregular, naked-eye nebulosity, easy to locate in Sagittarius. Use lowest powers for best effect, then shift to higher powers for the dark patches in this extended diffuse nebula.

| 21 | 6531 | Sgr | 10 | 7 | 8/8 | 1803 | −2230 | 9, 13 |

Surrounded on all sides by more spectacular objects, this fine open cluster has been neglected by most amateurs. Yet it is a striking object in itself and well worth attention.

| 24 | 6603 | Sgr | 4 | 5 | 8/11 | 1817 | −1826 | 9, 13 |

Bright but small, this open cluster is hard to find since it lies in a dense star field. But if you follow the curve generated by the handle of the Milk Dipper in Sagittarius, you will come upon it about 2 degrees beyond the end star, Mu.

| 16 | 6611 | Ser | 25 | 6 | 8/11 | 1817 | −1347 | 9 |

A bright open cluster of about 100 stars. But like M.24, it lies in a dense star field. It lies about 2 degrees north of the Omega Nebula (see below) in a patch of nebulosity.

| 18 | 6613 | Sgr | 12 | 8 | 8/11 | 1818 | −1708 | 9, 13 |

Even though this open cluster is small, it is easier to find than its companions in the area since it is silhouetted against a dark background.

| 17 | 6618 | Sgr | 46 × 37 | − | 8/12 | 1818 | −1611 | 9, 13 |

The Omega, or Horseshoe, Nebula. Beautiful, brilliant; a satisfying object even in small telescopes. Use your highest power for detail, but wait for that moment of best seeing.

| 28 | 6626 | Sgr | 4.7 | 7 | 8/12 | 1823 | −2453 | 9, 13 |

A relatively dim globular lying about 1 degree north of Lambda Sagittarii.

| 69 | 6637 | Sgr | 2.8 | 8 | 8/13 | 1829 | −3222 | 13 |

A small globular which you can find just below the bowl of the Milk Dipper in Sagittarius.

Messier number	NGC number	Constel-lation	Angular size	Magnitude	Date on meridian	1970 Position		Map No.
						RA (h/m)	Decl. (°/′)	
25	I 4725	Sgr	40	7	8/14	1830	−1916	9, 13

This sprawling open cluster of about 50 stars is rather undistinguished. But it does contain the variable star U Sagittarii near its center.

| 22 | 6656 | Sgr | 17.3 | 6 | 8/15 | 1834 | −2357 | 9, 13 |

A bright globular cluster lying above the handle of the Milk Dipper, northeast of Kaus Borealis. The stars are easily resolvable in small telescopes.

| 70 | 6681 | Sgr | 2.3 | 10 | 8/17 | 1841 | −3220 | 13 |

Another small globular cluster. About 2 degrees east of M.69, it is located halfway between Ascella and Kaus Australis.

| 26 | 6694 | Sct | 9 | 9 | 8/18 | 1844 | −0926 | 9 |

20 stars in an open cluster. Difficult because of the brilliant background of the Scutum star cloud. But it is almost on a line drawn through Alpha and Epsilon Scuti and extended to the east the distance the stars are apart.

| 11 | 6705 | Sct | 12 | 6 | 8/19 | 1849 | −0618 | 9 |

A triangular patch in northern Scutum made up of hundreds of stars. Just visible to the naked eye and a wonderful open cluster for a 6-inch telescope.

| 57 | 6720 | Lyr | 1 × 1 | 9 | 8/20 | 1853 | +3300 | 5 |

The lovely Ring Nebula in Lyra. You may not be able to see the central star unless you have a large telescope (12 inches or more) but you can see the "doughnut" in any instrument. Look particularly for the illumination in the center of the ring.

| 54 | 6715 | Sgr | 2.1 | 7 | 8/20 | 1853 | −3031 | 13 |

A small globular just above the bowl of the Milk Dipper. Don't confuse this with M.69 or M.22. The three globulars make an interesting variation of size and brightness, all in the same region of the sky.

| 56 | 6779 | Lyr | 1.8 | 8 | 8/26 | 1916 | +3007 | 5 |

Overshadowed by its famous neighbor, the Ring Nebula, this fine little globular cluster is often neglected. Take the trouble to find it.

Appendix I

Conversion of Mean Solar Time Interval to Sidereal Time Interval

Hours	Correction Min	Correction Sec	Min	Correction Sec
1		10	1-3	0
2		20	4-9	1
3		30	10-15	2
4		39	16-21	3
5		49	22-27	4
6		59	28-33	5
7	1	09	34-39	6
8	1	19	40-45	7
9	1	29	46-51	8
10	1	39	52-57	9
11	1	48	58-60	10
12	1	58		
13	2	08		
14	2	18		
15	2	28		
16	2	38		
17	2	48		
18	2	57		
19	3	07		
20	3	17		
21	3	27		
22	3	37		
23	3	47		

Example: What sidereal time interval corresponds to a solar time interval of 13 hours 22 min?

From table:

13 hours = 2 min 8 sec

22 min   =   4 sec

2 min 12 sec

or, 13 hours, 2 min, 12 sec

Appendix II

Sidereal Time at 0 Hours G.C.T. (Universal Time)
for the Meridian of Greenwich, 1960

Date	Jan.	Feb.	Mar.	Apr.	May	June	July	Aug.	Sept.	Oct.	Nov.	Dec.
	h m	h m	h m	h m	h m	h m	h m	h m	h m	h m	h m	h m
1	6 39	8 41	10 35	12 37	14 36	16 38	18 36	20 38	22 40	0 39	2 41	4 39
2	6 43	8 45	10 39	12 41	14 40	16 42	18 40	20 42	22 45	0 43	2 45	4 43
3	6 47	8 48	10 43	12 44	14 44	16 46	18 45	20 46	22 49	0 47	2 49	4 47
4	6 51	8 53	10 47	12 49	14 48	16 50	18 48	20 50	22 53	0 51	2 53	4 51
5	6 54	8 57	10 51	12 53	14 52	16 54	18 52	20 54	22 56	0 55	2 57	4 55
6	6 58	9 01	10 55	12 57	14 55	16 58	18 56	20 58	23 00	0 59	3 01	4 59
7	7 02	9 05	10 59	13 01	14 59	17 02	19 00	21 02	23 04	1 03	3 05	5 03
8	7 06	9 09	11 03	13 05	15 03	17 06	19 04	21 06	23 08	1 07	3 09	5 07
9	7 10	9 12	11 07	13 09	15 07	17 09	19 08	21 10	23 12	1 10	3 13	5 11
10	7 14	9 16	11 11	13 13	15 11	17 13	19 12	21 14	23 16	1 14	3 17	5 15
11	7 18	9 20	11 15	13 17	15 15	17 17	19 16	21 18	23 20	1 18	3 21	5 19
12	7 22	9 24	11 19	13 21	15 19	17 21	19 20	21 22	23 24	1 22	3 25	5 23
13	7 26	9 28	11 23	13 25	15 23	17 25	19 24	21 26	23 28	1 26	3 28	5 27
14	7 30	9 32	11 26	13 29	15 27	17 29	19 27	21 30	23 32	1 30	3 32	5 31
15	7 34	9 36	11 30	13 32	15 31	17 33	19 32	21 34	23 36	1 34	3 36	5 35
16	7 38	9 40	11 34	13 37	15 35	17 37	19 35	21 38	23 40	1 38	3 40	5 39
17	7 42	9 44	11 38	13 41	15 39	17 41	19 39	21 42	23 44	1 42	3 44	5 43
18	7 46	9 48	11 42	13 44	15 43	17 45	19 43	21 45	23 48	1 46	3 48	5 46
19	7 50	9 52	11 46	13 48	15 47	17 49	19 47	21 49	23 52	1 50	3 52	5 50
20	7 54	9 56	11 50	13 52	15 51	17 53	19 51	21 53	23 56	1 54	3 56	5 54
21	7 58	10 00	11 54	13 56	15 55	17 57	19 55	21 57	0 00	1 58	4 00	5 58
22	8 01	10 04	11 58	14 00	15 59	18 01	19 59	22 01	0 03	2 02	4 04	6 02
23	8 05	10 08	12 02	14 04	16 02	18 05	20 03	22 05	0 07	2 06	4 08	6 06
24	8 09	10 12	12 06	14 08	16 06	18 09	20 07	22 09	0 11	2 10	4 12	6 10
25	8 13	10 16	12 10	14 12	16 10	18 13	20 11	22 13	0 15	2 14	4 16	6 14
26	8 17	10 19	12 14	14 16	16 14	18 17	20 15	22 17	0 19	2 17	4 20	6 18
27	8 21	10 23	12 18	14 20	16 18	18 20	20 19	22 21	0 23	2 21	4 24	6 22
28	8 25	10 27	12 22	14 24	16 22	18 24	20 23	22 25	0 27	2 25	4 28	6 26
29	8 29	10 31	12 26	14 28	16 26	18 28	20 27	22 29	0 31	2 29	4 32	6 30
30	8 33		12 30	14 32	16 30	18 32	20 31	22 33	0 35	2 33	4 36	6 34
31	8 37		12 34		16 34		20 35	22 37		2 37		6 38

Although this table is correct only for the year 1960 it may be used as an approximate table for any year. None of the values will be in error by more than 3 minutes.

Compiled from the American Ephemeris and Nautical Almanac.

Appendix III

Conversion of Arc to Time

°	h m	°	h m	°	h m	°	h m	°	h m	°	h m	′	m s	″	s
0	0 00	60	4 00	120	8 00	180	12 00	240	16 00	300	20 00	0	0 00	0	0.00
1	0 04	61	4 04	121	8 04	181	12 04	241	16 04	301	20 04	1	0 04	1	0.07
2	0 08	62	4 08	122	8 08	182	12 08	242	16 08	302	20 08	2	0 08	2	0.13
3	0 12	63	4 12	123	8 12	183	12 12	243	16 12	303	20 12	3	0 12	3	0.20
4	0 16	64	4 16	124	8 16	184	12 16	244	16 16	304	20 16	4	0 16	4	0.27
5	0 20	65	4 20	125	8 20	185	12 20	245	16 20	305	20 20	5	0 20	5	0.33
6	0 24	66	4 24	126	8 24	186	12 24	246	16 24	306	20 24	6	0 24	6	0.40
7	0 28	67	4 28	127	8 28	187	12 28	247	16 28	307	20 28	7	0 28	7	0.47
8	0 32	68	4 32	128	8 32	188	12 32	248	16 32	308	20 32	8	0 32	8	0.53
9	0 36	69	4 36	129	8 36	189	12 36	249	16 36	309	20 36	9	0 36	9	0.60
10	0 40	70	4 40	130	8 40	190	12 40	250	16 40	310	20 40	10	0 40	10	0.67
11	0 44	71	4 44	131	8 44	191	12 44	251	16 44	311	20 44	11	0 44	11	0.73
12	0 48	72	4 48	132	8 48	192	12 48	252	16 48	312	20 48	12	0 48	12	0.80
13	0 52	73	4 52	133	8 52	193	12 52	253	16 52	313	20 52	13	0 52	13	0.87
14	0 56	74	4 56	134	8 56	194	12 56	254	16 56	314	20 56	14	0 56	14	0.93
15	1 00	75	5 00	135	9 00	195	13 00	255	17 00	315	21 00	15	1 00	15	1.00
16	1 04	76	5 04	136	9 04	196	13 04	256	17 04	316	21 04	16	1 04	16	1.07
17	1 08	77	5 08	137	9 08	197	13 08	257	17 08	317	21 08	17	1 08	17	1.13
18	1 12	78	5 12	138	9 12	198	13 12	258	17 12	318	21 12	18	1 12	18	1.20
19	1 16	79	5 16	139	9 16	199	13 16	259	17 16	319	21 16	19	1 16	19	1.27
20	1 20	80	5 20	140	9 20	200	13 20	260	17 20	320	21 20	20	1 20	20	1.33
21	1 24	81	5 24	141	9 24	201	13 24	261	17 24	321	21 24	21	1 24	21	1.40
22	1 28	82	5 28	142	9 28	202	13 28	262	17 28	322	21 28	22	1 28	22	1.47
23	1 32	83	5 32	143	9 32	203	13 32	263	17 32	323	21 32	23	1 32	23	1.53
24	1 36	84	5 36	144	9 36	204	13 36	264	17 36	324	21 36	24	1 36	24	1.60
25	1 40	85	5 40	145	9 40	205	13 40	265	17 40	325	21 40	25	1 40	25	1.67
26	1 44	86	5 44	146	9 44	206	13 44	266	17 44	326	21 44	26	1 44	26	1.73
27	1 48	87	5 48	147	9 48	207	13 48	267	17 48	327	21 48	27	1 48	27	1.80
28	1 52	88	5 52	148	9 52	208	13 52	268	17 52	328	21 52	28	1 52	28	1.87
29	1 56	89	5 56	149	9 56	209	13 56	269	17 56	329	21 56	29	1 56	29	1.93
30	2 00	90	6 00	150	10 00	210	14 00	270	18 00	330	22 00	30	2 00	30	2.00
31	2 04	91	6 04	151	10 04	211	14 04	271	18 04	331	22 04	31	2 04	31	2.07
32	2 08	92	6 08	152	10 08	212	14 08	272	18 08	332	22 08	32	2 08	32	2.13
33	2 12	93	6 12	153	10 12	213	14 12	273	18 12	333	22 12	33	2 12	33	2.20
34	2 16	94	6 16	154	10 16	214	14 16	274	18 16	334	22 16	34	2 16	34	2.27
35	2 20	95	6 20	155	10 20	215	14 20	275	18 20	335	22 20	35	2 20	35	2.33
36	2 24	96	6 24	156	10 24	216	14 24	276	18 24	336	22 24	36	2 24	36	2.40
37	2 28	97	6 28	157	10 28	217	14 28	277	18 28	337	22 28	37	2 28	37	2.47
38	2 32	98	6 32	158	10 32	218	14 32	278	18 32	338	22 32	38	2 32	38	2.53
39	2 36	99	6 36	159	10 36	219	14 36	279	18 36	339	22 36	39	2 36	39	2.60
40	2 40	100	6 40	160	10 40	220	14 40	280	18 40	340	22 40	40	2 40	40	2.67
41	2 44	101	6 44	161	10 44	221	14 44	281	18 44	341	22 44	41	2 44	41	2.73
42	2 48	102	6 48	162	10 48	222	14 48	282	18 48	342	22 48	42	2 48	42	2.80
43	2 52	103	6 52	163	10 52	223	14 52	283	18 52	343	22 52	43	2 52	43	2.87
44	2 56	104	6 56	164	10 56	224	14 56	284	18 56	344	22 56	44	2 56	44	2.93
45	3 00	105	7 00	165	11 00	225	15 00	285	19 00	345	23 00	45	3 00	45	3.00
46	3 04	106	7 04	166	11 04	226	15 04	286	19 04	346	23 04	46	3 04	46	3.07
47	3 08	107	7 08	167	11 08	227	15 08	287	19 08	347	23 08	47	3 08	47	3.13
48	3 12	108	7 12	168	11 12	228	15 12	288	19 12	348	23 12	48	3 12	48	3.20
49	3 16	109	7 16	169	11 16	229	15 16	289	19 16	349	23 16	49	3 16	49	3.27
50	3 20	110	7 20	170	11 20	230	15 20	290	19 20	350	23 20	50	3 20	50	3.33
51	3 24	111	7 24	171	11 24	231	15 24	291	19 24	351	23 24	51	3 24	51	3.40
52	3 28	112	7 28	172	11 28	232	15 28	292	19 28	352	23 28	52	3 28	52	3.47
53	3 32	113	7 32	173	11 32	233	15 32	293	19 32	353	23 32	53	3 32	53	3.53
54	3 36	114	7 36	174	11 36	234	15 36	294	19 36	354	23 36	54	3 36	54	3.60
55	3 40	115	7 40	175	11 40	235	15 40	295	19 40	355	23 40	55	3 40	55	3.67
56	3 44	116	7 44	176	11 44	236	15 44	296	19 44	356	23 44	56	3 44	56	3.73
57	3 48	117	7 48	177	11 48	237	15 48	297	19 48	357	23 48	57	3 48	57	3.80
58	3 52	118	7 52	178	11 52	238	15 52	298	19 52	358	23 52	58	3 52	58	3.87
59	3 56	119	7 56	179	11 56	239	15 56	299	19 56	359	23 56	59	3 56	59	3.93
60	4 00	120	8 00	180	12 00	240	16 00	300	20 00	360	24 00	60	4 00	60	4.00

Appendix IV

Conversion of Universal Time (G.C.T.) to United States Time Zones

Universal Time	Eastern Daylight Time	Eastern Standard Time and Central Daylight Time	Central Standard Time and Mountain Daylight Time	Mountain Standard Time and Pacific Daylight Time	Pacific Standard Time
h					
0	*8 P.M.	*7 P.M.	*6 P.M.	*5 P.M.	*4 P.M.
1	*9	*8	*7	*6	*5
2	*10	*9	*8	*7	*6
3	*11 P.M.	*10	*9	*8	*7
4	0 Midnight	*11 P.M.	*10	*9	*8
5	1 A.M.	0 Midnight	*11 P.M.	*10	*9
6	2	1 A.M.	0 Midnight	*11 P.M.	*10
7	3	2	1 A.M.	0 Midnight	*11 P.M.
8	4	3	2	1 A.M.	0 Midnight
9	5	4	3	2	1 A.M.
10	6	5	4	3	2
11	7	6	5	4	3
12	8	7	6	5	4
13	9	8	7	6	5
14	10	9	8	7	6
15	11 A.M.	10	9	8	7
16	12 Noon	11 A.M.	10	9	8
17	1 P.M.	12 Noon	11 A.M.	10	9
18	2	1 P.M.	12 Noon	11 A.M.	10
19	3	2	1 P.M.	12 Noon	11 A.M.
20	4	3	2	1 P.M.	12 Noon
21	5	4	3	2	1 P.M.
22	6	5	4	3	2
23	7 P.M.	6 P.M.	5 P.M.	4 P.M.	3 P.M.

From American Ephemeris and Nautical Almanac, 1960.

*The time used is Universal Time, which differs from ordinary time by an exact number of hours as shown in the table; an asterisk denotes that the time is on the preceding day.

Appendix V

A Table of Cosines and Tangents

Angle	Cos	Tan	Angle	Cos	Tan
1°	.9998	.0175	46°	.6947	1.0355
2°	.9994	.0349	47°	.6820	1.0724
3°	.9986	.0524	48°	.6691	1.1106
4°	.9976	.0699	49°	.6561	1.1504
5°	.9962	.0875	50°	.6428	1.1918
6°	.9945	.1051	51°	.6293	1.2349
7°	.9925	.1228	52°	.6157	1.2799
8°	.9903	.1405	53°	.6018	1.3270
9°	.9877	.1584	54°	.5878	1.3764
10°	.9848	.1763	55°	.5736	1.4281
11°	.9816	.1944	56°	.5592	1.4826
12°	.9781	.2126	57°	.5446	1.5399
13°	.9744	.2309	58°	.5299	1.6003
14°	.9703	.2493	59°	.5150	1.6643
15°	.9659	.2679	60°	.5000	1.7321
16°	.9613	.2867	61°	.4848	1.8040
17°	.9563	.3057	62°	.4695	1.8807
18°	.9511	.3249	63°	.4540	1.9626
19°	.9455	.3443	64°	.4384	2.0503
20°	.9397	.3640	65°	.4226	2.1445
21°	.9336	.3839	66°	.4067	2.2460
22°	.9272	.4040	67°	.3907	2.3559
23°	.9205	.4245	68°	.3746	2.4751
24°	.9135	.4452	69°	.3584	2.6051
25°	.9063	.4663	70°	.3420	2.7475
26°	.8988	.4877	71°	.3256	2.9042
27°	.8910	.5095	72°	.3090	3.0777
28°	.8829	.5317	73°	.2924	3.2709
29°	.8746	.5543	74°	.2756	3.4874
30°	.8660	.5774	75°	.2588	3.7321
31°	.8572	.6009	76°	.2419	4.0108
32°	.8480	.6249	77°	.2250	4.3315
33°	.8387	.6494	78°	.2079	4.7046
34°	.8290	.6745	79°	.1908	5.1446
35°	.8192	.7002	80°	.1736	5.6713
36°	.8090	.7265	81°	.1564	6.3138
37°	.7986	.7536	82°	.1392	7.1154
38°	.7880	.7813	83°	.1219	8.1443
39°	.7771	.8098	84°	.1045	9.5144
40°	.7660	.8391	85°	.0872	11.4301
41°	.7547	.8693	86°	.0698	14.3007
42°	.7431	.9004	87°	.0523	19.0811
43°	.7314	.9325	88°	.0349	28.6363
44°	.7193	.9657	89°	.0175	57.2900
45°	.7071	1.0000	90°	.0000	∞

Appendix VI

Astronomical Symbols

☿ Mercury
♀ Venus
⊕ Earth
♂ Mars
♃ Jupiter
♄ Saturn
♅ Uranus
♆ Neptune
♇ Pluto
☉ Sun
● New Moon
☽ First Quarter
○ Full Moon
☾ Last Quarter

☌ Conjunction. Where two bodies have the same right ascension but not necessarily the same declination.

☍ Opposition. Where two bodies differ 180° in right ascension.

□ Quadrature. Where two bodies differ 90° in right ascension.

Appendix VII

Greek Alphabet

A	α	Alpha	H	η	Eta	N	ν	Nu	T	τ	Tau
B	β	Beta	Θ	θ	Theta	Ξ	ξ	Xi	Y	ν	Upsilon
Γ	γ	Gamma	I	ι	Iota	O	o	Omicron	Φ	ϕ	Phi
Δ	δ	Delta	K	κ	Kappa	Π	π	Pi	X	χ	Chi
E	ϵ	Epsilon	Λ	λ	Lambda	P	ρ	Rho	Ψ	ψ	Psi
Z	ζ	Zeta	M	μ	Mu	Σ	σ	Sigma	Ω	ω	Omega

Glossary

ABERRATION OF LIGHT The apparent displacement of an astronomical object in whatever direction the observer is moving. It is most noticeable along the line of the earth's orbit around the sun and may amount to as much as 20.5 seconds of arc.

ABSOLUTE MAGNITUDE A measure of the intrinsic brightness of a star, independent of the star's distance from earth. It may also be defined as the apparent magnitude a star might have at a distance of 10 parsecs from earth.

ACHROMATIC LENS A lens with two or more elements designed to produce images free from false color.

AIRY DISK The disklike image of a point source of light as seen in an optical system.

ALBEDO The amount of light reflected by a heavenly body compared to the amount falling upon it.

ALTAZIMUTH MOUNTING A telescope mounting in which one axis (azimuth) is parallel to the plane of the observer, with a second axis (altitude) perpendicular to the first.

ANGSTROM UNIT A unit of wavelength measurement. It equals one hundred-millionth of a centimeter.

ANGULAR DIAMETER The angle subtended by the actual diameter of an object. The moon has an actual diameter of 2,160 miles, but subtends an arc varying from 33'30" to 29'21" depending upon its orbital distance from us.

APHELION The point of an orbit farthest from the sun.

APOGEE The point of an orbit farthest from the earth.

APPARENT MAGNITUDE The brightness of a star as we see it. A first-magnitude star is as bright as a candle flame at a distance of 1,300 feet.

ASTEROID A body large enough to be observed but smaller than a regular planet.

ASTIGMATISM A mirror or lens defect in which the size and shape of an image vary for different points of focus.

ASTRONOMICAL UNIT A unit of space measurement equal to the average distance between the sun and earth: 93 million miles.

AURORA Light emitted by the earth's atmosphere at heights of 50–600 miles. Usually ascribed to charged hydrogen particles (protons) and electrons coming from the sun.

AZIMUTH A measure of direction. It is the angular distance of a body, measured westward, from the south point of the horizon.

BARLOW LENS A negative lens used to increase both magnification and eye-relief when used in conjunction with ordinary eyepieces.

BINARY Two close-together stars moving in elliptical paths around a common center of gravity.

BOLIDE A bright meteor which apparently explodes during its flight through the atmosphere.

CELESTIAL EQUATOR An imaginary line in the heavens created by the intersection of a projection of the plane of the earth's equator and the celestial sphere.

CELESTIAL MERIDIAN A great circle which passes through the north and south poles of the celestial sphere, and also through the zenith and nadir.

CELESTIAL SPHERE The great imaginary globe upon whose inner surface we may imagine all the stars to lie.

CEPHEID VARIABLE A type of variable star, so named because the first one found was in the constellation Cepheus.

CHROMATIC ABERRATION A defect in a lens in which the various colors of the spectrum are not brought to the same focus. Produces a colored halo around the image.

CHROMOSPHERE   A reddish layer of the sun's atmosphere which lies outside the photosphere.

COMA   1. An umbrella-shaped stellar image resulting from a lens or mirror defect. 2. The glowing light around the nucleus of a comet.

CONJUNCTION   When a planet is in a position toward or beyond the sun. If it is between earth and sun, it is in *inferior* conjunction. If it is beyond the sun, it is in *superior* conjunction.

CONSTELLATIONS   The arbitrary groups into which stars are divided for easy reference and identification.

CORONA   The outermost portion of the sun's atmosphere.

CORRECTING LENS   A lens placed at the front of a catadioptric telescope whose function is to correct the spherical aberration of the primary mirror.

CORRECTION   The amount of deviation of an astronomical mirror surface from a perfect paraboloid. Overcorrection implies too deep a curve; undercorrection, too shallow.

CURVATURE OF FIELD   The apparent bending of the field of view of a telescope. Can be compensated for by changing the focus for the edge areas.

DALL-KIRKHAM TELESCOPE   A Cassegrain-type telescope which makes use of an ellipsoidal primary mirror and a spherical secondary.

DAWES' LIMIT   The smallest angular separation of two stars in which each is still observable with a telescope of given aperture.

DECLINATION   The angular distance of a heavenly body north or south of the celestial equator.

DEFINITION   Faithful reproduction of the characteristics of an object in all parts of the image.

DIFFRACTION   Spreading of light into an area ordinarily in shadow, resulting in a light and dark pattern because of the interference of light waves.

DISTORTION   Curvature of what should be straight lines near the edge of the field.

ECCENTRICITY (OF ELLIPSE)   A mathematical ratio which determines the shape of an elliptical orbit. If near zero, the ellipse is almost circular; as it approaches 1, the ellipse flattens.

ECLIPTIC   The great circle cut in the celestial sphere by an extension of the plane of the earth's orbit.

ELONGATION   Angular distance of an object east or west of the sun. The two inner planets, Mercury and Venus, have maximum values for elongation, 28° for Mercury, and 47° for Venus.

EPHEMERIS   A table of predicted positions of heavenly bodies.

EQUATORIAL MOUNTING   A telescope mounting in which one axis (polar) is parallel to the earth's axis, with a second axis (declination) perpendicular to the first.

EQUINOCTIAL   The celestial equator.

EQUINOXES   The two points at which the ecliptic intersects the celestial equator. The sun's passage from south to north is called the vernal equinox; from north to south, the autumnal equinox.

EQUIVALENT FOCAL LENGTH   The useful focal length of a compound optical system.

ERFLE EYEPIECE   A wide-field eyepiece which employs a third lens between eye and field lens.

ESCAPE VELOCITY   The minimum velocity which will enable an object to escape from the surface of a planet without further propulsion.

EXIT PUPIL   The image of the objective or mirror formed by the eyepiece; also called the Ramsden disk.

EYE LENS   The lens closest to the eye in an eyepiece.

EYE-RELIEF   The distance the eye must be placed from the eye lens to obtain sharpest vision.

FIELD, OR FIELD OF VIEW   The area of the sky visible at any one time through a telescope.

FLOCCULI   Clouds of very hot gas found near sunspots; when seen near the limb of the sun they are called faculae.

FOCAL LENGTH   The distance at which rays reflected from the surface of a mirror, or transmitted through a lens, intersect each other.

FOCAL PLANE   The area in which the rays reflected from a mirror, or transmitted through a lens, intersect to form an image.

FOCAL RATIO   The ratio between the effective focal length of a compound optical system and the aperture of the mirror or objective.

GALAXY   Any of the great systems of stars that occupy space. A typical galaxy may have as many as 100 million stars.

GEGENSCHEIN   A nebulosity of light directly opposite the sun.

HERSCHEL WEDGE   A wedge-shaped prism used in solar observation. Reduces heat and light intensity by directing most of the rays away from the eye.

HOUR ANGLE   The position of a heavenly body east or west of the meridian.

HUYGHENIAN EYEPIECE   A so-called negative eyepiece made up of two plano-convex lenses whose flat surfaces face the eye side of the eyepiece.

INTERFERENCE FRINGE   The dark lines caused by alternate interference and reinforcement of light waves coming from the same source.

KELLNER EYEPIECE   A positive eyepiece in which two plano-convex lenses, whose convex surfaces are oriented toward each other, are used for eye and field lenses.

LIBRATION   An oscillation (or apparent oscillation) of a heavenly body. The moon librates both east and west and north and south.

LIMB   The edge of a heavenly body.

LUMINOSITY   The total amount of radiation emitted by a heavenly body.

MAGNIFICATION   The apparent linear increase in size from an object to its image.

MAKSUTOV TELESCOPE   A catadioptric telescope made of a meniscus-type correcting plate, plus primary and secondary mirrors.

MERIDIAN   1. Terrestrial: the great circle on the earth's surface which passes through the poles and the geographical position of the observer.
2. Celestial: the great circle on the celestial sphere

which passes through the heavenly poles and the zenith and nadir of the observer.

METEOR   The streak in the sky resulting from the ionization of the atmosphere by the passage of a meteoroid.

METEORITE   That part of a meteoroid that has landed on earth.

METEOROID   A small chunk of matter in space.

MICRON   Unit used in small measurements. Equals 1 millionth of a meter or .00004 inch.

MONTH   One of twelve unequal periods which make up the civil year. For astronomical purposes there are four different types of months.

1. Anomalistic: interval required for the moon to pass from perigee to perigee (or apogee to apogee)—27.55455 days.

2. Nodical: interval required for the moon to pass from one node back to the same node again—27.21222 days.

3. Sidereal: interval required for the moon to pass from a fixed position with regard to the stars back to that same position, as seen from the earth—27.32166 days.

4. Synodic: interval from new moon to new moon—29.53059 days.

NADIR   Position in the heavens 180° away from the zenith.

NEBULA   Applied properly to any interstellar cloud of gas or dust. Often loosely to an indistinct heavenly body.

NEGATIVE EYEPIECE   One which produces an image between the lens elements. Such an image cannot be focused because of its position.

NODE   The points of passage of the moon, a satellite, a planet, or a comet through the plane of the ecliptic. From south to north, the passage is the ascending node, represented by the capital Greek letter Omega. In the opposite direction, it is called the descending node, and the same symbol is used upside down.

NOVA   A "new" star created by the explosion of a previously unobserved or undistinguished star. The increase in brightness is usually 100,000 times. When the increase is many times more than this, the new star is called a supernova.

OBJECTIVE   In a reflecting, compound, or catadioptric telescope, the objective is the primary mirror. In a refractor, it is the principal (front) lens.

OCCULTATION   The shutting off of the light from one body by the passage of another in front of it.

OPPOSITION   When the sun and another body are in opposite directions from earth, the second body is in opposition.

ORTHOSCOPIC EYEPIECE   An eyepiece which has a 3-element field lens and a single plano-convex eye lens.

PARSEC   An astronomical distance unit equal to 3.26 light-years or 19,160 billion miles.

PENUMBRA   Partial shadow in an eclipse in which most of the rays from the sun have been cut off.

PERIGEE   The orbital point at which the moon or an artificial satellite is closest to earth.

PERIHELION   The orbital point at which any body is closest to the sun.

PHASE   The ratio of lighted to dark surface of the moon and planets.

PHOTOSPHERE   That part of the sun's atmosphere nearest to its "surface."

PLAGE   A bright ragged blotch which appears near sunspots when the sun is viewed in calcium light.

PLANO-CONVEX LENS   A lens whose opposite sides are respectively flat and convex.

POLAR AXIS   The axis in an equatorial mounting parallel to the earth's axis.

POSITIVE EYEPIECE   An eyepiece in which the focal plane is outside the field lens.

PRECESSION   The cone-shaped motion traced in space by any wobbling body, such as a top or a gyroscope. The earth wobbles once during a period of 25,800 years. This is what causes the westward motion of the equinoxes.

PRIME FOCUS   The point at which the reflected rays from the primary mirror or the transmitted rays from the objective lens come to a focus.

PROMINENCE   A great volume of hydrogen gas emitted from the sun. When viewed against the solar background prominences appear as dark filaments. On the limb they appear as great flamelike projections.

QUADRATURE   Position of a planet at right angles to the sun.

RADIANT   The point in the heavens from which the meteors in a given meteor shower seem to emerge.

RAMSDEN DISK   Another name for the exit pupil formed on the eye side of an eyepiece.

RAMSDEN EYEPIECE   An adaptation of the Kellner eyepiece. The eye lens is an achromatic lens instead of a single plano-convex unit.

RAYLEIGH STANDARD   The requirement that rays converging to a focal point do not differ in path length by more than ¼ wavelength of light.

RESOLVING POWER   The power of a telescope to separate two close-together objects. It depends on the aperture of the telescope.

RETICLE   Ruled pieces of glass placed at the focal plane of an eyepiece. The rulings are superimposed on the image.

RFT   Abbreviation for "Richest-Field Telescope," usually a Newtonian reflector of very short focal length.

RIGHT ASCENSION   The angular distance of a celestial body measured to the east of the vernal equinox. It may be expressed in degrees or time units.

RILLES   Narrow lunar valleys, sometimes hundreds of miles long. They never occur near the centers of the maria.

RITCHEY-CHRETIEN TELESCOPE   A Cassegrain-type telescope which employs hyperboloidal curves on both primary and secondary mirrors.

SAROS   A time interval—about 19 years—used by ancient astronomers for the prediction of eclipses.

SCHMIDT CAMERA   A photographic instrument using a correcting plate and a concave primary mirror. The resulting focal plane is curved. Adaptations of the principle used in the camera produce Schmidt-Casse-grains, and others, for visual use.

SECONDARY MIRROR   A mirror other than the main or primary mirror of any type of reflecting telescope.

SECONDARY SPECTRUM   The color remaining on the fringe of images, even though the lens has been corrected for chromatic aberration.

SIDERITE   A meteorite composed of a nickel-iron alloy.

SIDEROLITE   A meteorite which is a combination of the materials which make up aerolites and siderites.

SOLSTICE   One of two points on the ecliptic midway between the equinoxes. The summer solstice is the longest day of the year; the winter, the shortest.

SPECTROSCOPIC BINARIES   Double stars whose dual nature can be identified only with the spectroscope.

SPECTRUM   The continuous band of color into which white light is separated by passing through a prism or diffraction grating.

SPHERICAL ABERRATION   The failure of a spherically ground mirror to bring rays reflected from all parts of its surface to a common focus.

TRANSIT   Motion of a small body across the face of a larger.

TROPICAL YEAR   The ordinary year—365.25 days.

UMBRA   The complete shadow in an eclipse where *all* rays from the sun are cut off.

WIDMANSTÄTTEN FIGURES   The crystalline markings which appear when meteorites are cut and then polished.

ZENITH   The point in the sky directly above the observer.

ZODIAC   The strip of sky, 8° wide, along the ecliptic.

ZODIACAL LIGHT   A wedge-shaped tongue of light created by reflected illumination from tiny particles along the zodiac.

Reference
Material

GENERAL READING

ALTER, D., CLEMINSHAW, C. H., and PHILLIPS, J. G. *Pictorial Astronomy.* Fourth rev. ed. New York: Crowell, 1974.

ASIMOV, ISAAC. *Asimov on Astronomy.* Garden City, N.Y.: Doubleday, 1974.

BAKER, ROBERT H., and FREDRICK, LAURENCE W. *Astronomy.* Ninth ed. New York: Van Nostrand Reinhold, 1971.

BIZONY, M. T., ed. *The Space Encyclopedia.* New York: Dutton, 1960.

BOK, BART J. and PRISCILLA F. *The Milky Way.* Fourth ed. Cambridge: Harvard University Press, 1974.

CLARKE, ARTHUR C., and BONESTELL, CHESLEY. *Beyond Jupiter: The Worlds of Tomorrow.* Boston: Little, Brown, 1973.

DIXON, ROBERT T. *Dynamic Astronomy.* Second ed. Englewood Cliffs, N.J.: Prentice-Hall, 1975.

DODSON, R. S. *Exploring the Heavens.* Rev. ed. New York: Crowell, 1964.

ERNST, B., and DE VRIES, T. E. *Atlas of the Universe.* London: Nelson, 1961.

HAWKINS, GERALD S. *Splendor in the Sky.* New York: Harper & Row, 1961.

HOYLE, FRED. *Astronomy.* New York: Doubleday, 1962.

————. *Frontiers of Astronomy.* New York: Harper, 1955.

HYNEK, J. A., and APFEL, N. *Astronomy One.* New York: Benjamin, 1972.

KAHN, FRITZ. *Design of the Universe.* New York: Crown, 1954.

KROGDAHL, WESLEY S. *The Astronomical Universe.* Rev. ed. New York: Macmillan, 1962.

MCLAUGHLIN, DEAN B. *Introduction to Astronomy.* Boston: Houghton-Mifflin, 1961.

MOORE, PATRICK. *Picture History of Astronomy.* Rev. ed. New York: Grosset & Dunlap, 1972.

PAYNE-GAPOSCHKIN, C., and HARAMUNDANIS, K. *Introduction to Astronomy.* Second ed. Englewood Cliffs, N.J.: Prentice-Hall, 1970.

SHAPLEY, HARLOW. *Beyond the Observatory.* New York: Scribner's, 1972.

SKILLING, W. T., and RICHARDSON, R. S. *A Brief Text in Astronomy.* Rev. ed. New York: Holt, Rinehart & Winston, 1959.

TELESCOPES, CHARTS, ATLASES

BEČVAR, ANTONIN. *Atlas Coeli.* Vol. II, Epoch 1950. Cambridge: Sky Publishing, 1959.

BROWN, PETER L. *What Star Is That?* New York: Viking, 1971.

HOWARD, N. E. *Standard Handbook for Telescope Making.* New York: Crowell, 1959.

INGALLS, ALBERT G., ed. *Amateur Telescope Making.* Books I, II, and III. Rev. ed. New York: Scientific American, 1956, 1957.

MOORE, PATRICK. *Seeing Stars*. Chicago: Rand McNally, 1971.

NORTON, ARTHUR P. *Star Atlas*. London: Gall & Inglis, 1959.

OLCOTT, WILLIAM, and MAYALL, R. NEWTON and MARGARET W. *Field Book of the Skies*. Fourth ed. New York: Putnam's, 1954.

PELTIER, LESLIE C. *Guideposts to the Stars*. New York: Macmillan, 1972.

REY, H. A. *The Stars*. Boston: Houghton-Mifflin, 1952.

SIDGWICK, J. B. *Amateur Astronomers Handbook*. London: Faber & Faber, 1956.

———. *Observational Astronomy for Amateurs*. London: Faber & Faber, 1957.

WEBB, T. W., and MAYALL, MARGARET W. *Celestial Objects for Common Telescopes* (2 vols.). Rev. ed. New York: Dover, 1962.

SUN, MOON, AND PLANETS

ALTER, DINSMORE. *Pictorial Guide to the Moon*. Third rev. ed. New York: Crowell, 1973.

JONES, HAROLD SPENCER. *Life on Other Worlds*. New York: New American Library, 1956.

MENZEL, DONALD H. *Our Sun*. Rev. ed. Cambridge: Harvard University Press, 1959.

MITCHELL, S. A. *Eclipses of the Sun*. Fifth ed. New York: Columbia University Press, 1951.

MOORE, PATRICK. *A Guide to the Moon*. New York: Norton, 1953.

———. *A Guide to the Planets*. New York: Norton, 1954.

———, and CROSS, CHARLES A. *Mars*. New York: Crown, 1973.

OLIVIER, C. P. *Comets and Meteors*. Baltimore: Williams & Wilkins, 1930.

WATSON, FLETCHER G. *Between the Planets*. Third ed. Cambridge: Harvard University Press, forthcoming.

WILKINS, H. P., and MOORE, PATRICK. *The Moon*. New York: Macmillan, 1955.

STARS

BINNENDIJK, L. *Properties of Double Stars*. Philadelphia: University of Pennsylvania Press, 1960.

CAMPBELL, LEON, and JACCHIA, L. *The Story of Variable Stars*. Philadelphia: Blakiston, 1941.

KRUSE, W., and DIECKVOSS, W. *The Stars*. Ann Arbor: University of Michigan Press, 1957.

PICKERING, JAMES SAYRE. *The Stars Are Yours*. Rev. ed. New York: Macmillan, 1958.

PERIODICALS

American Ephemeris and Nautical Almanac. Annual. Washington, D.C.: U.S. Government Printing Office.

Astronomy. Monthly. Milwaukee: AstroMedia Corporation.

The Observer's Handbook. Annual. Toronto: Royal Astronomical Society of Canada.

Review of Popular Astronomy. Bi-monthly. St. Louis: Sky Map Publications.

Scientific American. Monthly. New York: Scientific American Publishing Company.

Sky and Telescope. Monthly. Cambridge: Sky Publishing Company.

Sky Lines. Monthly. New York: Amateur Astronomers Association.

The Strolling Astronomer. Bi-monthly. Las Cruces, N.M.: Association of Lunar and Planetary Observers.

The World Almanac. Annual. New York: Newspaper Enterprise Association, Inc.

Publications of the Astronomical Society of the Pacific. Bi-monthly. Palo Alto: Astronomical Society of the Pacific.

Monthly Notices of the Royal Astronomical Society. London: Burlington House.

PHOTOGRAPHY

KEENE, G. T. *Star Gazing with Telescope and Camera*. Princeton: Amphoto, 1967.

PAUL, HENRY E. *Outer Space Photography for the Amateur*. Third ed. Princeton: Amphoto, 1967.

Index

aberration (*see also* coma), 209
  chromatic, 14–16, 22, 23, 26, 28, 29, 209
  eyepiece, 26–29
  spherical, 12–13, 22, 23, 26, 29, 212
    camera lenses and, 138
  zonal, 12, 13
absolute magnitude, 209
Acamar, 42, 165
accessories:
  camera, 136–145
  telescope, 30–32, 60
Achernar, 42, 44, 165
Achird, 165
achromatic doublet, 15
achromatic lens, 209
Acrab (Elacrab), 71, 165
Acubens, 165
Adara, 4, 165
Adhafera, 165
Adonis, 91
aerolites, 127–128, 209
Ain, 129, 165
air-spaced doublet, 15, 18
air-spaced objective, 18
Airy, Sir George, 5 fn.
Airy disks, *see* spurious disks
Albali, 165
albedo, 209
Albireo, 38, 165
Alchita, 165
Alcor, 6, 165
Alcyone, 129, 165
Aldebaran, 38, 71, 86, 165
Alderamin, 165

Aldib, 165
Alfard, 40, 166
Algenib, 40, 166
Algieba, 37, 166
Algol, 37, 40, 106, 166
Algorab, 166
Alhena, 71, 166
Alioth, 129, 166
Alkaid (Benetnash), 40, 45, 166
Alkaurops, 166
Alkes, 166
Allen, Richard Hinckley, 104 fn.
Almach, 40, 166
Alnair, 166
Alnilam, 166
Alnitak, 166
alphabet, Greek, 208
Alpha Triangulum Australe, 42
Alphecca, 166
Alpheratz, 40, 166
Alphirk, 166
Alrai, 37, 166
Alrami, 166
Alrisha, 40, 166
Alshain, 166
Alsuhail, 166
Altair, 38, 40, 42, 129, 166
altazimuth mountings, 18, 51, 56, 209
Alter, Dinsmore, 69
Aludra, 166
Alula Australe, 166
Alula Boreale, 166
Alwaid, 166
Alya, 166

Amalthea, 95
American Association of Variable Star Observers, 4–5, 56 fn., 106, 107, 110, 125–126
American Ephemeris and Nautical Almanac, 50, 56, 63, 91, 99, 100, 204 fn.
American Meteor Society, 130
Amphitrite, 92
Ancha, 166
Andromeda Galaxy, 11, 20, 33, 40, 44, 192
Andromedids, 188
angstrom unit, 15 fn., 209
angular diameter, 209
angular size, of spurious disks, 6
anomalistic month, 74, 211
Antares, 40, 71, 105, 165, 166
Antlia, 42, 44
aperture, diameter of, 2
aphelions, 82, 209
apogee, 209
apparent field, 9
    finding, 10
apparent magnitude, 3, 209
appulses, 72
Aquarids, 188
Aquarius, 40, 42, 44, 114, 116, 191
Aquila, 38, 40, 44
Arcturus, 37, 38, 129, 165, 166
Arecibo, Puerto Rico, radio telescope in, 83
Argus, 42
astronomical symbols, 208
astronomical units, 79, 209
astrophotography, *see* photography
Atiks, 167
Atlas, 167
atlas, star, 147 *et seq.*
atmosphere:
    earth, 33
    Jupiter, 92
    Mars, 90
    Saturn, 97, 98
    transparent, 11 fn.
    Uranus, 101
Auriga, 37, 44, 120
Aurora Borealis, 132, 133
    photographing the, 138
auroras, 132–133, 209
    photographing, 136, 138
autumn, *see* fall
Auva, 167
Azelfafage, 167
Azha, 167
Azmidiske, 167

background light, seeing conditions affected by, 5
Baily's beads, 75
ball-and-socket mounting, 51
Barlow lens, 26, 29, 105, 209
    photography and use of, 141
Barnard's star, 45

Baten Kaitos, 167
Bayer, Johann, 45
Beid, 167
Bellatrix, 38, 129, 167
belts, Jovian, 94
Bertele eyepiece, 29
Beta Eridani, 42
Betelgeuse, 38, 167
Biela's Comet, 124
Big Dipper, 6, 35, 37, 38, 40, 42
    photographing the, 137
binaries, 105–106, 209
    spectroscopic, 105, 212
    visual, 105–106
        list of, 172–174
Black-Eye Nebula, 198
"black holes," 110
Bode, Johann, 79 fn.
Bode's Law, 79, 91
bolides, 126, 128, 130, 209
Boötes, 37, 38, 44
Boss's General Catalog of Stars, 45
Botein, 167
Bouwers, A., 23
Braymer, Lawrence, 24
bright diffuse nebulae, 115
brightness:
    apparent star, 3
    image, 2–5

Caelum, 42, 44
California Nebula, 121, 182
Callisto, 95, 96
Camelopardalis, 44
cameras, 136–145
    Schmidt, 23, 211–212
Cancer, 37, 44, 46
Canes Venatici, 38, 44, 118
Canis Major, 38, 44, 120
Canis Minor, 38, 44
Canopus, 44, 167
Capella, 37, 38, 42, 129, 165, 167
Caph, 167
Capricornus, 40, 44
Carina, 44, 120
Cassegrainian telescopes, 17, 20, 21, 22–23, 52
Cassini, Giovanni Domenico, 99
Cassini's Division, 7, 98, 99
Cassiopeia, 37, 42, 44
Castor, 38, 167
catadioptric telescopes, 20, 23–26
Ceginus, 167
Celaeno, 167, 193
celestial equator, 47, 48, 49, 209, 210
celestial globe, model, 46
celestial meridian, 209, 210–211
celestial objects, locating, 35
celestial showpieces, 111–121
celestial sphere, 209

cemented doublet, 15, 16
Centaurus, 42, 44, 120
Cepheid variables, 107, 209
Cepheus, 37, 40, 44
Ceres, 91, 92, 140
Cetus, 40, 44
charts:
    heliocentric, 81, 82
    star, how to use, 45–46
    variable stars, 107–109
chromatic aberration, 14–16, 22, 23, 26, 28, 29, 209
chromosphere, 58, 75, 210
chrondules, 127
Chubb Crater, 127
Cincinnati Observatory Minor Planet Center, 91
Circinus, 42
Circlet of Pisces, 40, 42
clocks, sidereal, 49
clusters:
    galactic, 111, 112
    globular, 112–114, 193
        list of, 179–180
        photographing, 136, 145
    open star, 111–112, 121
        list of, 177–178
        photographing, 136
Cocon Nebula, 183
Columba, 42, 44
coma (aberration), 13–14, 16, 18, 22, 23, 26, 29, 210
    camera lenses and, 138
coma (comets), 123, 125
Coma Berenices, 38, 44
comes, 105
Comet Arend-Roland, 125, 126
Comet Ikeya-Seki, 122, 125
Comet Seki-Lines, 124
Comet Wilson, 125
comets, 106, 122–126
    Messier, Charles, and, 190
    observing, 125–126
    periodic, list of, 187
    photographing, 136, 138
compound telescopes, 1, 20–26
Cone Nebula, 182
conjunction, 80, 208, 210
    inferior, 80, 210
    superior, 80, 210
constellations, 120, 210
    circumpolar, 38, 44, 45
    fall, 40–42
    locating, by bright stars, 35
    month by month, 44–45
    photographing, 136–137
    southern, 42, 44, 45
    spring, 35–38
    summer, 38–40
    visible from 40° N, 44
    winter, 42–44
    zodiacal, 48

contact doublet, 18
Copernicus satellite, 130
Cor Caroli, 38, 167
corona, 58, 76, 210
Corona Australis, 40, 44
Corona Borealis (Northern Cross), 38, 44, 138
coronograph, 58
correcting lens, 210
correcting plate, 23, 26
correction, 210
Cor Serpentis, 167
Corvus, 37, 44
cosines, table of, 207
"cosmic smog," 115, 121
Couder reflectors, 26
counterglow (Gegenschein), 132, 135, 210
Coutchie, Raymond, 69
Coxa, 129, 167
Crab Nebula, 110, 114, 115, 181, 194
Crater, 37, 44
Crepe Ring, 98, 100
crescent phase, 80
Crux, 42, 120
Cursa, 167
curvature of field, see field curvature
Cygnus, 11, 38, 44, 45, 110, 120, 121, 141

Dabih, 40, 167
Dall-Kirkham telescopes, 22, 52, 210
dark nebulae, 115
Davis, Ralph, Mr. and Mrs., 144
Dawes, W. R., 6
Dawes' limit, 6–7, 210
day, sidereal (star), 49, 51
declination, 35, 42, 44, 210
    parallels of, 47
declination circle, 53
deficiencies, optical, 11–16
definition, 7, 210
Deimos, 90
Delphinus, 40, 44
Delta Cephei, 107
Delta Ceti, 42
Deneb, 38, 40, 129, 165, 167
Deneb Algedi, 40, 167
Deneb Kaitos, 40, 167
Deneb Okab, 167
Denebola, 37, 38, 167
descending node, 72, 211
Diadem, 129, 167, 198
diagonals, star, 30, 32
"Diamond of Virgo," 38
"diamond ring" effect, 75
dichotomy, 84
diffraction, 14, 210
diffraction pattern, 5
diffuse nebulae, 114–118
    list of, 182–183
Dione, 100

distances, planetary, 79–80
distortion, 14, 23, 26, 28, 29, 210
 negative (barrel), 14
 positive (pincushion), 14
Dorado, 44
double stars, 104–106
doublets, 15, 18
 achromatic, 15
 air-spaced, 15, 18
 cemented, 15, 16
 contact, 18
Draco, 38, 44, 127
Draconids, 127, 188
Dschubba, 71, 167
Dubhe, 37, 42, 167
Dumbbell Nebula, 113, 181, 191
Dziban, 167

earth, 79, 80
 atmosphere of, 33
 revolution of, 33, 72
 rotation of, 33, 44, 50
 symbol for, 208
earth satellites, see satellites, artificial
earth time, 49
eccentricity, 78, 79, 210
Echo satellites, 122, 130, 139, 189
eclipses, 72–77
 annular, 72
 during the year, 72–73
 lunar, 72, 76, 189
 observing, 74
 partial, 72
 paths of, 72
 periodic, 73–74
 shadows of, 74
 solar, 72, 73, 75, 189
 types of, 72
eclipsing binaries, 105, 106, 110
ecliptic, 47, 48, 210
Elacrab, see Acrab
elbow telescopes, 30
Electra, 167, 193
ellipse, see eccentricity
elliptical nebulae, 184 fn.
elongations, 80, 210
Enceladus, 100
Encke's Comet, 124, 187
Encke's Division, 98
English mounting, 52, 53
Enif, 167
ephemeris, 210
Ephemeris time, 50, 51
Epsilon Lyrae, 6
equator, celestial, 47, 48, 49, 209, 210
equatorial mountings, 19, 30, 31, 51–52, 56, 210
 aligning, 54
equinoxes, 210
 precession of the, 48–49
equivalent focal length, 141, 210

Equuleus, 40, 44
Erakis, 167
Erfle eyepiece, 29, 210
Eridanus, 42, 44.
escape velocity, 210
Etamin, 38, 167
Eunomia, 92
Europa, 95, 96
Euryscopic eyepiece, 29
exit pupil, 2, 210
 field size and, 11
 size of, 9
Explorer satellites, 130, 189
extragalactic nebulae, 118–119
 list of, 184–186
eye lens, 28, 29, 210
eyepieces, 8, 26–30
 achromatic Ramsden, 29
 Bertele, 29
 compound, 29–30
 Erfle, 29, 210
 Euryscopic, 29
 function of, 8
 Goerz, 29
 good, characteristics of, 26–28
 Herschelian, 32
 Huyghenian, 28, 29, 30, 210
 Kellner, 29, 30, 210
 Koenig, 29
 negative, 211
 orthoscopic, 29, 30, 211
 Ploessel, 29, 30
 positive, 211
 Ramsden, 26, 28, 29, 30, 32, 211
 single-element, 28
 stop, 9, 10
 thick-lens, 28
 thick-lens cemented, 28
 thin-lens, 28
 Tolles, 28
 two-lens, 28–29
 using, 30
 zoom, 29–30
eye relief, 210

faculae, 58
 dark, 58
fall:
 constellations visible in, 40–42
 Messier objects visible in, 190–192
False Cross, 44
field, 210
 apparent, 9
  finding, 10
 illumination, 10
 size:
  exit pupil and, 11
  importance of, 10–11
 true, 10–11
  sizes (table), 10

field curvature, 13, 22, 23, 26, 29, 210
field lens, 28, 29
filaments, 60
filar micrometer, 105–106
film, 136–145
filters, 30, 31–32
    colored, 31
    density of, determining, 31
    high-density, 30
    neutral density, 31
    variable, 57
finder telescopes, 30–31
First Point of Aries, 35
Flagstaff, Arizona, Naval Observatory at, 12, 22, 23
Flamsteed, John, 45
flocculi, 60, 210
Flora, 92
Florensky, Kirell P., 124 fn.
f-number, *see* focal ratio
focal length, 2, 210
    equivalent, 141, 210
focal plane, 1, 210
focal ratio, 2, 210
focus, prime, 211
Fomalhaut, 40, 42, 104, 167
fork mounting, 52, 53
Fornax, 42, 44
Fraunhofer objective, 18
full phase, 80
Furad, 167

galactic clusters, 111, 112
galaxies, 118–119, 210
    barred spiral, 184 fn.
    irregular, 184 fn.
    normal spiral, 184 fn.
    photographing, 136, 145
    types of, 184 fn.
Galilean lens, 28
Galilean refractors, 17–18
Galileo, 99
Gamma Cephei, 37
Ganymede, 93, 95, 96
Gegenschein, *see* counterglow
Gemini, 38, 44, 120
Geminids, 188
geography:
    celestial, 47–49
    lunar, 62–63
German mounting, 52, 53
Giacobinids, 127, 188
Gianfar, 167
gibbous phase, 80
Giedi, 40
Gienah, 168
globes, model celestial, 46
globular clusters, 112–114, 193
    list of, 179–180
    photographing, 136, 145
glossary, 209–212

glows, sky, 132–135
Goerz eyepiece, 29
Gomeisa, 168
Grafias, 168
Great Nebula, 117, 182, 191, 194
Great Red Spot, 94
Great Spiral Galaxy, 192
Gredi, 168
Greek alphabet, 208
green flash, 132, 135
Gregorian reflectors, 26
Gregory, John, 26
Gregory-Maksutov telescopes, 26
Grumium, 168
Grus, 44
"Guardians of the Pole," 37

halation, 138
Hale telescope (Mount Palomar), 12
Halley, Edmund, 190
Halley's Comet, 124, 187
Hamal, 40, 168
Haris, 129, 168
Harvard College Observatory, 107
Harvard designation, 107
Hasseleh, 168
Hatsya, 168
Hebe, 92
Heka, 168
Helical Nebula, 114, 181
heliocentric charts, 81, 82
Hencke, 91
Hercules, 38, 44, 114, 139, 193
Hercules cluster, 200
Hermes, 91
Herring, Alika, 69
Herschelian eyepieces, 32
Herschel wedge, 30, 32, 56–57, 210
Hevelius, Johannes, 190
Heze, 168
Hidalgo, 91
Hoba West meteorite, 127
Hoedus I, 168
Hoedus II, 168
Homam, 168
Horologium, 42
Horsehead Nebula, 115, 116, 182
Horseshoe Nebula, *see* Omega Nebula
hour angle, 210
hour circles, 44, 45, 48, 49
Huygenian eyepieces, 28, 29, 30, 210
Huygens, Christian, 190
Hyades, 38, 42, 71, 111, 112
    photographing, 136
Hydra, 40, 44
Hydrus, 44
Hyperion, 100

Iapetus, 100
Icarus, 91

illumination, field, 10
image:
    brightness, 2–5
    primary, 13
    secondary, 13
Index Catalog, 45
inferior conjunction, 80, 81, 210
Intelsat 4 satellite, 130
interference fringe, 210
International Astronomical Union, 62
International Date Line, 50
Io, 95, 96
Iris, 92
Izar, 168

Julian Day, 109
June meteor shower, 188
Juno, 91, 92
Jupiter, 72, 78, 79, 80, 81, 82, 92–97, 129, 144
    atmosphere of, 92
    drawing, 95
    observing, 94–97
    photographing, 144
    satellites of, 95–97, 106
    surface features, 94
    symbol for, 208
    telescopic details, 94–95
    transits of, 95
    vital statistics, 92

Kaffaljidhma, 168
Kajam, 168
Kaus Australis, 40, 129, 168
Kaus Borealis, 40, 129, 168
Kaus Medius, 168
Kelb Alrai, 168
Kellner eyepieces, 29, 30, 210
Kepler lens, 28
Kerb, 168
Keystone, 38
Kiffa Australis, 168
Kiffa Borealis, 168
Kirch, 190
Koenig eyepiece, 29
Kornephoros, 168
Kraz, 168
Kruger, 60, 45
Kuma, 129, 168

Lacaille, Nicolas Louis de, 42, 44, 45
Lacerta, 42, 44
Lagoon Nebula, 117, 118, 182, 193, 201
Lambda Scorpii, 40
lateral chromatic aberration, 15
least circle of confusion, 12, 13
lenses:
    achromatic, 209
    Barlow, 26, 29, 105, 209
        photography and use of, 141
    camera, 137–138
    coated, 30

correcting, 210
eye, 28, 29, 210
field, 28, 29
Galilean, 28
Kepler, 28
meniscus, 23
plano-convex, 211
Leo, 37, 38, 44
Leo Minor, 44
Leonids, 188
Lepus, 42, 44
Lesath, 168
Libra, 40, 44
librations, 62–63, 210
light:
    background, seeing conditions affected by, 5
    speed of, 33
light-gathering power of telescopes, 2–3, 5
light-grasp, 2
    secondary spectrum and, 15
light intensity, reduction of, 56–57
limb, 210
Little Dipper, 4, 37, 38, 40
Little Dumbbell Nebula, 114, 181
local hour angle, 49
local meridian, 44
logbook, 54, 72, 100, 109
longitudinal chromatic aberration, 15
luminosity, 210
Lunar Orbiter probes, 67, 68
Lupus, 44, 120
Lynx, 44
Lyra, 34, 38, 44, 114, 137, 196
    photographing, 136
Lyrids, 188

Maasym, 129, 168
Mackintosh, Allan, 26
Magellanic Clouds, 42, 44, 120
magnetic storms, 133
magnification, 2, 7–9, 210
    by the objective, 7–8
    excessive, effect on seeing conditions, 5
    limits of, 8–9
    nature of, 8
    relationship between true field size and, 10
magnitudes:
    limiting, 4
    stellar, 3–5
        representative, 129
        telescopes and, 4–5
Maia, 168, 193
Maksutov, D., 23
Maksutov Club, 26
Maksutov telescopes, 17, 20, 23, 24, 25, 26, 52, 210
Maraldi, 190
Mare Acidalium, 87, 89
Mariner IV spacecraft, 87, 89, 90
Mariner IX spacecraft, 88
Mariner X spacecraft, 83, 84, 90

Markab, 40, 168
Markeb, 168
Mars, 9, 78, 79, 80, 81, 82, 86–91
   atmosphere of, 90
   "canals," 87, 88, 89
   clouds, 89–90
   drawing, 90–91
   moons of, 90
   photographing, 144
   surface features, 89, 90
   symbol for, 208
   telescopic details, 87
   vital statistics, 86
Marsik, 168
Massalia, 92
Matar, 168
McClure, Alan, 137
Mebsuta, 168
Mechain, Pierre, 190
megaparsecs, 118
Megrez, 38, 42, 168
Mekbuda, 168
Melbourne Observatory Designation, 45
meniscus lens, 23
Menkalinan, 37, 129, 168
Menkar, 168
Menkhib, 168
Mensa, 42, 44
Merak, 37, 168
Mercury, 47, 78, 79, 80, 81, 82–83
   orbit of, 78–79
   symbol for, 208
   transits of, 83
   vital statistics, 82
Merez, 168
Merga, 169
meridian, 210–211
   celestial, 47, 209, 210–211
   local, 44
   terrestrial, 210
Merope, 169, 193
Mesarthim, 129, 169
Messier, Charles, 30 fn., 45, 69, 190
Messier Catalog, 190–202
Metallah, 169
meteorites, 126, 127, 129, 211
   metallic, 128
   stony, 127–128, 129
meteoroids, 126, 211
   origin of, 129
meteors, 122, 124, 126–130, 211
   annual showers, list of, 188
   observing, 129–130
   radiant, 126
   sporadic, 126
Meteor 12 satellite, 130
Metis, 92
Miaplacidus, 44, 169
micrometeorites, 128–129
micrometer, filar, 105–106
micron, 211

Microscopium, 42, 44
Milk Dipper, 40
Milky Way, 19, 40, 42, 106, 112
   photographing the, 141
   star clouds of the, 119–121
Miller, William C., 117 fn.
Mimas, 100
Minkar, 169
Mintaka, 169
Mira, 107, 169
Mirach, 40, 129, 169
Miram, 169
Miranda, 101
Mirfak, 169
mirror, secondary, 212
Mirzam, 129, 169
Misam, 169
Mizar, 6, 37, 40, 169
model celestial globes, 46
Monoceros, 42, 44
monochromator, quartz, 60
month, 211
   anomalistic, 74, 211
   nodical, 211
   sidereal, 211
   synodic, 72, 73, 74, 211
moon, 60–70, 143
   changes on the, 66
   comparisons of craters on the, 66, 69
   contrast on surface of the, 63
   drawing the, 69–70
   eclipses and the, 72–77
   features of the, 61–62, 69
   full, magnitude of, 4
   geography of the, 62–63
   observing the, 63–64
   photographing the, 136, 144
   ray systems, 69
   reference material, 214
   surface of the, 66
   symbols for, 208
   vital statistics, 61
moons:
   Jovian, 95–97, 106
   Martian, 90
   Neptune's, 102
   Saturn's, 99–100
   Uranian, 101
Moonwatch telescopes, 29, 125, 131
Moore, Patrick, 86
motions, planetary, 81, 82
mountings, telescope, 3, 18, 19, 30, 31, 51–52, 53, 54, 56, 209, 210
Mount Palomar, California, 4, 12, 34
Mufrid, 169
Muliphein, 129, 169
Museida, 169

nadir, 211
Naos, 165, 169

Nashira, 169
Nath, 169
Nautical Almanac, see *American Ephemeris and Nautical Almanac*
Naval Observatory (Flagstaff, Arizona), 12, 22, 23
nebulae, 211
   dark, 115
   diffuse, 114–118
     list of, 182–183
   elliptical, 184 fn.
   extragalactic, 118–119
     list of, 184–186
     photographing, 136, 145
   planetary, 114, 121
     list of, 181
     photographing, 136
negative eyepiece, 211
Neptune, 78, 79, 81, 101, 102
   moons of, 102
   orbit of, 78
   symbol for, 208
   vital statistics, 102
Nereid, 102
New General Catalog, 45
Newtonian-Maksutov telescopes, 26
Newtonian reflectors, 1, 14, 17, 19, 30–31
Nihal, 169
node, 211
   ascending, 72, 211
   descending, 72, 211
nodical month, 211
Nodus I, 169
Nodus II, *see* Aldib
Norma, 42, 44
North America Nebula, 121, 183
Northern Cross, 38, 42
North Star, *see* Polaris
novae, 107, 210
Nubecula Major, 42, 120
Nubecula Minor, 42, 120
Nunki, 169
Nusakan, 169
Nushaba, 169

Oberon, 101
object glass, 1
objective, 1, 2, 211
   air-spaced, 18
   diameter of, 2
   Fraunhofer, 18
   magnification by the, 7–8
   orthoscopic, 14
Observer's Handbook, 91, 107 fn.
occultations, 71–72, 211
occulting disk, 60
Octans, 42
off-axis telescopes, 1, 26
Olivier, Charles P., 130
Omega Centauri, 114

Omega (Horseshoe) Nebula, 117, 182, 201
Omicron Leonis, 109
open star clusters, 111–112, 121
   list of, 177–178
   photographing, 136
Ophiuchus, 38, 40, 44
Opik, E. J., 89
opposition, 80, 208, 211
optical axis, 10
optical deficiencies, 11–16
optical doubles, 105
orbits:
   artificial satellite, 130–131
   planetary, 78–79
Orion, 37, 38, 42, 44, 115, 116, 117, 120, 191, 194
Orionids, 188
Orion Nebula, photographing the, 145
Orion's Belt, 38
Orion's Sword, 194
orthoscopic eyepieces, 29, 30, 211
orthoscopic objective, 14
Owl Nebula, 181, 196

Pallas, 91, 92
Parkes, New South Wales, radio telescope in, 83
parsec, 211
Paul, Henry E., 137, 145
Pegasus, 40, 42, 44
Pegasus satellites, 189
Pelican Nebula, 182
penta-prism, unsilvered, 31, 32
penumbra, 58, 60, 211
penumbral shadow, 74, 76
perigee, 211
perihelions, 82, 211
Perseids, 188
Perseus, 11, 37, 40, 44, 112, 114, 120, 121
Phakt, 169
phase, 211
   crescent, 80
   full, 80
   gibbous, 80
Phecda, 38, 129, 169
Pherkad, 38, 169
Pherkard, 129, 169
Phobos, 90
Phoebe, 100
Phoenix, 42, 44
photography, celestial, 136–145
   fixed camera and, 136–139
   moving camera and, 139–141
   reference material, 214
   through the telescope, 141–143
photosphere, 57, 58, 211
Piazzi, Giuseppe, 40
Pickering, E. C., 4 fn.
Pickering, W. H., 69
Pisces, 35, 40, 44, 119
Piscis Austrinus, 40, 42, 44

plages, 60, 211
planetary appulse, 72
planetary nebulae, 114, 121
   list of, 181
   photographing, 136
planets, 78–103
   inferior, 80
   minor, 91–92
   motions of, 81, 82
   observing, 82
   orbits of, 78–79
   photographing, 136, 144
   reference material, 214
   relative distances of, 79–80
   relative positions of, 80–81
   superior, 80, 81
   symbols for, 208
planispheres, 46
plano-convex lens, 211
Pleiades, 4, 37, 42, 71, 111, 112, 193
   photographing, 136, 139, 140, 141
Pleione, 169
Ploessel eyepieces, 29, 30
Pluto, 47, 78, 79, 81, 102–103
   discoverer of, 89
   orbit of, 78–79
   symbol for, 208
   vital statistics, 102
pointers, 37
polar axis, 211
polar axis circle, 53
Polaris, 37, 42, 45, 54, 139
polarization method of reducing light intensity, 57
Pollux, 10, 38, 71, 169
poor seeing conditions, *see* seeing conditions
Porter, Russell, 69
positive eyepiece, 211
Praesepe, 37, 112, 195
   photographing, 136
precession, 33, 211
   of the equinoxes, 48–49
prices, telescope, 17
primary image, 13
prime focus, 211
prism, solar, 56
Procyon, 38, 42, 129, 169
prominence, 211
pulsars, 110
Puppis, 42, 44, 195
Pyxis, 42, 44

Quadrantids, 188
quadrature, 80, 81, 208, 211
quartz monochromator, 60
quasars, 78, 110
Questar telescope, 144, 145

radiant, 126, 127, 129, 211

Ramsden disk, 2, 11, 211
Ramsden eyepieces, 26, 28, 29, 30, 32, 211
Rana, 169
R Andromedae, 107
Ras Algethi, 169
Ras Alhague, 38, 169
Ras Elased Australis, 169
Ras Elased Borealis, 169
Rayleigh limit, 12
Rayleigh standard, 211
R Coronae Borealis, 107
records, keeping, 54
reference material, 213–214
reflectors, 3, 20
   Couder, 26
   Gregorian, 26
   Newtonian, 1, 14, 17, 19, 30–31
   objective in, 1
   simple, 19–20
refractors, 1, 3, 17–19
   astronomical, 18
   cost of, 17
   Galilean, 17–18
   types of, 17–18
Regulus, 37, 38, 40, 71, 72, 169
resolution, 5–7
resolving power, 6–7, 26, 211
reticle, 211
Reticulum, 42, 44
retrograde motion, 81
Rhea, 100
richest-field telescopes (RFT's), 14 fn., 19, 20, 211
Rigel, 38, 42, 165, 169
right ascension, 24, 35, 44, 45, 48, 211
right ascension circle, 53
rills, 211
Ring Nebula, 34, 114, 181, 190, 196, 202
Ritchey-Chretien telescopes, 22–23, 211
R Leonis, 109
Rosetta Nebula, 182
Ross 128, 45
Rotanev, 40, 169
Rucha, 37, 169

Sabik, 169
Sadalachbia, 129, 170
Sadalmelek, 170
Sadalsud, 170
Sador, 170, 191
Sagitta, 38, 44
   photographing, 136
Sagittarius, 11, 40, 44, 117, 120, 121, 136, 193
Saiph, 38, 42, 170
Sampson telescope, 26
Sarin, 170
saros, 74, 211
satellites, artificial, 122, 130–131
   observing, 131
   orbits of, 130–131

photographing, 136, 138–139
visible, list of, 189
Saturn, 7, 72, 79, 81, 97–100, 142
    atmosphere of, 97, 98
    drawing, 100
    moons of, 99–100
    observing, 99
    rings, 98–99, 100
    surface features, 98
    symbol for, 208
    vital statistics, 97
Saturn Nebula, 114, 116, 181, 191
Sceptrum, 129, 170
Scheat, 40, 170
Schedir, 42, 170
Schmidt, Bernard, 23, 66
Schmidt camera, 23, 211–212
Schmidt-Cassegrain telescopes, 23, 53
Schmidt telescopes, 23
Schwartzchild telescopes, 26
Scorpius, 40, 44, 114, 120
Sculptor, 42, 44
Scutum, 42, 44, 46, 136
secondary image, 13
secondary mirror, 212
secondary spectrum, 15, 19, 212
seeing conditions, factors causing poor, 4–5
Segin, 170
Serpens, 38, 112
Serpens Caput, 38, 44
Serpens Cauda, 44
setting circles, 30, 51, 52–54
Seven Sisters, see Pleiades
Sextans, 44
shadow:
    penumbral, 74, 76
    umbral, 74, 75, 76, 77
Sham, 129, 170
Shaula, 40, 170
Sheliak, 170
Sheratan, 170
Sickle, the, 37, 38
sidereal clocks, 49
sidereal day, 49, 51
sidereal month, 211
sidereal time, 49, 50
    charts, 50
    tables, 203, 204
    telescopes used to determine, 49–50
siderites, 128, 212
siderolites, 212
Sirius, 4, 33, 38, 42, 129, 170
Situla, 170
Skat, 170
sky, 33–46
    measuring the, 34–35
sky glows, 132–135
solar prism, 56
solar-radiation satellite, 130
solar system, dimensions of, 78

solstice, 212
Sombrero Nebula, 198
Southern Cross, see Crux
spectrohelioscope, 60
spectroscopic binaries, 105, 212
spectrum, 60, 212
    secondary, 15, 19, 212
sphere, celestial, 209
spherical aberration, 12–13, 22, 23, 29, 212
    camera lenses and, 138
Spica, 37, 38, 39, 40, 71, 165, 170
spring:
    constellations visible in, 35–38
    Messier objects visible in, 195–198
spurious (Airy) disks, 5–6, 209
Sputnik II, 122, 128
SS Cygni, 107, 165
standard stations, 71
star atlas, 147 et seq.
star charts, using, 45–46
star clouds, 121, 141
    photographing, 136
star diagonals, 30, 32
star magnitudes, see magnitudes
Star Names and Their Meanings (Allen), 104 fn.
stars, 104–110
    bright, locating constellations by, 35
    designations, 45
    distance of, measuring, 35
    double, 104–106
    list of, 165–171
    reference material, 214
    timing the, 49
    variable, 106–110, 165
        AAVSO charts, 107–109
        Cepheid, 107, 209
        finding, 109–110
        identifying, 107
        lists of, 175, 176
        long-period, 106–107, 176
        nonperiodic, 107
        short-period, 107, 175
        types of, 106–107
star trails, 139, 141
    photographing, 136, 139
stations, standard, 71
stellar magnitudes, see magnitudes
Stonyhurst Disks, 56
stop, eyepiece, 9, 10
Struve, Otto, 111
Sualocin, 40, 170
Subra, 170
Sulaphat, 170
summer:
    constellations visible in, 38–40
    Messier objects visible in, 199–202
sun, 55–60, 165
    direct observation of the, 56–57
    eclipses and the, 72–76
    features of the, 57–58

magnitude of, 4
photographing the, 141–145
projection of image of, 55–56, 74
reference material, 214
symbol for, 208
telescope accessories for work with the, 60
vital statistics, 55
suncaps, 57
sunspots, 58, 60, 145
superior conjunction, 80, 210
symbols, astronomical, 208
Syncom 3, 130
synodic month, 72, 73, 74, 211
Syrtis Major, 87, 89

Tabit, 170
Talitha, 170
tangents, table of, 207
Tania Australis, 170
Tania Borealis, 170
Tarazed, 170
Taurids, 188
Taurus, 38, 44, 120
Taygeta, 129, 170
Tejat Posterior, 170
Tejat Prior, 170
telescopes (see also reflectors; refractors), 1–32
    accessories, 30–32
        for solar work, 60
    Cassegrainian, 17, 20, 21, 22–23, 52
    catadioptric, 20, 23–26
    compound, 1, 20–26
    Dall-Kirkham, 22, 52, 210
    efficiency of, factors reducing, 4
    elbow, 30
    finder, 30–31
    good, functions of, 1–2
    Gregory-Maksutov, 26
    light-gathering power of, 2–3, 5
    Maksutov, 17, 20, 23, 24, 25, 26, 52, 210
    Moonwatch, 29, 125, 131
    mountings, 3, 30, 31, 51–52, 54, 56, 209, 210
    Newtonian-Maksutov, 26
    off-axis, 1, 26
    photography through, 141–143
    prices of, 17
    principle of, 1
    Questar, 144, 145
    reference material, 213
    resolving power of, 6–7, 26, 211
    richest-field (RFT's), 14 fn., 19, 20, 211
    Ritchey-Chretien, 22–23, 211
    Sampson, 26
    Schmidt, 23
    Schmidt-Cassegrain, 23, 53
    Schwartzchild, 26
    sidereal time determined by, 49–50
    star magnitudes and, 4–5
    true field of, 9–11

Telescopium, 42, 44
temperature, effect on seeing conditions, 5
terminology:
    photographic, 136–145
    telescope, 2–16
Tethys, 100
Theemin, 170
Theta Orionis, 194
Thuban, 170
time:
    earth, 49
    Ephemeris, 50, 51
    relationships, 50–51
    sidereal, 49, 50
        charts, 50
        tables, 203, 204
        telescopes used to determine, 50–51
    tables, 203–206
    universal, 50, 51
        conversion table, 206
time zones, 49
Titan, 100
Titania, 101
Toliman, 42, 170
Tolles eyepieces, 28
Tombaugh, Clyde, 89
transit, 212
Transit satellite, 130, 189
transmission factor, 2
transparent atmosphere, 11 fn.
Trapezium, 194
Triangulum, 40, 44, 191
Triangulum Australe, 42
Trifid Nebula, 117, 118, 182, 193, 201
Triton, 102
Trojan asteroids, 91
tropical year, 212
true field, 10–11
    sizes, table of, 10
Tureis, 170
Tyl, 170

umbra, 58, 60, 212
umbral shadow, 74, 75, 76, 77
Umbriel, 101
universal time, 50, 51
    conversion table, 206
Uranus, 78, 79, 81, 100–101
    atmosphere of, 101
    moons of, 101
    symbol for, 208
    vital statistics, 100
Ursa Major, 37, 37 fn., 38, 44
Ursa Minor, 37, 44
Ursids, 188

Van Maanen's star, 45
variable stars, 106–110, 165
    AAVSO charts, 107–109
    Cepheid, 107, 209

finding, 109-110
identifying, 107
lists of, 175, 176
long-period, 106–107, 176
nonperiodic, 107
short-period, 107, 175
types of, 106–107
Vega, 38, 40, 42, 165, 170
veiled groups, 58
Veil Nebula, 182
Vela, 44
Venator, Nicolaus, 40
Venus, 47, 72, 78, 79, 80, 81, 82–86, 144
    drawing, 86
    features of, 86
    magnitude of, 4
    observing, 84
    orbit of, 78
    photographing, 144
    symbol for, 208
    transits of, 86
    vital statistics, 83
vernal equinox, 40, 48, 49
Vesta, 91, 92
Vindemiatrix, 170
Virgo, 37, 38, 40, 44
visual binaries, 105–106
    list of, 172–174
Volans, 44
Vulpecula, 38, 44, 113

Wasat, 170

Water Jar, 40, 42
Wezen, 170
Whipple, Fred, 89
Whirlpool Nebula, 118, 198
white dwarfs, 110
Widmanstätten figures, 128, 212
winter:
    constellations visible in, 42–44
    Messier objects visible in, 193–195

year, tropical, 212
Yed Posterior, 170
Yed Prior, 170
Yildun, 169

Zaurak, 170
Zavijah, 170
Zebeneschamali, see Kiffa Borealis
zenith, 212
Zibel, 170
zodiac, 48, 212
zodiacal light, 132, 133–135, 212
zonal aberration, 12, 13
zones, time, 49
zoom eyepieces, 29–30
Zosma, 170
Zuben Elakrab, 170
Zuben Elakribi, 171
Zubenelgenubi, see Kiffa Australis
Zuben Hakrabi, 171